Clan Cleansing in Somalia

PENNSYLVANIA STUDIES IN HUMAN RIGHTS

Bert B. Lockwood, Jr., Series Editor

A complete list of books in the series is available from the publisher.

Clan Cleansing in Somalia

The Ruinous Legacy of 1991

Lidwien Kapteijns

UNIVERSITY OF PENNSYLVANIA PRESS

PHILADELPHIA

Copyright © 2013 University of Pennsylvania Press

All rights reserved. Except for brief quotations used for purposes of review or scholarly citation, none of this book may be reproduced in any form by any means without written permission from the publisher.

Published by
University of Pennsylvania Press
Philadelphia, Pennsylvania 19104-4112
www.upenn.edu/pennpress

Paperback edition ISBN 978-0-8122-2319-4

Printed in the United States of America on acid-free paper

10 9 8 7 6 5 4 3 2 1

To all Somalis whose lives have been forever changed by the seemingly endless violence in Somalia

Contents

Note on Transliteration ix
Introduction 1

1. Speaking the Unspeakable: Somali
   Poets and Novelists on Civil War Violence 21

2. Historical Background to the Violence of State Collapse 71

3. Clan Cleansing in Mogadishu and Beyond 131

4. The Why and How of Clan Cleansing: Political
   Objectives and Discursive Means 192

Time-Line of Major Events 241
Notes 243
Glossary 279
Bibliography 283
Name Index 297
Subject Index 302
Acknowledgments 305

Note on Transliteration

I have followed Somali orthography to transcribe Somali names and phrases, even if they are based on Arabic. This means that "c" stands for the (Somali and Arabic) consonant 'ayn and "x" for the aspirated "h," while long vowels are doubled. (Because other sources use other conventions, the reader will find other forms of names and phrases in direct citations.) This means the common name 'Ali is spelled Cali and Halima Xaliima. Many Somalis prefer the more conventional transliteration of their name and I have honored this when I was aware of such preference.

I refer to Somali authors who have published under a particular last name (often their third or grandfather's name) by that last name. In all other cases, Somali authors are referred to by their first, father's, and grandfather's name, in that order. Names in quotation marks indicate soubriquets or nicknames, a very common phenomenon in the Somali context, where such nicknames are often better known than a person's formal name.

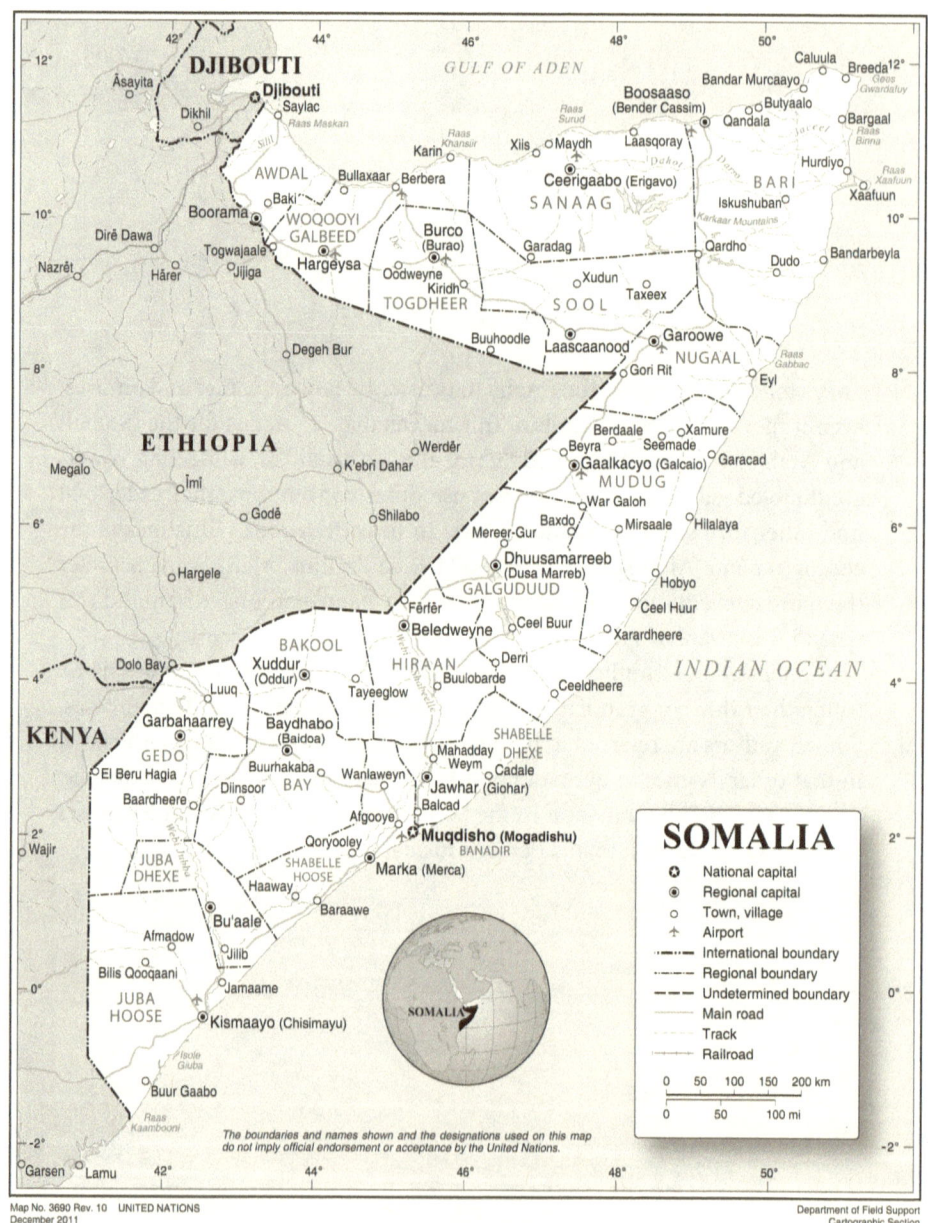

Figure 1. Somalia. Map No. 3690 Rev. 10, December 2011. Courtesy of the United Nations.

Introduction

> Our understanding of events, conceivably also of ourselves, is a process of bringing the disparate into a same frame of reference. It is like taking a photo: The unassimilable, the strange, the foreign and the menacing all become domesticable because artificially focused in a frame of fixed and isolated "seeing."
> —Breyten Breytenbach 1994

This book deals with the changing use of clan-based violence against civilians as a technology of power in the Somali civil war (1978–present). At its center is what I consider the violence of the "key shift,"[1] activated by politico-military leaders in the course of the armed uprising that culminated in the expulsion of President Maxamed Siyaad Barre on January 26, 1991. This study argues that the violence that accompanied and followed the moment of regime and state collapse was analytically, politically, and discursively something new, a transformative turning point and key shift that has remained largely unaddressed (and has been purposefully denied and concealed) both in the scholarship about the Somali civil war and in political efforts at social reconstruction and moral repair. Before explaining why I interpret the violence of January 1991 as a key shift and give it a central place in this study, I will sketch in outline what it consisted of and how it fits into the framework of the fast-moving political events and changing dominant discourse of this period.

1991 as Key Shift

When Barre, who had been president of Somalia since his military coup of October 1969, was toppled, his regime was morally, politically, and financially bankrupt. It had been an autocratic and patrimonial regime, in which an increasingly narrow elite of close family members and top political officials (the cream of the patrimonial clients or *serviteurs patrimoniaux*, as Compagnon 1995 calls them), increasingly devoured the national, public resources of the state for private, personal gain and gradually turned all national institutions that were not part of the repressive apparatus into empty shells. Moreover, in order to contain political and popular resistance against it, the Barre regime developed a calculated policy of using clan sentiment to exacerbate competition, conflict, and grudges among Somalis.[2] As we will see below, these divide-and-rule policies included campaigns of brutal collective punishment of civilians suspected of harboring sympathies for one or the other of the armed opposition fronts that from 1978 onward took up arms against the regime. In December 1990 and January 1991, the USC (United Somali Congress), supported by two other armed fronts, the SPM (Somali Patriotic Movement) and the SNM (Somali National Movement), captured Mogadishu and drove Barre out. However, when Mogadishu passed into its hands, the leaders of the USC, followed by USC fighters and civilian supporters, adopted a politics that defined as mortal enemy all Somalis encompassed by the genealogical construct of Daarood, which also included the president.[3] Although the vast majority of these individuals had not been associated with, or benefited from the regime—in many cases as little or even less than those now hunting them down—they were nevertheless targeted for elimination and expulsion not only in Mogadishu but also, over a period of two years, in central, south-central, and southern Somalia. This is the violence that is central to this study. It did not just represent violence against civilians based on clan, which is in itself not new in Somalia, but a shift to a new kind of collective, clan-based violence, namely that of clan cleansing, in a new political context and with a new dominant discourse.

Political violence targeting civilians on the basis of their clan background has deep historical roots in Somalia. It may well go back to precolonial times and certainly was, in the form of "collective clan punishment" and "punitive" expeditions, one of the foundations of colonial policy toward Somalis. During the decolonization process, the young politicians of the era of civilian administrations (1960–1969), who had inherited a deeply tribalized state from their colonial masters, built national institutions, and promoted a national Somali identity and imaginary. However, they also used political patronage and feelings of clan solidarity among their constituencies as a political instrument against each other. Nevertheless, political violence, though not negligible (e.g., around elections) was not pervasive. The use of large-scale violence against civilians on the basis of clan did not become common political practice until the military regime of Barre (1969–1991). The latter developed the targeting for large-scale violence of civilians who shared the clan background of significant political opponents as a tool used with increasing intensity for maintaining his regime's monopoly on power. Government actions in the Northwest in 1988–1989, which, as we will see below, exceeded in magnitude anything that had come before, exemplify this most powerfully. It is against the background of this kind of violence as a technology of power that 1991 presents a key shift or transformative turning point.

There are three reasons why the clan cleansing campaign of 1991–1992 represents a key shift in the political use of violence against civilians and a turning point in the Somali civil war. First, the particular form of clan-based violence unleashed against civilians in 1991 was a political instrument exercised outside of the institutions of the state that had framed and mediated relations among Somalis until this moment of regime and state collapse. Even though the politico-military leaders who devised and carried out this policy used it to gain control over the state, they did so outside of any mediating state institutions, drawing civilians into the direct experience of physical violence at each other's hands. The second aspect of this moment of key shift, related to the first, is that these leaders did not only make civilians the *target* of violence on the basis of their clan background but also rallied them in the name of clan to become *perpetrators* of such violence. In other words, 1991 marked the moment at which the nature of the political violence used as a technology of power changed and became communal violence, perpetrated and suffered by people who shared geographical and social space as neighbors, acquaintances, friends, maternal relatives, and in-laws. At this moment, "political entrepreneurs,"[4] in the pursuit of their political goals, encouraged, ordered, enabled, and allowed ordinary Somali people to humiliate, rob, rape, maim, kill, and expel other Somali people now constructed as the clan enemy who had to be eliminated and expelled. I will refer to this form of violence as a policy and campaign of clan cleansing.

A striking aspect of this new kind of violence was that it was activated to the full *after* the military regime had collapsed and President Barre had been put to flight. This brings us to the third dimension of the key shift, namely that it marked the abrupt change—sliding into place in Mogadishu in a matter of weeks—of the axis along which civil war violence (including the political use of violence against civilians) had occurred until now. Until this moment, the political dividing line had been that between the government and the (armed and unarmed) opposition. This alignment was abruptly replaced by one that pitted people against each other on the basis of a particular construction of clan identity: the groups associated with the genealogical construct of Daarood-ness were equated with the hated outgoing military regime. They were hunted down and targeted for violence by the militias and civilian supporters of the USC (associated with the genealogical construct of Hawiye-ness) and, in the north, of the SNM (associated with the genealogical construct of Isaaq-ness). One side, including both opponents and leading henchmen of the military regime, now set out to eliminate and expel the other side, also including long-term enemies and victims as well as leading members and supporters of the regime. The rationale for this political reversal took the form of a shift in discourse that at this moment—through the perpetration of violence by and against common people—slid into dominance. The reversal of the political axis of violence; the non-state and communal nature of violence that took the form of clan cleansing, and a new discourse that provided the rationale for that violence constituted the key shift that is central to this book.

The Concept of Clan Cleansing

The question of what to call the violence marking this key shift was one that occupied me for a long time. I tried to take into account how many victims it claimed, how long it lasted, over what geographical expanse it extended, the intent of the perpetrators, the concrete processes by which the victims were "othered," and so forth—all factors that will be considered in the course of this book. Although I found that the concept of genocide—so easily thrown around these days—is not an accurate or helpful term for the violence of 1991, situating the latter in the context of genocide studies proved analytically productive. Recent genocide scholarship agrees on the verdict that the definition in the 1948 UN Convention on the Prevention and Punishment of the Crime of Genocide is both too broad and too narrow to be helpful to scholarly analysis.[5]

A more recent definition of genocide is given by Hinton in *Annihilating Difference: The Anthropology of Genocide*. He proposes to apply the term to "those cases in which a perpetrator group attempts, intentionally and over a sustained period of time, to annihilate another social or political community from the face of the earth."[6] This definition can indeed be applied to the violence of the key shift in Somalia. The latter consisted of rounding up and killing individuals of the targeted groups as well as terrorizing them through acts of torture, rape, humiliation, and dispossession in order to expel them. It occurred over a large geographical space (the area framed by lines connecting Mogadishu, Galkaacyo on the Ethiopian border, Gedo on the border with Kenya, and Kismaayo on the southern coast) and over a period of about two years. Even today, a large part of this area remains devoid of the people who were expelled from it on the basis of their clan background in 1991.

Of more heuristic value than the term genocide itself is that of "ethnic cleansing," or better, "the campaign or policy of ethnic cleansing," which features prominently in the scholarship about the civil war in former Yugoslavia (Bringa 2002: 204). Bringa refers in this context to the final report by the United Nations Commission of Experts, which defines ethnic cleansing as "rendering an area ethnically homogeneous by using force or intimidation to remove from a given area persons of another ethnic or religious group" (204; compare Wyschogrod 2005: 209). The Commission did not make the means used in this campaign of ethnic cleansing part of its definition, but described these as including: "the mass killing of civilians, sexual assault, the bombardment of cities, the destruction of mosques and churches, the confiscation of property and similar measures to eliminate or dramatically reduce Muslim and Croat populations that lie within Serb-held territories" (Bringa: 204). This definition of ethnic cleansing applies, *mutatis mutandis*, to the violence of 1991, although the appropriate phrase in the Somali case would be a campaign or policy of *clan* (not *ethnic*) cleansing.[7]

The case of former Yugoslavia offers insight into the Somali case. In Bosnia, as in Somalia, the policy of ethnic (or clan) cleansing was an instrument of power used to reach particular political goals. In Bosnia, one central goal was, as Bringa puts it, to redefine "the enemy from being the outside foreign capitalist or Soviet powers to becoming the other competing 'Yugoslav' nations within" (2002: 207). In Somalia this meant, if we stay close to her words, redefining the enemy from Barre's military regime to the other competing Somali clans within. In both cases, it was violence that brought about this redefinition, namely communal violence in which perpetrators who were mobilized in the name of ethnicity/clan killed, terrorized, and expelled civilians now defined as enemies on the basis of their ethnic/clan (and in Bosnia also religious) backgrounds. In the Somalia of January 1991, it was those who aspired to becoming the sole heirs of Barre (rather than of Tito) who redefined the enemy in clan terms and used large-scale clan-based communal violence to achieve their political goals. And both in Bosnia and Somalia it was through this kind of violence that the political entrepreneurs and warlords involved were able to destroy all alternatives to their own political project and leadership. As Bringa puts it, "'Ethnic cleansing' then was not only, and perhaps not even primarily, about 'ethnic purification.' It was primarily... about the 'destruction of alternatives' and the elimination of people who represented alternatives by virtue of identifying or being identified with another ethnic or political community" (213).

In both Bosnia and Somalia the most violent "forced unmixing" of people took place in the cities that were most mixed and cosmopolitan,[8] where a good part of the middle class had chosen to emphasize a more cosmopolitan and shared (in the Somali case an explicitly national) identity over ethnic or clan-based ones. In cities such as Sarajevo and Mogadishu, the violence with which the would-be heirs of state-power tried to impose their new political order was thus all the greater because it had to undo the lived realities of many of its inhabitants. Robert Hayden put it this way for former Yugoslavia: "It is this lack of congruence between the present reality of life as lived and the objectification of life as it suddenly must be lived that produces the mortal horrors of ethnic cleansing" (2002: 233).

Episodes of (ethnic, clan, or religious) cleansing do not occur outside of political contexts and without the active agency of political entrepreneurs who mobilize and indoctrinate the individuals and groups who physically carry out most of the violent acts. What Shaw says about genocide is also true for clan cleansing, that genocidal violence results from leaders' political acts, whatever the socioeconomic hardships and inequalities that make common perpetrators so vulnerable to such incitement may be. Quoting Michael Mann, Shaw writes that "explanations must be '*essentially political*'" and "genocide is the product of (contingent) escalations in political conflict, which turn it toward violence and killing, and cannot be explained by underlying cultural, economic or even political conflicts" (2007: 466, my emphasis).

Shaw takes this thought even farther by specifying that it is not just the actions of political leaders that lead to genocide, but the actions of such leaders *in the context of violent conflict*. Thus he says: "it can be argued that military contexts are generally *more* directly instrumental than narrowly political

contexts in leading to genocide. Or to put it another way it is when political conflicts *become* violent or military that genocide is most likely to result." His conclusion that "there is nothing accidental about the role of war in genocide" is again directly relevant to Somalia in 1991 (2007: 467).

This brings us to the context in which incitement to clan cleansing could become so successful. Again, recent scholarship on genocide serves as a valuable heuristic. Hinton analyzes this kind of context in terms of genocidal priming, "a making ready for action or future operation, a charging or adding heat to a particular political situation" (Hinton 2002: 28). Such processes of priming include, he proposes, "socio-economic upheaval, polarized social divisions, structural change, and effective ideological manipulation" (29). The analysis below will examine such primes for clan cleansing in Somalia.

Apart from the concept of genocidal priming, Hinton also introduces the term of genocidal activation or trigger.[9] He writes that "when the priming is 'hot' and genocide does take place, there is almost always some sort of 'genocidal activation' that ignites the 'charge' that has been primed." He adds "that this 'push' often comes from leaders who use panic, fear, and material gain to incite their followers to kill" (2002: 30). In Rwanda, for example, Hinton notes, this was the shooting down of the airplane of Habyarimana. In Somalia, the activation of clan cleansing coincided with the collapse of the Barre regime, when, in the middle of violent political realignment, politico-military leaders decided to pursue their political goals through a particular kind of communal violence.

However, even if one acknowledges the role of political organizers, the participation in communal violence of ordinary people must be put into context and analyzed further.[10] Here a final insight from genocide studies that helps bring the violence of 1991 in Somalia into focus is its emphasis on the role of what Hinton calls "effectively disseminate[d] messages of hate" (29):

> Genocides are distinguished by a process of "othering" in which the boundaries of an imagined community are reshaped in such a manner that a previously "included" group . . . is ideologically recast (almost always in dehumanizing rhetoric) as being outside the community, as a threatening and dangerous "other"—whether racial, political, ethnic, religious, economic, and so on—that must be annihilated. (6)

The significance of discourses that provide the perpetrators of such violence with their motives and rationales also gets attention in Eltringham's analysis of the genocide in Rwanda:

> Words can kill—or at least motivate a person to kill. It is through language that the primal impulses, the likes and dislikes, the hatreds and enmities, the stereotypes and degrading and dehumanising characterisations of those who are not desirable or are rivals for political or economic power or status, are transmitted . . . words are the carriers of deeds. (Eltringham 2004: xii)

This insight too has important heuristic value for the Somali case, in which existing and newly minted clan hate-narratives served to motivate perpetrators to participate in the politically orchestrated communal violence as well as to justify it and to deny and conceal its real nature. The discursive dimension of the clan cleansing of 1991–1992 is one of this book's central themes and is addressed explicitly in the first and fourth chapters.

The Interpretive Framework and Organization of the Book

Chapter 1 is an examination of the ways Somali poetic and prose fiction texts mediate, that is to say, interpret and discursively intervene in the violence of 1991 and the civil war more broadly. It first focuses on what has traditionally been considered "prestigious" (or politically objective and morally legitimate) poetry. According to the Somali canon, this poetry, as I have argued elsewhere, is poetry by men, in men's prestigious genres of orature, about matters of general political importance that have long been regarded as men's business, and suitable to be performed or published in shared Somali public space (Kapteijns 2010a). Although its strengths as effective and emotive speech designed to move and change the mindsets of its audience are considerable, this genre of poetry also has limitations. This chapter therefore also examines texts that belong to more recent genres of Somali orature/literature not bound by the rules of "prestigious poetry," namely free verse and prose fiction in both Somali and English by Somali authors in Somalia and the diaspora.

The dominant discourse through which these texts mediate civil war violence is that of clan, whose important roles, as we will see below, their authors analyze with great rhetorical power and analytical sophistication. In their own ways, the texts all struggle with making the unspeakable speakable, that is to say, with articulating truths about the violence committed in the name of clan in ways that avoid deepening or reigniting communal hatreds and, instead, bring Somalis together. If, in these texts, the discourse of clan is the most explicit, the discursive strands emphasizing the concepts of nation and Islam, as I have analyzed elsewhere, are closely intertwined with it (Kapteijns 2010a). Even though the texts under study date from before the rise to political prominence of the Islamic Courts Movement in 2006, signs of a transformation of the discourse about Islam—from an understated, cultural, organic to a more emphatically political one—are already visible in Somali poems of the early 2000s, also examined in Chapter 1.

When I began the research that eventually led to this study, I was fully focused on identifying, translating, and interpreting those texts of Somali popular culture broadly construed that dealt with the Somali civil war in a nonhateful way and that situated themselves in shared Somali public space. Chapter 1 is based on that research. However, it was the aporia that marked these prestigious texts, the aspects that remained unspoken and proved to be largely unspeakable, that motivated me to pursue a fuller study, drawing on a wider range of sources, of the violence of 1991.

Chapter 2, therefore, presents a more conventional historical approach to the violence of 1991. The first part presents the historical background to state collapse up to July 1989, when the political violence that had proliferated in many parts of Somalia (and had developed from May 1988 into all-out war in the Northwest) exploded in the streets of Mogadishu and thus into full view of the world. Taking its cue both from the poetry presented in Chapter 1 and drawing on scholarly analyses of the military regime of Maxamed Siyaad Barre (1969–1991) such as Compagnon 1995, it shows how large-scale clan-based violence as a technology of power became increasingly entrenched in state institutions. This was expressed most clearly by the state's perpetration of large-scale violence against ordinary civilians for the (alleged) acts of political opposition committed by men associated with the same clan background. Without the long-standing policy of such clan-based collective "punishment" and the scale this assumed first in 1979–1982 and then in 1988–1989, the clan cleansing that accompanied state collapse in Mogadishu might have been unthinkable. How the Barre regime used large-scale clan-based violence against civilians as a political instrument to stay in power is the subject of the first part of this chapter. The second part begins with sketching the wider political and economic contexts that framed and constituted the "primes" for the violence of January 1991. It then analyzes the political events from July 1989 to the expulsion of Barre on January 26, 1991, the moment the campaign of clan cleansing came into full force. It also presents the key political organizations of that time, including those that orchestrated and went along with the clan cleansing campaign.[11]

The campaign of clan cleansing is the subject of Chapter 3. It draws on written sources and oral accounts of survivors to illustrate both the communal dimension of the violence—the intimate involvement of neighbors and friends—and the organized fashion in which it was orchestrated and implemented. It documents the kinds of violence that were committed and traces the clan cleansing campaign geographically from Mogadishu to central, south-central, and southern Somalia and temporally from January 1991 to the end of 1992, the eve of international intervention. How politicians, journalists, and scholars have overlooked, ignored, concealed, denied, and distorted the clan cleansing campaign of 1991–1992 from the time it was unfolding until today is also a theme of this chapter.

The clan cleansing campaign the USC conducted against the numerous, diverse, large and small groups associated with Daarood-ness was not the only form of brutal clan-based violence perpetrated against civilians in the period under study here (or since then). First, immediately after unleashing its campaign against "*the*" Daarood, the USC selectively attacked other civilian victims also on the basis of clan. Thus its militias and other supporters spared people associated with the clan-bases of some of its allies,[12] while enabling the brutalization of so-called minority groups, which had no militia leaders and militias of their own.[13] Second, in the wake of regime collapse and the reversal of the axis along which political opposition had taken place (and political violence had been perpetrated), the political and military realignments gave rise to the emergence of dozens of new armed fronts. These also consisted of clan-based militias and were intent on either assisting the USC in its campaign and bid for power over the state or on stopping, reversing, and avenging these. In what I call the War of the Militias, the parties generally did not honor the concept of civilian in theory or practice and often purposefully "punished" civilians for the alleged or real political acts of political and military leaders of the same clan background. Although the rank-and-file of all militias largely consisted of men who had until recently been civilians, in the War of the Militias the dimension of communal violence became less pronounced. Chapter 3 will trace some of the major episodes of violence perpetrated during the intense militia warfare of this stage of the civil war, in which the victims became perpetrators and vice versa, as clan-based militias attacked and brutalized civilians as a matter of normalized strategy. It was in this period that the lives of few Somali civilians remained untouched by the violence and that the numbers of those who streamed out of Somalia into Kenya and Ethiopia and to other destinations across the sea rose to hundreds of thousands. It was also in this stage (after it had been largely clan-cleansed) that Mogadishu was dismantled, with everything of any possible value ripped out, looted, and sold abroad. As the violence rolled back and forth across all of south, south-central, and central Somalia, it made productive activity impossible and deepened armed conflict over the control of food, causing the devastating famine that, in December 1992, became the rationale for the first U.S./UN intervention, Operation Restore Hope (see Glossary). This marked a new stage in the Somali civil war, which lies beyond the scope of this book.

For some readers, Chapter 3's account of the clan cleansing campaign and the War of the Militias that followed and overlapped with it may appear more detailed than necessary. There are, however, compelling reasons for such detail. Because clan cleansing has remained largely unstudied and constitutes a historical legacy with which Somalis as a group have not come to terms, documenting it is an important dimension of this book. Equally crucial is detailing the process that followed from this campaign, by which victims turned into perpetrators and perpetrators into victims. Without a careful reconstruction of who did what to whom, when, and in the name of what group construct, the increasingly widespread adoption of large-scale violence against civilians as a political instrument cannot be understood.[14] Such detailed analysis may also disrupt clan-based narratives that focus on the victimization of the in-group without any acknowledgement of the violence perpetrated in that group's name. Indeed, I chose 1991–1992 (for which Chapter 2 presents the historical backdrop) as the focus of this study in order to do justice to this history of events. This time-frame encompasses not only the clan cleansing that targeted "*the*" Daarood but also the large-scale clan-based brutalization of civilians by Daarood-based militias. These two years also witnessed the implosion of the political constructs of Daarood- and Hawiye-ness, as warlords and militias on each side turned inward and abused and massacred civilians of what had been their own side. This shows how a wide array of warlords and their clan-based militias used clan identity constructs as political instruments in the ongoing struggle over the remains of the state and public resources.

Given all this, the following deserves special emphasis. Although the clan cleansing campaign that gained full momentum in January 1991 lies at the heart of this book, this does not mean that the violation of the many civilians before or after that date—whether in Mudug and the Northwest before 1991 or in the Banaadir and riverine regions after that date—is any less grievous or unjust than that of January 1991, or that the culpability of those responsible for those gross human rights violations is any less real and enormous. My distinction is an analytical one. It is meaningful, I will argue, because when Somali civilians exercised lethal violence and conducted clan cleansing against other largely unsuspecting Somali civilians outside of the institutions of the state, this marked the shift to the dominance of a new logic and a new discourse and ripped Somalis apart in new ways that require moral repair and social reconstruction of a new kind and magnitude. This will be further elaborated below.

Insisting on this key shift, moreover, does not imply that responsibility and culpability lie with only one set of perpetrators, mobilized in terms of only one set of clan identities. As we will see, the preconditions for clan cleansing and many of the features that came to characterize it existed before January 1991 and were rooted in the military regime. It is therefore crucial to analyze the key shift in both its diachronic (or historical) and synchronic (or contemporary) contexts. If Chapter 1 presents the violence of the civil war as mediated by Somali *texts*, Chapters 2 and 3 present a historical narrative that focuses on Somali *contexts*.

Chapter 4 analyzes in greater depth two themes that underlie the narrative, the motives of the perpetrators of the major episodes of clan-based violence against civilians and the role the production of particular discursive meanings played in this violence. The first part of this chapter presents an analytical summary of the different political objectives to which politicomilitary leaders put the use of collective clan-based violence against civilians in the period under study. It asks what the Barre regime expected to achieve by targeting civilians of particular clan backgrounds, what constituted the political objectives of the clan cleansing of 1991, and why the armed fronts and militias that multiplied in the wake of clan cleansing and regime and state collapse brutalized civilians. What political goals did the large-scale rape and other forms of humiliation and torture serve in these successive moments of Somali history?

The second part of the chapter returns to the discursive dimension of the clan cleansing campaign, first raised in Chapter 1, by analyzing and contextualizing the clan hate-narratives that provided the rationales and justifications for the organized communal violence of clan cleansing. How did discourses about clan victimization and clan grievances get interpreted and publicized ("spun") in such a way that collective violence against "clan others" became acceptable, even meritorious behavior? Can the ways in which these hate-narratives interwove (and interweave) fact and fiction, past and present, and the everyday and the epic, be disentangled?

The chapter concludes with situating the violence in the context of a Somali past that is "unbewältigt," unabsorbed, undigested, and publicly largely unacknowledged, and that, partly in result, underlies the ongoing civil war in Somalia as a powerfully negative political force. This is so in spite of the many other episodes of violence that have occurred in Somalia since 1991–1992 and in spite of significant discursive shifts. In the period under study here, the dominant discursive strand of Somali political discourse pitted clan against nation and rooted for the latter in shared Somali public space and for the former in clan settings. Since then, especially from 2006 on, the discursive strand of Islam(ism) has become most prominent but remains interlocked with the discourse of nation and clan (including the "clan logic") in a (until now) deeply negative sense.[15]

As Somali politicians continue to rebuild a central (even if federal) government and political entrepreneurs and warlords continue to struggle over the resources that once belonged to the state, ordinary Somalis remain deeply divided. Publicly largely unacknowledged and scholarly largely ignored, the legacy of clan cleansing continues to undermine the unity with which Somalis might resist those who benefit from continued violence and civil war. This is a crucial area of drift sand in which attempts at social reconstruction continue to founder.[16]

This "unbewältigt" past of politically orchestrated, clan-based communal violence, which had leaders who directed it as well as many ordinary men and women who carried it out—is in need of critical engagement by many kinds of actors and in many forms. This book presents itself as one such engagement with, and mediation of this past, one that follows the conventions of historical analysis as an academic genre and draws on the sources and insights of this field as well as an array of interdisciplinary scholarship.

The Historiography on Which This Study Draws

This study has benefited from scholarship in four areas of study, which, though they overlap considerably, will be briefly reviewed separately. The first is that of the anthropology of violence and the largely anthropological field of comparative genocide studies. The writings of Alison (2007), Allen (1996), Benard (1994), Bowen (2002), Bringa (2002), Buckley-Zistel (2006),

Donham (2006), Eltringham (2004, 2009, 2011a, b), Feldman (1995), Hinton (2002), Lemarchand (1994, 1996, 1997, 2007), Lieberman (2006), Lubkeman (2008), Newbury (1998), Robben and Nordstrom (1995), Shaw (2007), and Zur (1998), many explicitly cited, have shaped my approach to the study of violence (Kapteijns and Richters 2010).

The second area of study on which this book draws deals with the relationship between ethnicity and the state. Especially the writings by Berman (1998), Berman and Lonsdale (1992), Cooper (2008), Fearon and Laitin (2000), Fortier (1999), Lonsdale (1994), Mamdani (1996, 2009), Schlee (1989), and Willemse (2005, 2009) have shaped my approach to the analysis of clan.[17] All these scholars teach us how to avoid attributing simple agency to the phenomenon of ethnic group or to take it for granted as a unit of analysis. They also try to explain how ethnicity and clanship nevertheless become such powerful political realities and how individuals and groups use it as a political tool or resource and "roll into" it a wide range of grievances and political ambitions that give ethnicity/clanship its particular meanings and power at particular junctions in time.

The third area of studies is the scholarship about the Somali civil war, of which this book is a part. Since my 2001 historiographical essay, a large number of new studies have come out, wide-ranging, multifaceted, and of uneven quality. The historiography consists of both broad surveys and specialized studies of particular aspects and stages of the civil war (including the ill-starred international intervention of 1992–1995). This study focuses on *Somali texts and contexts* and has a more limited thematic and temporal focus. It recognizes as highly significant such dimensions as the international political contexts (analyzed in Doornbos 2006; Issa-Salwe 1996; Lyons and Samatar 1995) and the struggle over economic resources exacerbated by international involvement (analyzed in Besteman and Cassanelli 1996; Menkhaus 1989; Little 1996), but does not make a new contribution to these areas of study. This must be a task for further research.

Two scholarly analyses in Somali studies have shaped my study in important ways. One of these is Daniel Compagnon's "Ressources politiques, régulation autoritaire et domination personnelle en Somalie: Le régime de Siyaad Barre (1969–1991)," which presents a dynamic and detailed study of the Barre regime up to its fall in 1991. Compagnon's conceptualization of clan as a political resource of "political entrepreneurs" trying to maintain control over a "patrimonial state" has shaped my own understanding of clan and clan-based violence against civilians as a technology of power.[18] Another work that has helped anchor this study is Abdisalam Issa-Salwe's concise political history of modern Somalia, *The Collapse of the Somali State: The Impact of the Colonial Legacy*, first published in 1994 (1996). One of the few written so soon after the collapse of the state in 1991, it distinguishes itself from many other analyses of the civil war by neither joining the war discursively nor skipping over the events of the clan cleansing.

A fourth area of scholarship, which has mushroomed in the wake of the establishment of the Truth and Reconciliation Committee in South Africa in 1991, concerns itself with subjects such as restorative justice, conflict transformation, postconflict reconstruction, and moral repair as represented by scholars such as Fletcher and Weinstein (2002), Michnik (1994), Neier (1994), Stover and Weinstein (2004), and Walker (2006), as well as Donham, Eltringham, and Newbury. This scholarship, on which I draw explicitly in Chapter 4, has helped me situate my study in relationship to the highly contested field of memory the violence of 1991 represents. Scholars in this field reflect on what truth means and what role it might play in bringing about justice and social repair. They conclude that, in the face of the sharply divergent and even diametrically opposed memories and interpretations of violence that different parties to large-scale communal violence often hold, no court of justice, not even as powerful a truth and reconciliation commission as that of South Africa or the International Criminal Court in The Hague, can hand down authoritative truth about such violence. This is even more true for a single historical study such as this book. Narratives of group victimization and denial of any group wrongdoing by members of groups in whose names large-scale violence was committed—however problematic or even "untrue" in the eyes of others (including legal judges and scholars)—reflect real and powerful attitudes toward the present and cannot be simply dismissed.

My project does not try to bring all these divergent memories and interpretations of the violence of 1991 into the open. Nor does it try to simply "correct" or displace them.[19] As a contextual analysis of a particular moment, political use, and type of large-scale clan-based violence against civilians that is often concealed and denied, it offers input into the debate about truth, justice, and social repair that Somalis in the long run may find impossible to avoid and in which the clan cleansing campaign of 1991–1992 has a rightful and central place.

The Source Base

The source base of this study is complex and diverse. For the first chapter it consists of texts that fall into the category of Somali popular culture broadly construed, that is to say, poetry, song, and prose fiction (mostly in Somali and English). I gained access to texts that mediate Somali civil war violence in a variety of ways. First, I spent June to September 2007 in Ethiopia, where I got to know aspects of the experiences of the Somali community at Bole Rwanda in Addis Ababa. I did research in the archives of the Institute of Ethiopian Studies at the University of Addis Ababa and visited Jigjiga in the Somali Region. From here, I also briefly visited Nairobi to take part in a UNESCO-sponsored conference about preservation of the Somali cultural heritage. Second, from September to December 2007, I did research in Djibouti, where I consulted with colleagues at the Halabuur Cultural Centre and Radio-Television-Djibouti. From here I also made a brief trip to Makalla in Yemen, where I was hosted by a family from Brava with a long tradition of religious leadership. Third, I visited and obtained texts from music stores on two continents, from Addis Ababa, Jigjiga, and Djibouti (Studio Arta) to Toronto, Columbus, and Minneapolis. In other places (such as London and Rome) friends helped me in my search. Fourth, as I discovered in Djibouti, the oral compositions of Somali poets and songwriters are increasingly recorded in writing and published as poetry collections called *diiwaans*. This is done by the poets themselves (as in the case of Cabdi Muxumed Amiin 2006 and Cabdulkadir Cabdi Shube 2007), or by scholars and editors such as Boobe Yuusuf Ducaale (2006), Fadumo Ahmed Alim (2008), Mohamed-Abdi (1994), and Mohamed Sh. Hassan (1998, 2007). Fifth and finally, Somali cyberspace, with its more than 700 Web sites and numerous radio programs and videoclips, increasingly constitutes the public space in which all these texts come together (Issa-Salwe 2005: 113–25). For this research, the following Web sites have proven most useful: www.wardheer.com; www.aftahan.com; www.doollo.com; www.golkhatumo.com; and www.mudulood.com.

A second category consists of accounts by authors who witnessed or played a part in at least some events of the civil war they describe. These include political memoirs that vary widely in quality of analysis, truthfulness, and degree of self-promotion. Some memoirs are more informative of the spiteful mindsets of their authors than of the events they purport to describe (e.g., Hussein Ali Dualeh 1994). Others, also written from particular perspectives, are very instructive, three in particular. Two of these are political memoirs of the events leading up to the collapse of the Barre regime by the two top Italian diplomats in Mogadishu at the time, ambassador Mario Sica (1994) and his second-in-command Claudio Pacifico (1996).

Pacifico had come to Somalia in February 1987. He loved hunting and the great Somali outdoors, and had made many friends, including Mogadishu businessman Ali Mahdi[20] and his wife Nuurto (then still adviser to the Barre regime). Sica only arrived in Mogadishu in March 1990 and was actively involved in attempts to persuade Barre to make meaningful concessions and stave off the full collapse of the regime. Both men were in close touch with the main political players in the capital, including Barre himself. Both accounts are specifically situated socially and geographically, because they view the Somali scene from the elite perch of an embassy in the Shibis neighborhood, close to Barre's presidential residence, and politically, because both men strongly defend Italy's then widely criticized decision to keep engaging and supporting Barre until the embassy evacuation on January 12, 1991, two weeks before Barre was expelled from Mogadishu. Both accounts provide a detailed picture of the events of the last two years of the Barre regime and are an important source for Chapter 2.

A third book-length account and analysis from the perspective of someone who experienced some of the events that constitute its subject matter is Daahir Cali Cumar "Deyr"'s *Qaran Dumay iyo Qoon Talo-Waayey* (*A Nation That Collapsed and a People at Their Wit's End*), published in 1997. Given that the author did research and made notes about the events he witnessed as they were unfolding, this account also has features of investigative journalism. The author appears to have been among those targeted for clan cleansing and his detailed narrative is at times quite passionate about the ways civilians were brutalized. His account is also analytical and quite critical of political leaders and military commanders of all sides. Daahir Cali was in Brava and Kismaayo when these towns were first taken by the USC in early February and late April 1991; his book is thus an important part of the evidentiary base of Chapter 3.

A third category of sources consists of contemporary news reports. It includes publications such as *Africa Confidential* and *Indian Ocean Newsletter* (bimonthly information sheets about major political developments and news makers in Africa, published in the UK and France respectively), as well as FBIS (Foreign Broadcasts Information Service), which provides daily transcripts from various international and African radio broadcasts, including Radio Mogadishu in the period under study.[21] As for the major international newspapers and news agencies (such as Reuters and Agence France Press), there appear to have been no (or hardly any) foreign journalists stationed in Somalia at the moment of regime collapse, though courageous journalists such as Peter Biles for the *Observer* and the *Guardian*, David Chazan for AFP, Aidan Hartley for the *Guardian*, Neil Henry for the *Washington Post*, Reid Miller for the Associated Press (AP), Jane Perlez for the *New York Times*, Robert M. Press for the *Christian Science Monitor*, and Todd Shields for the *Independent* wrote about Somalia and, after January 26, 1991, made brief visits from Nairobi. They were on the ground in Mogadishu immediately after Barre's expulsion and filed firsthand reports that offer crucial glimpses of the situation at that moment. However, neither journalists nor human rights organizations provided coverage of the clan cleansing proceeding at the time; this remained, as we will see below, outside their scope of vision.

The absence of outside observers was reversed later in the year, during the months of deepening famine that led up to the U.S./UN humanitarian intervention Operation Restore Hope (UNITAF). The heavy fighting that broke out in Mogadishu between USC-Caydiid and USC-Cali Mahdi, the large-scale subclan-based violence against civilians this involved, and, eventually, the famine that had been looming since 1989, were the subject of extensive field reports by representatives of human rights organizations such as Africa Watch, African Rights, Amnesty International, Human Rights Watch, Physicians for Human Rights, and so forth. Despite their limitations, the news reports from Mogadishu during this period (December 1990–April 1991) are an important part of the source base for Chapter 3.[22] Also featured among contemporary news sources are public statements and press releases by Somali action groups in the diaspora during the time the clan cleansing campaign was unfolding. Examples are a press release by Concerned Somalis, "Genocide in Mogadisho: Mogadisho After the Ouster of Barre's Dictatorship," Washington, D.C., March 11, 1991. I also acquired copies of some videotapes by Somali journalists in Mogadishu during 1991 and 1992.

The last category of sources on which this study draws, though only in a limited way, is oral accounts. I have spoken with individuals who witnessed the clan cleansing and other clan-based violence against civilians in Mogadishu and beyond[23] to bring to light aspects of 1991 that existing published accounts failed to notice or ignored, distorted, and even purposely concealed and denied. These oral accounts give evidence of both the intimate (communal) nature of the violence and the organized fashion in which it was implemented. With the exception of the poetry and songs examined in Chapter 1, the oral source base of this study does not extend beyond such interviews. A full-scale memory project of 1991 along the lines proposed by Lemarchand 2007, one that would bring the memories of individuals of all sides of the conflict—victims, perpetrators, bystanders, rescuers, and others—into public space, remains a task for the future. It would most likely require the participation of a team (or teams) of Somali researchers and must either find ways of negotiating the enduring divisiveness engendered by the campaign of clan cleansing or wait until the violence of the ongoing civil war subsides enough to make the politicization of everything related to 1991 less acute.

Chapter 1

Speaking the Unspeakable: Somali Poets and Novelists on Civil War Violence

> "History is the poisoned well, seeping into the ground-water. It's not the unknown past we're doomed to repeat, but the past we know. Every recorded event is a brick of potential, of precedent, thrown into the future. . . . This is the duplicity of history: an idea recorded will become an idea resurrected."
> —Anne Michaels, *Fugitive Pieces*

> "One of the most productive ways of thinking about discourse is not as a group of signs or a stretch of text, but as 'practices that systematically form the objects of which they speak.'"
> —Sara Mills, citing Foucault, *Discourse*

Introduction

The research on which this book is based began as a study of Somali popular songs and poetry as mediations of civil war violence. This is a continuation of my earlier work on Somali popular songs of the nationalist era, a genre that, as I have argued elsewhere, proved to be iconic for this era's will to modernity—its hopes for national unity and economic development as well as for a "modern," autonomous, and desiring selfhood. In the era after state collapse, some of the most popular and widely known poetic mediations of civil war violence have indeed continued to be popular songs. However, in the course of my research, it became clear that, as an expanding and rapidly changing genre, the popular song was neither the most authoritative genre of popular culture that dealt with civil war violence nor numerically the most significant. This led me to look beyond popular songs to poetry that was not sung or set to music.

These texts and genres of popular culture can be found wherever Somalis live.[1] They are disseminated through Somali music stores, local, national, and international Somali radio- and TV programs, and hundreds of sites in Somali cyberspace, which increasingly forms the junction of all these media flows. From Boston to Toronto, Columbus and Minneapolis, Addis Ababa and Jigjiga, but with particular success in Djibouti, I spent time listening to recordings and talking to the young men who managed or worked in Somali music stores. However, I also received direction. Given that the violence of the civil war has so divided Somalis, I allowed myself to be gently guided toward what my friends and colleagues (especially the literary scholars and specialists in Djibouti) considered legitimate poetry, poetry that does not divide its audience but rather tries to unite it in support of peace. When it deals with Somali civil war violence, this "prestigious" poetry, I have argued elsewhere, has enormous moral and rhetorical power.[2] However, the very fact of its prestige also produces limitations. Given the latter, the following will include an examination of texts the Somali canon has traditionally categorized as "nonprestigious" genres, including, for example, prose fiction, still a relatively recent genre.

This analysis will therefore address the question of how a selection of Somali popular culture texts of different genres mediate (that is to say, represent, interpret, comment upon, and intervene in) the violence that accompanied and followed state collapse, especially the campaign of clan cleansing of 1991–1992. This involves an examination of the dominant discourses of these texts, as they contain and articulate interpretations of the causes as well as potential solutions to the divide and mistrust that opened up among Somalis as a result of this violence. Before examining the texts, however, it is important to ask how well-known they are to Somali audiences and how representative the discourses are of the wider range of poetry and popular culture about the civil war. A truly authoritative answer must await formal audience research, which has not been part of this study. Informal indicators, however, suggest the following. First, in the hundreds of poems and songs about civil war violence read and listened to in the course of this research, hardly any did *not* engage the discourses of (anti-)clannism, nationhood and national feeling, and Islam. This is also true for the limited number of women's poetic contributions and even for texts dealing primarily with exodus and exile. Second, the poets and singers of some of the texts presented below performed them at one or more formal National Reconciliation meetings, as well as many other Somali gatherings in and outside of Somalia. This is true, for example, for Naaji's "Lament for Mogadishu" and Shube's "Sound, drum of wisdom." Somalis everywhere followed the former, first on audio- and videocassettes and later via the Internet. Third, most of the texts below, even those that predate the development of the Somali Internet in the early 2000s, have been included in Somali Web sites, the single, most comprehensive and continuously expanding depository of Somali cultural production in existence.[3] This inclusion in well known and popular general sites as well as Web sites specializing in poetry suggests that these texts circulate widely. They have also been included in the many *diiwaans* or poetry collections Somalis have begun to publish in the past decade. Finally, for some of the poems and songs available online we have the number of "hits" and thus know how often someone accessed them, but this is extraordinarily fragmented and impressionistic evidence.[4]

Somali Mediations of Violence: "Prestigious" Poetry

Poems of the Early 1990s

The first four texts presented here, three from the early 1990s and one from 2000, were authored by highly regarded members of that generation of artists that witnessed both the birth and collapse of the Somali state. They were key players in the creation of a national popular culture that emerged in the decade before independence (1960) and became an intrinsic part of the cultural nation-building project that the Maxamed Siyaad Barre regime first (in the 1970s) actively sponsored and, later, especially after defeat in the Somali-Ethiopian war of 1978–1979, subverted and helped destroy.

"Disaster"

"Disaster" (Masiibo) was authored in the early 1990s by Mustafa Sheekh Cilmi, a well-known poet who witnessed the clan cleansing in Mogadishu. Since 1991, the poet lived in exile in Nairobi, returned temporarily to Mogadishu, and has recently moved to Sweden. In "Disaster," a long poem in the genre of *gabay* alliterating in "m," Mustafa Sheekh goes into great detail about the violence that was committed in the first stages of the war.[5] First, he positions himself morally and explains how he despaired of the situation in his country when he saw that violence, greed, and other forms of unethical, unjust, irreligious, and un-Somali behavior went unchecked, without any possibility even for talks or mediation.

> When people moved away from religion and the path of justice,
> when greed turned sincerity and selflessness into something shameful,
> when people abandoned our way of life,
> I became an outcast.
> When they attacked any place that was at peace
> and readied themselves to prevent people from ever coming together again,
> when killing and robbing became permanent with no discussion possible,
> and there was no one to be seen who told the perpetrators to stop,
> that is when I gave up on the country, and folded and packed up my concern for it. (stanza 1)

However, it was the magnitude of the violence he saw that made the poet want to bear witness about the fighting; the loss of lives and property; the deaths of people of all kinds, from the poorest and weakest to the wealthy and strong; the destruction of houses, large and small; how people fled in a panic because of the shooting and the bombardments; how, as they ran, they were exposed to the wild animals of the bush and the sea; their exhaustion and starvation, and the rape of women of all generations, sometimes in each other's presence, even in mosques.

> Let me explain what moves me to speak today:
> Dear God, how much wealth was obliterated in the fighting.
> How many poor and destitute folks went down with it, people and property both destroyed.
> How many capable individuals and strong, brave, and brilliant men did we lose.
> How many tall houses were reduced to rubble, how many multistoried houses brought down and burned.
> How many mat- and mud houses were blown high into the sky.
> How many cannons were let loose on us without interruption.
> How many bullets did they shower down on us like rain.
> How we scattered in all directions indiscriminately!

How people moved now forwards and then backwards!
How they cut the ropes of our ships, throwing us to the wild beasts!
How many were thrown as food to the wild animals in forest and plain!

Every enclosed space they turned into a grave.
On how many bodies, dead since yesterday or the day before, did flies throng!
As we staggered on, we were no longer able to move our legs from exhaustion!
Our lips crusted over, none of their shine remaining.
How did exhaustion show itself on Dahabo and Fadumo!
How they mounted sweet-smelling girls and married women!
How many hijab-wearing girls had their belts torn from their waists?
How were women pursued into mosques they deemed safe!
Three generations of women raped on the same mat.
Time and again they stabbed virgin girls who had not yet been deflowered. (stanza 3)

To whom does the poet attribute responsibility and culpability for the events? First he mentions the Mooryaan, as the destitute young men who committed much of the actual violence came to be called in Mogadishu (Marchal 1993; Mohamed-Abdi 2001). The poet characterizes them as youth brought in from the countryside to do the dirty work of the more powerful and power-hungry men who incited them from behind the scenes (stanza 10). He also points the finger at the armed opposition fronts, which he accuses of deceiving the people. Here he does not single out the USC, the front that faced the Barre regime down in Mogadishu. He depicts the perpetrators more generally in a range of morally judgmental terms, from fools and intoxicated brutes (referring to the *qaat*, sometimes mixed with other, stronger drugs, chewed by the fighters), people with no sense of religious injunction or ethical principle (stanza 4), and bold-faced thieves who did not even try to hide the things they stole from those they robbed (stanza 6), to cruel tormentors who added humiliating insult to grievous injury (stanza 4). The images of the fleeing that reached the media were so graphic, the poet adds, that they shocked people all over the world (stanza 5).

They attacked us with youth brought from the bush.
How they jeered at us for how we were crushed.

How we were deceived by names and how did political fronts
tear us apart like wild animals.
How they tore off our skin, tearing and stripping it.
How we were violated by fools and worthless madmen.
How they deviated from the religion and the path of justice
How dead people were put into the earth without having been
    properly washed,
laid to rest by women while still wearing their clothes
How they perverted our way of life, walking all over it. (stanza 4)

How dogs put their teeth into the corpses of unknown people.
How people just walked by, as crows were pecking clean the bones of
    the dead.
How we staggered under the weight of grinding hunger.
Our bones bereft of any skin, we slowly stumbled away.
How the sight of us shocked the people who saw us.
The world was astounded at us, as if we were people
who had come back from Hell,
at our destitution, at how we had not eaten for six days, and
at how badly the skin of our legs was scraped. (stanza 5)

In the next thirteen stanzas, the poet gives more detail about the acts of destruction and looting. How the perpetrators looted and took away livestock, crops—even the soil, he claims—from the farms in and around Mogadishu, not even leaving people the bare minimal. How they slaughtered even the she-camel and its calf—the nomad's ultimate capital—just to sell their meat in the market. How they even robbed people of the clothes on their back. How they threw away books. How they stole people's cars, without even feeling the need to hide this. How they removed and exported private and public building furnishings and fixtures, any type of wire, even of a thumb's length, up to the air-conditioners of the morgues! They removed and destroyed everything, the poet argues, leaving no trace of modernity or memory of statehood:

They used hammer blows to make us respond to "tell us where the
    money is hidden!"
Our cars they carjacked from us in broad daylight,
not even taking them to a distant neighborhood, a valley, or beyond,
but driving around in them enjoying the sights. (stanza 6)

*　*　*

They sold abroad the refrigerators of the morgues.
They destroyed each trace of the memory of statehood.
Books with [important] writing were thrown away in dreadful places.
Any fast means of communication one might think to use, such as the
> telephone,
or the television one watches, or video cameras with which to record
> things,
anyone who might aspire to a better future they wiped out without a
> trace—
these Mooryaan, who were egged on by power brokers.... (stanza 10)

The poet also provides an explanatory framework for the violence when he refers to the destructive habit of clan vendettas. He says: "The whole shoreline is lined with our corpses, as clan grudges are acted upon time and again. It is in their nature to say, 'this man is of the Ducaale family, so kill him.'" He expresses regret about the spirit of clan cleansing that drove its victims to the areas from which their ancestors had once hailed. It was only recently, he says, that people had emancipated themselves from such homelands to become inhabitants of a national territory and citizens of a nation-state. Thus, the poet's meta-explanation of the violence is a lament—framed within an acknowledgement of God's omnipotence—about the fate of the nation and the flag of independent statehood, and about how foolish it is for people of common descent and culture to fight.

They destroyed our nation, the flood swept it away.
They threw our flag into the ditch, blown along by the wind.
The hearts that were entwined split apart and have been impossible
> to reunite.
This was the fate that befell people who
had only recently separated themselves from their places of origin.

We look to God for our reward, as He is the Always Generous,
but let me go back and add one last word of advice:
For people who were born together, of the same stock,
tracing their descent to the same origin,
with no differences in skin color, culture, religion or language,
to be divided by war and animosity is foolishness.

> Scrape the rust off your hearts and cleanse your inside.
> Hold on to your togetherness and strengthen your unity. (stanza 21)

"Mogadishu, You Have Been Violated" or "Lament for Mogadishu"

The second text, a poetic text alliterating in "x," "Mogadishu, You Have Been Violated" (Xamar waa lagu xumeeyeyeey)[6] was authored, set to music, sung, and performed to the accompaniment of the lute by Axmed Naaji Sacad, perhaps Somalia's most accomplished and versatile song-writer, singer, musician, and musical entrepreneur. Associated with the musical tradition of Mogadishu, of which he is one of the founders, he, too, had to flee Somalia and is now living in Yemen. The song dates from 1991 and became enormously popular among Somalis, for many of whom it captured the mood of the period. In this song, especially its refrain, Naaji dramatically presents the city as a woman who was raped, with no one to restore her honor. When a whole city is raped, who can restore its honor, Naaji appears to ask, especially when its violators are the very men who should have protected it! Equally dramatic is the juxtaposition of images of the city as the singer's (and, by implication, all Somalis') beautiful, safe, and regionally respected home, with those of the sudden and overwhelming force with which it was assaulted, violated, plundered, and robbed of its beauty and honor.

> Mogadishu, you have been violated,
> who will restore your honor?
> You are the place where my umbilical cord was buried
> —Mogadishu, you have been violated—
> the center of my kin folk and siblings
> —Mogadishu, you have been violated—
> Great was your stature on the shore of the Horn of Africa
> —Mogadishu, you have been violated—
> The fire they opened on you came down like a hot wind
> —Mogadishu, you have been violated—
> With furious force they obliterated your neighborhoods
> —Mogadishu, you have been violated—
> snatching away your beauty all at once.
> We used to reside in you calmly, safely and freely.
> Mogadishu, you have been violated, who will restore your honor?

* * *

Maternal relatives and in-laws became enraged with each other;
Mogadishu, you have been violated.
Those who freed you from the spiteful [collaborators] and the unbelieving foreigners;
—Mogadishu, you have been violated—
as well as our great thinkers were put into their graves;
—Mogadishu, you have been violated—
and the wisdom of our political and religious leaders was rejected;
—Mogadishu, you have been violated—
The families you sustained [crossed the borders];
—Mogadishu, you have been violated—
We used to reside in you calmly, safely, and freely.
Mogadishu, you have been violated, who will restore your honor?

In the second stanza, Naaji addresses the social relations that were violated during the fighting. These violent acts were perpetrated among people who were related through their mothers' side or by marriage, who had shared a political cause during and after the struggle for independence, and who had in the past subscribed to the same Somali social code, that of custom and religion as represented by elders and religious teachers. In just a few words, Naaji asserts the morality and cultural authenticity of Somali custom and of bonds of kinship that are wider than those imposed by the narrow "patrilineal absolutism" of the clan logic.[7] He reminds Somalis of the sacrifices their leaders made to obtain political independence and of the skills and talents with which they undertook building the independent state. Thus, he implicitly rejects clan thinking and explicitly evokes the common nation- and statehood that, anchored in religion and Somali tradition, had kept Somalis safe in their beautiful, highly regarded capital.

"To the Leaders of the USC"

Cabdi Muxumed Amiin, a prolific poet, songwriter, dramatist, and actor who died in 2010, is probably most widely known for his songs. Truly a poet in touch with the mood of the people, his repertoire reflects the Somali people's changing hopes for, and disappointments in the political developments in the country. A dedicated socialist and supporter of the Barre regime's "scientific socialist revolution," he authored some of the best known and most popular songs of the Barre era—such as Caynaanka haay! "Hold the Reins Forever"—which, later, as the personality cult around Barre became more obvious and oppressive, became greatly disliked. However, in 1989, on the eve of the fall of the regime, Cabdi Muxumed also authored the song "Land Cruiser." Sung by Saado Cali, who went to prison for performing it in front of Barre, this song dared to criticize the regime's conspicuous consumption even as the inhabitants of Mogadishu were without even water and light. You are driving fancy Land Cruisers, the song said, pampering them as if they are expensive mistresses, while you beg for grain from abroad. Cabdi Muxumed fled the violence in Mogadishu for Moscow, where he had studied and from where he continued his artistic production. He sent one of the songs he authored in 1991 to the legendary Somali diva from Mogadishu, Faduuma Qaasim. Now known as "My Country" (Dalkeygoow) or "I Did Not Leave You as a Tourist" (Dalxiis kaama imaanin), this song has become iconic of Somali nostalgia for the country they were forced to leave behind.[8] The poem "To the Leaders of the USC" (Ragga USC daadahshoow) is now available on www.youtube.com but appears to be less well known than some of this poet's songs.[9] This poem, alliterating in "d" and dating from 1991, addresses the very armed opposition front that actualized the key shift and unleashed the campaign of clan cleansing in Mogadishu in January 1991 and speaks to the order of events by which the shift took place. In the collection of his poetry published in 2006, the introduction to the poem read as follows:

> This poem criticizes the organization as well as the men who led it and who were unable to restrain themselves, failed to know how to do the right thing, allowed plunder, and failed to prevent the looting of both national and personal wealth, the killing of the common people, clan retaliation, and so forth. (Cabdi Muxumed Amiin 2006: 150)

The body of the poem begins with warm and respectful greetings to the men of the USC. The poet's next remark refers back to reasoning that was a common element of the "scientific socialist" thinking of the 1970s, namely to the different stages by which humankind has progressed through history—succeeding even in reaching the moon—not by luck but through hard work.[10] Then he turns to the events of January 1991. He evokes the picture of a city besieged by its own president, with shells raining down and dead bodies lining the streets. However, the people were united, he asserts, and stormed Barre's residence in Villa Somalia, making it possible for the USC leadership to take the lead and assure itself of an honorable place in history.

> During the days of fighting against
> the dictator who was brought down,
> when Mogadishu was resonating with explosions and artillery shells rained down,
> and dead bodies were everywhere lining the streets,
> while the people were one,
> like a branch and its bark,
> with only one purpose and desire;
> and when, in the early evening,
> every one flocked to "Afweyne"'s residence[11]
> and chased him out
> —for time caught up with him, now turning the tables—
> the people did their duty
> and gave you, leaders of the party,
> a distinguished position in history.

In the next two verses, the poet is at his most direct. He accuses the USC leaders not only of failing to think and plan well but also of becoming suspicious of other clans and of trying to monopolize state power even before peace, order, and basic services had been restored to the city. In the third verse, the poet appears to refer to the SNM, which had established itself as a regional administration in the north. Although he makes it clear that he is critical of the means it used in its armed opposition against the Barre regime, he cannot stomach the fact, he explains, that the USC failed to invite the SNM to participate before it formed a transitional government and grabbed the presidency.

> But feelings of suspicion took over
> and careless thinking.
> The illness that kills all of Africa
> has you in its grip.
> Before the families had settled down
> and were doing better,
> before the big gathering that the nation needed
> had been called,
> before the fighting was over
> and the bombing had subsided,
> before public services had been restored

and the bullets that were flying everywhere
in Mogadishu had ceased,
before the electricity had been turned back on,
and communications with the outside
and the water supply had been secured,
that you would engage in senseless fighting over who would be the head of state
is something I cannot stomach.

A high position is sweet only
when people hold a public celebration for you
and milk is poured and animals are slaughtered;
when one is elected
to the sound of "receive our blessings and benevolence."

But if someone, always says, as a wrongdoer would,
"it is me!"
and refuses to consult others
and undermines any alternative.
that is what destroyed our country and
has left us exhausted.
That you forget this so quickly is something
I cannot stomach
If we put this in historical perspective,
we [know that] we have fought before.

[But in regard to] the armed front that, in broad daylight,
smashed skulls, with a big hammer,
knocked out teeth and broke jaws;
the front that devoured people in secret
and fed them poison;
and about which nothing was done
with any urgency;
and that in part resides inside the country
forming a government itself—
That no delegation was immediately sent to it
—If it assumes its responsibility, justice will not stray—
is something I cannot stomach.

The poet then explicitly accuses the previous regime, the Barre dictatorship, for choosing force and violence in all its relations, in and outside Somalia, and for setting Somalis up against each other. Without an explicit reference to who did this for what reason and exactly at which moment, he goes on to criticize those who, in Barre's final hour, came to the failing dictator's help and proposed "to let the old man be":

> All the people who live and make their livelihood in the bush
> or on the vast sea or anywhere else in the Everlasting God's creation;
> in all corners of our Somali habitat,
> and even those parts of the world that were earnest
> in their rejection of oppression,
> said "let's fight" against the former government;
> "its misdeeds have destroyed us,
> and have set us up against each other."
> They called it "dalgub"—"wrecker of the country"—
> as no one will deny.
> How the city was bombarded
> when the fighting came to be concentrated in Mogadishu,
> and he [Barre] was dealt the final blows,
> and point after point was scored against him;
> and when he became bewildered and lost all sense of direction!
> That [at that moment] men came to his aid
> and his defense,
> and said "let the old man be,"
> is something I cannot stomach.

In the next two verses, the poet comes back to what he believes the "leaders of the USC" did wrong. First, he blames them, in relatively general terms, for lack of intelligence and political sophistication, miscalculation, and unethical behavior, and for thus embarking on a dead-end policy.[12] In the next stanza, he goes on to articulate what he regards as their political failures: to use violence and impose their will on the people without any discussion or explanation; to fail to control the criminal acts of clansmen; to engage in looting and in robbing women; to think and act as if one is superior to other people; and to run amok without constraint. Even though he uses a form of linguistic indirection ("it is not proper politics to . . ."), it is in this verse that his criticism is at its most direct: "to scare people into running away in a panic and kill them on the basis of clan" was a poor political decision, he asserts, implying that this campaign of elimination and expulsion on the basis of clan was a political decision, not just the failure "to control the criminal acts of clansmen."

Cabdi Muxumed, too, frames his mediation of the violence in terms of clan and nation, decrying the destructiveness of clan, the loss of human dignity implied in the destruction of the nation, and the blind acceptance of dishonest, greedy leaders. Here, however, he does not blame only the leaders of the USC, and the focalization of his poem, that is to say the subject of the actions he describes, shifts from "you, leaders of the USC" to "we," that is to say, "we, Somalis."

> The fire set by a hypocrite will burn
> those who are non-suspecting.
> Your lack of sophistication threw you
> off the right path and led you astray.
> It blinded and destroyed you,
> and guided you onto a dead-end road,
> an empty space.
> Only when we hit the wall,
> can we imagine how we got there.
>
> It is not (proper) politics to just fight
> and drive people along like cattle.
> *It is not (proper) politics to scare people into running*
> *away in a panic and kill them on the basis of clan.*
> It is not (proper) politics for clansmen to roam around
> and commit hit-and-run crimes.
> It is not (proper) politics to put out one's goats to graze
> on stubble left behind by the wild boar.
> It is not (proper) politics to be mindless and irresponsible.
> It is not chasing after loot and robbing women.
> It is not demeaning people and considering yourselves superior.
> It is not running amok like unleashed livestock.
> We should not give thieves high positions and let them be.
> Clan is destructive and should not take us down with it.
> It is not human dignity for our nation to be destroyed
> without anyone giving a damn.

The poet, finally, concludes with a very pragmatic agenda for the future, one that shows traces of his once passionately held socialist belief in the importance of economic context:

> To be sincere means to move towards
> To an era of receptivity and wisdom
> and to overcome sectarianism.
> We should look at the world
> and feel the pain of envy.
> No one should care about anything else
> than for us to become a state.
> To rebuild the economy of our country
> is the appropriate way to go.
> Everyone should refuse importing food from abroad.
> Cultivate your land and produce food instead.
> If not, our human dignity will be lost
> and we should just look towards the grave.

"Sound, Drum of Wisdom!"

The fourth text, Cabdulqaadir Cabdi Shube's "Sound, Drum of Wisdom!" (Durbaan garashoow diyaan!),[13] is authored by a poet of the same generation as the first three but at a temporal remove from the events of 1990–1991. Shube performed this poem (alliterating in "d") at the national reconciliation meetings in Djibouti in 2000, in front of the very political leaders, warlords, and clan bosses he criticizes in his poem. In his spoken introduction, he asked them to put up with his anger and frustration; after all, he had spoken to them many times, on similar occasions, in similar terms. The following focuses on excerpts from this long poem. In 2000 a fragile de facto absence of war existed in some parts of Somalia, but no national government worth that name had been able to establish itself. Perhaps this is one of the reasons why Shube's emphasis lies less on describing civil war violence than on interpreting it, diagnosing its causes, and harnessing his rhetorical powers to overcome it. From the very beginning of this poem, it becomes evident that the poet mediates the violence of state collapse with notions of clan and clan thinking as they relate to nation and state. In the first stanza quoted here, he presents himself (and indirectly all Somalis) as someone left destitute by the self-inflicted loss of state and nation. He announces he wants to rekindle the fire of national feeling and heal the mindset of clan hatred:

> My aim is larger than
> what fits in the space between my cheeks.
> I am without a country and a people.
> I am someone who used to have a state
> and destroyed an established nation.
> I am someone who used to live in a safe, shielded place
> but is now battered by the winds in an open plain.
> I am a man who used to have resources and
> caused the ruin of his own environment.
> I am someone for whom others go around and beg.
> If I pull myself together, gather the stragglers and
> collect those left behind,
> I am rekindling a fire that has gone out.
> I am carrying a drum to provide wisdom.
> I am bringing a doctor along for healing.
> I am healing a mind-set.
> "Eyes, look!," I say
> what our peers are accomplishing,
> while we are sitting in an empty space. . . .

In the following verse, the poet directly blames Somali leaders for misleading the common people by manipulating the latter's clan sentiment for their own personal gain and by making false promises of material rewards. Even though only God is all-powerful, he says, it is up to common Somalis to pull themselves out of their tragic situation.

> Give them what they need, you drum of wisdom.
> Tell them that God decreed this.
> Point out the responsibility that has been shirked.
> Explain to them who deceived them,
> who made stupid people out of them,
> led them astray,
> hid the truth from them
> pushed them towards disaster,
> and hid behind clan,
> working on their feelings by appealing to kinship,
> obsessed with greed,
> paying you off with something that does not even wet your lips,

> promising to give you wealth that they do not have,
> degrading what they advocate and egg you on to do,
> with no feeling whatsoever,
> and hiding from you
> that God is generous,
> endlessly munificent,
> and can give to whomever he wants,
> but that we must make an effort.
> Drum, tell the people this on my behalf....

The poet then describes what he calls the "calamity of clannism" and its doomed supporters in terms of illness, madness, disorder, lawlessness, injustice, darkness, and ignorance. If clan had anything positive to offer, he assures his listener, God would have made this clear to us.

> Clannism is a calamity.
> There is nothing that can improve or cure it.
> It is worse than malaria and fever,
> worse than fatal diseases.
> It turns people into something less than human
> and takes away their sanity.
> It destroys law and order,
> it extinguishes the light,
> it shies away from knowledge,
> it takes shelter in ignorance,
> it takes justice down,
> it shores up oppression,
> and its supporters will go down with it.
>
> If it had any benefit,
> our Lord would have told us
> and our religion would have clarified this.
> My people, I promise,
> my lips will utter words of advice
> as long as they can.
> Sound, you drum of understanding!

****

All four poets reflect in their own ways on the questions of what violent acts were perpetrated, by and against whom, and for what reasons. The most detailed description of the violence is that in Mustafa Sheekh's "Disaster," which lists in harrowing detail the horrific acts committed by the perpetrators, the harm suffered by the victims, and the physical and moral impact on state and society. The violence that becomes visible in his text consists of grievous harm inflicted on people because of their group identity. Civilians—men, women, children, and old people—were killed (shot, stabbed, beaten, blown up) on a large scale. They were attacked unexpectedly and irrespective of where they were and what they were doing—with some families even unsuspectingly asleep in their own homes. The dead bodies of the victims lined the streets, their flesh gnawed at by dogs and pecked at by crows. These corpses were either not buried at all or were put into the dirt without the prescribed religious ritual—just put into the ground with their clothes on and without having been washed. Those victims who escaped with their lives were thrown into a panic and put to flight, forming an exodus of exhausted, starving, thirsty, destitute, sick and wounded small groups and individuals, of whom many succumbed to the hardship or were harassed, attacked, and killed as they fled. Large-scale rape of women and girls of all generations, often in each other's presence and even in mosques, was an integral part of the terror that drove people out. The violent acts were accompanied by speech acts that further humiliated the victims, for the perpetrators "jeered at us for how we were crushed." The poet moreover makes it clear that there was intent involved, as the perpetrators put their victims at the mercy of wild animals and interfered with the ships that might have taken them to safety.

Who are the men who committed these acts or were otherwise responsible for them? In "Disaster" Mustafa Sheekh makes specific mention of two groups, the Mooryaan, the young men from the bush who carried out many of the violent acts, and the political entrepreneurs who used them as their instrument and egged them on. Who were these powerbrokers who were behind the violence? The poet is not specific about their identity. Are they the leaders of the armed opposition fronts, which, according to the poet, deceived the people, manipulated and destroyed them? And does he hold some fronts more responsible than others? This is unclear.[14] Thus the poet who is most explicit about the violence that accompanied state collapse does not attribute—and in the early 1990s perhaps does not *need* to attribute—specific responsibility or culpability.

The poet is, in contrast, very specific about what he sees as a deeper cause of, and solution to the violence of state collapse and he frames his emotional appeal to his audience in terms of national unity. Though he does not name clan or clan thinking by name, he appeals to his audience as people who have descent, culture, religion, language, and skin color in common and who therefore should be able "to scrape the rust of hatred and divisiveness"—the corrosion caused by the acid of clan thinking—from what he presents as the "natural" and "true" collective identity of nationhood. That their beloved nation is also a construct and that the nation-building project that became dominant in the 1960s and 1970s contained and produced internal inequalities is not on the poet's agenda in this text.

In "Mogadishu, you have been violated," Axmed Naaji *evokes* the violence of state collapse rather than describing it in detail. Though he mentions artillery fire, the obliteration of the city's neighborhoods, and the expulsion of its families, all of this is subsumed under the metaphor of the city's rape by those who should have been its protectors. Naaji's explanatory framework connects the loss of the moral and material benefits of nation- and statehood to the violation of traditional cultural values that lay at the root of that common nationhood. Though he associates Mogadishu, here symbolizing the nation itself, with the greatness of the anticolonial struggle for independence, his strongest rhetorical strategy is to appeal to another dimension of the discourse that had undergirded Somali nation- and state-building for several decades, the rights and duties of kinship Somalis used to hold sacred. What happened in Mogadishu was the reversal—as Naaji puts it, the rape—of the national Somali identity whose roots lay in the common descent and traditional culture that had been the heart of nationalist discourse.

Naaji opposes what may be called the "patrilineal absolutism" of modern clan thinking—a valuation of the group constituted patrilineally only—to what he considers the organic, customary, authentically Somali, inclusive conceptions of kinship that valued the ever-expandable social web of relations with affines and in-laws, and relatives traced through the mother as well as those traced through the father. Thus Naaji denaturalizes and deconstructs the concept of clan as a political instrument of violence and distinguishes it sharply from what he considers the old and revered Somali kinship values. He presents the clan concept of the killers as a kind of "containerized" identity construct, one that in 1991 denied and violently erased both the interconnecting bonds between Somalis and the physical existence and presence of those individuals and groups embodying them.[15] Naaji does not identify specific perpetrators or mention clan or clans explicitly in this poem and it is only indirectly that he presents the mindset that allowed for the rape of Mogadishu as a travesty of the Somali traditional kinship code.

If the strength of Mustafa Sheekh's "Disaster" lies in how it describes what happened in 1991, that of the third text presented here, Cabdi Muxumed's "To the Leaders of the USC," distinguishes itself by directly addressing those it held responsible. Of all the poetry surveyed for this project, this poet is the only one to have authored a poem that is widely regarded as prestigious and legitimate and yet have been this explicit.[16] In contrast to "Disaster," the poem "To the Leaders of the USC" does not focus on the suffering of those targeted for violence but articulates the political blunders and crimes committed, according to the poet, by the leaders of the USC. Their cardinal sin was, the poet argues, their arrogant, short-sighted, and unethical ambition to take control of the state all by themselves, ignoring the other armed opposition fronts, envious and suspicious of other clans, and disregarding the wishes of the people, who were united in their commitment to overthrow the dictatorship and clamored for a constitutional convention. In the process, the poet asserts, they looked down on others, tried to impose their will by force, chased after loot, robbed women, ran amok, and allowed simple clansmen to run wild and commit all sorts of crimes. The most explicit references to the clan cleansing the USC set into motion are the lines in which the poet accuses the USC leaders of suffering from "the illness that kills all of Africa," that is to say, tribalism (or its Somali equivalent, clannism or clan thinking) and points out to them that "to scare people into running away in a panic and to kill them on the basis of clan" does not represent sound politics.

This is strong language, softened only by two textual strategies. First, the poet also uses strong language to hold other individuals and groups responsible for the violence that accompanied state collapse. First and foremost among these is Maxamed Siyaad Barre himself, whom the poet calls "dalgub," a "country wrecker," and accuses of setting Somalis up against each other. The poet's judgment of the other armed opposition movements is equally harsh. In challenging the government, they resorted to blunt force, treated their recruits badly, led them poorly, and poisoned their minds (perhaps with clan chauvinism). Finally, the poet refers to men who broke ranks with the anti-Barre opposition and burst on the scene to come to the dictator's rescue in his final hour. It is not clear to which men the poet here precisely refers. Accounts that try to explain away or justify the turn to clan cleansing make precisely these kinds of accusations against the groups that were targeted.[17]

Reports from the ranks of the latter show that different individuals became aware of USC intentions at different times. As a result, they stopped resisting the regime and instead turned to defending themselves against the USC at different times.[18]

The second rhetorical strategy is a linguistic one and has to do with how the poet, precisely when his accusations of the USC leadership are most explicit, also succeeds in diluting the force of his attack. He uses two techniques here, that of indirect speech and of changing the focalization in certain crucial poetic lines. Thus he makes his speech indirect by using the passive tense and the impersonal third person singular. For example, when he accuses the USC of "senselessly falling out" over the control of state power, his sentence is constructed in the impersonal form—"that *one* would engage in senseless fighting over" (*madaxnimo in la isugu dudaa*)—a construction comparable to the French *on y va*.[19] The same indirection characterizes the stanza in which the poet takes the USC leadership to task for their political strategy: "Politics is not"—and should not be—"to drive people away in a panic and to kill them on the basis of clan," he says. While it is obvious from the context that this must be read as an accusation of the USC leadership, the indictment at the same time reaches beyond this specific organization. The way the poet alternates narrow, specific accusations with broad metaphorical admonitions further reinforces this wider focus. While there is, therefore, on the one hand, no doubt that the poet accuses the "leaders of the USC" of his poem's title, he does not accuse them alone and *also* blames Somali political and military leaders more generally. It is characteristic of so-called prestigious poetry that it elevates its analysis to an abstract level, and this is what Cabdi Muxumed here appears to do (Samatar 1982: 56–58).

This is even more obvious in a second linguistic technique with which he dilutes the force of his accusations, changes in focalization. Thus, in the stanza in which he accuses the USC of poor and unethical policies, he not only uses the impersonal form but in the last line shifts from the implied "you, leaders of the USC" to the "we" that implicates all Somalis. "We Somalis" should not settle for political leaders who are immoral and should not destroy ourselves through clan thinking, and be indifferent to the fate of our nation:

> We should not give thieves high positions and let them be.
> Clan is destructive and should not take us down with it.
> It is not human dignity for our nation to be destroyed
> without anyone giving a damn.

The poet concludes with a general principle, that "clan only destroys and should not be a permanent feature of life," and that indifference to the fate of the nation is below human dignity. The phrase "clan is destructive" (*qabiil waa wax dumiyee*), finally, lends further emphasis to his rejection of clan as a general political principle (and not a specific accusation to the USC leadership), as it is a powerful intertextual reference to a famous line of poetry by the nationalist poet "Timacadde," who said: "Clannism can provide no shelter as it can only destroy (*Dugsi maleh qabyaaladu, waxay dumiso mooyaane*).[20]

Like Cabdi Muxumed, Cabdi Shube, in "Sound, Drum of Wisdom," focuses on how deceitful and merciless political entrepreneurs manipulated the gullibility, clan sentiment, and greed of common Somalis. Authored in 2000 for the national reconciliation meetings in Djibouti, the poem does not dwell on the kinds of violent acts that were inflicted on people or on those individuals or organizations that were responsible for the violence that accompanied the collapse of the state. It is at this more abstract and conceptual level that Shube fashions his poem as emotive and effective speech. As in "Disaster" and "Mogadishu, You Have Been Violated," the interpretive framework of "Sound, Drum of Wisdom" consists of the opposing conceptual pair of nation as a collective identity and project that is moral and constructive (and remains largely un-interrogated) and clan, the political instrument and mindset that is nation's immoral and destructive other. Shube's poem is fully dedicated to drawing this distinction and to persuading Somalis to embrace national unity, resist the clan sentiment manipulated by unscrupulous leaders and cure themselves from its debilitating effects on individual and collective sanity. Authored at a temporal remove, Shube does not deny the culpability of unscrupulous leaders, but his emphasis is on how all Somalis, including himself, have been instrumental in, and thus responsible for what happened.

Religion, that is, Islam, does not figure prominently in the poetic texts presented above, but it *does* figure unemphatically in three of the four. In "Disaster," for example, it has an organic presence and appears to figure as a matter of course. The author refers to it at the very beginning of his text, as he establishes the temporal framework of his poem ("When people moved away from religion and the path of justice"). Moreover, when he begins his detailed description of the violence, he addresses himself to God: "Dear God, how much wealth was obliterated in the fighting!"

In Naaji's "Mogadishu, You Were Violated," the emphasis is on the ethical qualities of what he considers authentic Somali traditional culture, of which respect for "the wisdom of our political and religious leaders" was an intrinsic part. Naaji's text here is typical of much of the poetry and song texts of the nationalist era (1955–1991), in which Islam was present as an organic, self-evident, and integral part of the Somali cultural legacy that did not need separate mention (Kapteijns 2009). The moral values that were to anchor and restrain Somali nationalist modernity lay in the religious-*and*-cultural authenticity of this Somali "tradition," whose Somali cultural and Islamic religious dimensions only came to be questioned with the gradual emergence of a multifaceted Islamist movement.[21]

Shube's text fits the pattern of Mustafa Sheekh's and Axmed Naaji's poems, in which Islam provides a more or less emphatic frame of reference as a matter of course, as an integral part of the Somali language itself. Shube's poem, perhaps reflecting its later date, refers to religion twice. Once, he does so to encourage Somalis to accept their fate as decreed by God and perhaps to leave the past behind. The second time, toward the end of his poem, he leverages religion in several ways. While reminding his audience that God is generous and can make things right again, he also insists that they (that is to say, we, Somalis) "must make an effort." And he again turns to religion to back up his argument that the concept of clan has nothing to offer: "If it had any benefit, our Lord would have told us and our religion would have clarified this."

The only exception is Cabdi Muxumed's "To the Leaders of the USC," which instead frames his intensely moral plea for unity, mutual respect, autonomous, self-sufficient, and democratic nation- and statehood in terms of human dignity and the aspiration to find a respected place in the world: "We should look at the world, and feel the pain of envy. No one should care about anything else than for us to become a state." Thus, where other poets often conclude their poems with an appeal to God, Cabdi Muxumed resorts to a strategy common in the earlier era of "scientific socialism" and emphasizes statehood and economic self-sufficiency, especially in food production. This way of articulating the hopes he has for Somalia does not draw the poet's religiosity into question—after all, he refers to the world as the creation of God, the Ever-Lasting—but marks him and these other poets as representative of the national era, when for most Somalis, the struggle to fashion a moral and authentic Somali identity drew on "traditional culture" and Islam as an indistinguishable conceptual pair.

Three provisional conclusions deserve to be drawn here. First, poems dealing with the specificities of the violence that accompanied state collapse are not many, Mustafa Sheekh's "Disaster" constituting a powerful and graphic exception. Second, prestigious poems that are specific about the identities of perpetrators and victims are extraordinarily rare, with Cabdi Muxumed's "To the Leaders of the USC" forming an exceptionally carefully conceptualized and contextualized exception to this rule. It is likely that these poets, who addressed Somalis in Somali about relatively current events, could assume that the identities of the parties to the violence of 1991 were obvious, but this aporia is, nevertheless, significant. After all, many Somalis have interpreted and continued to interpret this violence from the narrow perspective of the victimization of their own clan. Third, a large number of poems and songs that deal with the violence of state collapse use an explanatory frame that has three intertwined discursive strands, those of (anti-)clan, nation, and Islam. If we imagine a barber's pole, a kind of glass or plastic tube in which three (red, white, and blue) vertical stripes turn around and upward—continuously appearing to take each other's place—then we can envision these three intertwined discourses as those three stripes. The poets discussed above diagnosed clan as the cause of civil war violence and nation (organically rooted in Islam) as the solution. In the next two poems, this diagnosis is largely the same, but the proposed solution—and thus the direction of the poetic intervention—begins to be couched in more explicitly Islamic terms.

We will pursue the analysis of poetic mediations of civil war violence by examining two later poems, both authored in the period 2003–2005, just before the war in Mogadishu reignited and entered a new stage (and discursive shift) in the ongoing Somali civil war, one involving Islamist militias that justified their violent actions in Islamist terms. The authors of these poems, Cumar Cabdinuur Nuux "Nabaddoon," and Maxamed Cali Cibaar, both prolific poets, represent a different generation than those examined above. They are younger (in their thirties or forties), have more formal education (both are engineers), live in the West (that is to say, in the diaspora outside of Africa), and post their poems in writing on one or more Somali Web sites immediately after authoring them. Their poetry is featured on a variety of such Web sites, in audiovisual or written form, and is part of a vast body of "Internet poetry" whose contents and audience reception deserve further study.[22] Like the poems presented above, these later ones interpret the violence accompanying and following state collapse in abstract moral terms and through the discursive lens of clan-nation-Islam.

Speaking the Unspeakable 45

Poetry of the Early 2000s
"Clan and I."

"Clan and I" (Aniga iyo Qabiil), a poem alliterating in "q," was composed and immediately posted to the Internet by Nabaddoon in October 2003. This was a moment in time at which the tenure of the Transitional National Government or TNG (established at the national reconciliation meetings held in Djibouti in 2000) was about to end and that of the Transitional Federal Government or TFG (2004), now under its second president (2009–present), was about to begin. It illustrates both the interdiscursivity outlined above and the increasing emphasis on Islam.[23] "Clan and I" focuses explicitly on the concept of clan and takes the form of a heated conversation between Clan (Qabiil) and the poet himself, standing in for every Somali. The poet starts out by blaming Qabiil (Clan personified) for all the violence and disasters that have befallen Somalia. However, Qabiil argues back. Is the poet sure that he himself is not Clan? The following is an excerpt from this text, in which the discourses of clan, nation, and Islam are clearly intertwined:

> Clan (Qabiil) and I had a discussion and disagreed with each other.
> I am without a nation (*qaran*) because of what you have caused: collapse, flight, and disaster.
> In the continents I reside now, I am naked because of you.
> Do you not acknowledge that I have been set back a century and a half?
>
> A Muslim people (*umma*) sustains a nation (*qaran*) with education and the pen,[24]
> but writing and arithmetic have lost their importance a long time ago.
> The gun has replaced them, children no longer have pens.
> Do you not acknowledge that I have been set back a century and a half?
>
> When you undermined the economy and destroyed its value
> and you locked some people up together, forcing others to go elsewhere,
> you took for yourself the role that Nation (*Qaran*) would have played.
> Do you not acknowledge that I have been set back a century and a half?

Of our beautiful centuries-old cities,
some you destroyed while other ones suffer from neglect.
I am lucidly aware of what I am against,
but I am no longer sure whether I am watching a movie or am already in my grave.

The city has no regulations and no one does any work.
For quite a while its garbage and rotten-smelling trash have not been removed.
Tuberculosis and typhus have befallen its pretty girls.
Do you not acknowledge that I have been set back a century and a half?

Because of you, Clan, paternal and maternal relatives have come to hate each other.
Because of you a family sleeping peacefully is being blown up
and a kin group that has done no one wrong slaughtered.
Will you not go to hell for this—I will not join you there.

Then Clan (Qabiil) said, now I, who loves clan, take the word.
I do not mean to wrong you but to tell the truth and stop you in your tracks.
You are ranting and digging yourself into a hole.
While you destroyed the nation (*qaran*), you are blaming me.
Let me explain your mistakes to you, take my advice.

Except for your clan, you despise and hate everything.
You are the one carrying the guns and bombs.
You are the one who follows the lead of warlords and accept what they say.
Do you not admit that you are Clan?

An eye for an eye, and this is true,
is mentioned in the Qur'an and is not clan talk,
but you reject God's law and go another way.
"I must punish you for your wrongdoing," you say, "and cut your throat."

* * *

You go abroad, to rotten foreign lands.
You help the warlords and send them supplies.
You are collecting clan payments and contributions that cause havoc.
Don't you admit that you are Clan?

A nation (*qaran*) without strong leadership,
which discriminates on the basis of clan and
without guiding laws is a shambles.
Once you content yourself with such a flawed set up and impotent anger,
what can I do for you?
Don't you deserve bad things?
. . .
You, who come after me, take this wisdom as a legacy.
Keep nation and clan separate; don't surreptitiously mix the two up.
Discern what is wrong and evil and don't deceive yourselves.
Don't look for a logic that can make light and dark into the same thing.

Follow God's word and value peace.
Take guidance from the law laid down by Abu Qaasim.[25]
Ask for forgiveness from God and stop this agitation.
At the time of Judgment there will be a reckoning and scorching flames.
Listen you all, your soul will be taken to the grave all by itself,
and your lips will form only one sound, laughter or lament.

In this poem, Nabaddoon holds Clan directly responsible for the destruction of the war and the loss of the nation; for the physical segregation and expulsion of people on the basis of clan; for the collapse of the economy; for having youth toting guns instead of pens; for tearing families apart into patrilineally and matrilineally related groups; for ongoing violence against unsuspecting civilians, and for the destruction of cities that are now without rule or regulation, without services such as garbage collection or clean water, and without structured employment, and that have become seedbeds of illness and infection. The poet accuses Clan for having taken the place that Nation should have occupied, causing society to become lawless, inequitable, and discriminatory.

However, in the form of Clan talking back to the poet, Nabaddoon also articulates the responsibilities individual Somalis neglected and perverted: You only follow clan leaders, Clan complains, and only take their orders. You go abroad and continue to collect money on the basis of clan and send it back to Somalia to buy more arms. Peace and reconciliation will require a moral transformation of Somalis on the individual and collective level, the poet warns. This means observing Islamic law and committing oneself to peace, he argues, as well as making a clear distinction, in thought and action, between nation and clan. After all, the poet concludes, just as, on the Day of Judgment, you will either weep or smile, not both, and reap heaven or hell, not both, so you must either choose nation or clan, not both.

For Nabaddoon, clan is a complex phenomenon. It represents an unethical, inequitable, and unworkable political ideology or set of values; a powerful political instrument in the hands of immoral and grasping warlords, and a popular mindset that is short-sighted, chauvinist, aggressive, gullible, and easily manipulated for violent purposes. The poet does not develop his concept of nation. Instead, especially when guided by God's laws, it presents in this poem the solution to all that is wrong with clan.

"Duty."

The last poem presented here is Maxamed Cali Cibaar's "Duty" (Waajib), posted on the Internet in late 2005,[26] in which the Islamic strand of the intertwined discourses of clan, nation, and Islam, lights up more brightly than in Nabaddoon's "Clan and I."[27] The poem is in the genre of the *gabay* and alliterates in "w." In it, the poet addresses Somalis as a flawed *umma*[28]—a term that highlights the Islamic dimension of Somali peoplehood and addresses Somalis as a community of Muslims—and calls on them to do their *waajib* or moral duty. It is striking that the poet, in blasting the Somalis for being an "*umma* of evil," is also highly interdiscursive in the way of the barber's pole evoked above. Apart from the concept of *umma*, he regularly uses the terms *qaran* (nation), *bulsho* (people, society), and *waddan* (homeland), and he fulminates, among many other things, against "the evil of clan." The poet equates and associates clan thinking with a host of negative features characterizing the Somali *umma*: with mutual suspicion, disunity, division, and lack of mutual trust and trustworthiness; with the tendency to pay allegiance to dishonest leaders rather than moral ones; with selfishness, short-sightedness, dishonesty, venality, greed, moral transgression, and oppression; with evil-mongering, destruction, and lack of freedom; with the inability to hold a dialogue that goes beyond insult and provocation, and with irreligiosity and being led astray by the devil. The poem concludes with verses that couch the duty (*waajib*) that awaits those who want a solution for Somalia in both religious and political terms.

> An umma that the evil of clan has divided into ghettos.
> An umma whose ruler[29] is a thief who is [nevertheless] trusted by everyone.
> An umma whose chiefs are guided by small-minded counsel.
> An umma that attacks and stones the person who is useful to it.
>
> An umma whose *weli* (model religious leader)[30] sells religious services for personal gain.
> An umma that is wallowing in what is outside of the *sunna* and *xaraam*.
> An umma that does not act upon the sacred oaths its takes.
> An umma that avoids what is good and wanders away from it.
> An umma that is bothered by what is good and that stirs up evil. . . .
>
> An umma that does not worry about the fact that
> the country in which it has always lived is torn to pieces.
> An umma that is not even aware of the traps set up all around it.
> An umma that rejects unity and whose people are suspicious of each other.
> An umma that has said goodbye to freedom and prefers oppression.
> A nation that is about to die but dances the *waalo* dance.
>
> A nation incapable of dialogue, except for taunting each other.
> A nation that prefers the words of a liar over a just and solemn agreement.
> A nation that is unaware, my brother, that the Qur'aan is real,
> that does not know its noble origin,
> that further amplifies what the devil entices it to believe,
> whose name-giving feast is a *fitna*[31] for which boys are slaughtered.

He ends his lengthy poem with the following optimistic lines:

> If you do good deeds and believe in God
> and if forbearance is your companion, you will be victorious. . . .

> Don't worry, one day the newspapers will publish good news.
> Don't worry, one day the river will take away the dirt. . . .
> Don't worry one day you will be free from all those who grow fat on misery.

Three things are striking about "Clan and I," and "Duty" by the two younger poets. First, to a somewhat higher degree than in the earlier poems, in which the victims were often represented as "we" ("Disaster") and the perpetrators as "you" or "they" (e.g., the texts by Naaji and Cabdi Muxumed), Nabaddoon and Cibaar, like Shube, hold all Somalis collectively responsible for destroying nation, state, and country.[32] Second, while the later poets mediate civil war violence in the highly interdiscursive terms of clan, nation, and, Islam, the latter now receives more emphasis. In their assessment of what happened and must happen in Somalia to put an end to violence, division, and immorality, it is a true commitment to Islam that is seen as capable of curing the clannist mindset of the Somali people and bringing back their nation- and statehood. This represents a change in the ways poets have interpreted the past and how they want their Somali audience to imagine and act on their political future.

Third, the earlier poems largely refer to the violence of 1991 as a discrete set of events that occurred at a particular moment. This is even the case in Naaji's metaphorical elegy, "Mogadishu, You Have Been Violated," in which he evokes the furious violence with which the city's neighborhoods were destroyed and close relatives turned against each other. The later poems are less graphic about the specific events and instead address and analyze the general state of affairs. They accuse self-interested and deceitful leaders for inflicting this disaster upon the common people and blame the ignorance, short-sightedness, and irreligiosity of the latter for embracing and supporting these leaders' ideas. The diagnostic of these later texts is therefore—and this is understandable after another decade or so of continued conflict and ongoing violence—further abstracted from the clan cleansing campaign and the moment of state collapse.

The Discourse of Clan and the Limits of Speech

Above we saw how six Somali poets mediate the violence of state collapse by unambiguously harnessing their work's emotive power to delegitimizing the political construct of clan. However, what is striking is that they make no direct mention of specific clan-names or of episodes and incidents committed by and against people identified by specific clan names. Even in the one poem that is an exception to this rule, that by Cabdi Muxumed, the victims—targeted for violence because of their clan backgrounds—are not named, and the clans in whose name individuals killed and died remain unmentioned. Why this silence? Since when have poets observed such silence? Do they all observe it? What exactly remains unspoken and who benefits from this? What are the advantages and disadvantages of this silence? These are some of the questions that will be discussed in what follows.

If one ponders the question of "why this silence," a number of possible reasons present themselves. First, perhaps the poets, who mediate the violence examined here in the Somali language, feel that there is *no need to* give any details of the violence of the clan logic, on the basis that Somalis know what happened and do not need to be informed. Second, perhaps the unwillingness and inability to speak is a function of the magnitude of the violence that took place and of the loss of mutual trust that has resulted. Attributing specific responsibility to named individuals and groups may either be too explosive in the ongoing civil war or such a vast task, involving so many individuals of so many groups, that only a truth commission or criminal court could hope to undertake it. Third, since the poets speak out so strongly against clan as power politics and popular mindset, speaking in terms of clans or clan members would mean using and reinforcing the very concepts that they reject. Perhaps they feel they cannot take down the house of clan with clan's own tools.[33] Fourth, the inability or unwillingness to speak clan specifics may well be the result of the continuing weight and power of almost half a century of nationalist discourse. Several generations of Somali embraced and internalized this discourse, which was powerfully shaped by poets and songwriters such as the first four presented here. For Somalis raised on this discourse, clan and clan talk may be so shameful they become unspeakable.[34]

However, fifth and finally, this question of silence or aporia also brings us back to the nature of the kind of poetic texts I chose for my study. The first time I heard a scholar at an academic conference cite a few lines of poetry about the Somali civil war that *did* mention clan names, the Somalis in his audience, young and old, male and female, became furious. They indignantly pointed out that they considered neither his speech nor that of the poets he quoted legitimate in the context of simultaneously shared public Somali space—an academic space to boot. Confronted with the mention of specific clan names in the context of the communal violence that had occurred between them, it appeared they suddenly found themselves differentially related both to the words that were spoken and to the speaker and the people around them. Rightly or wrongly, they insisted that, in that particular context, their common identity as Somalis—their national identity—was the only relevant and appropriate one and that the speaker was out of line to address and construct them differently.[35]

As I mentioned above, when I began my study of Somali popular culture about civil war violence, I purposefully looked for texts that were authoritative and legitimate, and this meant, though I was not fully aware of this at the time, poems and popular songs that had either been performed in public before a diverse Somali audience or were intended for circulation in such shared Somali public space. By choosing to study this kind of speech, I was buying into what the Somali literary canon constructed as prestigious, that is to say, legitimate, authoritative, and effective emotive speech. Two features of this prestigious speech are significant in the context of this study. First, the poetry I had chosen turned out to be gendered male in all its aspects. The poets themselves, the poetic genres they use, the audience they target, the space in which they disseminate their texts all turned out to be male. This is even true for the nature of the subject-matter, for issues of compelling general importance that go beyond the subjective experiences of private individuals have in Somali discursive space traditionally been the (allegedly) rational domain of rational men.[36] Second, in the public sphere this poetry has constructed for itself, legitimate and authoritative speech about clan-based violence is marked by aporia when it comes to the mention of specific clan names.[37] It appears that this so-called prestigious poetry in shared Somali public space cannot "rationally" contain or confront, and thus avoids, what is most contested and divisive, that is, the specifics of the violence committed in the name of clan.

One may justly argue that the poets deserve credit for not engaging the clan identities of Somalis, thus differentiating among them and, in the context of the civil war, further dividing them. However, there are also costs to this aporia. Does it, for example, not prevent the poets from engaging the political realities of clan in any way other than generally, metaphorically, and moralistically? Does it not also prevent them from attributing any specific responsibility to individual perpetrators, just because this would immediately engage these individuals' clans, groups they refuse to blame collectively? Does this aporia then not contribute to the impunity of those most culpable? One way to better weigh the costs and benefits of this aporia is to examine in more detail what exactly the poets leave unsaid. For this purpose, I will turn below to so-called "nonprestigious" genres that are not characterized by this aporia and do not stick to the unspoken rules of "prestigious" speech.

Speaking the Unspeakable: New Genres as "Nonprestigious" Speech

The "nonprestigious" popular culture texts presented below are of three kinds. The first kind consists of short poetic texts that were largely contemporary to the violence unleashed in January 1991 and are "nonprestigious" because they are partisan insults that name clan names. Two works of prose fiction about this same episode of violence make up a second category, "nonprestigious" to the traditional Somali canon partly because of the novelty of the genre and partly because the authors are young men, whose literary expressions in the past were considered less significant than those of married, adult men.[38] A third kind, finally, is the free verse, in English, from the pen of a unique Somali-Canadian poet whose head-on engagement with the clan hate-narratives that both fed into the violence and were shaped by it is in a class of its own. In what follows I will examine each in turn.

"Cheering on the Clan" and the Violence of 1991

The first text is part of a vast body of what the Somali literary canon considers "nonprestigious" poetry because its raison d'être is to take sides and support or vilify specific clans or subclans. This kind of poetry is often characterized as *guubaabo qabiil*—"cheering on, or inciting, one's clan"; it is intended for, and is primarily disseminated among those it constructs as in-group. It does not have the legitimacy and authority of "prestigious" poetry and it is not tolerated or considered legitimate speech in simultaneously shared Somali public space. It is hard to buy "over the counter" (so to speak) in a Somali music store but nevertheless circulates widely on audiocassette or videotape and is therefore not fully contained in the semipublic sphere of the in-group. Occasionally it "leaks" into print in scholarly publications, as is the case of the two short texts presented below.

The poetic taunt or sneer cited below dates from 1991 and was published three years later, in French, in a small poetry collection edited and translated by Somali anthropologist Mohamed-Abdi, better known as "Gaandi." It addresses and derides the victims of the USC's clan cleansing campaign of 1991–1992.

> "You, Daarood, without giving you a moment of respite,
> if we do not put the soil under your feet on fire,
> and if the militias with their matted hair
> and the Mooryaan do not capture you,
> and if general Caydiid does not catch up with you,
> to crush you under his feet,
> and if we do not thrash everything as far as Gedo,
> and if you do not become half-starved skeletons
> like frogs outside their pool;
> and if we were to leave even a handful of you alive
> for a new generation to take root;
> and if you do not become subjugated people
> slinking along the walls of the narrow alleys of Mogadishu,
> then we are not the strong Irir[39]
> who have conquered the place that we deserve."[40]

The poet of this short verse (in the genre of *shirib*) is using the form of a dare (an oath, almost) to egg on his in-group (defined in terms of the genealogical construct of Irir, encompassing, among others, the Hawiye and Isaaq) to exterminate and expel the out-group (associated with the genealogical construct of Daarood). If his own people are who they claim to be, the poet swears, the Daarood will be put to fire and sword. They will be attacked, captured, pursued, subjugated, expelled, and annihilated by the militias, the Mooryaan, and the USC leader who played a leading role in the clan cleansing campaign, General Maxamed Faarax Caydiid. Their means of livelihood will be destroyed; they will be reduced to starvation and become defeated skeletal figures slinking along the walls of the city streets. To prevent new generations to be born, not even a handful will be allowed to survive. Only then, the poet threatens, will the Irir, who form the clan bases of both the USC and the SNM, have proven themselves and reached their goal. When the poet mentions the "place" (or "space") "we deserve" or "that is due to us," he refers to both political space and geographical place. According to the clan hate-narrative that lies behind this verse, the poet's people have not only been physically displaced by the group they construct as outsiders, but also politically barred from state power by them.

Another poem of this type, by Cabdi Faarax in 1991, from the same collection, also speaks about the clan cleansing of 1991–1992. In this case, the poet gloats that the survivors of the violence will for always remember the defeat and the destruction wrought on them:

> You, Daarood, I have crushed you so thoroughly
> that all those allied with Siyaad howl with rage.[41]
> When I fired at you with my machine gun, how you ran!
> You ran past me faster than a terrorized horse.
> How many coalitions did we defeat!
> How many times did I shatter you! You will always be speaking of this.
> (Mohamed-Abdi 1994: 11)

Prose Fiction About the Clan Cleansing of 1991

A very different mediation of violence takes the form of prose fiction written by two young male Somali authors, Abdirazak Y. Osman's English-language *In the Name of the Fathers: A Somali Novel* (1996) and Faisal Axmed Xasan's Somali-language *Maandeeq* (2000).[42] The emotional and political engagement of both writers is immediately evident from their dedications. Abdirazak dedicates his book to the cousin on whose civil war experience he models his story, as well as, "to all young Somalis who were used, misused, misled and betrayed by their fathers, uncles and leaders whom they trusted, respected and obeyed." Faisal dedicates his book to a number of individually named people who lost their lives in the violence of 1991, most of them in Mogadishu. Both authors are also not afraid to "speak clan" and mention specific clan names throughout their narratives. However, even as they do so, they write against clan as a valid category of thought and action; namely, they both show how imposing a collective clan identity (on oneself or on others) and committing violence in its name, is wrong, that is to say both discursively false and morally improper.

Both novels have as their major protagonists urban young men who find themselves in Mogadishu when the clan cleansing campaign begins. Abdirazak tells the story of a young man who is drawn into the USC war machine and survives, while Faisal's protagonist refuses to "do his job" when he is assigned to a team of clan cleansers and is summarily executed.

In the Name of the Fathers is written in the voice and from the point of view of a young man in Mogadishu who is completely apolitical. At the time the fighting begins he is dreaming of soccer and of taking his girl-friend to a New Year's party. However, his father is deeply involved in politics, especially the clan-based politics of the USC.[43] Ali at first disbelieves his father's claims that, when push comes to shove, the faltering dictator will suddenly gain the support of his whole clan-family. He sees the huge demonstration of the residents of Mogadishu to protest the arrest and trial of the courageous elders of the Manifesto group, who challenged Barre in May 1990,[44] as evidence of the validity of this skepticism. But when violence erupts and areas of the city come under fire from the president's men, rumors and reports by relatives begin to change his mind. Ali's relatives have a garage in which Toyota Land Cruisers are being rebuilt into "technicals," with sawed off roofs and belt-fed machine guns mounted in the back. When several of his uncles are killed by the other side, Ali joins them, signs up as a fighter, and enters "the liberation war" (Osman 1996: 101–2).

The novel tries to capture the moral confusion, inner uncertainties, and outward contradictions Ali faces when he, as so many young men, is swept up into the violence. He has mixed feelings about his father, who speaks about "*the*" Hawiye and "*the*" Daarood as homogeneous entities with unified and stable sets of sentiments and tendencies. Ali moves between admiration for his father—the mention of whose name saves him several times during his escape to Djibouti toward the end of the book—and suspicion and dislike of him. Why did his father leave his son and the rest of the family in the lurch while he himself was safely ensconced in Nairobi before the fighting he predicted—and as a founding member of the USC even planned—broke out? The author shows how Ali keeps doubting and keeps hoping that his doubts are justified until the key shift to communal violence has already taken place and violence has touched his loved ones. It is, the novel suggests, only the violence itself—the violence that befalls his uncles—that removes these doubts and makes him accept, at least for the moment, the rationale of freeing his own people from the oppressive presence of the enemy clan family.

In the end, it is Ali's own experience as an active perpetrator of violence that makes him turn away from it, but this revulsion develops only gradually. Ali describes his first battle, his first execution (of a scared old man who tries to flee), as well as the obliteration of his technical and its crew when he, quite by chance, had just stepped down for a minute. He reflects:

> My six-man group was history. I could hardly even recognize their faces. They melted like ice cubes on a hot pan. I was not happy about it of course, but thinking back, I was not very sad about it either. Maybe because I was stoned, I don't know. Those days everybody was high.

Some drank liquor, others chewed khat non-stop, or smoked hash, marijuana or even heroin. Those who were not using things were also high. The flames, the smoke, the smell of bullets fired, the smell of the bodies were all making the people drunk. I can't remember anybody who was in his complete senses so long as he was in that war. (111)

After a number of bloody battles, Ali, then driving his own technical, hands it over to someone else and, together with his stepmothers, joins a big convoy of trucks heading toward Djibouti. At times, Ali justifies the violence in which he participated, for example by referring to people who exploited their association with the government for enormous, ill-gained wealth. Thus, while driving a looted, brand-new, super-expensive car given to him in the family garage, he finds the former owner's ID and discovers that the man had just been a humble inspector in the Ministry of Defense. Furiously, he addresses the dead man aloud:

"How can you afford a car like this when you're not even a general?" I asked the picture, this time almost in a whisper. "How can you?" . . . You started this civil war from the day you bought yourself a car like this which is twenty times more than your salary for the next twenty years! And now look at yourself. You are dead and probably sitting on a good chair in Hell, and here I am driving your fucking car!" . . . "This is what the civil war is about, asshole! Corruption and greed," I added. And this is your payback!" (118–19)

Only in the course of the fighting and, after he quits the war, during his escape from Somalia to Djibouti does Ali become aware that, once clan-based violence becomes the law of the land, no one, of whatever clan background, can ever be safe. When Djibouti and freedom finally come into view and he takes a moment to reflect on his experiences, he struggles with the complex question of accountability:

Random thoughts came into my head. . . . I remembered my days and nights in the war back home in Somalia. I wondered who really was responsible for this agony and the uncountable sufferings. How much blame should I throw on myself? My weak self who couldn't even say no to war like my uncle Hassan did? My cruel self who killed men and women and God knows who else? Should I blame people like my father who, by overthrowing the corrupt government, had brought about this situation? Or the government itself who had forced people like my father to resist in the first place? Or perhaps the people behind the scenes who had kept such a government in power over the long miserable years? Or should the blame be on those men and women who had invented the tribes, weapons, governments, politics and all? Or was it God Almighty who gave some people too much power and others too little? I decided to blame all of them. (206)

At the end of the novel, therefore, Ali is not sure whether this war was just or unjust, but he has come to feel that war itself is senseless. Certainly Ali's losses matched those of many of the people he had pursued as his enemies. Most of his uncles, the two young brothers he had tried to bring into safety with him, his best friend, his home and possessions, even the two thousand dollars he had collected as loot, and, most of all, his care-free, cosmopolitan, "cool" life as a teenager in Mogadishu, all had fallen victim to the violence. His heart is full of confusion and contradictory feelings. Throughout the escape to Djibouti, he sees his travel companions, a diverse group, targeted for violence or saved from it both because of clan and in spite of it. Sometimes they are able to save each other; sometimes they are not. Sometimes men who control the roadblocks and lay ambushes respect fellow clan members, sometimes they do not. At some point during this trip out of hell, after an attack on the convoy, Ali is deeply moved at the sight of a young woman who can hardly walk back to the trucks, because, he finds out, she has just given birth. He feels a wave of sympathy that he is acutely aware trumps the fact that she belongs to "the other" clan family (83). Thus the author shows both the power of the hatred Ali learned in Mogadishu in 1990–1991—the normalization and naturalization of clan hatred—and the power of specific human interaction—in this case between young people of the opposite sex—to undermine it.

In the second novel, *Maandeeq*, the protagonist, Axmed, is also a young man living in Mogadishu. Axmed, however, does not survive, as he is executed by a USC commander when he refuses to participate in the violent campaign carried out in the name of his clan. The author of *Maandeeq* describes in some detail the hunting down, murder, and rape of people whose clan backgrounds fitted the genealogical construct of Daarood. When the perpetrators in this account round up Somalis of other non-Daarood clans, they release them, allowing them to either go their way or join the killings.

The author also reflects on the issue of intent. The USC leadership, he suggests, intended to rid the country of those it regarded as an obstacle to its capturing the heights of government for itself. To the foot soldiers of this war, however, he ascribes other motives. These are, for example, Axmed's reflections when he suddenly finds himself among the rampaging militias. First, he does not recognize anyone, as these men appear to have been brought in from the towns and countryside around Mogadishu. He thinks to himself that they have no idea what they are fighting for, and no personal knowledge of the enemy they are asked to kill.

> They do not know what they are fighting for they were just mobilized in the name of clan and were told "The Daarood are your enemy." Most people had never even been friends with someone who traced descent from Darood. . . . They were incited in the name of naked robbery and a policy based on "destroy the Somali country for, if you do, the Europeans and Americans will rebuild it. Now you need to capture the capital." The leading principle inculcated in them was "let your clan rule the Horn of Africa." They would kill other people standing in their way even if they were not Daarood, but now they were killing Daarood. (Faisal Xasan Axmed 2000: 82)

If, in the author's view, these were some of the motives of the militia men and Mooryaan, he also depicts them as moved by hate-narratives. Thus the argument that the Daarood were not even native to Mogadishu and had therefore no right to be there came to serve as one of the rationales for the clan cleansing.[45] The novel relates how, during the time of the massacres, Radio Mogadishu regularly broadcasted a particular song that justified the killings and expulsions in those terms: "Death will trouble only those who had to travel to come here. Their time is up, they will have to go." Although this message was clear enough, the words *erya, erya!* ("chase them out"), followed by *Allahu akbar! Allahu akbar!* ("God is Great"), were added to these lines.[46]

Both novels present the violence as gendered and as having gendered consequences. *Maandeeq* is most explicit about the mass rape of women and girls by the USC fighters and the Mooryaan, whom the author shows inviting each other, in vulgar terms, to have sex with a woman "for free" (Faisal Xasan Axmed 2000: 80). A particularly poignant scene is one between Axmed's father, one of the commanders of the USC militias, and his wife. Fed up with her husband's justifications of the clan violence her son died resisting, she refuses to bring him tea. In response, he shoots her (132).[47] Thus the author presents the perpetrators as men whose masculinity is deeply militarized, chauvinistic, and dehumanizing. However, even in *Maandeeq*, with its explicit and passionate *j'accuse*—unthinkable in the poetry studied above—the author carefully avoids presenting clans and clan families as homogeneous entities that spontaneously act in unison. Instead, he presents the communal violence in Mogadishu as a set of policies decided upon by the leaders of a political organization who mobilized and incited their followers by appealing to their sense of grievance and shared clanship.

The novels mediate the violence of the key shift in powerful ways. Like the poetry examined above, they develop a discourse of clan that denaturalizes clan as an identity construct, even as they show—better than the poems can—the powerful and lethal attraction of clan thinking to ordinary Somalis. Moreover, unlike the poems, they depict how their protagonists struggle against the power of the key shift and the clan logic, with Ali succumbing to it and Axmed paying for his resistance against it with his death. They evoke and convey the murky power of rumor and group thinking that set in when security broke down and the fighting began, the pressure of peers and appeals to manhood, the intoxication and then the numbness induced by the experience of battle itself, as well as other subjective experiences of the individuals who lived through this moment. Individuals *did have* choices, the stories propose, and *made* choices—moral and immoral ones—with consequences of enormous magnitude for which they must be held accountable. However, while those ordinary young people who participated in the violence were all too human, they were not all bad, Osman suggests, and Faisal insists that the violence was not committed *by* a clan, but committed *in the name of* clan.

In these ways the novels deal with some of the specifics of the communal violence and clan cleansing that are unspeakable in the so-called prestigious poetry of shared Somali public space. Before asking what this information contributes to an understanding of this violence, let us examine one last kind of mediation by a poet who specializes in breaking taboos and speaking the unspeakable.

Togane: Speaking the Unspeakable in Free Verse

Mohamud Togane is a highly unconventional Somali contemporary poet who *does* speak clan. From his location in Canada, in English, and in free, associative verse, he purposefully and explicitly articulates and airs the stereotypes, prejudices, truths, and half-truths that make up clan thinking and feed, as they are fed by, clan hatreds. It is clear that Togane despises clan thinking, but, since he regards it as a disease, a vice to which every Somali, including himself, is addicted, he refuses to conceal it. In the spirit of a "Clanoholics Anonymous," he professes his own addiction and then holds up a mirror to show every Somali how ugly his clannist "mug" really is.[48] Every clan, every prejudice, clan bosses and warlords of every shade and color, all are fair game to Togane, who names, insults, and ridicules them all. His associative, multilingual, highly intertextual free verse is as brilliant as it can be vulgar. It is even footnoted! Of course that does not make it "true" in the way in which a criminal court might try to establish truth. Togane exaggerates, boasts, blunders, and bludgeons his way toward the "truths" of the tangled mess of deeply felt and widely held resentments, half-truths, and prejudices that shape clan narratives and are constantly worked and reworked as powerful, divisive political spin. These are the hate-narratives that exist and circulate among Somalis and are not speakable in the rational and national public sphere of the "prestigious" poetry examined above.

Togane regularly refers to the violence set in motion in January 1991, sometimes in his own voice and sometimes in the voices of clan bosses, warlords, and even Somali scholars whose thoughts he "quotes." An example is a poem from 2003, in which he presents his view of what may have gone on in the minds of those who participated in the massacres and expulsion of *"the"* Daarood (Togane 2003a). In Togane's poem, the perpetrators paint the latter all with the same brush. *"The"* Daarood were the embodiment of the military regime and its only political and economic beneficiaries. They were, moreover, trespassers upon the land of the Abgaal Hawiye clan. This articulation goes right to the heart of the discourse about clan cleansing of 1991.[49]

> For the last fifty years we the Abgal had been chanting,
> O Darod, move away from my land!
> And I don't give a fuck
> Whether you swim or take a boat!
> Twelve years ago the Darod and their Papa Doc Afwayne were defeated and
> driven by force from MOGADISHU and from all Hawiye territory!
> Some fled on foot! . . . .
> The Darod dog is dead!
> The days of Darod are done!
> The days of the Darod are gone! . . . .

> Now there is no Somali dream, it was brutally murdered by a dirty Darod called Afwayne!
> Now it is every man and his crazy clan! . . . .
> Some fled by tanks!
> Some fled by Russian Migs!
> Some fled by cars!
> Some fled by lorries!
> Some fled by trucks!
> Some fled by land cruisers!
> Some fled by hitchhiking!
> Some fled by boats!
> Some tried swimming and forgot how to swim and drowned!
> On the beaches of Mombassa, their Darod dead bodies washed laden with American dollars!

Another example is from a poem in which Togane puts highly provocative words in the mouth of a warlord called Mohamed Dhere (Maxamed Dheere) (Togane 2006). First the warlord characterizes the relationship between "*the*" Daarood and "*the*" Hawiye as one between foreign masters and native servants: "the Darod have always had an Anglo Saxon attitude towards us Hutu Hawiye natives; that is why they are so haughty, so dignified even when the poor beggars are stark naked and starving to death!" Implying that "*the*" Daarood therefore got what they deserved in 1991, Togane, in the voice of the warlord, rejoices that now the tables have been turned, that "the Darod can lump it:"

> The Darod dog is dead!
> The days of Darod are done!
> The days of the Darod are gone!
> This is a new day!

Second, the warlord "tells" the poet that, given that "*the*" Daarood have always lorded it over "*the*" Hawiye, Togane should be grateful that the warlord (and the "Habr Gidir Hawiye" clan) drove them from Mogadishu. But note the language Togane uses to report the warlord's boast:

> Togane, stop your Habar-Gidir-bashing!
> You and I should thank the Habar Gidir for making Mogadishu

Darod-frei
Free of Dirty Darod!
Darod-rein . . .[50]

After reinforcing the hate-narrative by expressing it in a powerfully concise way, Togane suddenly and unexpectedly totally condemns the clan cleansing and its perpetrators by comparing them to the génocidaires of Rwanda and Hitler's Germany. Togane's poetry lets no one off the hook.

The next poem is entitled "The Darod Fire Back" (Togane 2003b). In the first part of the poem, Togane explains how, in an earlier poem, he had purposefully provoked *"the"* Daarood so as to bring out what they really thought about "his own" Abgaal Hawiye clan. In it, he gives voice to the hate-narratives that both sides tell about each other mostly without bringing them out into shared Somali public space. This is precisely what the "prestigious" poetry we examined left unsaid. Togane uses very strong language, mercilessly pushing the most uncensored and unreconstructed notions of clan down his readers' throats. He refers to the clan cleansing campaign as the "Darod-Hawiye civil war" and, even more harshly, as the "Hutu Hawiye holocaust," which he juxtaposes with its alleged cause, Barre's "Darod dictatorship." The poet goes on to insist—and he cannot *but* be tongue-in-cheek here—that his own gentle and peaceful clan has only gained respect now that it has obtained its own horrendous "man of disaster" ("Nin Belaaya") and warlord.[51]

In this poem, Togane on the one hand explicitly distances himself from what he calls the "heinous" and "trashy ideas" that people "whisper behind closed doors" about each other. However, on the other hand, the poem appears to accept the "containerized" identities whose names it bandies about. This creates ambiguity of meaning. It appears that Togane understands that arguing back against such clan hate-narratives with logic is useless. Perhaps that is why he often just rolls them out—articulates, embroiders, exaggerates, and perhaps ridicules them—as they stereotype (and worse) different groups in different ways. Perhaps he hopes that his readers, when openly confronted with these spiteful generalizations in shared public space, will realize that these stereotypes do not fit the Somali individuals they actually know and perhaps will come to feel ashamed of such clan slurs. However, Togane also often reproduces and invigorates these hate-narratives with such energy and skill that one sometimes cannot but wonder about his impact and intent. Even so, the excerpt that follows ends with the poet's explicit claim that this kind of "straight talk" is necessary for peace and reconciliation.[52]

> In my last piece . . ., apparently I have stepped on Darod toes.
> I did so deliberately. I was running an experiment:
> I wanted to see what would happen if I repeated and aired publicly
> some heinous Abgal trashy ideas regarding the Darod
> that the Abgal whisper behind closed secure doors
> among the already converted and convinced bigots and bores of the Abgal.
> I did not have to wait long before the Darod began
> to shoot back, to fire back, from the lip, from the hip,
> from the hoof, from the roof, from the belt, below the belt
> fast and furiously, round after round, salvo after withering salvoes!
> Another reason which compelled me
> to commit the ugly unctuous and gratuitous gaffes I had,
> striking such strange & rich, graceless & strident & disharmonious notes
> resonant of, redolent of, the vicious Darod-Hawiye civil war,
> is that I got tired of my friends chiding & teasing me all the time
> about how I treat the Darod devils with kid gloves
> while I constantly and mercilessly bash
> the Hawiye and the Eedor[53] dunces in my oeuvre.
> Apparently, I knew the right Darod buttons to push;
> apparently, I treaded on some really still sore, tender Darod wounds.
> The reactions, the responses, the retorts, the ripostes I had received
> which I had evoked, which I had invoked, which I had provoked,
> which I had elicited from the Darod are indeed very revealing.
> The Darod black cat is out of the bag!
> Now we all know what the Darod really think of us, the Abgal. . . .
>   (2003b)

Togane then quotes from the bluntly prejudicial reactions he received, which refer to the Abgal as allegedly stupid and unfit to lead a government, and asks:

> How did we, the Abgal, earn this universal Somali contempt?
> How do the enemies of the Abgal justify their contempt for the Abgal
> How do they rationalize away their contempt for the Abgal?
> During the Darod MOD tyranny & terror of Somalia,[54]
> I'd often hear this catechism:
> Question: How would you know that Jaale Siyaad, the Darod Fiend,[55]

had finally overcome clan favoritism and created equality in Somalia?
Answer: When we would see an Isaaq volunteer guulwade (victory
   pioneer):
an earnest Issaaq supporter of the Darod MOD tyranny & terror,
an Abgal ambassador and an unemployed Marehan.

The reason that my clan, the Abgal, were held in
universal Somali contempt was that, because, we believed the Darod
when they had solemnly sworn to us
that we were all Moslem brothers and Somalis. . . .

Togane goes on to ask how his clan first invited this universal Somali contempt, and tells the widely known anecdote about his father. There was an incident during the Somali movement for independence when the Italians wanted to force the Somali men they stopped and questioned to state the clan to which they belonged. Most men refused to do so and, when they answered the question of "who are you" with "I am Somali," received a sound beating. When it was Siyaad Togane's turn, he is reported to have said: "I am Somali, but just for tonight I am Abgaal," the name of his clan. Togane asks:

What did that finally get him but
a Darod dictatorship and a Hutu Hawiye holocaust!
He was the only Somali
in a savage sea of deceiving Darods & their Hawiye dupes!
You see, our enemies hold us Abgal in universal contempt, because
it is the silly habit of Somalis to mistake Abgal goodness,
to mistake Abgal accommodating welcoming kindness,
for weakness & stupidity. Never again!

Now that we have Nin Belaaya
(a man of disaster! A bringer of disaster! Al-hajji Mudane Musse
   Soodi Yellahow)
like every crazy Somali clan, we, the Abgal, are feared now,
are respected now, are courted ardently now, by the Il-jex, by the
   Jaaji![56]

After devoting the next section of the poem to trashing the alleged nature of the Janus-faced, hermaphroditic Daarood in the most withering and vulgar terms, Togane suggests that "some harsh airing of the truth" might promote healing.

> Now that the Darod know what we, the Abgal, think of them, and vice versa,
> I have no doubt that this peculiar knowledge will lead
> to understanding, to truth, to peace, to bashbash, to barwaaqo[57]
> For there cannot be a lasting peace
> without some harsh airing of the truth.
> Let the healing begin!

At its best, Togane's work presents compelling insights into the history of the clan thinking and the clan hate-narratives that made the clan cleansing of 1991–1992 possible. The final section of the poem entitled "Afweyne's Swansong," provides an example of this (2003c). It suggests that the formula of the Barre regime—absolute power through political manipulation of clan identities—has poisoned the minds of all Somalis, warlords and ordinary people. You cannot say, the poet proposes in the lines preceding this quote, that Barre (nick-named "Af Weyne" or "Mighty Mouth") did not know his clans, or "did not know us Somalis." He knew us only too well and lives on in what is the worst in us.

> Afwayne was a Somali
> Afwayne was Somalia
> Afwayne is Somalia writ large
> There is a little Afwayne inside me
> Screaming to get out!
> There is a little Afwayne inside every Somali
> Screaming to get out!
>
> The French existentialist philosopher
> Jean-Paul Sartre
> Observed
> "Hell is other people"
> The people of Baydabo say[58]
> Hawiye Na-red!
> Hawiye is hell!
> And they are so right!
> Afwayne's mad MOD was Darod

Ergo
Darod is hell too!
There is no doubt about it
We Somalis have become each other's hell!

Once Afwayne opined
"When we Somalis all go to hell
Allah will haul us all to hell
In a street car called
"Qurun iyo Qabeel!"[59]
What Afwayne forgot to add
Is
"And I
Il Buono Condottore
Il Duce della Somalia[60]
Afwayne
Shall be driving the street car called
Qabeel iyo Qurun!"

For still
Right now
The politics we Somalis practice
Hither in the Diaspora
&
Thither back in what was once our homeland
Are
The politics of Afwaynisssimo
Without Afwayne
Which is what the French call
Le politics de pire
The worst sort of politics
The politics of
"The lesser breed without the law"
The politics of
Kaffirs
Who are
"Half devil
Half child"

* * *

Our Ma'alim
Our teacher had taught us very well
Our Master
Our Guru Afwayne has been teaching us Somalis very well indeed
For over two decades now!
&
What Baron Samedi Papa Doc Afwayne had taught us so well
What Afwayne is still teaching us Somali zombies so well
From the grave
Is
Far graver
Far worse
Far more menacing
Far more grievous
Far more damaging
Far more lethal
Than this endless pain
Than this endless suffering
Than this endless exile
Than this endless bickering
Than all that Afwayne & his apt pupils had inflicted upon us silly Somalis

That is why today
MOGADISHU
Our erstwhile capital of the Somali nation
Is clannish hell visible
Bearing Dante's invisible hellish inscription
Lasciate ogni speranza voi ch'entrate
"All hope abandon, ye who enter here."
Is there really no more hope? (2003b)

In this poem Togane puts the political strategies of the military dictatorship—and thus the way clan as a technology of state power corrupted the institutions of the state and poisoned people's attitudes toward it—squarely on the agenda.

* * *

The popular culture texts examined above provide many insights into the violence that accompanied state collapse in Somalia. They speak about what kinds of violence were inflicted on the victims, the nature of the perpetrators and their targets, the chain of events that unfolded in Mogadishu in December 1990 and January 1991, the crimes and blunders committed by the political leaders, and the impact on the physical infrastructure and moral fabric of society. In all texts the explanatory framework within which both the causes of the violence are interpreted and solutions to it suggested takes the form of a discourse about clan (as bygone stage of human development, as instrument of political manipulation, and as poisoned, unbalanced, or diseased mindset), against which the authors leverage a discourse about nation and shared Somaliness, as well as (to different degrees) religion.

However, there are differences between the so-called prestigious poetry and the texts that do not have to observe the genre rules specific to it. For example, Cabdi Muxumed did not explain what he meant when he blamed the leaders of the USC for "driving people away in a panic and killing them for reasons of clan." All texts appear to struggle with how to deal with the specifics of that question. The "prestigious" poetry sacrifices such detail for the sake of addressing all Somalis with as much legitimacy, authority, and emotional force as possible. The texts representing the newer genres, on the other hand, take up this challenge and throw light on the processes by which the clan logic became dominant and what clan hate-narratives accompanied and emerged from it.

All these texts, however, each in its own way, transform monolithic or static understandings of the concept and category of clan. Thus Faisal Axmed undermines clan as a monolithic category by giving his heroic protagonist a clan identity in whose name perpetrators were incited to violence. Abdirazak Osman presents the clan logic as a process and shows how its meanings emerge for Ali, the young man who gets caught up in it, in the specific context of increasing lawlessness and political fear and confusion. Togane's purposefully transgressive poetry, finally, outs all the clan hate-narratives the so-called prestigious poetry cannot and does not touch. It is also transformative, for it magnifies them, distorts them (by presenting them as seen through a magnifying glass), concentrates them by refusing to dilute them and by isolating them from other contexts than their own, and makes explicit their most hateful implications. More than anyone else it is Togane who forces his audience to swallow the bitter pill that clan discourse is a bloody dead-end and that alternatives discourses must be sought.

Togane asserts that there may be healing in such public airing of dirty linen as he pursues in his poetry. He may well be right. Understanding and coming to terms with the violence under study here may well require as wide a range of mediations of violence as possible. We will pursue this idea further in Chapter 4.

Chapter 2

Historical Background to the Violence of State Collapse

Introduction: Scholarship as a Mediation of Violence

Scholarly analyses of violence, including this study, also constitute a type of mediation and a genre with its own rules, expectations, and pitfalls. Many scholars who have taken violence as their subject of study have been keenly aware that violence is an especially challenging, perhaps even distinctive subject matter (see Nordstrom and Robben 1995; Donham 2006; Lubkemann 2008). Thus Donald Donham argues in his essay "Staring at Suffering": "violence is a different kind of representational object than market systems or kinship.... Violence is red. There is a kind of excess, an ambivalence of both attraction and repulsion that does not affect other subjects" (2006: 24). Because violence is such a volatile topic and often holds more emotional power and potential divisiveness than other subjects of scholarly study, Donham argues, its representation poses special problems. One danger is, for example, that the line between scholar and analyst becomes easily blurred:

> analysis itself—after all, only another narrative in the world of narratives—can "join" a conflict, and the analyst can become virtually indistinguishable from the participant. I do not mean to suggest that political "neutrality" is either possible or even desirable. I have argued ... that analysts distinguish themselves from participants to the degree that they deal critically and self-consciously with the demands posed by the epistemology of extraordinary situations. That

means retrieving the complexities of a situation that the experience of violence nearly always simplifies. (2006: 29)

What would such scholarship that resists the kinds of simplifications that emerge as a result of violence look like? To the minds of Donham and Eltringham (2004), it should guard against reproducing the definitions, concepts and categories of identity that result from violence and avoid reading these back into the past as if they were the causes. If one projects ethnic or clan identities and hatreds that resulted from violence uncritically back into time, Donham cautions, this may distort the past and make mutual hatred and distrust appear even more intractable and irreconcilable than they are:

> This tendency to read the present (after violence) into the past necessarily overemphasizes and overplays hatred of the other as an explanation of violence. Nothing "primordializes" identity more efficiently than the personal experience of violence, especially the violence that appears to be directed at one's group as a group. (28–29)

Writing about the Rwandan genocide, Eltringham's insistence that scholars resist the categories that the génocidaires through their violence intended to impose is even more passionate. Scholars must deny the ethnic categorizations of the killers even the slightest bit of intellectual oxygen, he insists; whether scholars decide that the Tutsis constitute a different ethnic group from the Hutus or not, they should understand that it was the killers' construction of them as *"the"* Tutsis that helped cause the genocide, not the Tutsis' ontological "groupness":

> one way in which external analysts can proceed is to turn the tables on perpetrators, depriving them of the pseudo-objectivity that fuels their murderous projects, to refuse to propose "general," "objective" definitions of ethnicity and place the full focus on the groundless imaginings of perpetrators. In this way, the external analyst cuts off the perpetrator's supply of "objective" oxygen. At the same time, it stops in its tracks the reification of social distinction in Rwanda. The genocide occurred because of a perception of racial difference. . . . *This must be communicated explicitly.* (Eltringham 2004: 33)

The approach Donham, Eltringham, and others call for in the study of ethnic, clan-based, and communal violence, therefore, is one that resists and critically examines the rationales for the violence produced by the perpetrators of that violence, including the ways in which they construct and define the groups targeted for that violence. They moreover insist on the importance of retrieving the complexities of the contexts of violence through a thorough diachronic and synchronic contextualization of a specific occurrence of violence, that is to say, by examining both its historical background and its contemporary circumstances.

In Somali studies, such a contextual approach to the study of clan and clan-based violence is not well-developed. Few are the scholars who critically examine the construct of clan rather than just accepting it, treating it as an unproblematic, "natural" category, and attributing agency to it as if it were a single body or a machine operating automatically. Those who did refuse to take the concept of clan for granted successfully uncovered other principles of social and political organization and behavior, and documented other constructs of group identity than clan in Somali history and society. However, they—including the current author—mostly did not engage how and under what circumstances clan as a feature of politics and society became a real historical political force.[1] The near-absence of contextual approaches to the meanings of clanship, that is to say, of research into the specific historical and contemporary contexts on which the construct of clan draws to gain meaning and significance at specific historical junctures, has had an especially negative effect on the scholarship about the civil war.

In the context of Somalia, the challenge to scholars is perhaps all the more daunting, because in many parts of Somalia, the civil war is, after more than twenty years, still ongoing, with little or no closure for those who were in many different ways affected by it. As a result, the historical memory of large-scale clan-based violence against civilians such as the clan cleansing of 1991–1992, as well as the constructs of clan related to it, are deeply contested and continue to underlie the war itself.

As one of the causes of the violence, further distorted by it, and deeply implicated in its continuation, historical memory has been and is still being actively manipulated. It is twisted and "spun" by spin doctors posing as casual bystanders or objective scholars, distorted, used and abused, as well as concealed. This is so much the case that, even though many Somalis often say that "Somalis know what they have done to each other," this may not even be fully true for the generation of Somalis who experienced the violence of state collapse firsthand. It is even less true for the generations of Somali children who have been born or come of age in the period since 1991 and who are often either told nothing or exposed to the same old clan hate-narratives.[2] Meanwhile, those who bore direct responsibility for the war crimes and mass human rights violations before and during the civil war not only remain unrepentant and unpunished but compete for high office and are called upon by the international community, including the UN, to help rebuild national institutions.[3] As a result, there are few detailed scholarly analyses that deal with the episodes of violence under study here, and what scholarship exists often has precisely the flaws against which Donham and others caution.[4]

Instead, we have accounts, scholarly and not so scholarly, that have taken sides and joined the ongoing conflict by twisting facts and distorting perspectives; by couching plain old hate-narratives in the latest theoretical jargon; by hiding clan animosities behind generic terms that oppose "farmers" and "nomads" or "southerners" and "northerners"; by projecting new hatreds like neat billiard balls into the distant and near past, or by simply skipping and hiding from view particular stages and massacres of the civil war.[5] Even the excellent and scrupulously objective political history of the Somali civil war by Issa-Salwe (1996) accepts the construct of clan at face value and, at times, explains the violence in terms of precisely those monolithic categories (such as "*the*" Reer Hebel or *the whole* Clan X) that at closer examination do not hold up and, indeed, need to be explained.[6] As a result, on the subject of the Somali civil war, there are few scholars (and other writers) who engage in the double task of (1) resisting categories of analysis that are so imprecise and so deeply implicated in the violence they are called upon to explain, and yet (2) taking on the task of analyzing how clan and clan discourse have become such a lethal, near-genocidal force.[7]

If one visualizes the moment of state collapse as a junction at which many different strands of history—strands of varying kinds, sizes, and significance—came together and intersected with an equally diverse set of threads constituting the contemporary context of this episode, then one can understand how complex a comprehensive scholarly explanation of that fateful moment would have to be and what kinds of sources one would need to write such a study. This study pursues a much narrower goal: the account that follows focuses on the clan cleansing of 1991–1992. However, in accordance with the core principle laid out by Donham, one that is moreover central to the historian's craft, it will do so by means of a thorough contextualization. Chapters 2 and 3 are therefore designed to provide a narrative that provides such a context, with an emphasis on the Somali dimension of this history.

Chapter 2 lays out the historical background of the collapse of the state and the clan cleansing of 1991–1992 in two parts. The first part traces the historical background of the state collapse up to 1989 when the political violence that had proliferated in many parts of Somalia exploded in Mogadishu and thus into the view of the whole world. It draws on two overlapping areas of scholarship—that about the historical formation and politicization of ethnic/clan categories and that about the military regime of Maxamed Siyaad Barre (1969–1991)—to show how clan and clan-based violence as a technology of power became more and more entrenched in state institutions. This was expressed, among other things, in the collective clan "punishments" meted out by the state. The clan cleansing campaign of 1991–1992 would have been unthinkable, this chapter argues, without (1) the long-standing policy of large-scale violence against ordinary people for the (real and alleged) acts of political opposition by some men who shared the same clan background and (2) the scale this assumed first in 1979–1982 and then in 1988. The second part of the chapter analyzes political events from July 1989 to President Barre's expulsion on January 26, 1991. This was the moment at which the clan cleansing campaign gained full force and the state collapsed. The clan cleansing campaign itself and the context in which it unfolded are the subject matter of Chapter 3.

Historical Background to State Collapse Until July 1989

The Construct of Clan as a Technology of State Power

Whatever the exact nature and functions of kinship and clanship may have been in the pre-colonial period, what Mahmood Mamdani has argued for colonial rule in Africa as a whole is also relevant for Somalia: clan as a construct of collective identity, as a group construct, was transformed under colonial rule because it became the only legal identity the "natives" were allowed and the only means by which they could gain access to the state (Mamdani 1996). Thus, in colonial Somalia (i.e., British and Italian Somaliland), clan became the instrument of a governmental technology of power by which the rulers coerced and co-opted—in classic divide-and-rule fashion—the ruled, and by which the ruled competed with each other to pry benefits (or just gain security) from the penurious state. The colonial state continuously reinforced this group identity both through its courts and its policy of collective punishment—a policy by which whole clans or subclans were punished for the transgressions of individuals—that remained the touch-stone of colonial administration up to the eve of political independence in 1960.[8]

Even if clan *had been* the dominant principle of political and social organization before the colonial powers imposed a state structure—and this is most likely a simplification of Somali social and political organization—the establishment of colonial state administrations transformed the playing field (Kapteijns 2010b). Since the colonial administration insisted on ruling the Somalis as clans and fractions of clans, the latter began to compete with each other through and for the state. Thus the construct of clan, drawing undoubtedly on its precolonial roots, became a technology of power, a political instrument in the hands of the colonial administrators and their Somali subjects alike. The state used it to manage groups of subjects whom it did not want to engage as rights-bearing individuals, and the subjects used it to compete with each other for the benefits or protection from harassment that might be obtained from the state. Such a view of clan refuses to see clan as a "natural" category that can be taken at face value, but, at the same time, does not downplay either the significance of the construct of clan or its deep implication in the violence of the civil war. It does, however, insist on analyzing clan as both a tool of the government in ruling its subjects (and of other political entrepreneurs competing with the government) and a mind-set of the ruled as they interpret and experience the state and, through the state, each other. To understand, therefore, how the construct of clan has become so implicated in violence among Somalis, it is as such—as government technology and popular mindset—that it must, at every point in time, be understood in its historical (diachronic) and contemporary (synchronic) contexts.

At the establishment of an independent Somali Republic in 1960, the civilian regimes (1960–1969) inherited an administration most of whose institutions in the countryside—in contrast to the new national political institutions set up at the center of the newly independent country—were completely based on clan. Whatever their initial intentions, as time passed, many members of government used political parties to engage their subjects just as their colonial predecessors had, namely as clans. Thus they mobilized their clan constituencies (to obtain votes, lucrative investment opportunities, influence, and so forth), while these constituencies looked to them for access to government jobs, scholarships, and other benefits. These kinds of patron-client relationships that involve state institutions—and that had characterized colonial rule—constitute what is often called neopatrimonialism. Compagnon articulated his view of the role of clan in this period as follows. It was not just a continuation of the precolonial era, he argued, but the product of a redefinition of the field of political competition with the establishment of the state at the end of colonial rule. At that moment lineage solidarity became for political entrepreneurs not only an axis of political mobilization . . . but also of a masking of personal ambitions. (Compagnon 1995: 458)

For those with political ambitions, then, clan was a political resource.

According to Laitin and Samatar, throughout this period, and even under the military dictatorship (1969–1991), clan-balancing (and unbalancing) in the major institutions of state was not only an important dimension of government policy but also shaped the overall discourse of clan in Somalia (1987: 70; A. I. Samatar 1988: 108; Lewis 2008: 47); groups that "had" ministers, generals, or members of parliament of their clan background considered themselves represented in government and counted on state patronage from such political figures. Given that the post-independence state was what Cooper has called a "gate-keeper state," which controlled what was practically the only "gate" by which wealth flowed into and out of the country, access to the state and state patronage was indeed a crucial political and economic resource (Cooper 2006: 21). For individuals who succeeded in making use of such connections, the benefits were real. However, trickle-down was largely an illusion, as the so-called home areas of even the highest state officials (including Barre) largely remained complete backwaters. In Somali these were called *lamagaaraan*, regions where nothing ever reached. As the gap in power and wealth—nationally between Mogadishu and the rest of the country, within Mogadishu between haves and have-nots—grew, the construct of clan obscured the nature of the class privilege of the new elite. The new elite's neopatrimonial generosity toward some of their clients deceived (as players in a lottery are misled) as well as divided-and-ruled the common people. Thus the construct of clan continued to be a powerful political instrument that mediated the relationship, on the one hand, between government and subjects and, on the other, among the subjects themselves.

The complex history of the Barre regime has been the subject of at least three major studies, of which the most recent is Compagnon 1995. Compagnon conceptualizes Barre's rule as neopatrimonial personal rule and discerns different stages in which what began as a military dictatorship increasingly (in the 1980s) became what he calls "sultanisme" or "sultanic rule"; the latter refers to a regime in which the ruler ("the prince") and his closest family members and "patrimonial servants" control and abuse the national resources of the state for private gain. As suggested by the title of his study—*Political Resources, Authoritarian Regulation, and Personal Domination in Somalia: The Regime of Siyaad Barre (1969-1991)*—he focuses on the political and institutional resources Barre used in different stages of his rule: his control of the top political decision-making organs; the army, police, and security apparatus, including the prison system; the propaganda machine; the one-party system and its mobilization of different social sectors of the population (women, youth, and so forth); his "scientific socialism" (and the Soviet aid it brought along); the cult of the presidential personality, and so forth. The defeat in the Somali-Ethiopian war of 1977–1978, in which the Soviet Union abandoned Somalia and threw its political, financial, and military weight behind Ethiopia, forced Barre to restructure his political resources. The loss of Soviet patronage was offset by his access to international aid from the West, military as well as humanitarian. The food and other aid provided through the United Nations High Commissioner for Refugees (UNHCR) and other organizations became a major source of the Barre regime's patrimonial practices and political survival and remained so until 1989, about a year before his fall.[9] Meanwhile the army became a less secure political resource for Barre, as he had responded to military criticism of the political handling of the war with summary executions of a large number (100 or more) of officers. In response to the military coup of 1978, the army was purged further. From then on out (but especially in the mid- and late 1980s), Barre strengthened those security forces that were immediately dependent on him (such as the Red Berets or Presidential Guard) and tried to assure his control of the army through hasty promotion of men of his own clan background.

Compagnon presents the 1980s as a period in which Barre, in order to impress his international donors, created a façade of constitutionalism behind which the patrimonialization of the state, as he calls it—that is to say the buying of loyalty and acquiescence of political clients by granting them access to public resources for private gain—steadily increased. It was in this period that he turned corruption and the manipulation of clan sentiment into crucial political resources. By allowing clients to be corrupt, he also controlled them, and through purposely differential treatment of individuals and groups of different clan backgrounds, he set individuals and groups against each other and undermined the potential for unified opposition to his rule.

The 1980s were also the decade when observers began to characterize the political basis of the regime as a clan-alliance of the MOD clans (Mareexaan, Ogaadeen, Dhulbahante), part of the genealogical construct of the Daarood clan family. The idea of MOD dominance originated with the SNM. It became a powerful political tool for mobilizing its constituency and was widely adopted by opponents of the regime who could claim non-MOD descent. The two major studies of the Barre era (Laitin and Samatar 1987; Compagnon 1995) both question its factual basis, noting that, at least up to 1988, high-level government positions were held by individuals of practically all clan backgrounds. Compagnon bases this conclusion on as comprehensive a list of such high-level appointments as he could gather.[10] This does not mean, of course, that clan background did not influence how individuals might access government patronage or that clans were equally represented in Barre's military administration. Barre's government was a dictatorship in which no group or individual had democratic representation. According to Compagnon, the top officials in this autocracy were above all else Barre's loyal clients who put their own interests first and were not representatives of their clans (1995: 468). After all, Barre did not rule for the benefit of any clans but through them for his own benefit.

However, Barre was not the only politician to use clan as a political instrument. Neither Compagnon nor Laitin and Samatar pay sufficient attention to the political construct of MOD as a powerful tool in the hands of the leaders of the SNM, many of whom had served in important positions under Barre and thus had been schooled—willy-nilly—in the use and manipulation of clan as a political resource. The MOD construct is an example of the weaving of powerful clan hate-narratives that was to become a major dimension of the clan logic that produced the clan cleansing of 1991–1992. Poet Togane was right in more than one way when he wrote that what Barre taught us is even worse than what he did to us (2003b).

However, if Barre proved a master in restructuring his political resources and mercilessly pulling the strings of his networks of clientage, in doing so he destroyed not only the very resources on which he relied for political survival but also laid the foundation for the collapse of the state itself. There are many examples of such destructive strategies, not in the least that of turning the national banks into the private purse of those closest to the president, high-ranking political clients as well as his wives and children. This is how Compagnon characterizes the regime toward the end of the 1980s: "The state having become a vast network of clientage with the President at its top, there was no third way between working for his patronage, directly or through his patrimonial servants, and popular opposition" (1995: 470).

The prime example of a policy that blew up in Barre's face and helped bring down the state itself was the regime's political manipulation of clan. Laitin and Samatar gave the following political diagnosis of the mid-1980s. By this time, they write, Barre had come to depend more and more on "tribalistic techniques to hold on to power, shuffling political appointments back and forth throughout the bureaucracy and building ever new and changing tribal alliances" (1987: 91). They draw an ominous conclusion from their assessment of the situation at that time:

> Today in Somalia, interclan enmity is worse and potentially more violent than in any period of Somalia's history. That even Siyaad's opposition is deeply divided by clan affiliations suggests that the social forces sustaining interclan tensions go well beyond the Somali government. Because interclan rivalries focus societal attention to the distribution of jobs and contracts and not on the creation of new wealth or development of the society as a whole, this enmity is a disease that has seriously weakened the body politic. (94)

These "tribalistic techniques" must be seen as part of a particular history, namely that of the construction and manipulation of group identities by and through the state. Violence played an important part in this history from the inception of the state in Somalia. For example, even before they had moved their "Resident" (as they called the colonial official in charge of the Somali Coast Protectorate) from Aden to the mainland, the first political instrument the British used against Somalis who interfered with caravan trade-routes to the coast was that notorious form of collective punishment, the "punitive expedition" (Walsh n.d.). Collective punishment of the whole clan group (or clan section) for the (alleged and real) political or criminal offenses of a few remained an important dimension of clan-as-a-governmental-technology throughout the colonial period and, to a more limited extent, after independence. The Barre regime, however, took the practice to new lengths, transforming both its scale and content. The history of large-scale government violence perpetrated against Somalis *as clans* during the Barre regime is therefore crucial to an understanding of the clan cleansing that occurred as the state collapsed in 1990–1991. I will focus on two episodes of large-scale collective clan punishment by the Barre government that have been documented by scholars and human rights organizations, namely that of 1979–1982 in the regions of Mudug, Bari, and Nugaal, and the one whose brutality culminated in 1988–1989 in the regions of Woqooyi-Galbeed

(Northwestern Region) and Togdheer, which has been much better documented and studied.[11]

The State's Clan-Based Violence Against Civilians in the Northeast (1979–1982)

The differences between these two episodes of large-scale state violence (and between them and the clan cleansing of 1991–1992) are as significant as the similarities, but the commonalities are nevertheless very telling. The first episode must be interpreted against the background of the military regime's long-term collective harassment of individuals of a particular clan background, that of the Majeerteen, ever since it came to power in 1969.[12] Such harassment included an attack on people's livelihoods (the confiscation of shops, dismissal from jobs, the withholding and withdrawal of trading licenses, scholarships, even passports), as well as town and house arrest, imprisonment, torture, and even execution on either trumped up charges or no charges at all.[13] However, the magnitude, intensity, and scale of this collective harassment vastly increased after Somalia's defeat in the 1977–1978 war against Ethiopia.

It was Barre's response to this defeat that set into motion the chain of events that led to the large-scale massacres of 1979. According to Issa-Salwe, immediately after the Somali decision to withdraw in March 1978, General Maxamed Cali Samantar and his subordinate General Maxamed Nuur Galaal were implicated in the execution of eighty-two high military officers still in the field in Jigjiga (part of the territory they had conquered on Ethiopia), for what the regime called "their opposition to the way the war was handled."[14] In April 1978, partly in response to this and other executions and punishments of the very men who had fought so well in the war, a number of officers in the army committed an unsuccessful coup d'état. Perhaps so as not to have to take on the whole leadership of the coup and as a further tactic of divide-and-rule, Barre decided to present it as a "Majeerteen coup" and of the seventeen men who were put to death, all but one were of this clan background.[15] Participants in the coup who were of other clan backgrounds were quietly separated from the latter and given prison terms.[16] In February 1978, this, in turn, led to the establishment across the Somali border in Ethiopia of the first armed opposition against the Barre regime, the Somali Salvation Front (SSF), later called the Somali Salvation Democratic Front (SSDF).

In retaliation for the establishment of this armed opposition front, the military regime exacted a nation-wide collective "punishment" from the whole group (except for informers and other individuals Barre was able to put to political use). Issa-Salwe (1996: 95–96) and Samatar (1991: 36–45) have given the most comprehensive accounts of the large-scale violations of human rights this entailed: hundreds of military officers were rounded up, the civil service was purged, and political leaders, elders, intellectuals, businessmen, religious leaders, even women, were sent to Barre's worst prisons. In the targeted areas, students were arrested and sentenced to death or given life sentences; schools and hospitals were closed or destroyed, and commercial vessels were confiscated and trade banned. On top of this, the government—reports especially mention General Maxamed Cali Samantar, a top member of the junta—responded to the SSDF's capture of two towns within the Somali borders at the end of June 1982 with what Issa-Salwe describes as a "scorched earth policy" (Issa-Salwe 1996: 96). This policy consisted of "destroying water reservoirs, burning 18 villages" (which he mentions by name), as well as planting land mines around the main centers and confiscating thousands of livestock, and subjected "both the urban population and nomads . . . to summary arrest, detention in squalid conditions, torture, rape, and all forms of psychological intimidation."[17] According to the estimates given by Issa-Salwe, more than two thousand people died, while tens of thousands of camels and other livestock were confiscated (96). Jama Mohamed Ghalib, commander of the police in 1970–1974, describes the collective violence against these civilians as follows:

> The response of the regime was direct military action and punitive measures against non-combatant civilian populations throughout their clan homelands in Mudug and Nugal regions, where the capitals were Galkayu and Garowe respectively. The destruction of water reservoirs in their rural areas was total and indiscriminate. Agents would kill many dissidents by torture or direct murder without accountability. There were neither inquiries nor inquests: just remembered resentment.[18]

There are indications that other Somalis, both at the level of government officials and the common people, found some satisfaction in seeing this particular clan group brought low (Samatar 1988–89). The fact that a number of top officials of the earlier civilian administrations had come from this group; lingering resentments about these leading men's proud roles in the SYL and its victories; perhaps the self-importance of some individuals; Barre's divisive propaganda; and even the suggestion by certain party intellectuals that, in the absence of a class enemy, this clan would have to fill the slot of *rijici* ("reactionary"), *kacaandiid* ("anti-revolutionary"), and enemy of the state,[19] all contributed to a construction of clan that served the government's divide-and-rule policies and fed popular illusions that the misfortunes of *"the"* Majeerteen would—as in a zero-sum game—allow other clans to benefit from the state.[20]

Much remains unknown about this episode of state violence of 1979–1982. It was not investigated in any detail by human rights organizations; even the numbers of casualties and of women raped by government troops remain mere estimates. However, it is a classic case of collective clan-based violence against civilians as a government technology and instrument of state power—the very stuff of which, to refer back to Donham, "primordialized" identities are made (Donham 2006: 28–29).

Although the SSDF, with Ethiopian and Libyan aid and established in Ethiopia, had initially been able to constitute itself as a well-armed, sizable army and had attracted Somalis from a range of class, clan, and regional backgrounds, now it increasingly lost its national character and was racked by serious internal divisions (Compagnon 1995: 507–8). The above-mentioned incursion across the border into Somalia at the end of June 1982 was disastrous for the Front. When the Ethiopian government insisted on hoisting its Ethiopian flag over the two Somali towns the Front had captured with its support, the Front's commander, Cabdullaahi Yuusuf Axmed, as some accounts have it, refused and, after escaping an Ethiopian government attempt on his life that killed three of his bodyguards, was imprisoned. The Ethiopian army surrounded and tried to exterminate the Front. While many of its fighters were killed or imprisoned and others melted into the nomadic population of the region, a sizable group of fighters broke free from the Ethiopian army and, deciding to trust their fate to Barre rather than Mengistu, reentered Somalia. Here the military regime astutely used their return as the foundation for a policy of co-opting its Majeerteen enemies at the very time it was cracking down on *"the"* Isaaq. Under the command of General Maxamed Saciid Xirsi "Morgan" and nicknamed "Dhafoorqiiq," some of these SSDF returnees would eventually play a role in the violence that was still to come.[21] However, these events marked the end of the SSDF as a meaningful military entity until 1991.

The State's Clan-Based Violence Against Civilians in the Northwest (1988–1989)

The second episode of large-scale state violence against a large population group constructed as enemy clan[22] had its roots in circumstances that bore some likeness to those preceding the episode of 1979–1982, as they were, at least in part, connected to the consequences of the Somali-Ethiopian war. The residents of northern Somalia had a number of long-standing grievances about what they considered the political underrepresentation and economic neglect of their region compared to Mogadishu and the south more generally.[23] They had, moreover, suffered specific harms as a consequence of the war. First, they deeply resented the presence and actions on the border of their region of the Western Somali Liberation Front and other military groups armed and trained by the government to fight Ethiopia. Second, their region was burdened by the presence of several hundred thousand ethnic Somali and other refugees from the Somali-Ethiopian war—many housed in refugee camps—which had a devastating impact on the resources, ecology, and living standard of the residents (Africa Watch 1990: 34). Due to international aid (vast amounts of which were continuously and increasingly siphoned off by the government and its patrimonial clients), these refugees, on the one hand, sometimes had better services than the local population and, on the other, were extremely vulnerable to pressures by the government to be recruited into its security forces and army.[24]

The situation first came to a head in 1981, when the Barre regime declared economic warfare on Somalis from the northwestern region who were identified with the genealogical construct *"the"* Isaaq.[25] This conflict became a major cause of the fall of the regime in January 1991. As in the case of the SSF/SSDF, large-scale government abuse became the catalyst for the establishment in London, in March 1981, of the second armed opposition front, the SNM, some of whose leaders had been part of the SSF/SSDF. The military branch of the SNM, like the SSDF, also established itself across the Somali border in Ethiopia and conducted military operations against the Somali government. As in the SSDF, so too within the SNM, there were sincere and partially successful attempts to broaden the Front's base and include Somalis from various regions and backgrounds (Compagnon 1998: 76).

The collective clan-based violence the Barre regime now inflicted on Isaaq civilians, meted out on its behalf by General Maxamed Xaashi "Gaani" and General "Morgan,"[26] was very similar to that unleashed against the civilians the government had associated with the SSDF in 1979–1982. In this case, however, the abuses were investigated and documented by Africa Watch, though only after the massive government violence had reached what had until 1988 been unimaginable heights. For this earlier period (1981–1988), Africa Watch Report documented, through interviews with the victims in 1989, the purging of many Isaaq from the civil service, the confiscation of their businesses, the withholding of licenses and permits, arrests and imprisonments (including solitary confinement, rape,[27] torture, and worse), and so forth. In Hargeisa, a group of thirty highly educated intellectuals and professionals, including doctors, engineers, economists, government employees, and teachers, was first arrested (in December 1981) and then (in February 1982), tried and given life and other multi-year prison sentences simply for having undertaken a self-help scheme to improve basic local facilities and services (Africa Watch 1990: 37–40).

The government meanwhile followed similar tactics in Mogadishu, where prominent Isaaq politicians, leading intellectuals, and accomplished professionals were imprisoned without being formally charged or sentenced. Emergency rule was declared in the northwestern region; mobile courts and the regional branch of the National Security Council had full and arbitrary powers, imposing curfews, controlling all movement, arbitrarily arresting and detaining men and women in the towns as well as the countryside, raping women, sentencing students to long prison terms, destroying water reservoirs and laying landmines in the nomadic areas, and engaging in extrajudicial executions.

In 1986 and then, officially, in 1988, Barre made an agreement with Mengistu Haile Mariam, the president of Ethiopia, that led to the withdrawal of Ethiopian support from both the SNM and what remained of the SSF/SSDF (which had its arms confiscated). The SNM responded to this change in fortune by embarking on what can only be called a reckless course of action, which was to trigger a grossly disproportionate response from the Barre government.

In May 1988, the SNM, condoned by Ethiopia and with some Ethiopian support, crossed the Ethiopian-Somali border into the Somali Republic, attacked two major towns of the northwestern region (as well as several refugee camps) and distributed fighters (with and without uniforms and distinctive markings) among the civilian population. Whether the leadership blundered into this strategy or whether extremists intended to bring the whole civilian population into the war in this way is highly contested;[28] neither scenario, in any case, justifies how Barre unleashed the full power of his still powerful military—air and ground forces—on all structures and people of the region (including, paradoxically, the officials of his own government together with their families, as well as numerous other non-Isaaq civilians living and working in the Northwest). Hargeisa and Burco were bombarded indiscriminately; what was not destroyed from the air was battered in the artillery battles between the Somali National Army (also referred to as the Somali Armed Forces) and the SNM.[29] Even when the SNM had been driven back from the main centers in July 1988, land forces set to work to dismantle and destroy these towns further and booby-trap the ruins. Throughout this period, the whole civilian population appears to have become a target, in their homes and anywhere they sought refuge. Even during their long and harrowing exodus—on foot, without water or food, carrying the young and weak, giving birth on the way—across the border to Ethiopia, planes strafed them from the air.

While estimates of the numbers of casualties are impossible to confirm, the Gersony Report, commissioned by the U.S. State Department in 1989, documented and extrapolated at the very least 5,000 deaths of civilians killed by government troops outside any battle zone for the simple reason of their clan background. The numbers of those who were killed either while fighting or in the crossfire between SNM and government forces, or from the air, or who died of exhaustion, hunger, thirst, and disease during their flight or in the Ethiopian refugee camps must be a large multiple of this. In Ethiopia alone, Somali refugees (not just Isaaq, of course, and including many individuals who had fled Ethiopia and had become refugees in Somalia in 1978) numbered, according to Gersony, 330,000 (1989: 45, 60–61).

The New Dimensions of State Violence in the Northwest

There is no doubt that the magnitude and scale of this collective "punishment" by the state of a whole clan group for alleged, real, or potential acts of political opposition was unprecedented and, for that reason alone, represented a new dimension of state violence in Somali history. Nevertheless, an analysis of how the violence the military regime unleashed against the Northwest compared to earlier forms of collective clan-based violence against civilians by the state is significant to understand the nature of the state and its moral and political degeneration.

In many ways, what the military regime did in the Northwest in 1988 and 1989 was a larger version of what it had done to the population of Mudug in

1979–1981 and 1982, namely collective "punishment" of the so-called "kinsmen" of an armed opposition front. As in Mudug, the civilian population was targeted for death and expulsion, either through direct military assault (in the Mudug case with tanks and not airplanes), or indirectly through the destruction of the means of livelihood. In both cases, the government responded with disproportionate violence—in the Northwest vastly more disproportionate than even in Mudug—against invasions of its national territory (in June 1982 in Mudug and in May 1988 in the Northwest). However, here important differences come in. The two villages conquered by the SSDF were also conquered by a foreign power, Ethiopia, while the SNM, though inevitably with some Ethiopian collusion, invaded on its own. Moreover, the two villages were not major population centers, while the SNM invaded the major administrative and population centers of the northwestern region and distributed its fighters among the civilian population. This provided the government with a rationale to define its actions as legitimate warfare against an armed violation of its sovereignty and its legally constituted borders. However, even if one accepts this reasoning, one must characterize the government's handling of the war, especially its aerial bombardments of the towns of Hargeisa and Burco that did not spare any civilians (Isaaq or otherwise) as constituting a particular category of large-scale human rights violations, war crimes.

Collective clan-based violence against civilians always represents a violation of human rights. However, when its goal is to exterminate and expel large numbers of people based on their group identity alone, it becomes clan cleansing. No one has suggested this term for the collective brutalization of the people of Mudug. However, for the Northwest, this and even stronger terms (such as genocide) are regularly used.[30] The scale and character of the collective clan-based violence committed against Isaaq civilians—who, although they were not the only civilians brutalized by the government, were especially targeted—suggest that this *dimension* of state-violence in the Northwest indeed amounts to clan cleansing. The evidentiary base for this has been laid out by Africa Watch and the Gersony report. The latter's above-mentioned conclusion that five thousand Isaaq civilians were killed in situations far removed from any military action are just one piece of evidence for such a conclusion. One may therefore categorize the gross human rights violations committed in the Northwest by Barre's military regime as war crimes. However, given that these war crimes included collective violence against civilians who were targeted for death and expulsion on the basis of their Isaaq clan background, this government violence constituted in one of its dimensions clan cleansing.

The responsibility and culpability for these gross human rights violations lie, to begin with, squarely with Barre as president of Somalia and head of its autocratic government. Responsibility also lies with the institution of the national army and the military leaders who gave or passed on orders to commit these violations. This raises the question of what the nature was of the armed forces that fought the SNM in the Northwest. Given that, in the years leading up to 1988, many institutions had become empty facades behind which the regime allowed a narrow circle of political clients to misappropriate national resources for private gain, one may ask whether there indeed still was a national army in 1988. This question is all the more significant because the SNM, in justifying the path of political secession it chose after Barre's fall, focused the blame for the war violence committed in the Northwest not just on the Somali government but on Somali clans other than the Isaaq who, they argued, dominated that government (Compagnon 1995: 464; Laitin and Samatar 1987: 156).

There is no doubt that the military regime had, from 1978 onward, actively undermined the professionalism of the national armed forces and built up the power of the National Security Forces and other paramilitary organizations. In this, the regime actively used and manipulated clan as a political instrument, a development that appears to have intensified from 1986 onward. Thus the regime began to appoint hand-picked political clients, for example by promoting young officers of the same clan background as the president at breakneck speeds. However, this was only a small dimension of what appears to have been a wider strategy of using clan as a technology of power. At the same time that the government was leashing out against *"the"* Isaaq, it adopted the political strategy of mobilizing support by promoting a particular identity construct—that of Daarood-ness—that encompassed and brought together a wide range of clans, including some that until now had been the target of government clan-based violence.

In 1982, Barre reportedly tried to use poetry to promote this political project by encouraging certain poets to call in verse for the cause of Daarood unity as an instrument of protecting the regime—this being Barre's goal. Certain poets heeded this call, and the poems that resulted are collectively referred to as Ergo Daarood ("A Daarood Delegation"). The refrain of one of these poems—"O Daarood, come together, now the disgrace has gone too far"—suggests a purposeful strategy of clan polarization.[31] However,

Cabdullaahi Macallin Dhoodaan, in a long, powerful nationalist poem called "Durraaqsi," gave them a good scolding. Your close-mindedness and arrogance are incompatible with nation- and statehood, he argued, and this idea of Daarood unity is just a part of Barre's divide-and-rule strategies.[32] In the context of the government's clan-based targeting of those it suspected of support for the SNM and the return of a group of SSDF fighters, which led to what became a partial government co-optation of "*the*" Majeerteen, such divisive discursive strategies, even if they succeeded only partly, helped set Somalis against each other.

Moreover, it was in 1981–1986 that Barre had begun to recruit clan-based paramilitary militias for particular defensive and offensive military tasks. By 1988 these militias surrounded the SNM from different sides. In the West, Barre had established a Gadabursi-based militia called Horyaal, initially to hold back Ethiopia and harass the opposition fronts and, in 1988, to fight the SNM. Barre sent his staunch supporter and former head of the NSS, Axmed Suleemaan "Dafle" to his own home area to persuade some of the Dhulbahante to establish a clan militia in the East and undermine the SNM by attacking the Isaaq subclans closest to them (Compagnon 1995: 480). At the same time, the government had turned the old WSLF into an Ogaadeen-based militia and, as was mentioned above, was recruiting Ogaadeen men from the refugee camps located in the Northwest (Africa Watch 1990: 34; Gersony 1989: 62).

It is, therefore, tempting to buy into the view that the war in the Northwest was collective, clan-based violence against the Isaaq clan by other clans associated with, and supported by the government. However, this view is not correct. First, the clan militias were organized, armed, and funded, and received their orders from the leading military officials of the government; in other words, they were part of the national army. Second, the clan militias did not represent their clans, but embodied the regime's manipulation of the construct of clan to serve its divide-and-rule strategies. It was the government army that set up these militias and provided political clients of a particular clan background with money, arms, training, bribes for the elders, and so forth, even as it remained at least indirectly in command. Moreover, in organizing such militias, the government exploited divisions and incited conflict between neighboring groups that had had close social relations (and had intermarried) for generations. If the government could persuade such neighboring groups to fight, then they would be so much less likely to unite in opposition against it. In the case of all three clan militias, the government was able to play on past competition for grazing and water between these communities and their Isaaq neighbors, and in all three cases it stirred up violence that tore the intricate social fabric that generations of intermarriage had created. The clan-based militias therefore first and foremost represented the policies of the military regime, not of the clan groups associated with them. They are evidence of the degree to which the regime politically manipulated clan identity and sentiment into a political resource for hanging on to power. Compagnon sees two political uses for the regime's clan divide-and-rule at this moment in time. In terms of the Somali context, the exploitation and incitement to clan conflict represented "a modality of the struggle against subversion" of government power, while in the face of an increasingly critical international community, clan conflict was a way of masking the regime's own political dishonesty and incompetence (Compagnon 1995: 480).

The regime's divide-and-rule and the violence it caused were indeed effective in deepening the social and political divides they had been designed to create. Just as the regime used the militias to fight the SNM and mete out collective "punishment" to its supporters, so the latter blamed across the board (and blame until today) the totality of the groups from which the clan-based militias that were unleashed against them were drawn. Thus, the same clan logic promoted by the government also took hold in the ranks of the SNM. An example of the virulent clan logic that emerged when tensions between local groups became intertwined with the government's differential clan-based treatment and manipulation of such groups is the enmity that developed between the SNM and the refugees of 1978.

After the Somali defeat of 1978, an estimated 600,000 to one million refugees had fled from Ethiopia to Somalia. Under the auspices of the UNHCR, about one-half to one-third of them had been resettled in forty-one camps all over Somalia. Twelve of these camps, with several hundreds of thousands of refugees, were located in northern Somalia.[33] As mentioned above, the pressure such an influx of impoverished people put on the local communities would have been hard enough to manage by itself.[34] However, the government aggravated the situation by using some refugees as pawns to intimidate, control, and undermine local people. It also manipulated refugee food aid, an extraordinarily powerful weapon to bestow or withhold (Maren 1997). It recruited refugees, often forcibly, as members of the Somali army, the security forces, and, as was mentioned above, a paramilitary militia. The government reportedly also failed to contain and empowered refugee militias or gangs that abused nomadic populations around the camps, however hard it is to substantiate such abuses statistically.[35] To this litany of unlawful and criminal acts were added reports of an alleged or real government policy to replace the local population with refugees, especially Ogaadeen refugees. Whatever the official intent of the government toward such territorial displacement may have been, once it defined the civilian residents of a whole region as its enemy because of their clan identity, and used terror and death to drive many into exile, the latter's fear that "outsiders" were being brought in to replace the "rightful owners of the soil" became a real force and further inflamed sentiments at the local level.

The hatred that emerged among the SNM and the local population against what came to be called "*the*" Ogaadeen refugees is a good example of how imprecise clan labels are and how constructions of clan became intimately connected to government policies. It appears that to the SNM and its supporters the concepts of "*the*" Ogaadeen and "collaboration with the government" came to mutually constitute each other and were collapsed into each other; this is how clan as a technology of power operates. This construction erased both Ogaadeen refugees who did *not* collaborate with the government and non-Ogaadeen refugees who *did*. The military regime encouraged the coding of particular relationships between the state and certain individuals and groups in clan terms, and used the discourse of clan as an instrument of power and an emotional tool for dividing people who otherwise might have joined in opposition against it. From such a construction of clan as "us" and "them" and such use of clan discourse, it is an easy step (or better, a slippery slope) toward blaming and targeting for hate or violence all individuals constructed as making up a whole clan group. This is indeed what happened in the case of the SNM and "*the*" Ogaadeen refugees.

According to Africa Watch, it was one of the SNM's principal goals to "ensure that refugees from the Ogaadeen/Western Somalia left northern Somalia and returned to Ethiopia" (1990: 196). From the beginning of their incursion, the SNM fighters indeed attacked, with indiscriminate armed force and often more than once, nine of the twelve refugee camps in the region, killing unarmed refugees, expelling them from the area, and at times summarily executing those who tried to escape or were simply traveling along. It is therefore hard to escape the conclusion that this policy also acquired the bad odor of clan cleansing.[36] Later reports (in November/December 1990) of similar attacks on the refugee camps near Beledweyne by supporters of the branch of the USC most closely associated with the SNM further underlines the lethal consequences of the adoption of such a clan discourse and constructions of clan.[37]

The SNM applied this clan logic not just to "*the*" Ogaadeen refugees. In contrapuntal relationship with the government's disproportionate and clan-based collective violence, the SNM, from 1988 onward, came to define friend and foe in clan terms. Thus, it came to regard everyone who was not Isaaq as associated with the government; and everyone in any way associated with the government (still the largest employer in the country, with innumerable low-rank employees such as teachers and clerks) as the non-Isaaq clan enemy. As we will see below, this is a major stage in the development of the clan logic that contributed to the clan cleansing of 1991–1992. That the leadership and rank-and-file of the SNM, which in the wake of the government onslaught turned into what was virtually a people's army, were not immune to this kind of mindset, is perhaps understandable. However, such an understanding should not obscure the fact that this SNM mindset was an obvious distortion of the historical facts of the situation and represented the slippery slope of buying into the political uses of clan and clan violence that helped produce the clan cleansing campaign of 1991 and the collapse of the state.

In spite of all the ways the military regime undermined national institutions, including the army, by manipulating clan, at the time of the government military campaign against the SNM in the first half of 1988, a wide range of Somalis were still represented in the Somali National Army. It was only in summer 1988, to an extent *as a result of* the government's brutal repression of the people of the Northwest, that the national army began to disintegrate.[38] Although the professionalism of the national army and security forces had degenerated since 1978, and although the government had armed and trained clan-based paramilitary militias, the war crimes in the Northwest, of which clan cleansing constituted one dimension, were committed on the authority and by command of the government and thus in the framework of national institutions (however brutal and oppressive) that Somalis at that moment in history still shared.

As the scholarship about genocide reminds us, constructions of group identities such as clan gain real political and destructive power when people experience violence that is perpetrated against their group *as a group* (Donham 2006: 29). It was through violence that "clan-as-a-technology-of-state power" and "clan-as-a popular-mind-set-of-collective-hatred," fashioning each other contrapuntally or dialectically, produced the violent clan logic. This is crucial to an understanding of the communal violence and clan cleansing that occurred in 1991–1992, when non-state political entrepreneurs, fighting over the shadow of what the state had been and might once again become, incited Somalis, without state institutions mediating their actions, to fall upon each other. Before zooming in on this transformative moment, this essay will first briefly move its lens out and present an overview of the state of Somalia in 1989.

Decline and Fall of the Military Regime 1989–1991

Economic Rot and Ruin

A crucial component of the context to state collapse was the dramatic deterioration of the economy.[39] To begin with, the whole northwestern region lay in ruins—its towns and villages abandoned, its people internally displaced or expelled across the Somali borders, its schools and hospitals closed, its institutions collapsed, and its economic activities ground to a standstill—all this in the context of an ongoing war. Meanwhile, the whole country, as we will see below, was sliding toward war and violence, disrupting all productive activities, including, for example, banana production and exports in the Lower Jubba.[40] Unemployment and inflation skyrocketed; urban services such as water and electricity ground to a complete halt, and urban delinquency rose dramatically. Yet Barre's high-ranking government officials, as well as his closest family members, including "Mama" Khadiija and son Maslax, kept up their systematic and large-scale looting of state resources. Financial kickbacks from foreign companies awarded ready-to-go "turn-key" projects by the government were part of business-as-usual in Somalia.[41] For corruption to become an international scandal, the scale had to be enormous. Examples of this are the large-scale poaching of ivory in neighboring Kenya, in which Barre's wife Khadiija and son Maslax played a leading role, and the infamous Craxi scandal, which showed how Italian development aid had become a huge racket providing paybacks to high-ranking government officials in Italy and Somalia.[42] Barre's clients and closest family also robbed the reserves of the largest banks such as the Central Bank and the Somali Commercial and Savings Bank (SCSB), which had one of Barre's daughters as one of its top managers.[43] On August 15, 1989, the SCSB announced that it could no longer honor withdrawals of more than 10,000 Somali shillings; it was officially declared bankrupt in June of 1990 (Compagnon 1995: 616, 620). This was truly, as Compagnon put it, *le politique du ventre*—"politics of the belly."[44] The state was literally and shamelessly consuming itself. Twenty-some years of war later, no one is even raising the issue of accountability for the economic predation of this time-period.

Somalia had already run up debts it was no longer servicing; its debt service in the 1980s was five to six times larger than its revenue from exports (Compagnon 1995: 617, 619). In 1989, Rawson reports, Somalia had debts amounting to $268 million, including $78 million in overdue balances to the International Monetary Fund (IMF) (Rawson 1994: 177). As a result of accumulating arrears in payment, it had run into trouble with the IMF, which had declared it ineligible for further IMF loans in May 1988. In the period 1982–1988, U.S. economic aid, which had to a large extent consisted of USAID-disbursed commodity and cash grants that were particularly vulnerable to be stolen by government officials, had amounted to $490 million.[45] Peter Bridges reports that, when he was U.S. ambassador in Somalia in 1984–1987, the USAID mission had about three times more permanent U.S. personnel and contractors than the military mission. It was so large it did not see itself as part of the embassy at all, and its director did not feel that he needed to inform the ambassador when he met with senior Somali officials, even when Bridges requested this.[46]

All this was separate from U.S. military aid to Somalia, which in 1980–1988 had amounted to $163.5 million. In 1980–1989, overall donor support to Somalia had amounted to $2.5 billion (Rawson 1994: 164). This did not include aid brought in by UNHCR, which, together with the WFO and the private corporation CARE, pumped millions of dollars into Somalia to feed the refugees, whose numbers, though continuously inflated by the government, were estimated at 400,000 to 1 million.[47] The collusion of these relief and aid organizations with the military regime's deceitful diversion of this refugee aid and the disastrous consequences for those who either tried to grow food in Somalia or grew dependent on hand-outs—analyzed with such blunt candor by Michael Maren—had deepened the political and economic crisis (Maren 1997). However, in November 1988, the UNHCR too had announced that it was pulling out of Somalia; this meant a loss of $60–80 million all by itself (Compagnon 1995: 654). Into this bleak context then erupted the international outcry about the regime's war crimes in the Northwest, which came to be accepted as gross human rights violations by the U.S. State Department in the summer of 1988 (647).

When this giant aid machine ground to a standstill between 1986 and 1989, this was catastrophic for a country (and government) that had at times derived two-fifth of its GNP from foreign donors (*Economist*, September 29, 1990). In response, the regime undertook a dramatic diplomatic campaign and promised economic and political reform and good government and reconstruction in the Northwest wherever its emissaries traveled.[48] It seemed for a moment that the aid machine would be cranked up again. In March 1989, the United States, especially USAID, was working on rescheduling Somalia's debts and bringing Somalia back into the IMF fold. The United States promised to pay $15 million to the IMF in order to unblock IMF loans to Somalia (Compagnon 1995: 616). U.S. military aid, though it had declined since 1986, had never really stopped. Military keenness for continued relations with Somalia was such that when the violence erupted in the streets of Mogadishu in July 1989, it interrupted a joint U.S.-Somali training exercise on Somali soil (Rawson 1994: 174; Compagnon 1995: 646). However, it was this very event, the bloody suppression of civil discontent in broad daylight in the Somali capital, as we will see below, that put an end to what had for a moment seemed to be a new lease on life for the regime.

Thus the economic house of cards that Barre's military junta had built was collapsing. As the Somali shilling kept losing value and the government found itself repeatedly forced to print bills of higher denominations, government salaries became meaningless, covering at best a family's need for tea and sugar for a few days. In the interior, Italian diplomat and avid outdoorsman Claudio Pacifico noted how scarce food and (because of the lack of fuel) even water was inland from Mogadishu; people appeared to have no meat, oil, rice, pasta, or flour, he related, but just sorghum or maize porridge with a little bit of tea and milk (1996: 286). Even in the capital city of Mogadishu, such basic services as water and electricity were failing, while government officials and cronies displayed their ill-gained wealth without any compunction. In 1989, several artists, including the courageous female poet and singer Saado Cali, with Barre in the audience, dared to express popular outrage at this in a song called Land Cruiser, composed by Cabdi Muxumed Amiin. In it they ridiculed how top government officials and beneficiaries pampered their Land Cruisers as if these were brides, while they went begging for food aid abroad. The artists were imprisoned, but their song reached and moved Somalis everywhere:

> It is crooked logic and an evil mentality
> to buy a Land Cruiser and go begging for grain at the same time.
> Wrap it in beautiful clothes to hide its interior
> and buy perfume for it as for a deserving wife.
> Persuade yourself that its whirring gives you a noble status
> Oh, Horn of Africa!![49]

Political Implosion into Violence

Though the Northwest was destroyed, the SNM was not, and the war continued. The Barre regime's atrocities against civilians targeted on the basis of their clan background now provided the SNM with a people's army (Compagnon 1992: 519). By June 1989, the SNM was again mounting attacks on the major centers, cutting off transport routes and interfering with government supplies to its garrisons. Gradually, the government lost control of anything but the major towns and, by the end of December 1989, even these were besieged by the SNM (Krech 1989).[50] As a result, government soldiers in Hargeisa were starving to death.[51] In this period, violence of different kinds and scales erupted throughout Somalia.

First of all, a number of new fronts appeared on the scene and took up the armed struggle against the regime. The most significant of these for the time period under study were the Ogaadeen-based SPM (Somali Patriotic Front) and the Hawiye-based USC (United Somali Congress). The SPM emerged from two mutinies in the army, one in April 1989 in Kismaayo, led by Bashiir Salaad Bililiqo, and one in Hargeisa in mid-June 1989, led by Axmed Cumar "Jees."[52] These rebellions may have been related to the peace treaty with Ethiopia Barre had formalized on April 3, 1988, thus officially abandoning the cause of Western Somalia/Ogaadeenia. Moreover, because he now distrusted his top Ogaadeen military officers, Barre had first demoted his Minister of Defense General Aadan Cabdullaahi Nuur "Gabyow," who had played a significant role in the war in the North, and later imprisoned him.[53]

Colonel "Jees," who deserted from the army with 300 soldiers, reportedly first helped the SNM forces to get very close to Hargeisa. His "call to the Somali army to desert en masse" was broadcast on Radio SNM. A more formal agreement between the SPM and SNM followed. "Jees" then marched his troops through the Ogaadeen to the South, where he and Bililiqo combined forces to establish the SPM, the front that was to attack the beleaguered regime from the southwest. From July 1989 onward, the SPM was engaged in active fighting with the government, temporarily capturing Dhoobley and Afmadow, and besieging Kismaayo. Government troops counterattacked in early September and, in their pursuit, even crossed into Kenyan territory. They also wiped out the residents of the border town of Dhoobley; clan-based collective violence against civilians had become business as usual for the regime.[54]

However, these events were just the tip of the iceberg. Sources such as *Africa Confidential* and the *Indian Ocean Newsletter* (ION), with all their imperfections, relate incident after incident that show how the South had slipped into chaos and violence. For example, the ION issue of March 1989 reported on a rebel group that called itself Abris, which emerged in the context of local conflicts over resources between herders of different clan backgrounds. It consisted of three thousand army defectors who were a law unto themselves and lived from smuggling and poaching, and later merged with the SPM.[55] Another issue, that of April 1989, reported under "conflicting news": an air force contingent having joined the rebels in Baydhaba; continued fighting between Ogaadeen and Mareexaan; the town of Luuq having been taken over by Ogaadeen and Oromo refugees tired of appalling conditions in the camps; Somali towns in the region having been bombed, and so forth.[56] Irrespective of whether all of this is literally true or not, it is evident that the government was no longer in control of these regions.

One ominous item of news reported in the same ION issue of August 1989 suggests that here too the Barre regime was fueling the fires of clan conflict, undoubtedly to prevent the emergence of a more unified opposition. It reported the following: "About two weeks ago a meeting was held between Ogadeni and Marehan dignitaries in Bardhere to denounce the regime's use of commandos to alternately massacre members of one or other clan [sic] so as to incite clashes between the two clans."[57] This kind of cynical divide-and-rule by the regime sacrificed the interests of ordinary civilians of both sides, including Barre's clan. No wonder that Compagnon concluded his analysis of the considerable power and wealth that had accrued to Mareexaan individuals in the course of Barre's twenty-one years of rule with the insight that "Barre had not ruled *for* the Marehan but *through* them" (1995: 472).

Many scholars and analysts, as well as Somali civilians who lived through these events, are convinced that the regime itself actively and deviously contributed to the intensifying clan polarization of this period. The use of violence was a crucial tool in this. In 1989–1990, government military campaigns under Maslax Maxamed Siyaad, "Morgan," and others were sent out against groups of defectors, guerillas, or simply bandits, and commonly used clan-based collective violence against civilians. In central Somalia, those targeted were often Hawiye, including Hawiye civilians.[58]

The USC, a second front that became active in this period, had been established in Italy in January 1989, with as its president Cali Maxamed Cossobleh "Wardhiigley," who had been vice president of the SNM until 1987 (Compagnon 1998: 76). Although the founding document of January 12, 1989, was couched in national terms, by this time, the USC, like other armed fronts, had become associated with a particular clan-base, that of the Hawiye.[59] On December 19, 1989, General Maxamed Faarax Caydiid, who had most recently held a lucrative ambassadorial position in India, arrived in Ethiopia and there, with Ethiopian support, established his own branch of the USC in close and formal relationship with the SNM. Together with his associates, he recruited and organized soldiers who had defected from the Somali National Army as well as guerilla fighters—he called them *mujaahidiin* ("fighters of jihad") as the SNM did—and raised a USC fighting force. According to his own account, he arrived at his headquarters in Mustaxiil, just to the west of the contested Somali-Ethiopian border, in early April 1990. From Mustaxiil, he began to oversee the recruitment and training of his fighters and began armed action.[60] That the USC was attracting mainly fighters and defected government soldiers from its clan-base (Hawiye), was, at this point in time, not unexpected or unique, as all armed fronts had become clan-based. However, that the USC and SNM were rallying their militias with anti-Daarood propaganda that presented all urban wealth and power as belonging to the Daarood enemy to be defeated and dispossessed was a dangerous new development whose significance would become clear only later (Pacifico 1996: 276–77. See also Chapter 4). This is how Caydiid described this period in the book Satya Pal Ruhela wrote about him:

> After I collected all the mujahideen who were in Ethiopia and all the military men who had deserted the Somali National Army and were actually living in the SNM area, I moved to Mustahil passing through Dagah Bur, Gabri Darre etc. Before reaching my final destination, I arrived at Balli-Gubadle on 31 March, 1990 to participate in the Sixth Conference of the SNM. The Chairman of SPM, Col. Ahmed Omar Jess, and Col. Abdi Hassan Awale (Qaybdiid) who was leading the USC forces inside the country, all participated in the Congress. (Ruhela 1994: 168)

At this SNM Congress, on April 1, 1990, Caydiid gave a speech, proposing an alliance between the SNM, SPM, and USC. In Mustaxiil, he was joined, he writes, by twenty-two intellectuals. According to his memoirs, on June 12–17, 1990, he convened a USC Congress, with 261 people in attendance, which elected him as chairman of the USC (Ruhela 1994: 168).

From Mustaxiil, Caydiid began his slow march on Mogadishu, attacking government seats and army bases and gradually wresting control of the central areas of the country (southern Mudug, Hiiraan, and Bakool) away from the government. In October 1990, representatives of the three fronts, SNM, SPM, and USC-Caydiid reportedly met in Diradawa, vowed to join forces to put an end to the Barre regime and laid out a strategy to attack Mogadishu from different directions: the SNM from the northwest, the USC from center-west, and the SPM from the south and southwest. They also outlined a joint power-sharing arrangement for the aftermath.[61]

In response to this growing opposition, Barre's army and other security forces fought back[62] —in the process, reportedly, often indiscriminately "punishing" civilians suspected of opposition because they were associated with the clan-base of the armed opposition fronts. The violence perpetrated by the army, which included violence against civilians associated with the USC, now came to be increasingly seen and experienced in clan terms. For example, according to Issa-Salwe, General "Morgan," whom Barre had sent out to clear the road between Mogadishu and Gaalkacyo, pillaged, abused, and even killed civilians, especially Hawiye civilians, in Dhuusamareeb (Issa-Salwe 1996: 106–7).[63] Maren reported a similar episode in Beledweyne (Maren 1997: 113–14). Thus grudges accumulated.

Apart from the emergence and consolidation of these three armed opposition fronts, a second development that accelerated Somalia's full slide into violence occurred when the national institutions, including the army, already compromised in make-up, capacity, and behavior, began to fall apart. This began in the north in the summer of 1988 and proceeded everywhere else in the country throughout 1989 and 1990, up to Barre's expulsion from the capital in January 1991. While many soldiers (and officers), no longer paid or under firm institutional control, deserted and joined the opposition fronts associated with their clan backgrounds, and others reportedly sold their guns for food and melted into the civilian population, some used their guns to secure a livelihood by looting and thus further undermined law and order.[64]

Third, in the absence of a functioning central government, regional conflicts between neighboring groups, in long-standing competition with each other over resources and power, multiplied. These conflicts erupted between groups that lived in close proximity and rarely involved whole clans. However, in this wider political climate, such conflicts engaging sections or subsections of clans fed into the increasingly clan-based struggle over the state.[65] The ecological and economic competition in the Lower Jubba area analyzed by Menkhaus and Craven (1996) and Little (1996) is just one of many examples. Fourth, arms became ubiquitous. Both the Soviet Union and the United

States had provided Somalia with enormous amounts of weapons—even though Barre was never satisfied and was always pushing for more—while both the regime and the armed opposition fronts actively acquired arms from the outside.[66] The fall of the Mengistu regime in Ethiopia in May 1991 reportedly also played a role in flooding Somalia with arms. As weapons normally available only to national armies fell into the hands of poorly disciplined militias and armed gangs, violent incidents increased in number and intensity.

Fifth, there are indications that, even before the end of 1989, three parties to the conflict were intensifying their use of clan as a political instrument. By further whipping up clan sentiment, they tried to make sure that the struggle between the brutal dictatorship and the vast majority of Somalis who opposed it and had suffered at its hands would be transformed into a war between groups defined in clan terms.

The first entity that used clan as leverage for very specific political goals was the regime itself, especially, the ever-narrowing clique at its top. When the regime began to totter, its long-time top-leaders must have been well aware of the human rights violations, crimes, and war crimes they had committed and the reckoning the Somali people would exact from them once they fell from power. What better strategy, then, to try to confuse matters by redrawing the battle lines along clan-lines. If the looming conflict between government and people could be changed into one that would turn the people's anger against another clan or clan-family instead of the government, this would mean that some top officials, simply by activating their clan identities, might be able to escape that reckoning altogether and emerge unsullied by association with the government. Others might be able hide their individual guilt behind the collective opprobrium now heaped upon a vast group of overwhelmingly civilian individuals, including many who had suffered greatly at the hands of the government.

The second entity that had a political interest in transforming the struggle against the regime into a conflict conceived of in clan terms was the leadership of the USC, especially General Caydiid. A major theme of Caydiid's political education or indoctrination practices (the "*dagaalgelin*" of his fighters) was to whip up his men's emotions vis-à-vis the Barre regime. He did this by emphasizing their marginalization as Hawiye and equating "all the wealth of Mogadishu," which was to become theirs in the hour of victory, as the wealth of "*the*" Daarood (see Chapter 4 for further analysis). Given that the president's clan group was part of this larger clan-construct, this reasoning became in the hands of shrewd leaders a "ready-made ideology".[67]

to channel the anger, suffering, and ambitions of their followers. This thread will be taken up again.

The third entity that contributed to the act of alchemy that converted the armed struggle against Barre into a war between clans and clan families was the leadership of the SNM. Of course, given government atrocities against the civilians associated with it, the Barre regime bears primary responsibility for this mind-set. However, on the SNM side too, political leaders molded the readymade ideology of clanship to fit their own purposes. At this moment in time, two objectives stood out. First, having sacrificed so much, they wanted to prevent any political compromises that would leave the Barre regime standing. Second, like the other armed fronts, they tried to predetermine the shape of the post-Barre political scene by excluding others with whom power may have to be shared, either because of these others' own long-term opposition to the Barre regime, or just because of the rights that would accrue to them under the terms of a post-Barre *democratic* dispensation.[68]

Some SNM leaders, especially the secessionists among them, appear to have been convinced that Hargeisa could never "become liberated" if the South came out of the civil war intact, in other words, unless Mogadishu burned. They therefore developed a set of discursive strategies that contributed to transforming the political conflict into a conflict between clans and that mocked and incited USC supporters who opposed plans to take the war into Mogadishu because they did not want it to become a second Hargeisa and be completely destroyed (see Chapter 4). Given that SNM armed resistance against the Barre regime had already led to the destruction of its regional base and its inhabitants, and given that clan as an instrument of power in the zero-sum struggle over the state was already well established, the SNM leaders, like their ally USC-Caydiid, rejected any political transition that fell short of overthrowing Barre by force. If this meant taking the war into Mogadishu and seeing the capital city burn, so be it.

This was the state of Somalia at the end of 1989. In the Northwest the war continued, with government troops practically starving and controlling only the towns and not the countryside. South and south-central Somalia meanwhile were destabilized because of the armed attacks on administrative centers and government centers by the SPM and USC, the reportedly often brutal and indiscriminate retaliation against civilians by government forces, and armed battles between army regiments now split into rival, clan-based factions. Armed bandits, deserting and marauding soldiers, and unmediated local conflicts deepened the violence in the country. The economy was in full collapse, food scarce, and drought looming. National institutions were in full collapse as well, with groups of soldiers crossing over to the largely clan-based opposition fronts or looting on their own account.

Although the country had been falling into violence throughout 1988–1989, the massacres perpetrated by the regime in Mogadishu in July 1989, in full view of the international community, marked a new stage in the Somali civil war and signaled to the outside world that Barre's regime was likely to be beyond rescue or reform. The massacres occurred in Mogadishu just after Barre had allowed a visit from Amnesty International (June 24–July 2, 1989) and when international aid organizations such as USAID were regaining some hope that Somalia could still be brought back into the IMF fold (Rawson 1994: 177). This new stage in the Somali civil war was to end with the expulsion of Barre and his die-hard supporters on January 26, 1991. The next section will zoom in on the history of events of the period July 1989–January 1991 and present them in three frames, focusing on three major sets of agents: The henchmen of the Barre regime, the Manifesto Group, and the USC leadership.

From the Mosque Massacre of July 1989 to the Expulsion of Barre on January 26, 1991

As in the course of 1989 power had shifted away from the government in the country as a whole, so this shift also occurred in Mogadishu. This stage of the civil war began with the Barre regime using disproportionate and lethal force against demonstrating civilians (July 13–14, 1989) and ended with the Battle for Mogadishu (December 29, 1990, to January 26, 1991). It was during the latter that the fighters of the USC, now distributed among a fully mobilized civilian population, drove out what was left of the besieged and beleaguered government, which did not hesitate to shell and train its heavy artillery on the residential quarters of the city.

The primary responsibility for the violence and massive human rights violations of this period (from 1989 to January 26, 1991) must again be attributed to the Barre regime, both because of the kind of violence it was willing to perpetrate against its own citizens and because of its refusal to move out of the capital city before it lay in ruins. Before analyzing the role and responsibility of the newly emerged opposition groups (a good part of whose top leadership had been part of the regime in the immediate or more distant past), we will therefore turn to the actions of the regime.

The Henchmen of the Barre Regime

The predominantly (but not exclusively) military men who throughout this period, even if in a continuously shifting formation, dominated the top positions in the government, armed forces, and security establishment bear great responsibility for Somalia's collapse into violence and the events of this period. These top military men included, apart from Barre himself, the following:

(1) Maxamed Cali Samantar, the number two man of the regime, had held (and until the very end continued to hold) a number of crucial positions such as chief of staff of the SAF, minister of defense, vice president of the Republic, and prime minister.[69]
(2) Axmed Suleemaan "Dafle" had been one of the main architects of the military coup of 1969; had founded and directed the notorious National Security System (NSS) for thirteen years; had served as minister of the interior, and was also a son-in-law of Barre (Compagnon 1995: 476, 560).
(3) Xusseen Kulmiye Afrax served as vice president of the Somali Republic from the beginning to the end of Barre's regime. He was an age-mate of Barre and had served with him from the beginning of his career, when he commanded the police. He also served as President of the National Assembly and held several important ministerial positions.
(4) Maxamed Xaashi "Gaani" had been deputy-defense Minister in 1987 and sectoral commander in the Northwest in the period 1980–1986, during which he had imposed a state of emergency that was characterized by major human rights violations against the civilian population.[70]
(5) Maxamed Saciid Xirsi "Morgan," who had started his career as Barre's body guard and married his daughter, was younger than these four, but began to play an increasingly important role in military affairs during the period under study here. He had succeeded "Gaani" in the Northwest, where he, after a brief change in policy, unleashed the full military power of the state against the SNM and civilian residents. In 1989–1990, "Morgan" led a number of military campaigns in various parts of the country, helped defend Villa Somalia and the president until the last moment, and was part of the leaders who,

with an armed convoy, managed to take Barre out of the city into safety.⁷¹

(6) Maslax Maxamed Siyaad Barre was Barre's oldest son and presumed heir. With his mother, the highly influential and corrupt "Mama" Khadiija, he had been a power behind the throne and a leading figure in the Barre kleptocracy for many years. In the late 1980s, he played a major role in political and military affairs, becoming both minister of defense and chief of staff of the army.⁷²

(7) Axmed Jilacow Caddow was head of the NSS in the Benaadir region (including Mogadishu) and of one of the most notorious prisons of the country, "The Hole" (Godka).⁷³

Lower in the chain of command were people such as Colonel Daahir "Koogay," commander of the Presidential Guards, or Red Berets, who were at the heart of some of the most brutal acts of the regime in Mogadishu in this period; Colonel Ibraahim Cali Barre "Canjeex," commander of the 2nd Tank Brigade in Mogadishu, whose name is associated with the Jasiira massacre of July 1989;⁷⁴ and Colonel Cabdullaahi Jaamac Warsame, of that same brigade, whom the Italian embassy held responsible for the death by beating of Italian professor Salvo on June 17, 1990 (Pacifico 1996: 352). The list goes on. In contrast to the seven top military men listed above, of various clan backgrounds, the three minor figures shared Barre's clan background, as appears to have been the case in 1989–1990 for most unit commanders in Mogadishu.⁷⁵

The nonmilitary high office holders of the regime included the following:

(8) Cabdiraxmaan Jaamac "Buluq-Buluq" was Barre's cousin and another pretender to the throne. In this period he served as minister of finance, minister of foreign affairs, deputy-prime minister, and so forth. He played a major role in Somalia's falling out of favor with the IMF and other ruinous economic policies.⁷⁶

(9) Maxamed Sheekh Cismaan had been a member of the original Socialist Revolutionary Council and served for many years as Minister of Finance of the Barre regime, one of the major sites of power and corruption. How much impunity the top men of the elite around Barre enjoyed is evident from what their sons could get away with. Thus the sons of Maxamed Sheekh, together with the son of Cabdi Xoosh, the business associate of Barre's wife Khadiija, reportedly went unpunished after having gang-raped a university student.⁷⁷

(10) Cabdullaahi Axmed Caddow served as Somali ambassador to the United States for almost a decade, during which his conspicuous consumption of real estate and blatant clan discrimination of ordinary Somali nationals became the talk of Washington. After the marriage of his daughter to one of Barre's sons, he returned to Somalia to serve the regime as minister of finance, Somali minister of state in the Presidency, and other functions. According to Ambassador Bridges, he and his wife continued to maximize their profits.[78]

(11) Cabdiqaasim Salaad Xassan was associated with the regime from beginning to end, holding several ministerial positions. He served as the regime's last Minister of the Interior, but had also held this influential position during the government's brutal war in the Northwest. This list too goes on.

It appears that the most influential men surrounding Barre were the military men of his generation who had been (and remained) steadfast in their loyalty to Barre and, in the case of Samantar, perhaps also to the political program of the regime. Having graduated from military academies (including Italian and Soviet ones) and having been important players in a military regime for twenty-one years, they were, as the Italian diplomat Pacifico put it, used to solving things "*a cannonate*," "by the gun" (1996: 127). This is precisely how the regime responded to political unrest in the capital city.

The mass demonstrations held in Mogadishu on July 14–17, 1989, centered on the Sheikh Sufi mosque and were a response to the arrest of a number of religious and political leaders who had criticized the regime shortly before (Krech 1989, July 14, 1989). The government's response was brutal. It ordered the armed forces to shoot into the crowd, killing and wounding hundreds of people and arresting many more.[79] Moreover, in the two nights that followed, after curfew, the Military Police and the Red Berets conducted house-to-house searches, hunting for suspects, arresting them, raping wives and sisters, and looting their property. The government's violence was directed at all civilians suspected of support for the opposition. However, the most well-known gruesome incident, which became public because one man accidentally survived, involved forty-six middle-class men, professionals, businessmen, and teachers, whom their captors believed to be Isaaq. These men were taken from their homes in the middle of the night, transported to Jasiira, a beach outside Mogadishu, and summarily executed.[80] According to Pacifico, who was present in the city and had influential friends, it was

General "Canjeex," the commander of the armored division present in Mogadishu, who personally oversaw the midnight arrests of these men and their transfer to Jasiira beach (1996: 305). This is how he remembered the violence of July 1989 in his book *Somalia: Ricordi d'un mal d'Africa italiano*:

> Horrible days and nights followed from this date to December 29, 1990, as the unexpected violence of the clashes and the speed with which the disorder, like an oil stain, spread over the whole city was even more unexpected than the beginning of the final battle at the end of December. (Pacifico 1996: 299)

The July 1989 mosque massacre is typical of one line of action the Barre regime pursued, that is to say, the collective "punishment" of civilian suspects that grew in brutality and scale throughout 1990 and up to his expulsion from Mogadishu on January 26, 1991. The other line of action consisted of political decisions and top appointments that zigzagged between, on the one hand, gestures toward reform and reconciliation with the opposition and, on the other hand, uncompromising repression that squashed any hope for peaceful transformation. Italian diplomats Pacifico and Sica, keen to justify Italy's continuing close ties to Barre well into January 1991, saw this political zigzagging as evidence that Barre had become indecisive and disoriented, turning now to the hawks and then to the doves of the regime. They believed that it was the hardliners of both the regime and the opposition (especially the USC) who made compromise impossible and were thus responsible for the total destruction of Mogadishu (Pacifico 1996: 196, 335; Sica 1994: 68, 97, 118). Another interpretation of Barre's sharply alternating political course is that he was completely disingenuous and purposefully tried to confuse and mislead all involved, especially foreign powers that might somehow be persuaded to resume their disbursements of the military and financial aid he needed.[81]

That gestures of reform and reconciliation alternated with bloody acts of repression is even evident from the limited record provided by international news sources. For example, at the end of August 1989, Barre announced the restoration of a multiparty system and sent General Samantar to Rome to improve diplomatic relations that had been shaken by the atrocities committed in the Northwest, the murder on July 9, 1989, of the Italian Catholic Bishop (Salvatore Colombo) in Mogadishu, and the mosque massacre that immediately followed it. In October 1989, the president appointed a committee for the reform of the constitution and in January 1990, on the occasion of the visit of the Italian president, he released a number of political prisoners.[82] However, when the Manifesto Group, an unarmed coalition of prominent citizens and former statesmen (about which more below) first published its Manifesto on May 15, 1990, Barre imprisoned forty-five of them and bloodily suppressed a demonstration they had organized.[83] It was only when the inhabitants of Mogadishu came out en masse to show support during their trial on July 15, 1990, that Barre, refraining from calling in the army to disperse or punish the crowd, allowed the arrested Manifesto elders to go free.

In the summer of 1990, Barre appeared to continue on the road of apparent reform and reconciliation and followed up with a barrage of reform proposals: He accelerated the approval of the new democratic constitution by the National Assembly and established a committee to prepare electoral laws and laws regulating parties. Moreover, although the country as a whole was no longer under his control, he announced—rather incredibly—a national referendum to approve the constitution for October 31, 1990, and free elections for February 1, 1991. Also among these reform measures was the establishment, on July 19, 1990, of a Reconciliation Committee, whose members were drawn both from the Manifesto Group and the USC leadership in Mogadishu (in this period still overlapping categories), as we will see below (Sica 1994: 59).

Yet, some of these gestures of leniency and reform came less than two weeks after Barre's Red Berets had shot into a large crowd of Somali soccer fans in the National Stadium. When, on July 6, 1990, the crowd had begun to hoot at Barre and call him Ceausescu (the Romanian dictator whose overthrow had begun with a similar mass meeting in Bucharest on December 21, 1989), the Red Berets had opened fire, killing seven and injuring tens of individuals.[84] Sica evoked the surrealist quality of this month of July 1990 for those who were seriously and conscientiously working away at a new constitution indicating: We held constitutional debates by day and at night we lived in a war zone (1996: 371).

Cabinet and other shuffles of top officials continued apace.[85] September 1990 witnessed the government's approval of the new constitution as well as the appointment as prime minister, perhaps under Western diplomatic pressure, of Maxamed Hawaadleh Madar, who replaced hard-liner General Samantar.[86] In October the (sham of a) National Assembly voted in favor of the constitution, but in that same month the Red Berets opened fire on another demonstration, wounding and killing a number of people.[87] As different government ministers in these last three months met with the Reconciliation and the Cease-Fire Verification Committees and discussed political pluralism on the radio, General "Morgan," since mid-November minister of defense and commander-in-chief of the armed forces, reportedly allowed new recruits he was about to take to war in the interior to settle a clan-based grievance against their neighbors, causing serious bloodshed and intensifying clan sentiment.[88] Incidents like these were not just a further setback to the reconciliation effort and any remaining hopes for peaceful transition but, given their explosive clan dimension, also ominously contributed to turning the political struggle between armed insurgents and their hated government into a fight between clans.

On the eve of the regime's demise, its spokesmen had become totally hypocritical and irrelevant to the political realities around them. The following incidents illustrate this. On December 3, 1990, less than two months after Parliament passed the new constitution, Cabdiqaasim Salaad Xassan, Barre's minister of the interior, announced on Radio Mogadishu that the police would shoot "bandits"—the word the government commonly used to refer to armed supporters of the USC—active in the neighborhoods of Wadajir, Yaaqshid, and Wardhiigley on sight. Yet, twenty days later, as the USC militias were at the gates of a city whose parameters the government no longer controlled, the same minister, on the same radio, formally announced the introduction of a multiparty system.[89] Similarly, a week later, on December 29, 1990, on the very day the USC began its full-scale armed assault on the city and the government began to subject residential neighborhoods to indiscriminate heavy artillery fire, Xusseen Kulmiye Afrax was ceremoniously opening the National Assembly.[90] This kind of willful duplicity had, at this time, become the outgoing regime's hallmark.

Before it had come this far, however, there were still political leaders who hung on to the hope that a peaceful political transition to the post-Barre era was possible. The reconciliation efforts that were mounted in Mogadishu by the prominent men of what became known as the Manifesto Group are the subject of the next section.

The Manifesto Group—The Council for National Reconciliation and Salvation

Separate from the government and the armed opposition parties was the group that called itself "the Council for National Reconciliation and Salvation" and became known as the Manifesto Group. This group of prominent citizens consisted, first of all, of political leaders from the pre-Barre era of civilian administrations (1960–1969), including a former president, a president of parliament, a president of the Supreme Court, a president of the national Chamber of Commerce, a commander of the Somali Police Forces, a president of a major political party (the Somali Youth League), a director-general of the Central Bank, ministers, members of parliament, regional governors, high-ranking army officials, and ambassadors. Other signatories were important businessmen and traders; professionals, including a number of lawyers and several engineers; religious leaders, and intellectuals, including the poet and songwriter Cabdi Muxumed Amiin.

On May 15, 1990, 114 signatories—a meaningful number as it is the number of the chapters of the Qur'an—issued a Manifesto in which they explicitly criticized the Barre regime and proposed what they believed to be a way of preventing further warfare and of reforming the political and economic system.[91] Addressing the president directly, the Manifesto Group laid out its concerns under six headings: (1) the civil war, (2) lack of security and respect for the law, (3) the violation of human rights, (4) governmental maladministration, (5) economic disaster, and (6) a national reconciliation and salvation conference.

Under the rubric of "the civil war," the elders expressed their concern about the destructive impact of the civil war raging between the government and the opposition; the killing of tens of thousands of innocent civilians, and the destruction and pillage of their property; the expulsion of hundreds of thousands from their homes into foreign countries including neighboring Kenya and Ethiopia, and the destruction and plundering of major townships—of which thirteen were named, including five population centers recently (May–July 1988) destroyed by the government in the North and Northwest. Under the rubric of "lack of security and respect for the law," the signatories described the lawlessness and "tribal feuds" that had resulted from the government's divide-and-rule policies and that were taking their toll in such a way that "the peaceful co-existence of Somali Communities" was endangered. On the subject of "the violation of human rights," especially the lawyers of the group appeared to have found their voice. They criticized the suppression of freedom of speech; imprisonment in subhuman conditions, torture, and death during detention suffered by individuals merely suspected of sympathizing with the opposition; and the abolition of habeas corpus, a right that Somalis had enjoyed, they pointed out, even under foreign colonial rule. The signatories added that, according to Amnesty International, Africa

Watch, and other human rights organizations, Somalia was among the worst human rights violators in the world.

On the topic of "governmental mal-administration" the signatories barely succeeded in hiding their contempt, arguing that "the present regime is normally characterized with unconstrained corruption, from top to bottom, tribalism, nepotism, tyranny and injustice and inefficiency." Public administration at all levels had failed, they noted, and they complained that "all public services..., throughout the land, such as maintenance of law and order, protection of life and property, public health, basic education, water and electricity, transport and communication and the economic system have practically ceased to function." They elaborated on two examples, the failure of the Somali Commercial and Savings Bank (SCSB)—the same institution that David Rawson identified as the big black hole into which foreign economic (especially USAID) aid had vanished throughout the 1980s (Rawson 1994: 167)—and the purposeful mismanagement and unscrupulous politicization of the army. As for the SCSB, this bank had even stopped honoring the credit papers it had issued to its own account holders and had been closed to all clients for eight weeks. This was disastrous to both ordinary citizens and the community of Somali traders and businessmen, well represented among the signatories. The elders did not mince their words when diagnosing the causes of bank collapse:

> This has come about as a result of political and tribal interference and pressure brought to bear on the managerial banking authority from the highest governmental circles that ended up in facilitating easy credit to the tune of hundreds of millions of shillings, to the wives, the sons, the daughters, brothers and other relatives, as well as tribesmen and other political favorites of the governing echelons, most of which later proved irrecoverable, since they were not covered or guaranteed by any assets or equities.

As for the National Army, they expressed outrage at how the government had corrupted the army, "involving it in party politics and tribal interests," and "promoting the officer corps on the bases [sic] of political and tribal loyalty as opposed to ... 'professional merits.'" They concluded this section of the Manifesto as follows:

> The irresponsible, egoistic and power hungry instrumentalization of the national Army in order to maintain dictatorial power and tribal

interest, has reduced the national Army [sic] to the point where it has lost all respect and credibility in the eyes of the Somali people. It has now practically disintegrated into tribal factions, sadly and painful as this may sound to all sensable [sic] Somalis.

The fifth section of the Manifesto, dealing with economic disaster, opens in a moving and dramatic way: "There is no doubt today that hunger and misery have been felt in every Somali house except in those of the very few privileged ones and that the entire national economy is in shambles" (106). The signatories spoke about the consequences of this for Somalia in terms of not only a brain drain but also "the humiliating condition of being international beggars." The latter, the Manifesto authors contended,

> is an end-product of the mismanagement and corruption as well as the arbitrary imposition of the Marxist Economic system which is contrary to our Islamic beliefs and cultural heritage. By the way, this philosophy has now been universally acknowledged as a failing system as demonstrated by the events taking place in Eastern Europe.

There is bitterness in the words of these men who ruled Somalia prior to Barre's takeover in 1969. Before this date, they write, Somalia had a large reserve fund of over sixty million dollars, in addition to "a sum of stand-by hard currency capable of covering all import requirements for the whole country for four months."

In their introduction to the sixth and final section, entitled the "National Reconciliation and Salvation Conference," the signatories insisted on "a radical change of the present regime, to be replaced by a care-taker government which enjoys the respect of the Somali people in general." They added, "The sooner we recognize the Godly given rights of the Somali people to freely choose their own government at every level, the better." The signatories referred to the government's recent statements about constitutional and political reform and a transition to a democratic multiparty system. The Somali people no longer believe such promises, they suggested, but if the regime is serious about democratic reform, it could take up their two concrete proposals. First, citing seven specific laws by number and date, they asked the government to abrogate all repressive laws as well as the oppressive security forces: the NSS, the Military Intelligence Organization (Hangash), the Military Counter Intelligence Organization (Dabarjebinta), the Red Berets or Military Police, the Party Investigation Organization (Baarista Xisbiga), and the Guulwadayaal or Victory Pioneers, the party militia, to whom most Somalis referred as the "Green Dogs." Second, they demanded the restoration of the old penal codes of Somalia, again cited by name, number, and date.

In its sixth and final section, the Manifesto laid out a concrete action plan to prepare for a conference on national reconciliation and salvation that would be held outside Somalia, on neutral ground. It should be constituted, they argued, "according to our traditional 'Shir' system," and consist "of the most popular political, tribal, religious and business leaders from all regions of Somalia, leaders who enjoy the full respect and confidence of their local and national constituents."

There is no doubt that the voice of the Manifesto elders was the rational and reasonable one of Somalia's first truly "modern" generation.[92] Wide open to the best of what the West and the world as a whole had to offer in terms of education, law, administration, medicine, technology, and economic development, yet deeply rooted in Somali culture and religion, this generation had worked for national independence and had midwifed Somali statehood. While a number of them had actively resisted the political manipulation of clan (both as administrative tool and as popular mindset), they were neither naïve about it nor blind to its power. Thus they appear to have aspired to a clan-balance among the signatories, though they would later be disparaged for not having achieved this.[93]

On the one hand, the Manifesto Group represented a particular generation, status/class, and gender—not clan backgrounds—and symbolized the national spirit and national identity of that moment in history at which Somali hopes for modern nationhood had been vibrant and strong. On the other, they formed a group of people whose history and fortunes during the two decades of Barre's rule could not have been more different. Some (such as Cabdullaahi Hoolif[94]) had spent years first in Barre's prisons and then under town arrest, without any hope of opening a business or leaving the capital even for a day, while others (such as Cismaan Axmed Roobleh and Cali Mahdi Maxamed)[95] had seen their businesses flourish and wealth grow. On the one hand, they had come together to write this courageous and compelling Manifesto; on the other, some already harbored plans, it would turn out, that excluded the others. For example, when some Manifesto members were in detention, in June–July 1990, they talked about their hopes for a rebirth of national feeling and the establishment of different political parties along the lines of the former Somali Youth League. Suddenly one person, Abshir

Kaahiye Faarax,[96] took exception, saying "I will not trust the Daarood." He later became a close adviser of Caydiid and was killed when Caydiid's house was targeted by a U.S. helicopter and was totally destroyed.[97] In other words, the Manifesto elders were, to use a Somali concept, *isma-dhaxal*, that is to say individuals whose lived experience during the military regime and long-term goals for the future were so different that the short-term alliance to bring down the Barre regime was doomed to failure.[98] This, however, would become fully evident only later. If the Manifesto elders, therefore, from hindsight, deserve criticism, then it must be, first, because a number of them were not sincerely committed to the political alliance they had formed and second, because they may have overestimated their own political relevance and underestimated the brutality of the struggle over the state that was already in full swing.

With their Manifesto and their proposal for a National Reconciliation Conference, the 114 senior statesmen explicitly and purposefully placed themselves between the government and the armed opposition fronts. As one of the four duties of the preparatory committee for this conference, which was to consist of thirteen of their own number, they proposed to: "conduct and oversee all necessary discussion with the government and the opposition groups, with the principal aim of laying the foundation ground for a peaceful political solution to the present crises." To the generals of the Barre regime as well as the leaders of the armed fronts (often former high-ranking military officers of the Somali army themselves), this group of prestigious politicians and other middle-class men—mere civilians, with no power but that of their conviction—may have seemed extraordinarily self-important and completely out of touch with the realities of the country. For those whose military struggle had already been extremely costly (as, for example, in the case of the SNM), the Rubicon had been crossed a long time ago. For them the road forward could only be one of further military struggle.

When it was published on May 15, 1990, the Manifesto immediately caused national and international excitement. Barre appeared to hesitate (Sica 1994: 45–46), but then, on June 11, 1990, he imprisoned those who did not recant (or were out of town or able to hide) in Laanta Buur. Initially, they were charged with five offenses under the 1962 Penal Code: offending the honor of the head of state (article 220), political conspiracy through association (article 233), civil war (article 223), instigation to civil war (article 230), and slander (article 287). Later, perhaps because the Italian ambassador contested these initial charges on legal grounds, they were charged on the basis of the much more oppressive national security law of 1970—ironically, one of the laws whose abrogation they had demanded (Sica 1994: 48). To Sica, at least, the accused appeared to be in real danger. The government had decided to charge them in three groups, he explains: the two instigators (Maxamed Abshir Muuse and Axmed Maxamed Darmaan), the twenty-five collaborators, and the signatories. He added:

> The voices from the palace said that Barre would settle definitively with his arch rival Mohamed Abshir, his former superior in the Italian military school and the Somali Police, and the most coherent and inflexible of his opponents during the twenty or so years of dictatorship. (58–59)

On July 15, when the accused were brought to court, the inhabitants of Mogadishu took to the streets in great numbers and brought all traffic in the streets leading to the court to a halt. The accused all confessed to the same offense: "I, in person, conceived of the Manifesto and persuaded the others to sign on."[99] When, after a long wait, the verdict came back as "released on the basis of lack of evidence," the demonstrators were jubilant and many political observers took hope. When the government appointed a Reconciliation Committee on July 9, 1990, it included several members of the Manifesto Group.[100]

Throughout the rest of the year and up to and beyond Barre's expulsion from Mogadishu, the Reconciliation Committee, including its Manifesto elders, tried to work out a compromise solution by which all parties would agree to a cease-fire, in return for which Barre would accept an honorable political exit[101] and law and order would be reestablished. The skeptics were many. Robert Press of the *Christian Science Monitor* visited the city on December 31, 1990, as the Battle for Mogadishu was under way and Mogadishu was resonating with the sounds of heavy artillery.[102] He met with several Manifesto elders, namely Cali Jaamac Cali, Xaaji Cali Shiddo, Maxamuud Nuur Fagadhe, and Axmed Darmaan, some of whom expressed concern for their safety.[103] Across town, Press interviewed one of their prominent critics, namely Maxamed Ibraahim Cigaal,[104] who had been prime minister in the last civilian administration and had only recently been released from prison. Though he commended the Manifesto elders for having inspired and raised the awareness of the Somali people back in May 1990, now, he argued, there were only two choices open to them, to either step aside and let the opposition fronts come in and form a transitional government, "or face a showdown." More dismissive, though not disrespectful, was the president of the

SNM, Ibraahim Meygaag Samatar, not present in Mogadishu but also cited by Press in his news report. To him the remaining members of the Manifesto Group were "brave, but belated elders," whose hope that Barre would listen to reason was nothing but an illusion. The reality that mattered now, Manifesto critics appeared to say, was the one visible through the barrel of a gun. Even so, as we will see below, some Manifesto elders, especially those who were associated with the Reconciliation Committee, did not give up.

However, we will first turn to a third set of political and military leaders who played a crucial role in this period, namely the leadership of the USC, whose responsibility for the violence that destroyed the city of Mogadishu and led to the brutalization, death, and expulsion of so many of its inhabitants exceeded even that of Barre's military regime itself.

The USC Leadership

The leadership of the USC in this period was complex and far from homogeneous. International radio broadcasts and other news media of the period featured a range of USC spokesmen commenting on the evolving events from Rome, London, Nairobi, and occasionally Radio SNM. In Rome, USC founder Cali Maxamed "Wardhiigleh" had died, as had his expected successor, human rights lawyer Ismaaciil Jumcaale Cossobleh, who had also been a Manifesto elder.[105] It was therefore the USC leadership in Mogadishu and that of the military branch under General Maxamed Faarax Caydiid that were most influential.

As for USC-Mogadishu, even fairly knowledgeable outsiders such as Italian diplomats residing in Mogadishu had trouble distinguishing the Manifesto Group and the USC leaders, because the latter evolved from the Manifesto Group in the course of the year or had been an entity within it all along. Manifesto signatories who emerged as key USC figures included Dr. Xusseen Xaaji Maxamed Bood, head of USC-Mogadishu,[106] Cali Mahdi Maxamed, a wealthy businessman and former parliamentarian (20/22 on the list), Abshir Kaahiye Faarax (mentioned above), Axmed Maxamed Darmaan, former ambassador to China (44/46),[107] and others.

The Italian diplomats in Mogadishu saw the Manifesto Group, USC-Mogadishu, and USC-Caydiid as a continuum, from moderate, reasonable, and not clan-based (the Manifesto Group), to moderate and reasonable (USC Mogadishu), to intransigent and hard-line (USC-Caydiid). They felt very close to the Manifesto Group and felt a kind of proprietary pride in it because so many of the Manifesto elders had studied in Italy and had cut their teeth as administrators and politicians during the Italian Trusteeship era before independence. However, USC-Mogadishu included not only men of such a background but also individuals they regarded as personal friends (such as Cali Mahdi and his wife Nuurto Xaaji Xassan).[108] This is how Sica described his impressions around May 1990:

> All the nuances were at that moment not yet clear to me, but a difference in tone between the Hawiye component of the Manifesto, more open to the power sharing with other clans, and the USC leadership (in particular Hussein Bod), more reserved and more sensitive to the territorial aspect ("In Mogadishu, Hawiye territory, the Hawiye must rule") did not escape me.[109]

This philosophy of autochthony, a sense of entitlement based on being native to Mogadishu, would become even more politically charged in late 1990 and fuel the violence that was to take place.

Sica saw the "intransigent wing" as consisting of two parts. The "belligerent" USC representative in Rome was a thorn in his side because he had on his side Italian public opinion, which was largely against the continuation of Italian diplomatic support for the Barre regime. Caydiid, meanwhile, still remained largely outside his scope of vision. This is how he described those he saw as the USC hard-liners:

> A separate position—more militant and with often more gratuitously polemical declarations—was taken up by the USC representative in Italy, Abdulkadir Mohamed Abdulle "Mahaddey," who had the title of "Secretary for the Exterior." Different again was the position of Aidid, who for the moment remained a distant figure for me, whose representativeness (even his belonging to the USC) was contested by all the representatives of the USC I met. (Sica 1994: 69)

The biggest bone of contention between moderate and hard-line USC leaders appeared to be about what military strategy should be followed in the struggle to overthrow Barre. The moderates wanted to see armed force used to put Mogadishu under an increasingly tight siege, so that Barre would be forced to accept a political solution and step down. Mogadishu should not become a battleground. As Pacifico put it, "The moderates did not want the battles in the streets of Mogadishu, because, having seen what had happened a little more than a year ago in the capital of the North, Hargeisa, they knew very well that Mogadishu would be destroyed" (1996: 336).

Pacifico, who had been in Somalia since 1987 and, as an avid hunter and outdoorsman, loved its unspoiled nature and tough "dubats,"[110] had a particularly low opinion of the heads of the armed struggle against Barre. He was extraordinarily critical of the SNM leaders and felt that, by invading northwest Somalia and hiding among its residents, they had "played a cynical game with the suffering of their own civilian population" (1996: 290). As he saw how the hardliners of both the armed opposition and the regime (he claimed to despise both equally) not only failed to protect the population from violence but actively involved them in it, he registered an interesting insight:

> Gradually I understood that the involvement of their own civilian populations was necessary for the new guerilla heads, not only to impress western public opinion with their suffering as an entitlement vis-à-vis respective adversaries, but above all to sweep aside the traditional command structures (the councils of elders) within their tribal groups and to take their place." (290–91)

Indeed, whether by intent or not, both the regime and the armed opposition contributed to making the city ungovernable even before the Battle for Mogadishu began on December 30, 1990. Barre's subcommanders and soldiers ran amok in the city, either because he could no longer control or pay the army whose competence and morale he himself had actively undermined, or in the hope of discouraging resistance by making its price too high. It is possible that USC hardliners too committed acts of violence to provoke the civilian population further and thus to ensure its full popular participation in the armed struggle against the regime. As each side had an interest in making the other side appear brutal and partisan, neither observers nor victims of the violence that swept over Mogadishu were fully sure who at any moment was behind it. Thus, incidents such as the murder of the Catholic bishop, Salvatore Colombo, or the murder of the German Lufthansa employee and the rape of his wife in June 1990 did not have clear authors and rumors about what each side might have hoped to achieve through them kept minds buzzing.[111] On September 29, 1990, more than a year after this had become a common saying in Somalia, the *Economist* called Barre "the mayor of Mogadishu," implying that he no longer had any power in the country outside the capital, and commented on the enormous surge in violent crime.[112]

Thus, as law and order broke down ever further, most observers were unable to distinguish between the violence committed by marauding soldiers, USC fighters and supporters, or simply armed bands of robbers.[113] Similarly opaque was the identity of the armed men who carjacked the four-wheel drive vehicles in the city irrespective of who owned them, the USC, General "Morgan" and the army, bandits, or, what is most likely, all of the above.[114] What is clear, however, is that in the months leading up to the Battle for Mogadishu the USC leadership had different strategies. One strategy, pursued by the so-called "moderate" USC leadership in Mogadishu, as part of or in collaboration with the Reconciliation Committee, consisted of trying to prevent full-scale warfare inside the city and thus to find a political compromise by which Barre would step down and be allowed an honorable exit. This strategy appears to have been backed by military pressure that took two forms. First, in July 1990, the USC adopted a strategic bombing campaign, hitting, to start with, embassies of countries perceived as supporting Barre (the Chinese, Libyan, and Iraqi embassies, but not the Italian)[115] and then public government buildings such as the Telephone Exchange, Radio Mogadishu, and the Ministry of the Interior (Pacifico 1996: 376). Second, at some point in time before December 30, 1990, USC-Mogadishu—perhaps to protect themselves against Barre's duplicity and Caydiid's ambition—organized its own armed militia, which would play an important role in the USC's final assault on Mogadishu. As *Africa Confidential* later reported,

> The decision to have an essentially Abgal [Hawiye] force was taken in Mogadishu by a group which later called itself the USC Executive Committee. Leading members—all prominent Manifesto signatories—included the new President Ali Mahdi Mohamed; Hussein Haji Mohamed "Bod," an ex-parliamentarian and the committee chairman;[116] and a former ambassador to Iran, Ahmed Mohamed Darman. The financial backing for the new guerilla force came from Ali Mahdi Mohamed, a wealthy businessman who had also been a parliamentarian in civilian governments before Siad took power in 1969. Gen. Mohamed Nur "Galaal," a former Deputy Defense Minister, became its commander.[117]

Distinct from (and to some extent contrary to) this first strategy, that of negotiation backed by military pressure, there was the clear-cut military one of slowly marching on Mogadishu and entering it when enough government garrisons in the central and southern regions had been dismantled and destroyed. This was the strategy pursued by General Caydiid, supported by the SPM under Axmed Cumar "Jees," which had established itself in Bay and Bakool, and the SNM, which was supporting Caydiid with advice, supplies, and perhaps also troops.[118]

In these last three months, both the "reconciliation-plus" option (reconciliation with a military backup plan) and the military strategy were both pursued with increasing intensity. As we will see below, the Reconciliation Committee succeeded in making Barre sign a cease-fire agreement and to appoint a new prime minister from among the members of the Committee (Cumar Carta Ghaalib) on January 20, 1991. On January 23, they even negotiated that Barre would step down in return for a constitutional handover of power and resignation from the presidency. Overtaken by events, this success came too late and thus proved to be meaningless. Meanwhile, the military strategy succeeded in gradually bringing central Somalia under USC control and, with the help of "Jees" and the SPM operating in south-central, in tightening the noose around the capital. That the slow march on Mogadishu involved, most ominously, armed attacks on the refugee camps around Beledweyne, where the USC killed and expelled refugees regarded as "alien" Daarood, would reach the outside world only much later (Maren 1997: 113–14, and see below). On both the government and the USC side, however, there appear to have been elements purposely transforming the armed insurgency against the state into communal, clan-based violence.

That there were tensions between the two strategies and thus political competition between USC-Mogadishu and USC-Caydiid is not surprising. These differences, moreover, mapped onto different clan-constructs, that is, those of the Abgaal Hawiye and the Habr Gidir Hawiye.[119] Even before USC-Mogadishu hurriedly seized the presidency just days after Barre's expulsion at the end of January 1991, these tensions came into the open. On October 12, 1990, about three and a half months before Barre's fall, Xusseen Xaaji Maxamed Bood, a prominent member of the Manifesto Group, the leadership of USC-Mogadishu, and the Reconciliation Committee, called General Caydiid "a subversive figure and not really part of the USC" (Sica 1994: 86). From his side, General Caydiid, speaking on the radio of the SNM, on December 11, 1990, declared that there could be no peace with Barre and that those who wanted to make peace and reconcile with him were not members of the USC, adding, "They are henchmen of the Mogadishu regime and serve it."[120]

Like the Barre government, therefore, the USC also alternated between diplomacy and violence. As Xusseen Bood and the Reconciliation Committee were speaking of peace, the USC was also sharpening its knives. Like the Barre regime, moreover, it contained in its ranks men who had elevated clan-based grievances to the level of policy and had chosen clan-based violence as their most powerful political instrument.

The Battle for Mogadishu (December 30, 1990–January 26, 1991)

The progress the USC fighters had been making ever since the fall of 1989 was not linear but had taken the form of attacks that doubled back on themselves and were then repeated to come on more strongly, like waves. The fighters attacked and withdrew, succeeded in capturing government weapons and transport and withdrew, and then came back stronger putting the captured hardware to work.[121] Founded to represent a particular clan, the USC gained much support from the population in the areas where it operated and also attracted soldiers and military officers who defected from the Somali National Army and switched sides. In that wavelike motion, USC militias slowly but surely moved toward the capital. By the end of August 1990, Caydiid's militias were reported to be at a distance of one hundred kilometers from Mogadishu and to have captured Beledweyne, Dhuusamareeb, Ceelbuur, and Buulo Barde (Pacifico 1996: 375). The attempt by General "Morgan" to recapture Buula Barde in late November or early December had apparently failed, for by this time USC fighters were attacking along the whole axis of Buulo Barde, Jowhar, and Jalalaqsi, down the Shabeelle River. General Caydiid, whose earlier headquarters had been across the Ethiopian border, was now reportedly based in Ceelbuur, deep inside Somalia and northeast of Mogadishu (Sica 1994: 99). However, it was not until January 21, 1991, that Radio SNM reported the USC's (or perhaps the SPM's) capture of the two important towns of Xuddur and Baydhaba in the Bakool and Bay regions, well to the west of the axis mentioned above.[122] At the same time, at Beledweyne, as mentioned above, militias associated with the USC reportedly attacked six refugee camps housing about 75,000 Somalis and others who had fled Ethiopia during the 1977–1978 war and killed or expelled the residents.[123] A British doctor who flew over western Somalia reported that all refugee camps near the Ethiopian border and along the Shabeelle and Jubba Rivers had emptied out and showed signs of destruction and looting.[124]

On December 2, a French journalist, Michel Sailhan, reporting on a visit to Mogadishu, found the city poorly protected and was able to travel in and out with USC representatives.[125] For the rest of the month, the situation in Mogadishu deteriorated. As foreigners fled the city, they spoke of ever deteriorating security, with bandits, marauding soldiers, and rebels all resorting to violence. Arms were everywhere and were sold openly in the street. Four-wheel drive vehicles continued to be stolen by government, USC, and bandits alike.[126] One eye witness reported seeing a car whose driver, when shot at, shot back![127] The security forces now had orders to shoot rebels on sight. Even the delegates of the National Assembly in mid-December "complained that discipline in the armed forces had collapsed and voiced concern about frequent looting and gunfire in the capital."[128]

This was the background to the Battle for Mogadishu, which erupted on December 30, 1990.[129] On the day after it began, Prime Minister Maxamed Hawaadleh Madar, soon to be replaced by Cumar Carta Ghaalib (or Qaalib), announced that heavily armed "bandits" had entered the neighborhood of Wardhiigley (closest to Villa Somalia, the presidential palace where Barre had made his stance) and that "the armed forces had fought the bandits using weapons similar to those being used by the bandits and even heavier weapons."[130]

It appears that two transformative events were happening at the same time or in very quick succession. First, inside the city, USC supporters had risen en masse and had stormed Villa Somalia with any arms they could muster, or even without. Second, though USC fighters had been infiltrating the capital for several months, this uprising is said to have triggered—perhaps somewhat earlier than had been planned—the USC's all-out final military assault on Mogadishu. Although the capture and liberation of Mogadishu had been part of a long-term military strategy, it appears that USC-Mogadishu, with the recently defected General Maxamed Nuur Galaal as commander of operations in the capital, may have launched the final attack on Barre in advance of the arrival of the bulk of Caydiid's fighters. However, the popular uprising was at least in part a spontaneous outburst of pain and anger at the Barre regime.

The uprising was reportedly a reaction against the latest brutalities committed by the Red Berets—by now almost exclusively consisting of men of the president's clan. In response to the killing of some government representatives, they had hunted down rebels in private homes, singling out and shooting individuals because of their clan background—undoubtedly Hawiye, but perhaps also Isaaq and Ogaadeen.[131] There are several reports by people who were in the city when these events occurred. Thus Sica, not one of Barre's harshest critics, described the regime's provocation as follows:

> That same afternoon, for three consecutive afternoons, the Red Berets launched an extremely bloody combing of three Mogadishu quarters in search of guerilla dens. The regime that had boasted to have come to power in a bloodless coup 21 years before, as it bragged on some city walls, instead ended in a terrible bloodbath.[132]

Pacifico's description is even more graphic:

> It was practically on Christmas Day that the Red Berets had begun a wide-ranging combing action in some of the quarters of the capital, to begin with that of Wardhiigley, where—this they knew—numerous groups of guerillas and arms deposits were hidden ... As always, and more than ever, the actions of the Red Berets were particularly violent and brutal. With the search as an excuse, the houses were plundered, the women raped, and any kind of abuse committed. And the indignation over these violent actions ignited the violence.[133]

At this point, some groups of USC supporters, already in the city and acting perhaps without explicit orders from the top, made secret plans to retaliate. The attacks on "the houses of high-ranking Marehan notables and government officials," the uprising in the Wardhiigley neighborhood, and the people's storming of Villa Somalia, were thus not completely unorganized but emerged, it appears, also from popular indignation at the brutal acts of the Red Berets. The people could not take it anymore.[134] While Villa Somalia was stormed and USC fighters attacked government officials all over the city, residential neighborhoods, especially Wardhiigley, came under heavy fire from the heavy artillery that surrounded the Villa. Italian diplomat Claudio Pacifico, who was taken to see Barre in Villa Somalia by Toyota Land Cruiser on January 4, 1991, in the middle of intense crossfire, was an eyewitness of these scenes. He saw corpses everywhere and noted the armored cars whose booming 155mm cannons pointed downward toward city. Moreover, from the relative safety of the car, he also saw smaller-scale, equally brutal incidents of violence. Thus he saw how the Red Berets had thrown "a group of youngsters, probably captured guerillas" to the ground and were hitting them with the butts of their guns, presenting a "scene," he explained, "that had every sign of a summary execution" (1996: 405).

The uprising in Mogadishu appears to have caused USC-Mogadishu to call in the militias under General Maxamed Nuur Galaal. This is the point of view of *Africa Confidential*, which reported:

> Originally the USC Committee in Mogadishu had hoped to re-open discussions with the well-armed Hawiye guerillas operating very successfully in central Somalia in conjunction with the SNM, under Aydeed's command. The events of late December forced a reappraisal. Galaal and 1,500 men, who had already been operating only 50 kilometers from the capital, arrived at the end of the first week of January. They were relatively ill-trained and lightly armed, and it wasn't until more heavily armed men of the SPM under Col. Ahmed Omar Jess reached the city on 23 January that the guerillas were able to break through and force Siad out a few days later.[135]

According to *Africa Confidential*, it was therefore General Maxamed Nuur Galaal, a former deputy minister of defense under Barre, who had overall control over the final assault on Mogadishu, with lieutenant-colonel Maxamuud Maxamed Xaashi "Shabeel" commanding the fighting.[136] Indeed, General Galaal later insisted that General Caydiid was not around when Barre was expelled and could thus take no credit for the victory.[137] This appears disingenuous. It is true that Caydiid was leading the war in Mogadishu's hinterland, but privately taped video-footage shows him meeting with members of USC-Mogadishu in the city on January 9.[138] At this meeting, he unambiguously rejected any negotiated compromise with Barre. However, it is possible that the arrival in Mogadishu of the USC militias led by Galaal was not only a response to Barre's final provocation and the popular uprising but also an effort to stay ahead of, or keep up with General Caydiid.

In London, the USC spokesman interviewed by BBC World Service was confident the end was near. He said: "The men that are under arms with the USC are in the thousands. Apart from the ex-army soldiers and officers, a large number of the nomadic population in the area of central and southern Somalia have been given training and are armed now."[139] Pushed by the interviewer to comment on the clan background of the thousands of rural fighters the USC had recruited and now brought to Mogadishu, he noted that their clan background was largely Hawiye but that Somalis of other clan backgrounds in south and south-central Somalia also supported the USC.[140] Indeed, at this point, innumerable Somalis, in and outside the USC and in and outside Somalia, still believed the USC would overthrow the Barre regime for all Somalis who had opposed and suffered at the hands of the regime and were cheering the USC on.[141]

The Battle for Mogadishu was accompanied with large-scale looting, both by government and rebel forces. Pacifico described the advance of the USC fighters as they gained control over the neighborhoods, including Lido, his own, and thoroughly sacked them, as follows. The first to arrive, he wrote, were groups of USC fighters, who, with a minimum of military organization, liberated a particular zone from the government. Then came common criminals and ordinary civilians who followed the fighters in search of loot. These included, he writes, "thousands of poor wretches, among whom women and children, who had decided to fight for the noble cause of looting" and who carried everything, but truly everything, away in a very brief period of time (1996: 400). Pacifico's own house too was looted this way and, in his memoirs, he registers his bitterness at two elements of the looting spree in particular. First, he was convinced that the USC used the license to plunder as an incentive for the common people and bands of criminals to gain support for its cause, in which they would thus, moreover, become deeply complicit. Second, he fumed at what he called Caydiid's deliberate campaign of disinformation, which blamed the Red Berets and, more generally all "Faqash" for looting and pillaging by his own fighters.[142] "The truth was, as always, very different," he writes. "We were well aware," he writes, that "many imams in the mosques preached in those days that robbing the houses of the government and the infidel gaal (whites) did not constitute a sin" (401).

Leaving the grounds of the embassy on January 3, 1991, Pacifico witnessed what he called a "lunar landscape": "deserted streets; burned cars; walls knocked down or riddled with bullets; corpses in the middle of the street, some quite decomposed, and furniture and other remnants of looting." All the familiar sites he had seen every day for four years had changed, "heavy with the stink of the corpses of the dead and a sense of abandonment and death." Near the airport and KM 4, he saw throngs of people, whole families, loaded down by either their sparse belongings or loot—he could not tell—walking out of the city toward Afgooye (403–4).

Other eyewitness accounts of Mogadishu in the first days of January featured in a report filed by Neil Henry of the *Washington Post* on January 6, 1991. Henry had traveled to Mombasa, where he interviewed people who had just been evacuated from Mogadishu by an Italian cargo plane. The evacuees described a Mogadishu in the grip of anarchy and terror, "a place where armed robbery, mass looting and clan violence spurred by fervent desires for retribution," he wrote, "appear to take precedence over more generally accepted ways of warfare." Some of the non-Somali evacuees reported seeing USC fighters with "white headbands adorned with the letters 'USC' in red and armbands proclaiming in Arabic, 'God is great'" in the streets of the city, though these seemed "to constitute only a fraction of the anti-government combatants fighting in Mogadishu." Among the Somalis Henry interviewed was Maxamuud Aadan Yuusuf, a forty-five-year-old engineer who taught at the University of Turin, Italy, and had been in Mogadishu to visit his family during the Christmas break. His account emphasized three aspects in particular.

First, he described with shock and horror that it was common people who had picked up weapons to participate in the violence. Henry reported: "much of the fighting is being done by 'petrol station owners, taxi drivers' and many other Hawiye civilians with weapons taking revenge on the government and the Marehan people." "'This is not war,' said Yusuf. 'It is chaos, anarchy.'" Second, the evacuees marveled at the omnipresence of automatic guns, telling Henry that "you could buy an AK47 for less than $300." Engineer Yusuf confirmed this: "So many people have arms in Mogadishu—some are even walking around with axes in their hands." Third, engineer Yusuf commented on the looting, listing the places that had been pillaged: the United Nations compound, the University of Mogadishu, the Ministry of Veterinary Medicine, the American Apartments. "I saw three soldiers carrying a computer thinking it would be good to hold water," he told Henry, and he added, referring to the participation of civilians, that the looters were not just soldiers but also other men, as well as women, and even children.[143]

If Barre had been willing to step down and leave the capital, events might possibly have taken a turn for the better.[144] However, Barre stayed put and turned his heavy artillery indiscriminately against residential neighborhoods—especially the nearest one, Wardhiigley—causing large numbers of civilian casualties. Given that some of these guns could deliver shells of fifteen or more pounds and reach many kilometers far, and that the USC fighters increasingly returned fire with similar weapons they had captured from the government or otherwise acquired, the destruction of the city and slaughter of its residents that the Manifesto Group and part of USC-Mogadishu had hoped to avoid had nevertheless become a reality.[145]

Throughout this period, in an attempt to prevent worse violence, different groups and parties continued to push for a negotiated settlement that would bring about a cease-fire, protect Mogadishu and its residents from the onslaught of total war, and secure the reform but also safeguard the continuity of government institutions. One such attempt was a proposed Peace and Reconciliation Conference, to be sponsored by Italy and Egypt, and planned first for November 21–24 and then for December 11–13, 1990.[146] It failed. USC-Caydiid and the SNM rejected it out of hand and the government hemmed and hawed; temporarily arrested some of the Manifesto and USC-Mogadishu leaders;[147] dragged its feet and finally, in a blatant show of insincerity, invited the opposition fronts instead to a reconciliation meeting in Mogadishu, promising to pay everyone's expenses and guaranteeing their security.[148]

Throughout January and up to three days before his expulsion, as the big guns boomed and Mogadishu burned, Barre kept up negotiations with different groups and continued to add to the committees he had already established. What really went on in his head is hard to know and few people who saw him in these last days have written about his state of mind. Pacifico saw him in Villa Somalia on January 4, as the war raged around and inside Villa Somalia. According to his memoirs, the Italian diplomat was strongly affected by the mayhem around him and emotionally appealed to Barre to accept a ceasefire and not to let his generals destroy the city and its inhabitants. Barre responded that he had established "un fracco di comitati" ("a whole bunch of committees") to bring this about and, to Pacifico, looked weary and lethargic. He "showed regret about what was happening," Pacifico felt, "but there was in his words no admission of guilt or responsibility" (1996: 407).

Already on January 2, 1991, Barre had used the radio to announce a cease-fire and meetings with local elders.[149] Manifesto elders such as Xaaji Xaashi Weheliye Macallin, Xaaji Muusa Boqor, and Maxamed Saciid "Gentleman" had been asked to mediate between the government and the USC. Xaaji Muusa Boqor, who had been a minister of the interior in the era of the Italian trusteeship, and Xaaji Xaashi Weheliye, whom Sica called the most gifted person in Mogadishu (1994: 42), paid for their efforts with their lives. On January 8, 1991, they were hit by a rocket in the very house in which they were negotiating, either by regime hardliners or by the USC.[150] Attempts to stop the military showdown that was in full swing nevertheless continued. On January 10, 1991, Radio Mogadishu broadcast speeches by minister of information Cumar Maxamed Cabdiraxmaan "Dheere" and two leading Manifesto elders, Xaaji Cali Shiddo Cabdi, former ambassador in Paris, and General Xaaji Maxamed Abshir, commander of the police in the era of the civilian administrations. The minister "reviewed the resolutions passed by the meeting between elders and government officials in Mogadishu. They included the appointment of a cease-fire committee, the burial of those who had died in the fighting, and the restoration of the water supply and communications."[151]

Of all the frantic efforts at a negotiated political transition, two deserve further mention: Barre's appeal to Italy and Egypt to sponsor a last-minute peace plan and his reconstitution of the Reconciliation Committee. The first last-ditch attempt at a negotiated political transition was an offer delivered to Egypt and Italy (including Ambassador Sica, who was in the city until January 12). Barre would leave in return for an honorable exit, he promised. Sica, who first heard about the offer on the 4th,[152] and received a direct message from Barre on the 6th or 7th, drew up a proposal that resembled the one for the canceled Cairo meeting and included the following. The state would continue to exist but Barre's repressive regime would end. Barre would remain titular head, constitutional head of state without power, and a new government would be constituted independent from him. A reconciliation process would be started. The Red Berets, Party Militia, National Security Service, and Military Police would be immediately disbanded and new elections would be held with international assistance and under international supervision (Sica 1994: 116).

On January 8, Sica transmitted the proposal to both parties (Barre and USC) and invited them to a meeting on the embassy grounds. The government never responded, Sica reports, and when he met General "Morgan" in person, the latter snubbed him, saying that the government would call a reconciliation meeting without intervention by foreign powers such as Italy. The response of USC-Mogadishu—drawn up by Xusseen Bood, Sica believed—politely pointed out that it needed more time to consult other political players, but to Sica's deep chagrin, the USC spokesmen in Rome and London, as well as that of the SSDF in Nairobi, all rejected the idea that negotiating with Barre was still an option.[153]

As for the second last-ditch attempt at a negotiated transition, on January 12–13, the Barre regime formally reconstituted a Reconciliation Committee of 100 members—3/4 representing the people and 1/4 the government—led by Prime Minister Mohamed Hawaadle Madar and a six- (later seven-) member committee. This executive committee included the head of USC Mogadishu, Xusseen Xaaji Maxamed Bood, Manifesto elders Axmed Maxamed Darmaan and Cabdiasiis Nuur Xirsi, as well as Cumar Carta Ghaalib, a prominent politician who had fallen from presidential grace in the early 1980s and had since been imprisoned, sentenced to death, pardoned, and released into house arrest.[154] The initiative was ridiculed by Radio SNM, which pointed at what it considered Barre's hypocrisy, as he was, on the one hand, destroying the city and its residents by means of heavy and indiscriminate shelling and, on the other hand, asking for a cease-fire and the restoration of peace. It added:

> The so-called committee appointed to supervise a cease-fire and discuss peace is just a sign of desperation.... The meeting was originally scheduled to be held in the People's Assembly Hall, but at the last minute its venue was changed to Villa Baydhoa [Baydhaba or Baidoa]. The change was brought about by the capture of the site of the Assembly Hall by USC fighters. We therefore wish to tell the remnants of Siyad's regime that whatever proposals they come up with will be ignored by the Somali people.[155]

If one were to believe the Minister of Information's almost daily reports on Radio Mogadishu, the Reconciliation Committee made immediate progress, as it had entered in dialogue with USC-Mogadishu. In the name of Somali unity and the religion of Islam, the Minister made a passionate appeal to observe the cease-fire, wage "a merciless war against the gangs of looters in the city," and "uphold your unity and cohesiveness, accept peace, and thank God:"[156]

> Somalis, you should know your interests. There is nothing which you might want individually. You are the same people, one family, brothers; you speak one language and share the same religion and tradition.... The shedding of your blood is sinful since you are Muslims. To shed the blood of a Muslim without obvious reason and justification is sinful. You know the teachings of Islam, so salvage the remaining property and lives. Let those who ran away from Mogadishu, from their homes, who now feel worn out, return. Let the children, the elderly, and the women be brought back to their homes by the assurance of peace....
>
> You are a sovereign people, you have a national flag, you are a nation.... You have been pillaging foreigners' property [words indistinct] those are diplomats. What can we achieve by slapping and harassing them? Today in our country there is not a single embassy open, none. How can we possibly do things? We have been disgraced. First let us restore peace and order. Let us listen and respect each other.

Next day, January 17, the minister was back on the radio, announcing that, although a full cease-fire had not yet been achieved, a subcommittee had "drafted a reasonable and respectful letter of advice to the President," which proposed a constitutional way forward and which the president had promised to accept. This time the minister had brought four other prominent men to Radio Mogadishu to address the people. Xusseen Xaaji Maxamed Bood, here called chairman of the implementation committee of the USC, and Axmed Maxamed Darmaan added their voices to the appeal for peace and calm, as did Sheikh Xusseen Xassan Cali, who reminded the Somali people to look to the future, let go of the grievances and problems of the past, and preserve and protect important national institutions such as "the radio station, the post office, the airport, the port, national [public] buildings, telephones, fuel depots, hospitals, schools, underground fuel storages and water wells, which belong to all Somalis." The broadcast concluded with a pledge by Brigadier-General Cabdullaahi Axmed "Cirro," representing the Ministry of Defense, that the Somali Armed Forces would obey these resolutions and effect an immediate cease-fire."[157]

Just a few days later, on January 20, the president accepted some or all of the Committee's proposals. He dissolved the government of Prime Minister Maxamed Hawaadleh Madar and appointed Cumar Carta Ghaalib, the nominee of the Reconciliation Committee, as prime minister charged with forming a new government.[158] USC London immediately rejected the new development. It "criticized the role of the peace committee describing it as a cheap propaganda ploy" and stated that no cease-fire could come into effect before Barre resigned. It moreover claimed that the USC was now in effective control of Mogadishu and that the three main opposition movements (USC, SNM, and SPM) were in the process of forming a transitional government.[159] The former would prove to be more in line with reality than the latter.

By then the futility of the reconciliation efforts must have become clear to even the members of the Reconciliation Committee themselves. It cannot have escaped them that the concessions Barre made only three days before he was expelled from Mogadishu were laughably minimal and unacceptable to the three armed opposition movements that had vowed to overthrow him.[160] It must have been obvious to them that they had failed to keep the war out of Mogadishu or limit the destruction it brought in its wake. However, something else had occurred in Mogadishu as they had been making a last-ditch effort to preserve the state from collapsing and preventing a political free-for-all: the violence in Mogadishu had become a campaign of clan cleansing and a massive episode of organized communal violence. It had been set in motion by the second week of January and intensified after Barre's expulsion from Mogadishu on January 26 and the hurried establishment of a transitional government by USC-Mogadishu on January 28, 1991. It is to this episode of large-scale clan-based violence against civilians we will now turn.

Chapter 3

Clan Cleansing in Mogadishu and Beyond

Introduction

From mid-December 1990 on, the number of foreigners who remained in Mogadishu dwindled.[1] The U.S. embassy, where foreign nationals of many backgrounds toward the end had taken refuge, was evacuated on January 5, 1991, the Italian embassy on January 12. Both evacuations involved dramatic rescue actions by land, sea, and air.[2] Groups of stragglers, especially Italians who worked in the city or the agricultural areas of Jubba and Jannaale, also managed to arrange for escape but had to leave all their possessions behind.[3] By January 10 even most humanitarian workers had left the country to escape the violence. A rare exception was Austrian Willy (Wilhelm) Huber of SOS Children's Village, who, with a small Somali staff of doctors, nurses, and aides, stayed put and provided emergency aid to the wounded. As this hospital was located in a zone captured by the USC early on, Huber was able to bear eloquent testimony to the human costs of the indiscriminate shelling of the city by heavy government artillery.[4] However, for reasons that may include the relentless pressure of the work in the hospital, his dependence on the USC to be allowed to continue it, or even an attempt to stay above the fray, he never bore witness to the violent clan cleansing that began to happen even before Barre was expelled.

Most international news reports of this period describe, apart from the cannon fire with which Barre's men blanketed parts of the city from Villa Somalia, indiscriminate violence perpetrated by a mix of criminal gangs, marauding former government soldiers, USC militias from the countryside, and ordinary people running amok. Chaos, a free-for all, urban poor looting at will, government officials making off with ill-gained wealth or a final bribe,[5] impoverished rural guerillas and ordinary criminals on a rampage, a people pushed to the limit taking mass revenge on the supporters of the regime, clan vengeance, and leaders unable to exercise control—this is what has constituted the framework for many journalistic and scholarly accounts alike.[6] There was truth to such representations, for all of this was indeed *also* happening. However, all the need, greed, and anger that under the cover of war were injected into the dramatic moment of regime collapse gave a lethal charge to a dimension of the violence to which these news reports did not pay attention, namely organized clan cleansing.

Yet it was this clan dimension that, for whoever was willing or able to see it, constituted the most sinister aspect of the violent events in Mogadishu in January 1991, one that showed that a significant dimension and amount of the violence was not random but organized and did not pitch government against armed opposition but common people against common people. If the violence had been a popular outburst against the benefactors and supporters—even alleged benefactors and supporters—of the regime alone, then men who had been central pillars of the military regime and its policies until the very end would have *all* become primary targets of such anger. They were not. A closer examination of who was *not* attacked and who *was* targeted for violence provides crucial insights into that dimension of the violence that was part of an organized strategy of clan cleansing, a strategy in which the agency of particular politicians and military men, as well as popular fury, played a crucial role.

"Recycling in Tribal Key": Some of Barre's Henchmen Embraced as Heroes by the USC

The evidence that the violence perpetrated by the USC leaders and rank-and-file from January 1991 on was not random lies in the fact that even top generals who had been the heart, muscle, and brain of the Barre regime from its inception did not become targets for violence when they were of the clan background associated with the USC, that is to say, when they were Hawiye. The Barre regime fell on January 26, 1991, when an armed convoy took Barre out of the city toward Kismaayo in the South. Within two days, on January 28, 1991, the leadership of USC-Mogadishu (including Xusseen Bood) hurriedly proclaimed a transitional administration with Cali Mahdi as president, a move immediately rejected and deeply resented not only by USC-Caydiid but also by the two other fronts actively engaged in the armed struggle, the SPM and SNM. What took many observers by surprise, however, was that at this moment, within two days of Barre's expulsion, those top men of the regime who had the "right" clan background not only remained unharmed but were enthusiastically welcomed into the top ranks of the USC leadership. This was part of the key shift of January 1991.

Mario Sica, Italian ambassador in Mogadishu, responded with sarcasm to the claim of the new Cali Mahdi administration that it was engaged "not in a clan fight but in a struggle against the remnants of Siad Barre"; as he pointed out, "not a few of those 'remnants' found refuge in its ranks, as advisers or in other roles."[7] Listing their names and former roles in the Barre regime, Sica wrote:

> This is the case of Hussein Kulmie, one of the fathers of the "revolution" of Siad Barre, and extremely loyal to him, who is part of all the assemblies of elders convoked in Mogadishu; of the super-rich ex-Minister of Finance Mohamed Sheikh Osman (who now claims to have played a double role by financing the guerilla secretly); of the ex-Minister of Finance Hussein Mohamed Siad "Atow," connected to numerous regime affairs; of the former head of the National Security Service of the Benadir, Ahmed Gilaò [Jilacow] Addow, up to the end the mayor of Mogadishu, whom Ali Mahdi without batting an eyelash made his very security adviser; of Abdullahi Ahmed Addow, formerly governor of the Somali Central Bank in the first Republic, then ambassador of Siad Barre in Washington for almost ten years, then minister of Finance and of the Presidency, one of the technocrats most listened to by the dictator, of whom Aidid will make one of his advisers; of Abdikasim Salad, the last Minister of the Interior of Siad Barre, young, intelligent, and very cultured . . . who could have been the man of the democratic turning point we had hoped for; but who instead, despite our frequent meetings, stuck until the end to the hardest positions of the regime.[8]

Sica's second-in-command Claudio Pacifico mentions some of the same names and gives further details. Because of his clan background alone, he notes, even Xusseen Kulmiye Afrax, the former vice president of the Somali

Republic, who with Barre and General Samantar had been one of the founders of the military regime, was immediately recycled into the new political establishment. However, this "recycling in tribal key"[9] did not stop at the highest level but was also extended to men in lower positions "who had been sullied by participating in these crimes and depravities that were the source of the fall of the regime of Siad Barre and that were now attributed to only the old president." "And soon," Pacifico added with some bitterness, "we would find ourselves dealing with delegations, in which would sit, brotherly, side by side, men who had not killed each other a few days earlier only by pure chance" (1996: 446).

Somalis following events from the diaspora also commented on this development at the time. In a public statement entitled "Genocide in Mogadisho: Mogadisho after the ouster of Barre's dictatorship," issued in Washington, D.C., on March 11, 1991, a group called Concerned Somalis wrote with great bitterness:

> In fact, over thirty of Barre regime's top officials are among USC's leadership in Mogadisho. Hussein Kulmiye Afrax, Siyad Barre's right hand man and Vice-President throughout [the] regime's tenure, today remains as the principle leader of the USC in Mogadisho. In contrast, the wives and the children of poor non-Hawiye janitors have to run for their lives.[10]

A press release from the Canadian Network on Human Rights in Somalia in Toronto, March 9, 1991, listed some of the same individuals (Xusseen Kulmiye Afrax, Cabdullaahi Axmed Caddow, and Axmed Jilacow). However, it also pointed out how the very men who now organized and financed the purge of what they called the "remnants of the Barre regime" were actually regime remnants themselves, as they had until just a few days before formed an intrinsic part of that regime. They presented Cali Mahdi, the new president-hopeful, as a close business associate of the Barre family; Colonel Maxamed Xaashi "Shabeel" as "a former division commander in the Barre regime who was responsible for the Genocide in Northern Somalia in 1988," and General Maxamed Faarax Caydiid as "a former aid de camp and bodyguard" of Barre as well as Barre's ambassador to India until 1990.[11]

This "recycling in tribal key" of the central pillars of the Barre regime powerfully demonstrates that the violence that surrounded the collapse of the regime was not just about popular anger at those regarded as its supporters, but, as I will elaborate below, about adopting clan cleansing as a strategy for capturing the state.

Clan Cleansing in Mogadishu: The Victims

While some of the men who had been long-time key players in the Barre regime were thus welcomed into USC ranks as heroes on the basis of their clan background, other such key players, as well as large numbers of ordinary people who had had nothing to do with the regime or had suffered more at the hands of the regime than those who now wanted them dead, were being purposefully targeted for violence on the basis of their clan background. And it was not just people who had the same clan background as the president and his Red Berets, although they were among the targets. All those associated with "*the*" Daarood—a genealogical construct that encompassed a score of clans and a large percentage of the inhabitants of Mogadishu and the country as a whole—now, irrespective of their individual histories, came to be seen as enemies to be killed and driven out.[12]

Most of those who were now targeted, even prominent individuals such as the Manifesto elders, were caught unaware by the USC pogrom. "I did not see it coming until the last moment," said one Manifesto elder, though "we did see the violence against civilians coming and even bought guns, to defend ourselves as civilians." Then, even as it was happening, "we believed that the massacres could be stopped" (Interview 3). Another Manifesto elder reported that he and some of his fellow signatories had been so focused on trying to end the dictatorship and get Barre to step down that, when news of the clan cleansing first began to reach them, they initially suspected Barre of trying to scare them and weaken their political resolve (Interview 9). Many Manifesto elders paid a high price for their refusal to accept the victory of the new clan paradigm and for their conviction that the USC leadership, especially the moderate leadership of USC-Mogadishu, would want to reconstitute a government that was nationally representative, not one based on the extermination and expulsion of a large part of the population.

Somalis in exile too were often equally unsuspecting. On January 3, 1991, in Toronto, Paul Watson of the *Toronto Star* interviewed Maxamed Cadirashiid Sharmarke. As the son of the Somali president who had been assassinated just before Barre's coup d'état, he had long been in exile from the regime. "Justice is drawing near," Maxamed was quoted as saying. Anxiously awaiting Barre's fall and making preparations to send humanitarian aid to Mogadishu in the wake of this eagerly awaited event, he had no idea that his own relatives would be hunted down as if they had been Barre beneficiaries or supporters.[13] Nuruddin Farah, the internationally renowned Somali novelist and essayist who interviewed some of those who had fled the clan cleansing in a Kenyan refugee camp soon after their arrival, registered his own resistance to accepting, let alone identifying himself with, the new identity categories to which the victims of clan-based violence referred with such deep emotion. He clearly felt like a man from another era:

> I was nonplussed by the tempestuous outpouring of strong sentiments and emotions expressed in intense clan terms. There was such venom in their recollection that I was taken aback, maybe because I had been unprepared for it. Shocked, perhaps not so much by any of what my interlocutors said, as by the severity and the depth of their hurt, which now ran in their blood. . . . "We know who *we* are," several of them repeated again and again, their voices bitter as the bolus of poison. "What has occurred in Mogadiscio has taught us who we are." What do they mean by "us"? This was not some sort of double-talk, saying one thing and meaning something totally other: they were wholeheartedly committed to a new form of Somali-speak, in which "us" refers to a post-colonial realpolitik governed by the anachronistic sentiments of clannism. I found myself needing to make it clear to every single one of them that I belonged neither to "*us*" nor "*them*." (Farah 2000: 5)

It is hard to imagine a more eloquent and poignant epitaph to the discourse of "Somaliness" and the nationalism of an earlier time—here represented by Nuruddin Farah—and the mindset of the refugees that was born out of their experience as victims of clan cleansing.[14]

What follows is a narrative of the events that made up the clan cleansing campaign, first as it began to unfold in Mogadishu in January 1991 and then as it extended to other parts of central, south-central, and south Somalia. The following vignettes illustrate that much of this violence was organized and purposeful; that many victims were selected, rounded up, and killed on the basis of their clan background in ways that were not haphazard but constitute recurring patterns; that there was widespread, popular participation in the violence—just as there was in saving targeted victims from it—and that perpetrators and victims often knew each other intimately; and finally, that this violence was ordered, directed, organized, and supervised by USC leaders.

Scenes of Clan Cleansing in Mogadishu

The first vignette dates from the first stages of the clan cleansing in Mogadishu. It shows the communal nature of the violence and the intimate knowledge perpetrators and victims often had of each other, as well as the unwillingness of the USC leadership to acknowledge the violence for what it was, let alone to try to prevent or contain it.

Vignette 1: "We Lined Them Up in the Garden and Shot Them All"

Mohamoud M. Afrah (Maxamuud M. Afrax) was a journalist when the Battle for Mogadishu began on December 30, 1990, having worked for many years for the only English-language papers published by the Ministry of Education. His memoirs of this period (up to July 1991) were among the very first ones to be published. Writing about himself in the third person as Ali Duhul (Cali Dhuxul), the author describes the period of the Battle for Mogadishu culminating in the expulsion of Barre from the city and the capture of the presidential residence, Villa Somalia, on January 26, 1991, part of which the author (for a little while "embedded" with some of the USC youth he knew) witnessed. By the first week of January, the government had turned the heavy artillery present in the presidential compound on the residential areas of the city below, destroying houses and killing and wounding civilians. Ali Duhul reports seeing the decaying bodies of hundreds of civilians, including women and children, on the side of the roads. He assumes that they were "killed in crossfire as they tried to flee the inferno" (Afrah 1992: 51). He asks USC fighters about the unburied bodies: "'How can we bury the dead when government forces continuously shell residential areas from their positions inside the Presidential Palace?' one of the rebels retorted. 'The city is rapidly becoming a massive open grave,' one man who lost all members of his family told me" (53).

However, Ali Duhul also reports on other forms of violence perpetrated by common people, both against government officials and against people of the same clan background as the president. He asks Cumar Raage, whom he calls "the Chairman of Mogadishu Committee of the USC," about this:

> Several top officers of the dreaded National Security Service (NSS) have been murdered in their villas. A number of people who belonged

to the President's minority Marehan clan were also murdered during the week, but Mr. Rageh attributed the revenge killings to angry citizens who "thought that the time was ripe for settling old scores." (50)

After Barre's expulsion, journalist Afrah continues his research and, in this context, interviews a "neighbor who joined the guerrillas," who tells him,

> I was in charge of a group of youngsters between the ages of fourteen and seventeen all carrying AK47 assault rifles when an old woman told us that there was a house full of the President's clansmen in one of the liberated sections of the city. She swore that some of them were members of the Presidential bodyguards, the red berets, fully armed. So we went to the house, a two-storey affairs [sic], and since I knew the area, I could tell immediately they were Marehan clansmen. (59)

Author Afrah (through his character Ali Duhul) asks what happened and the neighbor answers: "we lined them up in the garden and shot them all," adding as a kind of justification that the victims were "Marehans still hiding in the liberated area fully equipped." The author then asks whether the latter did not put up a fight. No, says the neighbor, for our guide used to come to the house to sell eggs. When asked what happened to the women and children, the neighbor answers: "We shot them all" (59). Afrah does not draw explicit conclusions from this account, but he appears to wonder whether fully equipped and armed men would have allowed themselves, with their wives and children, to be lined up and shot without putting up any resistance. It appears that a family considered of the "wrong" clan was betrayed by a casual acquaintance, who led armed neighborhood kids to their house to kill them and loot their possessions. Whether Afrah believed the leadership of USC-Mogadishu when it claimed that it was not involved in such incidents, is less clear, as he simply reports: "Rebel leaders consistently denied killing unarmed civilians, saying there were people who took the law in their hands by settling old scores" (59).[15]

This first vignette illustrates first, that USC fighters and supporters did not kill randomly but selected their victims on the basis of their clan background, and second, that the violence was communal violence in the sense that ordinary civilians, including neighbors and acquaintances, participated in the clan cleansing.

Vignette 2: The Looting of Pacifico's House

As Pacifico relates it, the incident described here occurred January 8, 1991, when the Lido neighborhood was overrun by USC militia and his house was attacked and looted. The gunmen who climbed the wall of his house were so numerous, his guards told him, that they understood that, though they were well armed, the situation was hopeless. The USC fighters disarmed them and put them up against the wall. They were looking specifically and by name for one man—in Pacifico's words, "an Ogaden and an old policeman whom the guerillas were seeking to kill" (1996: 422). Even though he was lined up against the wall right there with the other guards, the latter, who shared the clan background of the attackers, refused to give him away and saved his life. After the attackers had destroyed the gate and warned the men not to offer resistance to those who would come after them, they took the car, petrol, and weapons, and left. At dawn, Pacifico relates, others had come—looters and thieves, but also common people from the neighborhood whom he knew and who, he believed, had nothing against him personally. Together they stripped the house of its belongings, even the toilet bowls. He concludes, in rather patronizing terms: "Now that they had been unleashed, now the outbreak of the war, of the tribal feud (*faida*), had given them a moral justification, the temptation to loot the inaccessible riches of the whites was stronger than any other sentiment."

This episode suggests that these particular USC militias were at least somewhat organized and that the looting of the house and neighborhood had been planned and agreed upon beforehand. Destroying the gate, so that it could no longer be closed, served, among other things, as an invitation to common people to become implicated in the violence through looting.

Vignette 3: The Murder of Professor Abyan and Other Manifesto Elders

The third set of incidents consists of what happened to some of the key signatories of the Manifesto, the elite opposition group at the end of the Barre era discussed above. They too were sorted by clan background. This meant not only that their fortunes diverged dramatically but also that some of them now obtained the power of life and death over the others. Thus Manifesto elders of the clan associated with the USC such as Cali Mahdi, who was nominated president of a hastily USC-proclaimed transitional administration, and Xusseen Bood, who became the head of the Executive Committee of USC-Mogadishu, gained in power and influence. Manifesto elders of the "wrong" clan backgrounds, however, became targets.

One of the patterns discerned by survivors was the explicit targeting, early on during the clan cleansing project, of middle-class men of distinction (*niman magacleh*) such as intellectuals, professionals, politicians, or established businessmen. To refute arguments that such deaths were due to random looting, one survivor cited the murder of Xusseen Xassan, former Director-General of the Ministry of Foreign Affairs, who was killed early on and was found in the middle of a busy neighborhood with his golden Seiko watch still on his wrist.[16] The murder of Professor Ibrahim Abyan, the director of SIDAM (the Somali Institute for Development Administration) and a principal author of the text of the Manifesto of May 1990, who had, moreover, taught a whole generation of Somali students, also fits this pattern. His murder shows that there was nothing incidental about the killing of such highly accomplished Somali individuals.

Dr. Abyan and three friends were stopped by armed USC supporters when they were trying to leave the city at a place called "Ex-Control-Afgooye," in the Madiina neighborhood of Mogadishu. He was recognized by a general called General Maxamed Cabdi, who was of the same clan background as the gunmen. The general failed to persuade the gunmen to let Dr. Abyan and the others continue their journey, but obtained their permission to take them to the USC command center in the neighborhood of Yaaqshiid. At the control center, where General Maxamed Nuur Galaal was in command, there was at that moment an interrogation underway of a man who was suspected of being Daarood but who, because of his dialect, could also be a northerner from another clan background (Isaaq), not a target of clan cleansing. When the cars pulled up, General Maxamed Cabdi got out of the car first and, while he knocked the door, the four men including Dr. Abyan also got out of their car. As Galaal opened the door, fire was opened and the four men were killed. The man who was being interrogated was then put to the test and asked whether he recognized the body of Dr. Abyan. Though the man had grown up with Abyan in Laas Caanood, he denied that he knew him and thus saved his life.[17]

French scholar Daniel Compagnon commented as follows on Dr. Abyan's death:

> The USC leadership endorsed the witch-hunt against Daarood people, who were shot on the spot without trial, or even a minimum assessment of the role they had personally played in the ousted regime.

> This is how Dr Abyan, a member of the Manifesto Group, was killed in the yard of the house where several Hawiye leaders (including Ali Mahdi, the new provisional president) were meeting, without one of them making any attempt to save their colleague's life, even though they had been struggling for democracy together less than a month earlier. (Compagnon 1998: 78)[18]

Several members of the Manifesto Group and the Reconciliation Committee of the "wrong" clan background insisted on staying put and did not leave the country until after they had had a number of narrow escapes. One of these elders was twice taken away by armed men toward certain death. Both times he was saved by young neighbors who recognized him and were unable or unwilling to make the sudden transition to regarding him as an enemy. "Adeer" ("Uncle")—here a term of respect toward an older person—"is that you?" they said. "Where are they taking you?" "I do not know, nephew, just stay close to me, the elder answered anxiously" (Interview 4). In many cases everyday relationships trumped the new construction of clan otherness.

Equally poignant is the experience of two other Manifesto elders, one Hawiye and the other Daarood, who continued to hope that the USC leadership would see reason and could be persuaded to halt the clan cleansing campaign. Both had close female relatives raped in front of them; one because he was himself Daarood and the other, who was Hawiye, because his wife and in-laws were of the "wrong" clan (Interview 3).

Vignette 4: Jailor and Jailed Together on the Run

Of course some of the people now targeted for violence indeed *had* been high officials of the Barre regime. Some of these had escaped by plane or by car convoy to neighboring countries much earlier—at times bringing along ill-gained wealth to sweeten their exile.[19] As happened among the victors so too among the victims, men who had been on different sides of the political aisle just a few days or weeks before now ended up squeezed into the same clan category and sharing the same fate. A poignant fourth incident, related by Mario Sica, illustrates this. When Sica accompanied an Italian C-130 plane with food and medicines from Nairobi to Kismaayo in the beginning of March 1991, he met at the Kismaayo airport "two old acquaintances." One was Maxamed Jaamac Cumar "Dhigic-Dhigic," one of the Manifesto signatories whose arrest on December 4 Sica had worked so tirelessly to reverse. The other was Cabdirasaaq "Jurile," who as vice-minister of the exterior had refused to assist Sica and had defended the arrest (1994: 137). "What had brought the person who had shared responsibility for the arrest and the one who had been its victim together," Sica concluded, was that they shared the same clan background and had both been forced to flee the killing fields of Mogadishu.

Vignette 5: The Narrow Escapes of Engineer Axmed Aadan Yuusuf

Many victims of the clan cleansing campaign were rounded up from or summarily executed in their homes. The former happened, for example, to a former parliamentarian of the era of civilian administrations, Nuur Xaashi Calas, who had a son and two other male relatives killed in front of him but survived because the gunmen did not want to waste a bullet on someone so old and sickly. However, many others victims were stopped, sorted, and shot at checkpoints, or taken to holding pens and executed en masse. The story of engineer Axmed, even though he survived, illustrates this.

At a checkpoint near the university and close to where his brother, the narrator of the incident, lived, Axmed and his passenger were pulled from their car and made to stand in the street together with other captives. Among the men who were lining them up was someone with whom he had studied in Germany and who recognized him but did not say or do anything to set him free. However, another man drove by, a friend of the narrator and of the same clan background as the captors. He recognized Axmed. "Are you not that engineer (*injiniirkii*)? What are you doing here?" "They are holding me here." "Come with me." That was how he was saved. The other captives were killed on the spot.

Engineer Axmed had another narrow escape before he was able to leave Somalia. Stopped by armed USC men who asked him about his clan, he claimed to be of the clan of his brother-in-law, who was Hawiye. They did not believe him and took him to Hotel Tawfiiq in Mogadishu's Yaaqshiid neighborhood, a notorious USC holding center, where many other men, some of whom the narrator mentioned by name, were at that moment also kept. As he was held there, someone recognized him and ran to his sister to tell her that her brother was held at the hotel. The sister gathered her sons (who were Hawiye) and sent them to collect her brother. The narrator concluded his account by saying: "None of the other Daarood men held there survived" (Interview 2).

Vignette 6: What Should We Do with Aunt Maryan?

A sixth incident shows that ordinary people committed acts of clan cleansing under direct orders from USC leaders. This particularly telling incident occurred to the wife of a Manifesto signatory who survived the massacres in Mogadishu concealed in different places by different friends. They called us *laheystayaal*—hostages uncertain of their fate—the elder noted.[20] One day, his wife was rounded up by young gunmen who recognized her as "Eeddo Maryan" (Aunt Maryan)—here again a title of respect for an older person one knows well. They took her to their commander, a man who later became internationally known as the financier (and later rival) of General Maxamed Faarax Caydiid. They said to him: "Here is Eeddo Maryan. What shall we do with Eeddo?" Embarrassed, their commander told them to let her go, but before she was out of earshot, she heard him bark at them: "Next time, do not bring people like that to me; take care of them on the spot!"[21]

Something very similar happened to three other individuals, all Manifesto elders who were Daarood by background. They were abducted by USC supporters and taken to the house of Xassan Dimbil, a former Manifesto elder then supporting the USC.[22] Dimbil knew them well as they had been prisoners of Barre's regime in Laanta Buur together. He showed no surprise at seeing them hauled in front of him and just angrily told the captors: "Why did you bring them here? You should decide what to do with them yourselves." Though they were let go, the abducted men were forced to face the fact that this man, who had been their colleague just a few weeks ago, now had the power of life or death over them (Interview 4). This vignette also suggests that active concealment of individual responsibility for the clan cleansing characterized the campaign even as it unfolded.

Vignette 7: A Gang-Rape Averted

A seventh incident shows how hard it was for the armed gunmen who perpetrated much of the violence to distinguish between people of the "right" and the "wrong" clan background. The young sister of another narrator was captured in the street and dragged in the direction of a small building where the gunmen wanted to rape her. She told them that they would have to shoot her first. However, she also claimed to belong to the clan of the men threatening her and was able to give great detail because one of her best school friends was of that background. The young men were suspicious, but one believed her and managed to set her free.[23] Large-scale rape was part of the clan cleansing campaign, with thousands of women and girls purposely gang-raped in front or within earshot of relatives and friends who would have done anything to protect them.[24]

Vignette 8: The Narrow Escape of a Quick-Witted Wife

Another glimpse of the clan cleansing campaign comes from the account of a young wife who had just packed up some of her belongings to flee the city. In the absence of her husband, she had just stepped out to say goodbye to a (non-Daarood) neighbor when gunmen entered her home looking for a Daarood family. As she left her neighbor's house, she saw her young niece, flanked by a group of fierce-looking armed men, coming toward her. She appealed to her neighbor for help, as she could perhaps have claimed her as a relative, but her friend stayed silent. The young wife was taken inside her house. When she was asked what clan she was, she had to think on her feet. "You are right, I am a Daarood woman," she said, giving them the name of a relatively small Daarood clan. However, "my husband is not," she lied, claiming that he belonged to a clan associated with the USC. "The packed bags you see here are what he and his friends yesterday looted from the Daarood." The gunmen believed this and left her alone, perhaps, she later thought, because they were still new to their roles. On their way out—and this is what persuaded her that they had been specifically directed to her home—the gunmen commented to each other that the information they had been given was not *all* wrong. The wife and her husband fled the city that same night.[25]

Vignette 9: Contradictory Moral Imperatives

It is striking how many of the stories of survivors involve the active or passive agency of relatives, friends, and even acquaintances who decided to honor concrete social relationships that predated and proved immune to the logic of clan cleansing. It is clear from these examples that real-life everyday relationships often trumped the hate-narratives that constructed these friends, school-mates, colleagues, neighbors, and in-laws as despised and dangerous clan "others" who deserved to die or be expelled. However, for many individuals, the opposite became so much the norm that supporting the clan cleansing of people one did *not* personally know was fully compatible with saving the ones one knew. The story of Eeddo Caasha (not her real name) and her daughter illustrates this.

Mother and daughter had fled the capital at the height of the fighting in December. Once Barre had been expelled, they believed calm would return and came back to Mogadishu. This is when their problems began. First of all, their house was marked with a "D" (for Daarood), so they became a target even for people who did not already know them. However, the first people who showed up to take away their furniture and belongings were their neighbors. That these later stooped so low as to return next day to collect the special griddle for making *canjeelo* (a kind of unleavened bread) mother and daughter cannot comprehend until today. However, another friend and neighbor, also Hawiye, came to their aid. She prevented the rape of the daughter and paid a high price for doing so, as she was raped herself instead. This woman friend also arranged for her brother to take Eeddo Caasha and her daughter to the airport. As they were driving along, the brother received a phone call that reported successful attacks on Daarood targets elsewhere in the country. The brother asked his caller to repeat the message several times, and when Eeddo Caasha asked him why he did so, he answered, oblivious to the irony of the situation, that the news made him so happy that he could not hear it often enough.[26] Other accounts confirm that those who saved people they personally knew, nevertheless, also participated in the clan cleansing of those they did not.

In spite of the efforts of individuals who refused to participate in the clan cleansing or actively resisted it, at the end of three months, Mogadishu was largely, as poet Mohamud Togane phrased it, "Darod-rein" (Togane 2006).

Although the wider context of war and destruction and the complete disruption of normal services affected all inhabitants of the capital, those Somalis who did not fit the construct of *"the"* Daarood enemy remained largely untouched by the clan cleansing campaign the USC unleashed in Mogadishu. The most notable exception were a group of Somalis now often referred to as a minority, the Benaadiri people associated with the earliest history of the towns of Somalia's southern coast, including Mogadishu. Hard on the heels of the launching of the clan cleansing campaign members of this group too were "othered" and abused because of their clan background. Their othering, however, differed from that of *"the"* Daarood (about which more below), for they were constructed as outside of the Somali clan construct altogether, and thus as "foreign," "Arab," and unprotected. It appears that greed and lust, deprivation and intoxication, real and imaginary slights—such as resentment at the endogamous preferences of the Reer Xamar—and opportunity-with-impunity, served as rationales for the abuse. For the victims who survived, the experience of being put beyond the pale of Somaliness and witnessing how gangs of fighters purposefully debased and destroyed what was most dear to them—their religious standing, the integrity of their family and womenfolk, the family home and business—destroyed any trust they might have once had. More research is needed to establish whether the USC leadership in Mogadishu intended this to happen, simply ignored it, or tried but failed to contain this violence.[27]

Clan Cleansing Overlooked, Ignored, Concealed, and Denied

Silence in Contemporary News Sources

It is surprising that, as the clan cleansing was unfolding in Mogadishu, the English-language press never reported on this dimension of the violence in Mogadishu in any detail. Although it was true that very few foreigners remained in the city after the evacuation of the Italian embassy on January 12, 1991, a number of intrepid journalists visited the city immediately after Barre's expulsion of January 26, when the clan cleansing was in full swing, and reported on what they saw.[28] How could they have missed this?

It is evident from their reports that these journalists were hosted by the USC and taken on joint or individual tours by USC "handlers" appointed for that purpose.[29] These tours appear to have had many of the same "highlights," which included the bloated bodies of Barre's Red Berets in Villa Somalia (as well as a heap of uniforms that had been abandoned at the moment of flight); the bodies of sixteen executed civilians (including women) who had their hands tied behind their backs; scenes of looting, including common people collecting bank notes on the road before the looted Central Bank; and views of the destruction of the city, especially extensive in the neighborhood of Wardhiigley that bordered on the presidential palace.[30] What is striking from hindsight is how (relatively) passive the journalists were and how they refrained from asking questions from the people with whom they met beyond their handlers.

For example, Neil Henry of the *Washington Post*, who visited the capital on January 29, three days after Barre's expulsion, when the clan cleansing was in full swing, wrote the following:[31]

> this sun-swept capital on the Indian Ocean remains full of human agony and lingering scenes of horror. . . . Lime-covered corpses of

slain government soldiers lie in the middle of Sinai Road near downtown, three blocks from a vacant lot where chickens peck amid the unburied bodies of a dozen civilians executed by soldiers—men and women, shot in the head, their hands bound behind their backs with faded strips of cotton.

Aidan Hartley of the *Guardian* appears to have been shown the same scene and wrote:[32]

On a street corner, rebels showed the bodies of 16 executed men and women with their hands bound behind their backs. . . . In a district said [to be] inhabited mainly by Mr. Siad Barre's own Marehan clan, bodies have lain unburied for at least a week and are partially eaten by dogs.

Reid Miller of the Associated Press too appears to have seen the same corpses, in his case on January 28:[33] "But not all victims were killed by shellfire. At one intersection in the northern suburbs, reporters counted 16 bodies—men, women and children, some with their hands tied behind their backs and clearly shot on the spot." None of these journalists asked who these victims were and how, why, and by whom they were killed. The same is true for Robert Press of the *Christian Science Monitor*, who on February 5 described meeting one of the USC fighters:[34] "Sitting on the turret of a burned-out government tank in the middle of a main street here, rebel Abukar Cali Mohammed said: 'I shot a lot of people—to get democracy and make Somali free from the dictatorship of Mohamed Siad Barre.'" Press did not report on who exactly "young Abukar," as he calls him, was, where he came from, and whom he killed on whose orders.

The journalists took the same passive approach toward the scenes of looting they witnessed. Neil Henry reported:

Citizens, including children, tote, tug and wheel the most inexplicable array of ill-gotten trophies through the city streets—washing machines, a piano, beds, grease-laden electric generators, silverware sets, light fixtures, armfuls of books from a downtown library.[35]

Todd Shields described similar scenes of looting as "the processions that now pass along the city's streets":

Looters have free rein, using wheelbarrows, lorries or their bare hands to haul away items ranging from kitchen sponges to four-wheel-drive vehicles. On one street, a farm tractor with four men aboard dragged a giant shipping crate; on another, a woman plucked the keys from an overturned grand piano. At the gutted Roman Catholic cathedral, rebel gunmen watched indifferently as a crew hitched the church's electrical generator to a lorry and patiently maneuvered it from a tight courtyard. ... Presiding loosely over the chaos are hundreds of young men in mufti, bearing weapons of all types, from pistols to grenade launchers.[36]

Aidan Hartley wrote in the same vein: "In the city centre, looters went about their business, carrying a startling array of goods—chairs, desks, sponges, a sink, tires, books—from wrecked shops and homes."[37] While some of this loot clearly came from public buildings and the Roman Catholic Cathedral built during Italian rule, reporters in the city did not report on who these looters were, what motivated them, and whose homes they were looting. They did wonder what the sounds of gunfire they heard day and night meant. French journalist Michel Sailhan reported the kinds of answers they were given:

"You'll have to excuse them, they have just come out of the bush," a USC cadre told an AFP reporter startled by the sporadic bursts of machine gunfire during a guided tour of the city Friday. At night, celebratory salves of gun-fire, phosphorous flares and tracer bullets light up the sky like a fire-work display. "They captured the city and their magazines were fully loaded with ammunition looted from state stores," the USC guide said.[38]

Even though this description of the shooting is undoubtedly also true, it is nevertheless uncanny that the international reporters were unaware of the clan cleansing that was occurring in the city as it were under their very eyes.

Sailhan went beyond the guided tour and succeeded in interviewing one of General Caydiid's lieutenant colonels, fresh from "the bush," steel rod still in hand, as he was celebrating the USC victory in what appeared a large villa abandoned by its foreign owners. The French reporter found thirty-nine-year-old "Lieutenant-Colonel Mohamoud Mohamed Ashe alias 'Shabel' (Leopard) reclining in front of an Italian T.V. 'soap opera' swigging Johnnie Walker whisky from an exquisite crystal glass," surrounded by his wives, his men, and many guests in varying states of intoxication from alcohol. Shabeel was euphoric, Sailhan reported:

> "I don't give a damn about the politicians," roared "Shabel," his flowered shirt falling open to display a leopard emblem. "Now I can die. We won this war, you understand that," he insisted, his pepper and salt beard swaying three centimeters (two inches) from the nose of his interlocutor. Shabel let drop the steel rod he had used since December to mobilise his troops in the bush. "I'm a Somali civilian now. Just call me ex-colonel," he said.[39]

The victory party of drunk, boisterous, armed men was hardly an auspicious setting for an in-depth interview. Moreover, Sailhan had no way of knowing that Shabeel, now a close associate of General Caydiid, had committed or was to commit major human rights violations in the Northwest (1988), Brava (March–April 1991), and Gedo (August 1992).[40]

One must salute these war correspondents for their courage. They came to a city and country in chaos and at war, with limited background knowledge or language skills, and were kept on a short leash by their USC hosts. It appears that the key shift that turned the uprising against the military dictator into a campaign of clan cleansing occurred so unexpectedly that they simply did not catch on. It was not until April 7, 1991, that Chris McGreal of the *Independent* acknowledged what had happened: "It was the mainly Hawiye United Somali Congress (USC) which seized Mogadishu in January, promising consensus government and free elections. Instead, its warriors turned on the Darods. No one knows how many died; the Darods say thousands, the USC hundreds."[41] It was only in 2003 that Aidan Hartley provided a first-hand description of civilians being summarily shot for belonging to the wrong clan at a road block in Mogadishu shortly after Barre's expulsion (169).

Silence and Denial Among USC Moderates

Meanwhile the provisional administration of Cali Mahdi remained as silent as the grave about the clan cleansing that was going on in the city and refrained from any acknowledgement or comment. At his swearing-in ceremony at the police headquarters, Cali Mahdi boasted that the USC was "adhering to its ideology of fighting for liberty, justice, and equality." He reassured his listeners that he would "give first priority to the interests of the Somali people and their unity before anything else, with respect for the sacred religion and the age-old heritage of the Somali nation."⁴² His speeches to the Reconciliation Committee, now headed by Maxamed Hawaadleh Madar, were reported on Radio Mogadishu. The following, transcribed from a Radio Mogadishu broadcast of January 29, is the closest he came to admitting that clan cleansing was taking place both in and outside of Mogadishu: "It is not good to inflict harm on tribal basis on the Somali people who are a totally Muslim nation," he said and called "on those who authorized the pillaging, looting, and killing to refrain from these offenses," as "these people would not be tolerated."⁴³ Characterizing the unabated "murders and robbery" a deviation from Somali culture and Islam, Cali Mahdi instructed the Committee "to counter the ugly incidents in Mogadishu and proceed to the regions, districts, and villages" for the same purpose.⁴⁴

In a speech broadcast on Radio Mogadishu on that same day, Cumar Carta Ghaalib, a northerner and the man whom Cali Mahdi had given the premiership of his provisional administration, admitted that innocent civilians were being killed on the basis of their clan background. Like Cali Mahdi, he called on the religious leaders and the intellectuals to admonish people wherever possible to stop the looting and killing:

> I also want to clarify here, as is seen by the president and the committee, as Hussein Haji Mohamed Bood said, that any event that happens as a mistake, God has its [word indistinct], but we should distance ourselves, and those who work with us should do the same; our followers should also do this. *To kill a Somali man whose struggle is known to God and who has no other interest and is not part of the government is impermissible* because what God has forbidden we have been told to leave as such.⁴⁵

Two weeks later, the provisional administration brought the man who had been the first president of independent Somalia, Aadan Cabdulla Cismaan "Cadde," to the Radio to appeal for an end to the killings. Aadan "Cadde" reminded his listeners that Somali independence had been won through unity and "not through regionalism and tribalism," and "also spoke of the evil of tribalism, saying that tribalism plays a divisive role among the people." Calling on armed rebels and other citizens to fight mercilessly against what he called "a few disgruntled elements bent on killing people for clannish motives," he too spoke largely in euphemistic terms.⁴⁶ Even the small opening created by such minor gestures of acknowledgment cited above quickly closed.

Clan Cleansing in Mogadishu and Beyond   151

At the end of January, at the same time as the radio speech cited above, Prime Minister Cumar Carta gave a command that many interpreted as an endorsement of the clan cleansing campaign. He ordered "those among the Armed Forces of the government deposed by the Somali people" to surrender to either the USC (if they were in the South), the SPM (if they were in the central regions), or to the SNM (if they were in the North). To their minds, asking ex-government soldiers to surrender to the USC and its allies at the very moment that USC fighters and civilian supporters were engaging in a clan cleansing of even people who had had no association with the government was a blatant denial of what was going on. It meant for the soldiers, as Nur Ali Qabobe put it, that they should "give, without resistance, their heads to their arch enemies."[47] Moreover, the command represented a deliberate disregard of the SSDF, which had begun to reconstitute itself in the central and northeastern regions and was about to play an important role in stopping the reach of the clan cleansing campaign beyond Gaalkacyo.

On February 6 and again on March 5, 1991, the BBC reported two allegations that the USC was engaging in clan cleansing. The first person to sound the alarm was the politically compromised Cabdiraxmaan Jaamac "Buluq Buluq," Barre's cousin and major beneficiary of his regime until it fell. A spokesman for Cali Mahdi's Minister of Information and National Guidance called his allegations "devoid of substance and sense."[48] On March 5, 1991, the BBC aired an interview by reporter Peter Biles with an individual who had more credibility than "Buluq Buluq," namely Maxamed Cumar Jaamac "Dhigic-Dhigic," the Manifesto signatory mentioned above.[49] Again the Cali Mahdi administration, responding to this accusation via Radio Mogadishu, strongly denied that the USC was "massacring members of the Darod ethnic group" and characterized the allegations "as baseless and unfounded lies." Its spokesman went on to illustrate the administration's own clannist mindset by trying to undermine "Dhigic-Dhigic's" character in particular ways. He not only associated "Dhigic-Dhigic" with the ousted president, whom "Dhigic-Dhigic" (in contrast to Cali Mahdi himself) had long opposed but also with men who had indeed been part of Barre's military top but with whom "Dhigic-Dhigic" shared nothing but his Daarood background. The broadcast said:

"Dhigec-Dhihec's motives are no different from those of ousted dictator Siad Barre, who used to divide the Somali people along tribal lines throughout his long dictatorial rule," the spokesman added. . . . [I]t is important to recall the massacres directed by Siad Barre [words indistinct] against Somali society and perpetrated by the self-styled generals such as Morgan, Cirow, and others too numerous to name, who were very close to the dictator. Together these men created problems among the civilians through clannish ploys, all against the wishes of the Somali people who did not want to be divided.[50]

A third report about the USC clan cleansing campaign was made to the BBC by Maxamed Yuusuf Ismaaciil "Bari-Bari" on March 15, 1991. A spokesman for the Somali News Agency again called the allegation "that the USC was massacring those who sought shelter in Kismaayo town" unfounded and instead—note the clannist implications—accused,

> the self-styled generals such as Morgan, Gani, Ciro and others who destroyed Mogadishu, Hargeisa and other towns using heavy guns and artillery in an inhuman fashion. As a result many innocent people have lost their lives and some survivors fled to Kismaayo town where they have been forcibly told to fight with the aim of seeing Kismaayo town destroyed.[51]

The spokesman was correct that "Morgan," "Gaani," and Axmed Cabdullaahi "Cirro" had been top generals in the Somali National Army under Barre, with the names of the former two without any doubt associated with the war and the violence against civilians in the Northwest, as discussed above. However, "Bari Bari" had a completely different political history. After he had been the incorruptible head of the Ministry of Education's examination board, as well as cultural attaché in Egypt, he had joined the armed opposition against Barre (the SSDF) in the early 1980s. This contrasted sharply with the USC president-hopeful whose spokesman was now equating "Bari Bari" with the Barre regime. Both Cali Mahdi and his wife Nuurto had been closely connected to the regime (and, in case of Nuurto, even with Barre's closest family) until the very end. "Bari Bari" shared nothing with the generals mentioned by the spokesman except his Daarood descent. This kind of USC rebuttal was hardly reassuring, but it is difficult to know whether, apart from the FBIS employee who dutifully transcribed broadcasts like these, anyone in the international community was listening.[52]

Thus, even the so-called moderate political leaders of USC-Mogadishu, who appear to have initially wanted a negotiated and nonviolent transition to the post-Barre era, remained silent about the clan cleansing that was implemented around them. They were therefore minimally guilty of complicity. As a result of their silence, all leaders, fighters, and supporters of the USC organization of that time today remain enveloped in a cloud of suspicion. An eyewitness and survivor of the violence in Mogadishu, one of *lahaystayaal*, remembered encountering Xusseen Bood, then the head of the USC Executive, somewhere in the city. He knew Xusseen Bood well, as they had both signed the Manifesto of May 1990. Asked about the clan cleansing, Xusseen Bood claimed that he was powerless and blamed Caydiid for what was going on. Cali Mahdi, with whom the eye witness spoke later, answered in a similar vein: Because the rural fighters had been recruited and mobilized under the motto that they could exact revenge from *"the"* Daarood for all their grievances, they could not be stopped or contained. The eyewitness was not convinced by this and felt that, at the very least, the leaders of USC-Mogadishu condoned the elimination and expulsion of Daarood because they expected to benefit from it politically. And in any case, at this stage, they made no efforts to put a stop to it (Interview 3).

Not until the reconciliation meeting in Mogadishu in 2007, under the auspices of the Transitional Federal Government of Cabdullaahi Yuusuf and the chairmanship of this same Cali Mahdi Maxamed, did any leader of the USC, moderate or not, publicly acknowledge and express regret about for the clan cleansing of 1991–1992. Cali Mahdi apologized for, as he put it, the clan-based atrocities committed by *"the"* Hawiye against *"the"* Daarood.[53] By attributing agency to the overly broad construct of *"the"* Hawiye, he continued to sidestep the responsibility of the USC leadership, of which he was a part, and put the blame on ordinary Hawiye individuals, many of whom were passive bystanders or even rescuers.

Silence, Denial, and Distortion in Scholarship, Political Memoirs, and Human Rights Reports

It is not uncommon for analyses of violence to "join a conflict," as was noted by Donham above (2006: 29). However, the big and small acts of omission and commission to which this has led and leads nevertheless deserve to be pointed out, especially because academics and human rights experts, in contrast to the journalists quoted above, have had the benefit of hindsight and the duty of taking it into account. More thorough and less biased accounts exist (as referred to in this study's Introduction and footnotes).[54] However, the following examples are nevertheless indicative of the sloppy oversights, glib denials, and willful misrepresentations and understatements that mar scholarly analyses, personal and political memoirs, and even human rights reports about the clan cleansing of 1991–1992. Silences, misrepresentations, and denials have been part and parcel of episodes of large-scale violence such as genocide and ethnic cleansing; they are therefore relevant to documenting such episodes and providing insight into their nature and contexts.

Instances of analyses that simply skip the clan cleansing campaign the USC unleashed in Mogadishu in December 1990–January 1991 are abundant. They tell the story of the collapse of the Barre regime as a simple sequence of three scenes. Scene 1: From its last remaining perch in Villa Somalia, the falling regime's heavy artillery pounds the residential neighborhoods of Mogadishu, accompanied by arbitrary looting and violence by government soldiers. Scene 2: Fighting and chaos follow Barre's expulsion. Scene 3: USC-Caydiid and USC-Cali Mahdi fall out and turn Mogadishu into a new Beirut. In these accounts, there is no mention of the clan-based violence (let alone an organized campaign of clan cleansing committed by the USC), until the USC splits into two parts, each based on (sub-)clans, which turn their weapons against each other.[55] Stanley Cohen, in *States of Denial: Knowing About Atrocities and Suffering*, has a name for such denials and speaks in this context of "literal," "factual," or "blatant" denial, and even of "the classic cover-up" (2001: 7, 138).

Almost equally abundant are accounts that add to the second scene of the three-scene scenario mentioned above. They report the revenge killings exacted by the clans that had allegedly been victimized by the military regime from the clans that had purportedly been its supporters and beneficiaries. By uncritically accepting both clan as the relevant category of analysis and the logic of revenge, these accounts imply that the victims were punished for wrongs they had actually committed and sidestep any attribution of responsibility to political leaders. In reality, both perpetrators and victims of the clan cleansing had victims and beneficiaries of the regime in their ranks. Moreover, it was not a clan (or clans) that perpetrated clan cleansing but political leaders who mobilized and organized ordinary people to commit violence in the name of clan.[56] Hussein Adam exemplifies this second type of explanation when he casually summarizes the events of 1991 by writing: "In a primordial society, the anticipated reaction followed, as most of the Darod communities had to flee Mogadishu following Siyad's overthrow by the Hawiye-based USC" (2008: 92). Analyses of this kind simply throw the blame on justifiably angry mobs of clansmen and ignore the question of political intent and responsibility.[57] According to Cohen's typology, this kind of denial constitutes "interpretive denial," that is to say, a failure to acknowledge that what happened was the purposeful brutalization of uninvolved civilians constructed as clan "others" (2001: 7, 8, 61). Such misrepresentations constitute a continuation of the clan cleansing under study here and are therefore an integral part of its history. The examples below shed more light on what was and is at stake in the clan cleansing of 1991.

An egregious example of "interpretive" denial is provided by Hussein Ali Dualeh.[58] In his political memoirs, he describes what happened when the USC brought the fight to Mogadishu on December 30, 1990, in terms of the simplistic or perhaps even cowardly mindset of the victims of the clan cleansing campaign:

> No less than four hundred thousand Darod Clansmen—the total population of the Darod in Mogadishu and surrounding towns—escaped from Mogadishu to the Kenyan border. They were all ordinary citizens who had no links [126] whatsoever with the government. *But they simply felt insecure.* A Darod president had been ousted. The Hawiye through their USC movement had taken over Mogadishu. The Darod of the capital therefore feared Hawiye reprisals against them.[59]

Other examples of such "interpretive denial" abound. In his political memoir, former police commander Jama Mohamed Ghalib blames the clan cleansing, which he calls "ethnic Darod-Hawiye retributions," on the attempt by one of Barre's top military men, Axmed Suleemaan "Dafle," to organize the Daarood of the capital (1995: 211). Similarly, in *Understanding Somalia and Somaliland: Culture, History, Society*, I. M. Lewis simply blames Barre for "exhorting all the Darod in Mogadishu to kill the Hawiye citizens whether they were Abgal or Habar Gidir." He attributes no other responsibility (2008: 73). Even if the accusations directed at Dafle and Barre are true—and this is certainly possible even if no source is given—completely sidestepping the agency and direct responsibility of the USC leadership means concealing a major stage and dimension of the Somali civil war and sidestepping a crucial dimension of the truth. Moreover, equating the Barre's military regime with "*the*" Daarood means accepting the categories of the clan cleansers.

Interpretive denials are sometimes bolstered by prestigious human rights organizations. Rakiya Omaar, through her position at the head of Africa Watch a powerful opinion maker at the time, in 1992 published the following blatant half-truth:

> The fiercest clashes occurred on December 30 [1990], with fighting between members of the Darod clan (many of them armed by Siad Barre) and the Hawiye clan. Thousands of civilians lost their lives, particularly those belonging to the Hawiye, the largest clan in Mogadishu.[60]

In the absence of even thorough news coverage of episodes of mass violence, reports by human rights organization become an important part of the evidentiary base. However, sometimes these reports fall short, and because the focus always moves forward toward a new and pressing crisis, such misrepresentations may go uncorrected. This has been the case with the August 1992 report by Amnesty International, *Somalia: A Human Rights Disaster*, which ignored the intentional nature of the violence, was blind to its geographical scale and temporary scope, and seriously underestimated the numbers of victims.[61]

All these kinds of distortions constitute "interpretive denial," which, as Cohen puts it, "ranges from a genuine inability to grasp what the facts mean to others, to deeply cynical renaming to avoid moral censure or legal accountability" for oneself or others (Cohen 2001: 9). Thus interpretive denial overlaps with what Cohen calls "implicatory denial," applicable to situations in which individuals or groups do not deny the facts or their conventional interpretations but fail to acknowledge their significance and thus avoid any "moral or psychological demands" that these facts may make on them. In many cases such misrepresentations also constitute "a denial of the victim," as they imply that the victims somehow deserved what was done to them (2001: 7, 8, 61). Such denials have been an integral part of the histories of genocide and ethnic cleansing everywhere. Their existence and persistence in the Somali case are therefore not only a powerful diagnostic of the clan cleansing of 1991–1992 but also evidence of how *unbewältigt* this past continues to be. We will return to this in Chapter 4.

The historical narrative of the clan cleansing campaign is not complete until we follow it geographically and temporally beyond Mogadishu 1991 and unless we bring the focus back to the struggle over the state, for which this clan cleansing was an instrument and without which it cannot be understood. Three important developments, which together marked the complete collapse of not just the regime but also the state itself, characterize this stage of the civil war. First, the USC, in alliance with the SDM and a changing combination of other clan-based militias, took the campaign of clan cleansing out of Mogadishu into central, south-central, and southern Somalia, as far as the Indian Ocean on one side and the Ethiopian and Kenyan borders on the other. The USC's unexpected attack on its SPM ally in Afgooye (early February), its attack on Gaalkacyo at the end of February, and its capture of Kismaayo toward the end of April 1991 are all stages of the campaign. This campaign continued even when, first in April and then in November 1991, the USC split into two, with USC-Caydiid and USC-Cali Mahdi turning their heavy artillery and followers' fury against each other.

Second, the extension of the campaign of clan cleansing mobilized and brought together in an (up to then) unthinkable armed alliance—one that mirrored the USC's—all those who had been targeted by the USC clan cleansing campaign. This new Daarood-based coalition of militias encompassed former members of the armed opposition fronts that had fought against the military regime (such as the SSDF and SPM); a former military commander who had been a major pillar of the regime; and ordinary men who, in the wake of their victimization, joined the alliance as rank-and-file fighters. In March and April 1991, this coalition combined its forces to fight the USC and, unsuccessfully and at a great cost of lives all around, tried to capture Mogadishu and thus the heights of the state. Coalition fighters made it to the gates of Mogadishu, from where Caydiid's men drove them back into Gedo and Kismaayo.

Third, as the violence now rippled outward from Mogadishu (as it had surged toward it in 1989–1990), it became ever more general and indiscriminate, increasing further in scale and brutality. The geographical extension of the USC's clan cleansing campaign became part of what I call the "War of the Militias," which began in this period and is, even if in a different form, still ongoing. As clan-based militias mushroomed and battle lines moved back and forth, the lethal, collective clan-based brutalization of civilians associated with the other side became the strategy of habit, if not of choice, of the militias of military commanders such as Caydiid, "Shabeel," Xassan Cabdi Awaale "Qaybdiid," "Nero," "Jees," "Gaani," "Morgan," and Maslax Maxamed Siyaad Barre. In this period, terror warfare, characterized by large-scale rape, torture, and humiliation, appears to have intensified, with mutilation before execution and the desecration of bodies even before death had been ascertained becoming widespread. At this stage of the war, all civilians became the grass trampled by two fighting elephants. However, the violence they suffered was always specific to their clan background. In this context, the experiences of communities (now called "minorities") that had historically not been regarded as competitors for political power and had no militias of their own to protect them were especially grievous. Like the Reer Xamar in Mogadishu, so the people of Brava and the communities of so-called Somali Bantu of the Jubba valley, were constructed and targeted for dispossession, humiliation, and heinous bodily harm as "outsiders." The extension of the USC's clan cleansing campaign, the widening and deepening terror of the War of the Militias that developed parallel to it, and the plight of the victims are the burden of what follows.

Beyond Mogadishu

Although Barre had been driven out of Mogadishu and had fled first to Kismaayo and then, in early February to Gedo (i.e., Buurdhuubo) in the southwest, he still remained in the country and had thus not been definitively defeated. Even apart from Barre, neither for the SNM nor the USC was the war over. The SNM was to gain major victories in late January and early February of 1991. By February 3, it had recaptured Hargeisa and Burco[62] and—conducting a "full-scale assault on Borama" on February 5, and armed operations in Zeila later in the month—went on to subdue those areas that had not supported it in the course of the month.[63] Although the SNM information secretary in a broadcast to the people of the Awdal region said "that the offensive launched in the region was not meant to harm the people there" and was instead "a mopping up operation against the remnants of the soldiers of ex-dictator Siyad," here, too—though on a much smaller scale than in Mogadishu—civilians were targeted for violence on the basis of clan.[64] By then it was public knowledge that a powerful faction of the SNM was pushing for the establishment of an autonomous administration and secession from the Somali Republic.[65] This was formalized on May 18, 1991.

Meanwhile General Maxamed Faarax Caydiid had publicly rejected the transitional administration announced by Cali Mahdi and USC-Mogadishu on January 28, within two days of Barre's expulsion. However, instead of dealing with Cali Mahdi, Caydiid first turned to the establishment of USC control over those parts of the country not conquered by the SNM. Extending the clan cleansing campaign was part of this bid for control. However, especially after the USC capture of Kismaayo, which was a major stage in the clan cleansing campaign, the War of the Militias, in which the frontlines between changing configurations of competing militias rolled back and forth, caused death and destruction throughout south and south-central Somalia.

The War of the Militias Begins: The USC Attack on the SPM in February 1991

Afgooye, just outside Mogadishu, and Baydhaba, farther to the northwest, came to represent a stage in the anti-Daarood clan cleansing campaign and the first site of the War of the Militias. Here the USC and SPM, the two military fronts that had been allied in their capture of Mogadishu just two weeks earlier, clashed.[66] The USC attack on the SPM of February 6, 1991, was totally unexpected. The USC fighters crept up on the SPM from the southwest (and not from the main road from Mogadishu), at mid-afternoon, as the SPM fighters were relaxing and chewing *qaat*. According to Daahir Cali, many were killed both in that first attack and during the USC's motorized pursuit of the SPM fighters as they fled to Brava, Buulo Mareerto, and beyond. SPM commander "Jees," who had been in Baydhaba at the time of the attack, was unable to turn the situation around (1997: 167).

Why did the USC attack the SPM, which under "Jees" had played such a significant role in pinning down Barre in Mogadishu and taking down the regime? Was it to prevent the SPM from sharing the fruits of victory? Looking back on this episode, "Jees" explained what happened in terms of the USC's unexpected betrayal of the three-pronged political alliance of October 1990, on the one hand, and its full-fledged campaign of clan cleansing, of which the clan-base of his own SPM was not exempted, on the other.[67] This is what he said to David Chazan, who interviewed him on the road between Kismaayo and Mogadishu in late March:

> "When Siad Barre ran from Mogadishu to Kismaayo, in the south, we tried to pursue him. But the USC betrayed us and attacked us at Afgooye," 30 kilometres (18 miles) from Mogadishu, Col. Cheiss [Jees] said. The USC advanced some 400 kilometres southward, "*killing and molesting civilians* and forcing us to regroup and counter attack to drive them back," he said. "That is what made us leave Siad Barre alone."[68]

Another interview with "Jees" and another SPM commander called Major-General Aadan Cabdulle Nuur "Gabyow," Barre's former minister of defense, whose dismissal and imprisonment had triggered the founding of the SPM, was published at the time of the fighting itself in the *Nairobi-Star-on-Sunday*. In this interview, held at the "heavily guarded and fortified command post" in Afgooye, on February 10, 1991, "Jees" expressed regret at having been forced to continue the fighting. "Gabyow," however, bluntly stated: "Forget about any talk of negotiations. There can be no settlement to the latest problems. We will talk through the gun." As they spoke, the reporter saw wounded fighters being brought in from the battlefield to be treated in a makeshift surgical ward. He reported that he was struck by "the smell of rotting flesh and thick blood splattered over the rough cemented floor," adding, "the stench is overwhelming."[69]

Three days later, the international press reported that the USC had captured the town of Afgooye.[70] Cali Mahdi's Minister of Planning, Maxamed Abshir—the most opaque and unflappably spokesman for the Mahdi team—emphasized that the SPM was still welcome to attend the National Reconciliation Conference planned for later that month, Cali Mahdi himself, however, took a different approach. He referred to the SPM in terms of what had now became another code word for those targeted for clan cleansing, "Remnants of Barre" or "*haraadiga Siyaad*," about which more below. Playing down the fighting in Afgooye, Cali Mahdi told Sailhan that "the USC fought last Thursday with troops pretending to belong to the SPM but who were actually remnants of units loyal to Siad Barre." Thus, he skillfully erased that "Jees" and "Gabyow" did not fit the term "Barre remnants" or "Barre loyalists" any more than Cali Mahdi or General Caydiid and many of their closest associates. In other words, they all were.

Two aspects of Sailhan's report from Mogadishu on this date, as we now know from hindsight, did not bode well. First, he emphasized that "the lack of food was among the most pressing problems in the city" and that Willy Huber of the SOS Children's hospital was treating one hundred children a day for malnutrition. Second, he reported that USC officials accused the SPM of mistreating the townspeople of Afgooye, while Willy Huber accused the USC of pillaging the town after its capture.[71] It is obvious that, if there is any truth to these reports, the mindsets and strategies of the leaders on both sides of the divide were becoming all too similar.

After having taken control of the roads through Bay and Bakool, General Caydiid immediately launched a three-pronged campaign and, with the support of other clan-based militias such as the Raxanweyn-based SDM, launched offensives against Mudug (Gaalkacyo), Kismaayo, and Gedo. As Caydiid proudly acknowledged in a later interview with journalist Hamish

Wilson quoted below, by driving the SPM west and south-west and sweeping down the coast toward Kismaayo, the USC had made a bid for sole control of all the central and south-central regions (Hiiraan, Middle and Lower Shabeelle, Bay, and Bakool) and positioned itself favorably for the conquest of Kismaayo itself.[72]

Caydiid and Cali Mahdi were in full agreement about this military-political goal. In the same broadcast in which he rejected the allegations of clan cleansing in Mogadishu "as devoid of substance and sense," an Ali Mahdi spokesmen justified the USC attack on the city of Kismaayo, filled to overflowing with refugees from the clan cleansing in Mogadishu and other central and south-central towns. Because "troops loyal to former President Mohamed Siad Barre . . . are holding out in the Kismaayo region," the international press reported him as saying, "the military sweep to the South serves "to clean up this region.'"[73] A rag-tag Daarood-based alliance was indeed taking shape in Kismaayo and Gedo. It consisted of three types of fighters: some of Barre's die-hard top military officers, members of armed opposition fronts that had opposed and fought Barre for decades, and other men capable of bearing arms recruited there and then. Although this Daarood-based alliance emerged in the wake of the USC clan cleansing campaign, for the USC leadership it became a justification for that campaign and a rationale to pursue it further. The reference to "troops loyal to Barre" evoked the term *haraadiga Siyaad*, the blanket term that cloaked the USC's massive human rights violations of this period more generally. Meanwhile, in Kismaayo, Daahir Cali writes, the refugees noted with bitterness that the "remnants of the Barre regime" in Mogadishu were actually doing just fine. They noted that "most top officials of the Barre regime who were Hawiye, Isaaq, Raxanweyn, Dir, Sheekhaal, and so forth, and who were *not* Daarood, had been able to stay behind in Mogadishu without any fear of the USC that had captured the city" (1997: 194).

An Episode of Clan Cleansing in Gaalkacyo (Late February 1991)

On February 11, French journalist Michel Sailhan, in an article entitled "USC mounts 'wide-scale' operation to south," reported that the USC had reached Brava and Merca the week before and was now in Jilib and Jamaame, north of Kismaayo.[74] However, as the bulk of USC fighters were on their way south, a small strike-force was sent 400 kilometers north(east) of Mogadishu to execute another stage in the clan cleansing project: the brief and deliberate slaughter of the unsuspecting civilian population of Gaalkacyo, targeting especially its leading elders, who were loaded on trucks never to be seen or heard of again.

The strike-force suddenly attacked on February 26, 1991. In the military communiqué issued by General Caydiid on March 3, he stated that he had "smashed the rest of Faqash (enemy) forces and liberated Galkio [Gaalkacyo], Central Somalia" and had confronted "the so-called SSDF."[75] The attack had come completely unexpected. As mentioned above, although the SSDF had been the first armed front to be established against Barre, it had been plagued by internal conflict and had ceased to exist as an active military force since the early 1980s. It had, however, survived as an organization under the civilian leadership of Maxamed Abshir Walde and Muuse Islaan. Its spokesman in Nairobi, Xassan Cali Mirreh, who was regularly quoted by the international press, had scrupulously supported the USC as it tightened the noose around Mogadishu. After Barre's expulsion from Mogadishu, on February 14–19, 1991, the SSDF held its fourth congress in Gaalkacyo, which also initiated a regional reconciliation process, in which leaders representing a wide range of groups participated (Daahir Cali 1997: 94–95).

Only three days before the USC surprise night attack on Gaalkacyo, Radio Mogadishu had reported that an SSDF assembly, with representatives from different regions, had met with one of Cali Mahdi's ministers and decided to accept the provisional administration's invitation to attend a National Reconciliation Conference wherever and whenever it would be called.[76] There were therefore no Barre supporters from which this area needed to be "liberated" by General Caydiid nor had there been for over two decades. Caydiid's attack on Gaalkacyo had thus nothing to do with the war against forces loyal to Barre; it was a stage in the clan cleansing of Daarood Somalis from that large sweep of Somalia General Caydiid and his associates wanted to dominate. This area, which Caydiid, as he made progress with the project reportedly colored yellow on his map, extended from Burtiinleh, just south of Garoowe (itself northeast of Gaalkacyo, in the Nugaal region) to the borders with Ethiopia and Kenya, and along the coast from Ayl to Kismaayo (Interview 2).

This is how the group called Concerned Somalis, which issued a statement entitled "Genocide in Somalia: (USC Assault on the Mudug Region)," described the attack on Gaalkacyo:

> At 3:00 A.M. on February 26th, 1991, the USC attacked Galcayo, the capital of the Mudug region in the central rangeland of Somalia.

Initially, 1,000 highly trained commandoes infiltrated the city, entered the homes of the civilian population and slaughtered the women, the children, the disabled and the elderly. Simultaneously, professional soldiers armed with heavy artillery and rockets bombarded Galcayo indiscriminately. Recent reports estimated the civilian casualty to number 500 dead, 1000 wounded and 200 hostages.[77]

Oral accounts express grief and indignation about all victims of the attack, but especially dwell on the rounding up of the very elders who had spent effort and money from their own pockets to have the houses of absent USC supporters resident in the city protected from any theft or other interference. While the public statement by Concerned Somalis mentioned five elders of more than seventy years of age by name, oral accounts insist that sixteen elders were taken away on trucks never to be seen again. These accounts interpret Caydiid's elimination of the elders as a way of making sure that future reconciliation would be out of the question.[78]

No wonder that, when journalist Hamish Wilson "caught up with Caydiid in Northern Somalia," as he put it, on February 28, 1991, the latter was pleased with the military victories that had made him indispensable to the Cali Mahdi administration, which, in his words, "had hijacked power." Wilson reported that "Aidid asserted with confidence that he, and not Ali Mahdi, was the *real* leader of the USC, both because he had been locally elected and because he, with his *mujahidiin*, had, in the course of ten months, captured most of the central regions of Mudug, Galgudud, Hiran, and Middle Shabeelle."[79] However, as long as the campaign in the south of the country was still in progress and Barre still at bay, the alliance between USC-Caydiid and USC-Cali Mahdi was getting a lease on life. In the Gaalkacyo area, meanwhile, the SSDF was able to regain some control in April of 1991. According to Daahir Cali, from this time to June 1993, the war came to Gaalkacyo twenty-six times (1997: 97).

The Plight of the Expelled

Just as the clan cleansing campaign in Mogadishu was at the time not recognized as such in the international press, so its execution in the towns of Lower Shabeelle (such as Afgooye, Wanlaweyn, Merca, Qoryooley, and Jannaale), Middle Shabeelle (such as Balcad and Jowhar), Bay (such as Baidoa/Baydhaba), and Bakool (such as Xuddur) did not make headlines. Yet the killing and expulsion of Daarood civilians occurred here as well, both by the

USC and by other clan-based militias that immediately joined the USC such as the Raxanweyn-based SDM. The latter's participation in the USC capture of Kismaayo in April 1991, to be discussed below, is well established and was announced on Radio Mogadishu at the time of the victory.[80] The active and armed participation of many common people of the riverine region (including some of the people now called Bantu Somalis), encouraged and organized by their political/military leaders, has received little attention. Yet the evidence for this is overwhelming.

Many Daarood residents of the southern and south-central towns were expelled or killed.[81] Those who took refuge in or passed through the area as they fled Mogadishu were attacked, shot at, robbed of their vehicles and whatever possessions they might have had with them, and so forth. A young man who was then still a teenager vividly remembers how the convoy of cars in which he escaped from Mogadishu was time and again ambushed and shot at; in Qansaxdheere (Bay region), their car was hit by an RPG (rocket-propelled grenade) and they had to continue on foot. In Baydhaba the boys were sent out to fetch water in the late afternoon, but found that people were firing at them.[82] This is how Daahir Cali, who lived through these events, described the clan cleansing campaign as it unfolded in the riverine areas:

> They mercilessly killed the people they hunted down in the name of Daarood who were residents of the towns of B/weyne, B/barde, Jawhar, Muqdisho, Afgooye, Qoryooleey, Jannaale, Merka, Baraawe, Baydhabo, as well as others. Those who escaped death they made destitute, allowing them a small piece of cloth to wear and a cup with which to drink water. The writer of this was present in southern Somalia when the worst of these acts were committed, so what I write is not hearsay, as I was a witness. (1997: 132)

An individual from Baydhaba who was also present in the area at the time confirmed that local leaders planned and organized these acts of clan cleansing. Siyaad Sheekh Daahir blamed especially a local political entrepreneur called Barbaar Amar, who decided to side with the USC and take part in the clan cleansing campaign. This is how Siyaad described a meeting attended by his uncle at which this decision was made. As it happened, Siyaad and his uncle identify as part of the Raxanweyn (Yantaar) but also as of Daarood descent. In the riverine area, social organization is based on regional co-residence rather than constructs of biological descent more explicitly than in other parts of Somalia. This is how Siyaad has remembered it:

> After Barre was driven out, the responsible men (functionaries) of the city met and some said: "We need to clean out the Daarood. Otherwise we will not have the power." Sayyid Ahmed Sheekh spoke up against this plan. "Daarood ha la xasuuqo" ('Let's exterminate the Daarood') is not a plan I can support; we are here because we want to come together, he said. And if you want to commit genocide against them, begin with me, for I am of that origin. But I am here as a man of the Raxanweyn, of the people of Baydhaba.[83]

In spite of people like Siyaad's brother, political entrepreneurs and civilians of the area sided with the USC in its clan cleansing campaign from its very beginning.[84] Why so many ordinary people could be persuaded to join this campaign is a question that will be pursued in Chapter 4.

As clan cleansing swept through and out of Mogadishu and spread to other towns and areas of central and southern Somalia, the exodus of an ever-growing stream of people swelled to proportions that even surpassed that from the Northwest in 1988. Many of them were on foot, without anything to eat or drink. Maxamed Aadan Yuusuf, who was able to take his family to safety by car, described the scenes he saw on the road from Mogadishu to Kismaayo, as the USC, pushing south and capturing Merka, Brava, Jilib, Jamaame, and so forth, pursued the refugees. These scenes match those described in Mustafa Sheekh Cilmi's "Disaster" (Masiibo) quoted in Chapter 1.

> They chased after the refugees, who had nothing. I passed them by. I swear to you, what I saw, I swear on the Qur'an . . . there is a verse of the Qur'an that says, when you approach the end of the world, people will scatter; even parents, kids; no one will support anyone else. That is what I saw: on foot, by car, people dying on the road. You cannot imagine what took place. When I remember. . . . I was driving, with my kids in the car, for we were well off in Somalia. But what I saw was hard to watch: from Mogadishu, from Afgooye, a mass of people moving along without anything. (Interview 2)

News of the plight of the refugees reached the international community only gradually and mostly in the form of statistics; these events, after all, preceded the emergence of Somali cyberspace, cell phones, blogs, and tweets by four to five years. Though journalists such as Jane Perlez of the *New York Times* reported extensively on the violence of the Somali civil war, there were generally no interviews with victims and—beyond generic war and violence—no detailed analyses of what the events were from which these refugees were fleeing.

On January 28, 1991, Peter Biles reported from Mombasa that thousands of Somalis were streaming into Kenya. Just in the last two weeks, he wrote, 1,000 refugees had arrived by boat to just one city, the port of Mombasa, where they were housed in a special camp; by March 18 this same camp was housing about 30,000 Somali refugees.[85] About 600,000 internally displaced had swollen the population of the southern city of Kismaayo to several times its original size.[86] Refugees were also streaming into Kenya and Ethiopia, where the government appealed for urgent food aid, as "the dry eastern provinces of Ethiopia, where most refugees are housed in camps, have had no rain for the past three years."[87] Of those Somalis who escaped the clan cleansing by trying to head north, many too were killed, including the respected and well-known intellectual Faarax M. J. "Cawl," author of the historical novel, *Ignorance Is the Enemy of Love*, who was summarily executed at a checkpoint.[88]

As the statistics from this period are far from clear or consistent, the individual incidents and accidents reported by the international press and confirmed by oral accounts as common occurrences gain great significance. There was a spate of reports in early March 1991, when an overcrowded sixty-foot dhow, the *Christiana Hama*, which had left Kismaayo on February 26 with approximately 700 Somali refugees on board, struck a reef off the Kenyan coast, close to its destination, Malindi. When the media published the final count, it amounted to 153 dead and 515 survivors, with 132 bodies recovered, of whom 21 were inside the boat. Some had been trapped in the lower deck, while others had been trampled to death. Some 150 bodies were buried together in a mass grave. One news report related the words of a Kenyan diving instructor who said: "We found some mothers still holding their dead children with their arms wrapped around one another."[89]

Describing this period from hindsight in September 1993, African Rights confirmed the deaths of many refugees "in overcrowded, leaky, unsafe boats, as Somali, Kenyan, Yemeni and other businessmen and ship-owners cashed in on the plight of the refugees, charging them exorbitant fares" (1993: 5). It also mentioned specific incidents, some of which exacerbated because the Kenyan government did not want to allow refugees to land and even tried to forcibly ship some back across the Somali border. Thus it mentions the MV *Christian*,[90] which had a capacity for fifty people but carried 700, of whom 140 drowned and 40 were missing; the MV *Ras Kambooni*, with 450 refugees on board, which was denied food and medical supplies for eight days; and, most damningly for the Kenyan government, the case of a small ship that was towed back across the Somali border by a Kenyan navy patrol boat. It had a capacity of fifteen, but 130 refugees were forced on board, with further passengers brought to the vessel by small fishing boats. The ship became detached on the Somali side of the border and ran onto a coral reef, which resulted in injuries among the refugees, about 48 of whom were forced onto a fishing boat, which capsized and caused 37 of them, mostly women and children, to drown. African Rights added: "According to the accounts of survivors, instead of rescuing the refugees who clung to the navy boat, the Kenyan sailors snatched the gold bracelets from the wrists of the women, and abandoned them to their fate." There were scores and scores of accidents like these, though often involving smaller boats and fewer casualties.

Tens of thousands (and eventually hundreds of thousands) of refugees fled on foot. Those with means were able to cross into Kenya and Ethiopia more easily, though Kenya put many legal and illegal obstacles in the refugees' way. According to African Rights, "The refugees were actively discouraged from setting foot on Kenyan soil, and when they had done so, were treated poorly and abusively in the hope that they would return home."

The War of the Militias: A New Darood-Based Alliance (SNF) and the USC

The exodus from Mogadishu and areas to its west and southwest had caused the population of the southern city of Kismaayo to swell. Toward the end of March, during the fighting that would end with the capture of the city by USC fighters commanded by Caydiid, a news report by David Chazan described the situation as follows:[91]

> Rotting corpses are strewn along the dusty road from Kismaayo to Mogadishu, littered with smashed cars and trucks, pockmarked with bullet holes. Trucks packed with refugees fleeing the carnage rumble south under the merciless desert sun. . . . "There's hardly any food," said Erwin Koenig of the International Committee of the Red Cross (ICRC), the only relief organisation still in the southern city of Kismaayo, where local officials estimate there are up to 600,000 displaced

people, mostly Darods who fled Mogadishu.[92] Most are sleeping in the streets in makeshift cardboard shelters, while others have taken refuge in the church and in a disused Soviet-built meat processing factory, now home to hordes of undernourished, barefoot children, many with running sores. Wounded civilians and fighters lie groaning in the dusty courtyard of Kismaayo hospital, while the onset of the rains, expected any day, will make life almost intolerable for the refugees, already wracked by water-borne diseases such as dysentery.

At the time of Chazan's writing, the battle for Kismaayo was well underway. On the Kismaayo side, those who rejected peaceful accommodation were a mixed group and not all present in the city. Though Barre had initially fled to Kismaayo, where he stayed several days, he had been persuaded to move to the Gedo region, where he settled in Buurdhuubo, still receiving journalists and proclaiming his intention to take the country back.[93] Some elements of his entourage had stayed behind in Kismaayo, where they now mixed with people they had oppressed for decades! There were thus indeed "remnants of Barre" in Kismaayo, as there were in Mogadishu itself. Some of these Barre supporters still hoped to take the country back for Barre (Daahir Ali 1997: 173). Generals such as "Gaani" and "Morgan," though they may have been physically in Gedo, belonged to this group.

These were the military leaders who put together the Daarood-based alliance called the SNF,[94] whose allied contingents moved north toward Mogadishu. Initially successful, they drove the USC fighters led by General Maxamed Nuur Galaal back, passed through Brava and, by March 22, 1991, had succeeded in capturing Shalambood, where 170 USC fighters were said to have surrendered. Chris McGreal of the *Independent*, who passed by this road on the way to visit the front in early April, described vividly what he saw:

> The road north out of Kismayu is unremarkable for the first 40 miles, except for the dying, wasted banana crop. Then suddenly the ground is covered with bodies, shell casings and wrecked trucks. This is where the USC onslaught on Kismayu from the north was halted before being driven 200 miles back toward Mogadishu. Few structures have escaped the conflict, and towns have emptied.[95]

According to the field commanders of the alliance, Yuusuf Maxamed Ismaaciil of the SSDF and Cabdullahi Siraaji of the SPM, their combined forces, reportedly about 8,000 men, advanced toward Mogadishu from the south and west.⁹⁶ In Mogadishu, residents appeared nervous and hundreds of demonstrators were reported to have taken to the street to put pressure on the provisional government "to send troops against rival armed factions in southern Somalia."⁹⁷

On March 26 the alliance had captured Buufow, fifty miles south of Mogadishu. French journalist David Chazan visited the frontline and interviewed the SSDF and SPM field commanders there. Traveling south from the capital, he wrote: "The road south from Mogadishu is littered with rotting corpses and burned-out trucks, testifying to the seemingly endless agony of Somalia as rival clan-based factions battle for power."⁹⁸ He found the field commanders optimistic about their chances to capture Mogadishu. Chazan was well aware of the irony of the situation, for the two fronts that had resisted the Barre regime (the SSDF and the SPM) had now made common cause with the SNF fighters who displayed "a thinly veiled sympathy for the septuagenarian who ruled Somalia with an iron hand for 21 years." He raised the issue with Colonel "Jees." The latter admitted that "some of the contingents fighting with us are close to Siad Barre," but, as we saw above, he blamed the USC for the SPM's decision to leave Barre alone. When the USC had betrayed him and attacked him in Afgooye (back in February) and its fighters pushed south "killing and molesting civilians," he said, the SPM had had no choice but to make a stand, turn around and drive them back.⁹⁹

General Cabdullaahi Maxamuud of the SSDF, probably the well-known commander known as "Gardheere," who did not survive this campaign, clearly had the USC's clan cleansing on his mind.¹⁰⁰ He told Chazan,

> the USC, composed of Hawiye clansmen, had systematically massacred Darod tribesmen. "Everywhere they raped our women and slaughtered civilians. In all areas we liberated as we pushed north we found evidence of wanton slaughter and looting. It was just as if they wanted to destroy everything. They even stole the roofs and the windows from buildings. Anything they could move they took."¹⁰¹

"We do not recognize the legitimacy of the so-called provisional government set up by the USC in Mogadishu," the general told Chazan and added that the other groups would not attend the National Reconciliation Conference the USC proposed to hold in the capital because "Mogadishu is not secure for us."¹⁰² To British journalist McGreal, the mood of the fighters appeared as bitter as that of their commanders. On the front line, "the young men humping bazookas are not keen on peace," he reported. "Driven more by a thirst for revenge than clan difference or any views on the make-up of the government, they are waiting for ammunition supplies."[103]

By April 8, the Alliance had reached Afgooye and now stood at the gates of Mogadishu.[104] However, now the lack of ammunition, petrol, and even food and water for at least part of the SNF Alliance, the complete absence of unity of purpose and disagreement about Barre's potential future role, and perhaps even betrayal among the fronts making up the Alliance weakened them at this crucial moment.[105] It became General Caydiid's finest hour. After giving a rousing speech at Mogadishu's National Stadium, he set out to take charge of military operations and defeated the Alliance and drove its scattering fighters into two directions, toward Kismaayo on the coast and beyond Baydhaba into Gedo.[106]

The War of the Militias in Brava

The enormous human costs were not restricted to the fronts themselves.[107] The population of the Jubba Valley, including those we today call Somali Bantu, some of whom had sided with the USC, suffered loss of life, limb, and property as the battle line swung back and forth as often as three times between February and April 1991 alone.[108] The Raxanweyn-based SDM was led by Dr. Abdi Musa Mayow. Although he was allied with the soon-to-be-victorious USC-Caydiid, he could not prevent the harm done to the area and its residents.[109] Below I briefly examine the even less documented events in the coastal city of Brava, 120 miles south of Mogadishu.

Like Afgooye, Brava became a stage in both the USC clan cleansing campaign and the War of the Militias that developed from that campaign. On February 2 (or perhaps February 9), USC militias entered the city with armed force and demanded to be guided toward the houses of Daarood inhabitants. One eyewitness recounted that the attack came as the early afternoon news program on Radio Mogadishu was still in progress. By the time he went to the mosque an hour or so later, there were many dead bodies in the street, among which he recognized a number of Dhulbahante. The eyewitness had cheered on the USC in its campaign against what many considered the "Daarood" military regime of Barre. However, what happened that day, he reminisced, came as a shock. Moreover, although the militias hunted down residents who were Daarood and spared those who could claim Hawiye descent, even before nightfall all shops, including those of the

Reer Brava (like the Reer Xamar in Mogadishu associated with Brava's earliest history), had been looted.[110]

These events marked the beginning of a long series of episodes during which Brava was brutalized by fighters from both sides. As Issa-Salwe points out, between February 1991 and May 1992, Brava changed hands nine times (1996: 120). In the oral accounts to which I had access, these different episodes are not clearly periodized and have to a large extent been collapsed into each other. They are crystal clear, however, about the kinds of harms the Chimini-speaking families of the Reer Brava suffered at the hands of both the Hawiye-based militias of the USC and the Daarood-based ones of the SNF. As the song by Bravanese singer Abubakar Salim "Abu Dhera" put it: "One group leaves then the next group comes. They loot and take away your possessions. I can't tell one from the other; they are like ants of the same color."[111]

Some episodes and incidents stand out in the memories of Bravanese survivors. None have been precisely dated. They are included here because they speak to the way the Reer Brava simply did not seem to matter to the military commanders and fighters of either side. The first two are incidents experienced by individuals. First, a highly prominent Reer Brava citizen had this humiliating experience when USC fighters threatened to pillage his house. His own standing in town meant nothing and his house was spared only because a Hawiye neighbor came out and told the looters that it was *his* house and should therefore not be interfered with.[112] A second incident of "othering" was related by an individual who had joined the militias led by Lieutenant Colonel "Shabeel," the same colorful character that had been interviewed by French journalist Sailhan in Mogadishu just after Barre's expulsion. This person's wife was a Reer Brava woman. He was therefore outraged when he heard "Shabeel," in anticipation of moving into Brava, raise his fighters' morale by encouraging them to go and find "relief and release in the beautiful light-skinned girls of Brava."[113]

Two more widely remembered episodes also illustrate the construction of the Reer Brava as other, as a community that was politically and morally irrelevant, and that could thus be abused with impunity. The first episode may have occurred around May 1991, at a time of USC dominance in Brava. According to Bravanese eyewitness accounts, Cali Mahdi and Caydiid made a joint visit to the town. They were met by leading citizens of Brava, who complained bitterly about their treatment at the hands of the USC. Confronted with an eighty-year-old rape victim, Caydiid especially expressed regret and sorrow, explaining he had been imprisoned in Brava under Barre and considered it his city. This would stop at once. However, the accounts report that, after the two USC leaders had left the city, that very night the pillaging and raping continued as before.[114]

A second episode widely remembered occurred in October 1991, a time at which a Daarood-based military alliance dominated Brava. Again the town's population was subjected to extensive violence—now reportedly perpetrated by fighters of Colonel "Jees," under the overall command of General "Morgan."[115] The following is a report of how survivors remember it:

> Everybody says that the worst month during the stay of the Darood was October 1991. They were a mixture of Dhulbahante, Ogaadeen, Mareexaan and other small groups, trained soldiers mixed with looters. Most of them were ruthless killers. In the night of 26 October alone they entered 65 houses and killed several people. . . . The "officers" of these groups, men such as "Gaani," Bashiir "Bililiqo," Axmed Cumar "Jees" and "Morgan" were apologetic toward the Bravanese and were ready to hear their complaints, but they had very little hold on their "troops."[116]

One particular memory of this period is of a gunman associated with the Daarood-based alliance. Holding a gun to the head of a young Bravanese man, he boasted, "I can do what I want with you." When the youth refused to beg for his life, the gunman just shot him (Interview 7).

These stories represent just a fragment of what happened, both in Brava and in other communities that found themselves in the line of fire. On the one hand, this was simply the kind of impunity that existed in Somalia in this time period. On the other hand, when militias dealt with a so-called minority population, which was categorized as outside the Somali genealogical construct and the struggle to monopolize state power, impunity took on a whole extra dimension that was not lost on the people of Brava and those like them.

In the long run, before and after the U.S./UN intervention of 1992–1995, it was USC supporters of various backgrounds who settled in Brava and came to dominate it socially, politically, and economically. With the rise to political prominence of the al-Shabaab Islamist militias in 2009, the latter also established their control over Brava, expressing their contempt for the rich, *tariqa*-based Islamic culture of Brava by desecrating and destroying the city's places of worship and ancestral graves. At the time of writing the al-Shabaab occupiers are still in place.

The USC Capture of Kismaayo

When it became clear that the USC capture of Kismaayo was impending, a difference of opinion had arisen among the men who had political clout in the city. Those who believed that a peaceful accommodation with the USC and Cali Mahdi's provisional administration was still possible, such as Dr. Cumar Macallin, the political spokesman of the SPM, found allies in political leaders of the other side such as Cabdulqaadir Aadan Cismaan, a former Manifesto elder now close to the Cali Mahdi administration, and Maxamed Abshir Muusa, the only minister of that administration formerly associated with the SSDF. The latter two, together with Cabdirasaaq Xaaji Xusseen,[117] traveled to Kismaayo on March 28, 1991, to negotiate a peaceful takeover of the city. Maxamed Abshir was the same minister who had counseled peaceful accommodation in Gaalkacyo just days before the USC massacre of the local residents there. Now his message that the USC and the provisional administration could be trusted caused confusion, fear, and anger. Some residents of the city felt that Kismaayo should at all costs be spared the fate of Mogadishu and supported negotiations. Others, who had themselves experienced the events in Mogadishu, in contrast, wondered why Maxamed Abshir was providing the USC with the fig leaf behind which it could hide the clan cleansing he himself had witnessed? "When word spread of his presence there was talk of throwing him out, even killing him," reported Chris McGreal of the *Independent* from Kismaayo. McGreal interviewed Maxamed Abshir there: "'There are angry people here,' he told me. 'I am Darod, I should side with them. On the other hand, people like me need to put tribal consideration aside. I hold the USC masses responsible for the killings and lootings, but not the leadership. I am trying to explain that here.'"[118]

As these words show, many civilians rejected the peace option as completely unrealistic and saw submission to the approaching USC militias as suicidal, even more so in the light of the purposeful and unprovoked massacre of innocent civilians and potential peacemakers in Gaalkacyo on February 26. Many of the men who were recruited to defend Kismaayo and push the USC back to Mogadishu and beyond were, therefore, in a very emotional state of mind.

When Caydiid's forces reached Jilib, they reportedly paused, as the "peaceful accommodation" party led by Maxamed Abshir and others tried to persuade him to take over the administration of the city without sending in his militias. On April 4, it appeared for a moment that they had indeed managed to bring about a provisional cease-fire.[119] Even on the morning of the USC takeover of the city itself, the leaders of the peace-party reportedly drove through the city streets announcing this by megaphone.[120] However, the USC military men in the field were set on another course. What happened was, therefore, the opposite.

According to eyewitness and survivor reports, this stage of the clan cleansing was perhaps even crueler than that in Mogadishu because this time the purposeful humiliation and brutalization of Daarood individuals and families was even more personal and ruthless. Individuals were hunted down by people who had known them in everyday life and who now purposefully chose to torture and mutilate them, cutting off limbs while they were still alive and expressing joy at being able to gang-rape their female relatives in front of them, under their very eyes. To one eyewitness, this kind of behavior could no longer be understood in terms of a desire to take over the heights of the state; it now appeared motivated by deep personal and clan-based hatred and resentment (Interview 6). He was there when a young man led other gunmen in the lethal attack on his maternal uncle, when a former university student headed the hunt for a former department administrator, and so forth. When a group of middle-class victims approached Xiirey Qaasim Weheliye, a former Manifesto signatory now serving as Caydiid's governor of Kismaayo, to allow them to arrange for a boat with which to leave, he refused their request. Holding up one of his hands, he told them their clan had been like the middle finger of the hand, adding: "All we are doing today is making all fingers the same length."[121] Below we will return to this kind of hatred and hate-narratives and analyze them more fully.

Extreme brutality such as torture, mutilation, and gang rape with or without sharp objects had been part of the clan cleansing campaign all along. However, by the time Kismaayo was captured on April 23, 1991, it had become a major aspect.[122] Gang rape was a large part of terrorizing the population and driving them out. Daahir Cali, who was in Kismaayo at the time, reports the account of a friend who had been away when the USC took the city and now came back to rejoin his wife and children. The first people he met, at 5:30 in the morning, were eight girls who had been abducted from their homes the night before and had been cut with knives and raped all night, after which the men had left them. The girls could barely move, Daahir Cali writes, and left a trail of bloody footsteps where they walked (Daahir Cali 1997: 191). The author witnessed attempted rape himself when four armed men forced one of the young women who cooked lunch for the small group to which he belonged into a room in order to rape her. They called for help, he wrote, and men drinking tea nearby, including a USC man, intervened and apologized for such behavior. This incident occurred in broad daylight, this author writes; what happened at night was much worse and, from his perspective, completely beyond the pale of Somali culture (191–92). He concludes his account as follows:

> The killing of people was continuous except for those who entered the compounds of the Saleebaan[123] and found safety and support there. On April 23–26, Kismaayo was a town with residents but without life, for clothes, medicine, bedding and furniture, utensils, in some cases even windows, doors, and roofing, food, and so forth were looted. (193)

According to this author, many of those who fled on foot were killed by the local rural population—perhaps suggesting an element of class as well as clan-based antagonism—but the big rains that fell made their pursuit by USC fighters impossible. The road out of Kismaayo to Dhoobley, on the border with Kenya, acquired the name of "Habaar waalid" ("Parents' curse") because of the hardships people suffered. From Dhoobley, former officials of the Barre regime or people with some wealth crossed the Kenyan border to the main cities, as they did not need any help beyond a grant of political asylum. Others crossed into Kenya and were settled in refugee camps, first Libooye, and then Ifo 1 and 2, and Xagardheer. Some, however, stayed in Dhoobley and began to plan a counterattack (193–94).

Like the refugees who had preceded them, those who fled Kismaayo now made international headlines only when the misfortunes with which they met were especially horrific. This was, for example, the case with the *Kwanda* incident. The MS *Kwanda* was a relief ship that was hijacked in Kismaayo on April 24, as the USC troops of General Caydiid were about to capture the port. With the help of the harbor guards, who were said to belong to an "Islamic fundamentalist armed faction,"[124] 900 refugees forcibly boarded a relief ship that had come from Mombasa to unload 250 tons of food. After a week-long odyssey during which thirteen babies were born, the ship was finally able to reach Mombasa (Sica 1994: 149). There, however, it was refused permission to land. Mario Sica, who visited the ship, spoke of "a Dantesque scene of stench and dirt everywhere" (150). It was not until the first of May and after Italian diplomatic intervention that the refugees were finally allowed to land.

On board were a number of prominent men, including the vice-governor of Kismaayo, retired general Maxamed Xusseen Da'uud Xiirane, as well as the two Sica had described as such an unlikely pair back in March: Dhigic-Dhigic and "Jurile." Not on board, although he had been present in the city until it was captured, was Maxamed Abshir Muuse, who made it back to Mogadishu unharmed.[125]

Radio Mogadishu reported the USC-SDM "liberation" of Kismaayo and Baydhaba on April 23, 1991:

> According to the Central Command of the United Somali Congress (USC) and the Somali Democratic Movement (SDM), the towns of Kismaayo and Baydhabo in Jubbada Hoose [Lower Jubba] and Bay Regions have been completely cleared of the *remnants of Siad Barre's soldiers* who were hiding there. The report from the USC and SDM added that the administration of Kismaayo and Baydhaba towns and their surroundings are under the full control of the two armies . . . [with] the gallant forces of the USC and SDM . . . in hot pursuit of the fleeing, defeated soldiers.[126]

The USC was, however, unable to capture Gedo or drive Barre out of Buurdhuubo (Daahir Ali 1997: 250).

Nevertheless, even if it had done so at an enormous cost in human life and material destruction, the USC had established hegemony over a large part of central and southern Somalia, which included Mogadishu, Baydhaba, and Kismaayo, and some of the richest natural resources of the country. However, the state the USC had hoped to capture no longer existed. In the North, the SNM had decided upon secession and, on May 18, 1991, proclaimed the independent Republic of Somaliland. In the Northeast, a sizeable part of the area that would become the regional state of Puntland (consisting at the time of its foundation of Bari, Mudug, Nugaal, Sool, and Sanaag) had been, for the moment, secured from further USC attack by fighters of the SSDF.

The war did not end here. In May 1991, the military commanders expelled from Kismaayo regrouped at Dhoobley and established a second Daarood-based front, the SPM Alliance, with "Gabyow" as commander in chief and "Morgan" as his deputy (Daahir Ali 1997: 195). In June–July 1991, it would take back Kismaayo and Brava from the USC. However, the national political ambitions of commanders such as "Jees," "Morgan," and others, as well as the competition and internal divisions among them, continued to be an obstacle to peace and kept law and order for the local residents of the areas they controlled out of reach.

The situation inside Somalia was in some ways further exacerbated by the outcome of the National Reconciliation Conferences in Djibouti in June and July 1991. The decision to confirm Cali Mahdi as the president of the Transitional Government further alienated Caydiid; by November 1991 Mogadishu had exploded into full-scale warfare between the two. The decision to recommit all forces to drive former president Barre, still in Gedo, out of the country permanently angered the SPM Alliance, whose clan-base had been the target of USC clan cleansing and some of whose leaders still hoped to bring Barre back to power (Daahir Cali 1997: 252). Below we will examine how these political developments played themselves out up to the end of 1992.

The Plight of the Expelled Revisited

Many of the refugees from Kismaayo who survived the "Habaar waalid" road were unable to cross into Kenya. It is estimated that in May 1991 there were 100,000 refugees living on the Somali side of the border, especially near Liboi and Maandheera (Mandera): "Many were prevented from entering Kenya by the security forces and lived under trees and in make-shift shelters in no-man's land, under threat of attack from both Somali bandits, Kenyan shifta [brigands] and the Kenyan security forces" (African Rights 1993: 5). The wife of Manifesto elder Maxamed Sheekh Faruur, who later, together with her husband, received asylum in Germany, remembered how people had been dying of hunger and thirst; how she had been able to brew some tea from wild plants; and how a relative from Zambia, who had come to the border to search for relatives and people he knew, had found her and helped her reach Nairobi.[127]

African Rights also documented the conditions in the refugee camps in the period January–April 1991, accusing the Kenyan government of standing in the way of improvements in the Liboi, Ifo, and Hulugho camps. In May 1991, it reports, as a result of Caydiid's military offensive (and the USC's capture of Kismaayo), tens of thousands of refugees crossed the border at Maandheera, Ceel Waaq, and especially Liboi. Many of these were taken to what were then two new camps in Dadaab, Dagahaley, and Hagadera (1993: 6). The abuse of refugees in these camps, detentions, disappearances, beatings and torture, killings, rapes, robberies, and so forth by gangs of thugs as well as the Kenyan security forces are best documented for 1992 and 1993. However, they occurred in this earlier period as well (13–22).

As is often the case with disasters of this scale, it takes time before the perspectives of victims and eyewitnesses begin to be represented in writing. As a result, it is only more recently that one finds moving accounts of Somali refugee experiences in more personal narratives. Thus Ayaan Hirsi Ali's 2007 memoir, *Infidel*, gives a harrowing account of the circumstances in which the refugees from Mogadishu found themselves as they reached the Kenyan border. In the novel by the Somali-Italian writer Cristina (Ubax) Ali Farah, *Madre Piccola* (*Little Mother*), also from 2007, the drownings of fleeing refugees are not only evoked but seep into the atmosphere of the whole narrative, as the sound of a slow, persistent, ominous base in a piece of music (Farah 2007, 2008, 2011).

Ayaan Hirsi lived in Nairobi at the time of the clan cleansing. She tells the story of how she joined a male relative who had fled Somalia ahead of his family by boat to Mombasa and now wanted to go and look for his wife and children on the Kenyan border. Ayaan relates how they had to bribe their way across the border to Dhoobley on the Somali side, where an innumerable crowd of refugees were waiting to find some way to get into Kenya as they were slowly starving. "The children had lice visibly trailing along their necks," Ayaan wrote, "and there I was with my sporty little duffel bag, with a toothbrush and toothpaste and a change of underwear and clean clothes. It was surreal" (Ali 2007: 155). When she happened upon relatives from Mogadishu whom she had seen just ten weeks before, she found them completely transformed. She had known them as well off, plump women. Now they were filthy, starving, scared, and desperate, in a place without food and water, crawling with scorpions, snakes and other vermin (152–55).

Ayaan was one of thousands of Somalis who traveled from all over the world to look for relatives in the vast and numerous refugee camps and save whomever they could save.[128] Without money to bribe the Kenyan officials, without the resources to pay for transport from the border to a camp or town, and without the physical and moral strength to fight off ruthless fellow refugees, many of whom were armed, no Somali could even reach the miserable centers of death, disease, and rape that were the Kenyan refugee camps. Over time, these camps would come to hold the most vulnerable of all categories of refugees—categories that crossed clan lines but coincided with the social break-lines of class, caste, age, and gender.[129]

How many people were killed in this stage of the civil war—in the countryside during the USC's long march on Mogadishu; in Mogadishu, as a tottering regime lashed out at civilians; during the month-long battle for

Mogadishu with its indiscriminate government bombardments of residential areas; during the clan cleansing of 1991, and due to other clan-based and opportunistic violence that followed; during the massive exodus of refugees who fled Mogadishu and other southern and south-central towns, without food or water, in overloaded vehicles that were often intercepted and on boats that regularly capsized; and, eventually, in the refugee camps in Kenya, Ethiopia, and Yemen, where hunger, disease, rape, and other forms of violence kept taking their toll—is beyond any dependable estimate. The number amounts to tens of thousands dead, unknown numbers traumatized and wounded, and hundreds of thousands displaced.

In September 1991, two NGO researchers on an assessment mission in the Bari, Nugaal, and Mudug regions of Somalia, then administered by the SSDF, estimated the number of displaced in these three regions at 165,000, while SSDF estimates were 250,000–300,000. They also reported about the harsh conditions faced by refugees fleeing southern Somalia by way of Ethiopia to the Northeast: "Men are at risk of being killed, children at risk of disease, and whole families at risk of looting."[130]

Even before the USC campaign of clan cleansing had run its course, even the *concept* of civilian noncombatant had been completely abandoned by all sides in the War of the Militias. Moreover, the fighting that broke out in Mogadishu between USC-Caydiid and USC-Cali Mahdi reportedly claimed approximately 14,000 dead and 27,000 wounded from mid-November 1991 until the end of February 1992 alone (Africa Watch and Physicians for Human Rights 1992). This excludes the large numbers of deaths, wounded, purposefully maimed, and displaced that accompanied and followed in the wake of a second attempt by a Daarood-based alliance to capture Mogadishu from the USC (the SPM Alliance, defeated in April 1992). By then, the largely man- and war-made famine that is said to have killed over 200,000 people (especially the very young and old) was already spreading throughout the region. It would not attract world attention until the fall of that year (Maren 1997: 214).[131] In December 1992 it would trigger the U.S./UN intervention, which marked a whole new chapter in the Somali civil war. This new stage lies beyond the scope of this chapter but it was one in which the Goliath of UNITAF gradually became entangled in the Lilliputian dynamics of the political violence analyzed here.

Imploding Armed Fronts and Shifting Alliances

The outbreak of war between the USC factions of Caydiid and Cali Mahdi and the tensions within the Daarood-based SPM-Alliance had political dimensions that were personal (competition between individual warlords), local (competition between groups inhabiting certain regions), and national (ongoing competition over control of the state). Together these produced the continuously imploding and expanding armed fronts and the constantly shifting alliances of the continuing War of the Militias.

There are compelling reasons for extending the history of events that makes up this chapter beyond April–May 1991 when the USC capture of Kismaayo marked an important stage in the clan cleansing campaign and the War of the Militias that had evolved from it. Extending the narrative from this date to December 1992, the eve of the U.S./UN military humanitarian intervention (UNITAF) serves the following purposes. First, it demonstrates that the clan cleansing campaign by USC-Caydiid continued to be a significant dimension of the violence of this period. Since this subject is central to this book, establishing its geographical scope and time-range is therefore important. Second, extending the narrative to December 1992 illustrates further that militias drawing their fighters from the groups targeted by the clan cleansing themselves became perpetrators of clan-based violence against civilians. This is a crucial dimension of the history of this period and pertinent to considerations of postconflict reconstruction. Third, this stage of the civil war provides strong evidence for a central proposition of this study, namely that it was the political use of group identity constructs to take over control of the state, not those groups or identities themselves that lay at the root of Somali civil war violence. The history of May 1991–December 1992 shows this in vivid color, as it witnessed the political implosion on both sides of the 1991 divide. This meant that each side turned violence inward and reached for allies across the divide of 1991 to help them destroy all the more thoroughly those who were part of their in-group just a few weeks ago. As the political usefulness of the Hawiye/Irir and Daarood identity constructs diminished, warlords and other warmongers effortlessly turned to other such constructs and subconstructs to promote their cause. Fourth and finally, one of the central objectives of the "evenemential" history presented in this chapter is to establish why politico-military leaders adopted this kind of violence and how they persuaded so many ordinary people to join in. Although a full analysis of this question is part of Chapter 4, the episode of violence in Kismaayo in

Clan Cleansing in Mogadishu and Beyond 181

December 1992, with which this chapter ends, illustrates clearly how warlords who massacred civilians associated with the clan-base of a rival warlord did not just do so to weaken that rival but also to eliminate any hope for alternative local leadership by civilians.

The final section of this chapter will briefly analyze four major episodes of violence: (1) the violence that resulted from implosion of the USC in Mogadishu (November 1991); (2) the final defeat of Barre and the atrocities committed against civilians in the inter-riverine area by both the Daarood-based SPM Alliance in January–April 1992 and its victorious opponent, the alliance centered on USC Caydiid; (3) the atrocities committed by the victorious USC in the Gedo region in April–May 1992 against civilians it associated with the SPM Alliance clan base; and finally, (4) the hunting down and slaughter of about 120 prominent middle-class individuals in Kismaayo in December 1992, on the eve of the U.S./UN intervention, by SPM leader "Jees" in close alliance with USC General Caydiid. These episodes round out the account of the changing political uses of large-scale clan-based violence against civilians (including the final stages of the USC clan cleansing campaign) in the stages of the civil war examined in this book.

The Implosion of the USC

In November 1991, the USC imploded. Already in April 1991, fighting had broken out in Mogadishu between USC-Caydiid and USC-Cali Mahdi, but it was not until November 1991, after the Djibouti National Reconciliation conferences, that a full-scale war broke out between the two sides, each mobilizing its own subclan base. As in January 1991, Mogadishu's residential neighborhoods came under indiscriminate fire from even the heaviest weaponry, including Stalin organs, missile throwers, and anti-aircraft guns fixed to specially outfitted pick-up trucks. And as in the earlier stage of the civil war, disregard of the civilian population associated with the other side was common military strategy. Although the largest part of the city came under the control of Caydiid, Cali Mahdi was said to have larger popular support, even inside Caydiid territory. This episode of the Somali civil war, while punctuated by cease-fires and Caydiid-embracing-Mahdi photo-ops, lasted even beyond the U.S./UN intervention of 1992–1995, which energized it with huge infusions of money, food, arms, trucks, and so forth. In terms of the loss of human lives and the destruction of the city, this stage of the civil war was, by all accounts, extraordinarily costly. According to the estimates of human rights and relief organizations cited above, as many as

41,000 Somalis were wounded or killed just in the first four months of this intra-USC conflict.[132]

The USC split had repercussions for the other parties to the civil war. As we will see below, here too unstable configurations and reconfigurations of genealogical constructs and clan templates, stretched and shrunk, twisted and reversed, invoked and disavowed, provided the rationales for shifting political and military alliances. However, even as the war between the USC factions raged in Mogadishu, the old battle lines between a more or less united USC and a more or less united Daarood-based alliance were redrawn once again in January–April 1992, in the context of Barre's last comeback as the symbolic head of (part of) the SPM Alliance.

The Final Defeat of Barre and the Atrocities in the Riverine Areas

In the wake of the defeat of the Daarood-based SNF-Alliance of February–April 1991, Gedo had remained unconquered and its militias had been able to defend Luuq, Baardheere, and Buur-dhuubo, Barre's humble headquarters, against the USC. Meanwhile the commanders defeated in Kismaayo had regrouped and had retaken Kismaayo and Brava in the early summer of 1991 (Daahir Cali 1997: 250). Their combined forces, under the name of SPM Alliance, then made another attempt to capture Mogadishu, this time spearheaded, it appears, by the Gedo militias of the SNF. These moved Barre to Baydhaba in January 1992 and kept pushing on toward Mogadishu until they were routed by Caydiid on April 24, 1992 (254). As we will see below, this time Caydiid's forces pushed deep into Gedo and, with SPM-Jees on his side again, took Kismaayo for the second time on May 14, 1992. Barre fled to the Kenyan border and gave himself up to the Kenyan authorities at Wajeer, on April 29, 1992 (256). He received asylum in Nigeria where he died in January 1995. In the course of this campaign, the areas alongside and between the rivers (parts of Bay, Bakool, Lower and Middle Shabeelle, and Lower and Middle Jubba) became the site of clan-based atrocities against the civilian population associated with the other side, from among whom the Daarood residents had to a large extent already been displaced or purged. For the Baydhaba and Xuddur areas of Bay and Bakool, these atrocities have been movingly described by the U.S.-based Somali scholars Mukhtar and Kusow (Mukhtar 1992; Mukhtar and Kusow 1993).

As we saw before, some militias and civilian supporters of the Raxanweyn-based SDM had actively participated in the USC clan cleansing campaign in the areas in which they lived. During its unsuccessful attempt to capture Mogadishu in February–March 1991, the SNF Alliance, which included many survivors of this clan cleansing, had not only lived off the population through which it passed but had also been in a mood for revenge and keen to guarantee itself a route for retreat. When it was routed, the Raxanweyn-based SDM had participated in the USC conquest of Kismaayo in April 1991 and had launched ongoing attacks on the population of the towns and villages of Gedo.[133] When the Daarood-based front (now called the SPM Alliance) regrouped and made a second attempt to capture Mogadishu in January–April 1992, it committed large-scale atrocities against civilians of Raxanweyn (and other Digil-Mirifle) clan backgrounds.

Somali historian Mukhtar interviewed people who had fled the Upper Jubba area in Nairobi in the summer of 1992. His informants, he reported, "were outraged by the inhumane methods used by the Marehans and their allies since the downfall of Bar[r]e. They burned cities, villages, and grain storage structures. . . . They looted livestock, raped women and indiscriminately killed people" (1992: 7). More details emerged when Mukhtar visited the region itself in the summer of 1993, at which time the SDM had fallen out with Caydiid, whose new SNA alliance had abused the SDM's civilian base similarly to how the SPM alliance had treated it. The atrocities committed by the latter, Mukhtar reported, included the use of local women to load and unload looted goods from and onto trucks; their rape in front of their families; the torturing and killing of men, including respected religious leaders; locking as many as fifty people into a mud house and setting them on fire; wrapping people inside straw mats and burning them, and hanging men accused of not cooperating at hanging stations erected in every village (Mukhtar and Kusow 1993: 20–21).

As in the case of Brava, the victims related that commanders did not only condone but actively licensed such behavior, irrespective of what they would say to local elders in day-time meetings. Elders in Baydhaba reported that, when "Jees" was in charge of that town, he had explicitly encouraged his fighters to put the land he had conquered for them to good use.[134] The rank-and-file fighters who actually committed the abuses, Mukhtar and Kusow explain, were expected "to fight for their warlord, but once the city was secured, they had a free hand in robbing and looting whatever they laid their hands on as compensation." This was in lieu of "a weekly salary and daily Qat." When elders would reach an agreement with a warlord, nothing would change, for the warlord would claim that his fighters could not be controlled

(22–23). Moreover, as in Brava, the victims of these abuses felt targeted not just because of their perceived political association with the actions of the SDM or the USC but also because the militias despised and looked down on them because of their clan identity. When in April 1992 the USC militias subjected them to the same kind of atrocities, they spoke of being targeted for genocide and expulsion by both sides (idem, 16, 21). This study does not use these terms but it fully acknowledges the suffering of the victims of these clan-based atrocities.

Another place where the battle lines of the War of the Militias swung back and forth, sometimes from day to day or week to week, was the Lower Jubba valley. Here too agricultural production was disrupted, crops and seeds, water pumps, and tractors stolen, villages destroyed, and the local people reduced to gathering "famine food" and displaced.[135] Here too the many militias that struggled over the control of Kismaayo and the rich grazing and agricultural lands of the area accused the local population of taking sides. As in Brava and Baydhaba, the victims, who here included people we now call Somali Bantu, experienced the cruelty and humiliation that accompanied the violations as an expression of callous indifference to, and contempt for their group identity. So many people were targeted for death and expulsion on the basis of that identity that in this context too the word genocide has been used.[136]

USC Atrocities in Gedo

The atrocities committed in the Gedo area can be seen as both a stage of the clan cleansing project the USC had launched in Mogadishu in January 1991 and a brutal episode in the War of the Militias. When Caydiid's fighters had beaten the brutal offensive of the combined militias of the SPM Alliance (including the SNF) back from the outskirts of Mogadishu in April 1992, they pursued their opponents, including former president Barre, as far as and beyond the Kenyan border. One episode of the collective "punishment" of civilians that followed took place at Buulo Xaawo, where USC commanders committed atrocities both against the fighters and commanders of the SNF section of the alliance and those civilians of the Gedo region it could identify as Daarood. Amnesty International documented these atrocities as part of a report called *Somalia: A Human Rights Disaster*, dating from August 1992. Amnesty acknowledged how unusual its report was:

> For much of the past 18 months, Amnesty International reports that it has been difficult to obtain details about Somalia's human rights

situation from impartial sources. However, it is clear that throughout this period armed groups have deliberately killed other Somalis simply on account of their clan origin.[137]

However, in spite of its implicit apology for not reporting on the gross human rights abuses committed on all sides of the conflict, Amnesty insisted on the credibility of its report, asserting that, "Though unable to corroborate it in every detail, this chilling account is broadly consistent with other reports of abuses by General Aideed's forces which Amnesty International has received" (Amnesty International 1992: 1). Amnesty was careful to try to provide some context for the Buula Xaawo massacres by referring back to the clan-based violence committed in the riverine area, where the forces of the SPM Alliance (including the SNF) had targeted civilians "suspected of supporting the USC, such as Hawiye and Raxanweyn communities around Baydhaba and Afgooye." Amnesty moreover added some harrowing details about these atrocities that confirm the gist of Mukhtar and Kusow's 1993 report: "surviving Rahanweyn clan victims who were later treated in hospital in Mogadishu had apparently had their noses and ears mutilated and their genitals burnt with acid" (2). This clearly indicates the level of brutality that had become standard practice in the War of the Militias.

The atrocities committed by USC forces as they pursued especially the SNF to Buulo Xaawo, Doollo, Ceel Waaq, and Garbahaare, in April and May 1992, were similarly brutal. They reportedly began on April 28, 1992 and lasted for thirty-three days, for as long as General Caydiid held Buulo Xaawo from April 28 onward. The USC chased SNF fighters and commanding officers into Kenya and forcibly fetched some of them back to Buulo Xaawo to be executed.[138] USC fighters, the report said, "gathered people in the town centre, going round all the houses, and separated people by clan, marking out the Darods—Majar[t]en, Marehan and Ogadenis. Their own people—Hawiyes—they left alone." After they had been sorted out this way, they were tortured, mutilated, and bayoneted or shot, and the women raped and, if they were pregnant, disemboweled. After that, the report said, "The bodies were burnt with kerosene and firewood and the bones left lying there."[139]

One survivor testified to Amnesty that he had been spared because he was already crippled, while his companion, a former teacher in Mogadishu, was shot. The arbitrariness with which individuals were able to take or spare the lives of other individuals often haunts those who survived this way. One such survivor was a teenager at the time. He had been forced to flee Mogadishu in early February 1991 and had taken refuge in Gedo, where he had spent his early youth and where his father had worked before having been imprisoned by the Barre regime. During the USC pursuit of the SNF in the area, he was literally driven into the barbed wire that marked the Kenyan border. In pursuit of him was a USC "technical" that was driven by a man but whose big gun mounted on the back was commanded by a woman. As he lay face-down on the ground, covering his head with his *macawis* (sarong) in an attempt at "playing dead," the latter's eyes briefly met his. In that very instant, this female fighter determined whether he would live or die; for some (to him unfathomable) reason she chose life.[140]

The USC had vindicated itself, providing another link in the long chain of collective "punishment" that had become the Somali civil war. Journalist Scott Peterson visited Caydiid twice in this period, once in Baydhaba, on June 23, 1992, and once in Baardheere, a little later that summer, when the famine that was just about to make headlines all over the world was already claiming victims. Caydiid was pleased with his military feats. Peterson wrote:

> We sat in the covered veranda of Aidid's Baidoa base. With an exuberant toothy grin the warlord pointed at the map beside him. It was almost all colored bright yellow, the color of the colonel's fiefdom. Peace had come, he said, just in time to save the 4.5 million Somalis who might otherwise die from famine. (Peterson 2000: 42)

During the second visit, Caydiid denied what had been well established by the ICRC and other relief agencies, namely that he was (jointly) responsible for compounding suffering by letting his gunmen block the relief effort (49).

Caydiid himself wrote about his achievements of this period from the perspective of late 1993 in his memoirs: In three months, he wrote, he had captured all central regions and destroyed the army of the twenty-first military sector, created the alliance between SNM, SPM, and USC, formalized on October 2, 1990, and removed Barre from the capital on January 26, 1991. Three days later, in a five-hour meeting, he had advised Cali Mahdi not to proclaim himself president of the transitional administration—a political move that indeed proved disastrous, but largely because Caydiid himself had refused to accept this. He had defeated what he called "Barre's counter offensive" and captured Kismaayo in April 1991. Moreover, on July 5, 1991, he had been elected as the chairman of the USC for the second time, with 80 percent of the vote. In February 1992, he had created what was to become

SNA-Caydiid, bringing the USC, SPM, SDM, and other fronts together under one political umbrella. He had defeated USC-Cali Mahdi, and finally, though this was not to happen until 1993, he had brought about the Addis Ababa agreements between the warring factions (Ruhela 1994: 169).

There was much truth in what General Caydiid wrote, although his emphasis on his own agency at the expense of that of anybody else was obviously at least somewhat of an exaggeration. What is most stunning about his proud resume is that it did not make the slightest reference to the costs of his political and military victories or to the political failure of using clan cleansing to obtain a monopoly on state power. He, indeed, succeeded in cleansing *"the"* Daarood from the city of Mogadishu and much of the inter-riverine area. However, in doing so he had played a seminal role in the destruction of the state and the people for which he had in public articulated such a lofty, unified, democratic, and economically optimistic vision (Ruhela 1994).

Kismaayo Again: Warlords Versus Civilians on the Eve of
International Intervention

The USC had retaken Brava and Kismaayo in the first half of May 1992.[141] It had defeated "Morgan," who had been forced to flee to Kenya, where he was disarmed by the Kenyan government. However, against all odds he had regrouped, raised new funds, recruited fighters from the refugee camps, and reentered the war. The SNF of Gedo also regrouped and took back the major cities of the region in the second half of May. It was in the fighting over Buulo Xaawo on May 31, 1992, that the notorious USC commander Lieutenant Colonel "Shabeel" was killed. According to Daahir Cali, USC supporters in Kismaayo took this loss so badly that they killed more than forty (mostly Mareexaan) men to "avenge his death" (Daahir Ali 1997: 258).

In August 1992, a triumphant Caydiid, using Baardheere (in Gedo) as his headquarters, established a new alliance, the SNA-Caydiid, which counted SPM-Jees among its ranks. In response, Cali Mahdi, together with SPM-"Morgan" and the SNF, established the SNA-Cali Mahdi in October 1992. By this time, the famine that would trigger UNITAF, that stage of the U.S./UN intervention that lasted from December 8, 1992, to May 4, 1993, was already in full swing, with food an increasingly crucial weapon of war. Both Cali Mahdi and Caydiid were actively courted by the international community to allow a humanitarian intervention to bring food to the starving. When "Morgan" and the Gedo militias of the SNF retook Baardheere in October 1992—Caydiid had returned to Mogadishu—they did so under the very eyes of the ICRC and other food aid agencies. As Somalis, especially in the riverine areas, were dying by the tens of thousands, the presence of the international NGOs and the imminent arrival of the U.S./UN troops gave the complex politico-military enterprise of the warlords a whole set of new dimensions. This is the context of the massacre by Colonel "Jees" (then leader of the SPM-Jees branch of SNA-Caydiid) of over one hundred men of the middle class of Kismaayo.[142] This incident, which because of the impending arrival of Belgian and U.S. troops in Kismaayo was exceptionally well documented, illustrates the different political uses clan-based violence against civilians had come to serve at this point in the Somali civil war.

The massacre occurred in Kismaayo between December 8 and 19, 1992, over a period of nine to eleven days. The political moment was deeply fraught. First, U.S. troops had already landed in Mogadishu on December 9 and were expected in Kismaayo on December 19. This was a threat to the status quo. Second, though the city was still in the hands of Colonel "Jees," closely allied to Caydiid, General "Morgan," who had already retaken Baardheere in October 1991, was poised to reconquer Kismaayo.[143] The strategy "Jees" and Caydiid employed in this context was one that had been used before in the Somali civil war, namely that of exterminating the *niman magacleh*—the most distinguished male citizens of the city. In this case all men were Harti, the genealogical construct that encompasses four of the clans making up the category of Daarood.[144] Jane Perlez, of the *New York Times*, reported the following on December 29, 1992:

> More than 100 religious leaders and business executives, a doctor and other prominent residents of this port city were hunted door to door and killed in three nights of terror that began on the eve of the Americans landing in Mogadishu, Somali witnesses and U.S. diplomats say.[145] ... The night the killings began trucks roared through town and wild gunshots could be heard as Harti were pulled from their homes and killed on the edge of town, Somali witnesses said. ... Grim details of what happened in the killing spree were pieced together from Somalis who escaped or who hid Harti, and from Western relief workers whose agencies have tried to protect Harti employees.[146]

On the authority of a member of the SPM central committee, Perlez related that the killings had been preceded by a visit from General Caydiid on December 6 and by a rally at which Colonel "Jees" had said that "the town needed to be 'cleared' of people who would cause trouble." Reginald Moreels, the president of Doctors without Borders who had been in Kismaayo when the violence took place, testified that the victims had been shot in the head, the abdomen, and the thorax, that is to say, had been purposely killed. A U.S. army investigation later led to the discovery of sixteen bodies in one mass grave, "shot and missing genitals, hands and feet."[147] This mass grave, discovered in Gobweyn, just outside the city, contained the bodies of several distinguished elders, still blindfolded and sometimes robbed of their sarongs.

Perlez reported that Moreels had gone to meet with "Jees," who had called the massacre "just a little problem of one night and that things would be better." Moreels denied this, as in this period "clannic cleanings" were a nightly occurrence. On the basis of quotations from local interviews conducted by Perlez and Richburg, the animosity between the residents was deeply entwined, as it had been in Mogadishu, with sentiments about who was truly indigenous to the city and the area.[148]

Two further aspects of the account by Perlez are worth emphasizing, for they show that neither the local leadership of the SPM nor the people who made up the clan-base associated with it were united in their support of this violence. Perlez reports that Kismaayo residents who were *not* Harti had concealed and protected those targeted for violence and that many had wanted to speak out but feared retaliation.[149] She also provides evidence that the massacres planned by "Jees" did not have the support of the whole SPM Central Committee, one of whose senior members, Cali Haydar Ismaaciil, had reportedly criticized "Jees" and called him a criminal. In response to this critic, Perlez writes, "Jees" had referred to a decision of the Security Committee of the SNA, headed by Caydiid, which had decided that this was necessary "for the security of the country." General Caydiid's shadow thus indeed loomed large in this episode.

Because it was relatively well documented, it is possible to discern the political rationales of this episode of clan-based violence with some confidence. It is clear that "Jees" and Caydiid planned and carried out the massacre in the hope of maximizing their political advantage before the arrival of UNITAF troops. By killing middle-class civilians of the clan-base they associated with their rival "Morgan" (as part of SNA Cali Mahdi), they undermined the position of these rival warlords but also any other approach to resolving local conflict and competition for power than that of warlords using clan sentiment and clan-based violence as their instruments. The following illustrates these two points.

In the immediate aftermath of the violence, the Jees-Caydiid strategy appeared to pay off. One day before U.S. and Belgian troops landed in Kismaayo, Perlez reports, Colonel "Jees" gave President Bush's special envoy to Somalia, Robert Oakley, a warm welcome, full of references to "the emerging democracy in Somalia." When reporters asked about what the U.S. response would be to the gross violation of human rights that had just occurred, Oakley pointed out that the United States could do very little, because, under the Security Council Resolution that had sanctioned the intervention, it had little authority: "We are not an occupying power. We have no power of arrest. There is nothing in the Security Council resolution about war crimes, as there is with Bosnia."[150] All he could do was to try and isolate "Jees," Oakley said. He proposed to do so by—note the irony—encouraging traditional elders to participate in new town committees. He meant, of course, those "traditional elders" who had not been clan cleansed. Thus "Jees" and Caydiid were able to (temporarily) consolidate their advantage over "Morgan" (and SNA-Cali Mahdi) and literally got away with murder. Their expectation that the United States would choose strategic pragmatism over human rights concerns proved correct.

The second strategic advantage is related to how warlord-instigated clan-based violence undermined all alternative ways of channeling local conflicts and inequalities. Such violence increased the likelihood that, for local residents, clan identities and clan hatred would be the most compelling form of association, and clan-based violence the most common way of dealing with conflicts and inequalities among them. With the U.S./UN intervention bringing hopes for a new era, Kismaayo's leading middle-class citizens presented a potential alternative to the reign of warlord violence. However, by targeting only certain middle-class leaders for violence, in other words, by making local people's clan identities a matter of life and death, "Jees" and Caydiid undermined an alternative group identity for the people of Kismaayo: a middle class, urbane, cross-clan identity and esprit de corps that might have united them and given them a chance at providing local civilian leadership and conflict resolution.

The massacre of a particular group of the middle-class leadership of Kismaayo illustrates the different uses to which political entrepreneurs and warlords put clan-based violence against civilians. First, given that "Jees" was collaborating closely with Caydiid who, according to contemporary news reports, had visited Kismaayo the day before the killings, the conclusion that this massacre was a stage in the clan cleansing campaign that had first gained strength in Mogadishu in December 1990–January 1991 is unavoidable. Nevertheless, the circumstances of the killings were also very different, among other things because the commander who ordered the massacring of middle-class men was himself part of the genealogical construct of Daarood. This leads to the second insight, namely that the political alliance imagined in the name of Daarood-ness had imploded to such an extent that massacring Daarood civilians had become an acceptable political strategy. This matched the comparable implosion of the political alliance imagined in the name of Hawiye-ness (the war between USC-Caydiid and USC-Cali Mahdi in Mogadishu in November 1991), which had made the massacring of Hawiye civilians accepted political practice. In other words, the political construct of "*the*" Daarood proved to be just as unstable a category and discourse as, in the context of the USC, that of "*the*" Hawiye.

Given that the massacre was part of the wars "Jees" and "Morgan," as commanders of armed fronts of different names and composition, fought over the control of Kismaayo, the massacre also represents an episode in the brutal War of the Militias that had begun in early February 1991.

The third insight the massacre of December 1992 allows is that when warlords violently eliminated the potential competition for leadership presented by prominent local, civilian stakeholders, this violence reflected but also exacerbated clan differences.[151] The fourth and final insight one may draw from this episode of violence is the chilling one, already visible in the atrocities committed in the riverine regions and Gedo, that the brutal collective "punishment" of civilians constructed as "of the other side" or even "without a side" had become "politics as usual." Atrocities against civilians on the basis of their clan background were now committed in Somalia "by force of habit."[152]

This chapter has presented a *histoire événémentielle* of the clan cleansing and other forms of large-scale collective violence against civilians that took place in Somalia in 1991–1992. Chapter 4 will analyze two central themes underlying this narrative in more depth and detail. These are the political goals of the leaders who organized and allowed large-scale clan-based violence against civilians, and the reasons why so many ordinary people participated in it. For those who participated in it, discourses of clan hatred mediated this violence in crucial ways. Chapter 4 will therefore also return to the themes raised in the Somali popular culture texts presented in Chapter 1.

Chapter 4

The Why and How of Clan Cleansing: Political Objectives and Discursive Means

> What is dearest to us is often dearer than the truth.
> —Anne Michaels, *Fugitive Pieces*

Introduction

The chapters above have traced the changing use of large-scale clan-based violence against civilians as a political tool in the hands of politico-military leaders at three historical moments, namely during the Barre regime, at the moment of its collapse, and during the factional militia warfare in its wake. They have outlined the historical background and contemporary circumstances of what I have called the violence of the key shift, that is to say, a campaign of clan cleansing that turned ordinary civilians, outside any mediating state institutions, into both perpetrators and victims of communal violence. Since this key shift in the Somali civil war is often misrepresented and concealed, Chapter 3 has presented a narrative of some of the events that made up this clan cleansing campaign, especially focusing on its organized nature and its intimate character as communal violence, tracing it (and the other kinds of violence against civilians accompanying it) geographically beyond Mogadishu to other parts of the country and, temporally, from December 1990 to December 1992, the eve of international intervention.

This chapter will examine two important themes underlying that narrative in more detail. First, what political goals did politico-military entrepreneurs expect to achieve with the clan-based violence against civilians they organized and allowed, and what outcomes were they able to realize through it? Second, what propelled the men who were recruited into the militias as well as the ordinary civilians who joined in to participate in the clan cleansing? To answer these questions, this section will sum up and further develop some of the insights that emerged from the second and third chapters to identify what conditions and events primed the situation in Mogadishu and in Somalia as a whole for clan cleansing and what triggers appear to have activated its implementation and thus individual participation in it. The latter cannot be understood without further analysis of the discursive dimension of Somali civil war violence, with which the book opened.

The popular culture texts presented in Chapter 1 mediated civil war violence through a discourse that analyzed and cautioned fellow Somalis against clan thinking and struggled to make the communal violence Somalis had committed against each other speakable in various ways. In this final chapter, I will attempt to do something analogous to the work done by these poetic texts by coming back to the discourse of clan, this time as a discursive tool that provided the rationales for the clan cleansing and helped galvanize the perpetrators. These clan hate-narratives, as I call them, constituted the discursive dimension of the clan cleansing campaign, which itself was an instrument in the struggle different politico-military entrepreneurs waged over the state and what had been national resources. They constituted the discourse that persuaded, indoctrinated, and incited perpetrators to commit violence and the interpretive lenses through which the latter came to understand and justify their actions. Clan hate-narratives, therefore, helped determine the form that the violence took and, as I will argue below, continue to shape the kinds of social and moral "irrepair" that still underlie the politics of the ongoing Somali civil war.[1] In what follows, I first turn to how and with what results the Barre regime and the armed fronts that struggled to displace it used clan-based collective violence against civilians.

The Changing Political Use of Clan-Based Violence Against Civilians

The Politics of Clan-Based Violence Against Civilians During the Barre Era (1969-1991)

According to Compagnon (1995) and Latin and Samatar (1987), Barre was a master in exploiting clan feeling as a political resource and, for a long time, used it to reinforce his monopoly on power. This political practice had direct consequences for the well-being (or lack of such) of clan groups and thus also reinforced such group construction. Barre's manipulation of clan-based violence, however, became a major cause of his own fall from power and the collapse of the Somali state itself. He appears to have targeted civilians in his suppression of the armed opposition fronts for several reasons. First, he used large-scale clan-based violence against civilians to keep the opposition against him divided, as differential victimization strengthened clan-based identities, highlighted differences and inequalities, and gave those who were not targeted the illusion that they would be safe from government harassment. Second, through terrorizing civilians, Barre tried to raise the political and social costs of opposing him so high that the armed fronts and the civilians supporting them might be discouraged from challenging him. Thus, Barre further developed the tried and true colonial policy of "collective clan punishment" by intensifying and magnifying the violence involved.

That the civilians Barre targeted for violence probably, at least in their hearts, supported the armed opposition fronts with which Barre identified them is not in dispute. These fronts had, to a large extent, emerged as the *result* of the clan-based oppression, harassment, and dispossession of these civilians by the government. What made the Barre regime's actions illegal and immoral is that it turned its assumption that civilians sympathized with the armed opposition into a sufficient cause to target them for violence.

In regard to the SSDF, this opposition movement had lost its impetus in the early 1980s; internal dissension among the leadership and conflict with the Ethiopian government landed some leaders in Ethiopian prisons, while many rank-and-file supporters melted away and returned to their families' rural encampments or diaspora domiciles. However, some commanders and crack units reentered Somalia and surrendered to the Barre regime, which welcomed them with lots of fanfare and reincorporated them into the military command structure at the very moment it began to target the civilians suspected of supporting a new enemy, the newly established SNM. By coopting certain elements of the now crippled SSDF and making peace with certain Majeerteen elders and groups precisely at the time that the regime frontally attacked the economic base of the Northwestern region and Isaaq businessmen in the whole country, Barre succeeded in further dividing-and-ruling the opposition. However, this political "accomplishment" was not a direct pay-off of the regime's earlier clan-based attacks on the civilian population of Mudug, which had strengthened rather than weakened the SSDF.[2]

Barre nevertheless used the same policy of massive violence against civilians in response to the establishment (in 1981) of the armed opposition front called the SNM, an offshoot of the SSDF. The front was a response to government oppression in the Northwestern region and its success rose and fell in direct proportion to the increasing or decreasing intensity of government oppression. Before the SNM incursion into the Northwest triggered the government's vastly disproportionate and lethal violence against its own citizens there, the SNM had been a compact, relatively small armed front with relatively well-trained and disciplined fighters. The armed violence against civilians that were part of the government's retaliatory actions of 1988–1989, however, turned the SNM into a people's army, consisting of civilians-turned-fighters whose Isaaq identity had been reinforced because of the suffering bestowed on them in its name. In this case, Barre's policy of involving civilians politically and targeting them for violence not only had politically and morally unacceptable results but also completely backfired. Even though the SNM and the people of the Northwest were defeated and paid a terrible price, the government never reestablished full control over this region before it totally collapsed in January 1991.

The violence that caused civilians to become involved in the SNM's political project was, as was mentioned above, first and foremost government violence. However, the SNM itself too decided to involve civilians in political violence, namely in two ways. First, the SNM leaders did so by moving their fighters inside Somalia and having them fan out and conceal themselves among civilians. This took away any choice or alternative to full-scale war the latter might have favored, as it, predictably, brought the full military power of the state down on them. Whether the SNM commanders chose to involve (and sacrifice) civilians as a purposeful political strategy or whether they blundered into this decision is not clear. However, it is irrefutable that the large-scale clan-based violence against civilians that resulted was *also* an outcome of this SNM strategy—even if nothing can justify or smooth over the disproportionate violence the Barre regime unleashed in response to the SNM incursion. The ruthless armed violence the SNM helped provoke destroyed any possible alternative to its political project and war effort and solidified popular support behind it. Intentional or not, forcibly involving Isaaq civilians in the war with the regime paid off, in a disturbing kind of way, for the hardliners and secessionists of the SNM leadership.

From his vantage point as an Italian diplomat who hoped to reconcile Barre with the opposition, Claudio Pacifico had little sympathy for what he considered hardliners such as the SNM and USC-Caydiid. Even if the suffering of Isaaq civilians did not leave him cold, he wrote in his political memoirs, he had developed bitter feelings toward the SNM leaders, who, in his view, had played "a cynical game with the suffering of their own civilian population" (1996: 290). As we saw in Chapter 2, he believed that, in their eyes, civilian suffering would legitimize their cause and further undermine that of the Barre regime in Western eyes. Moreover, Pacifico suggested, the SNM obtained the full support of the civilian population of the Northwest only after the latter had experienced large-scale violence from the regime—violence that, however disproportionate—the SNM had helped provoke (290–91).

Pacifico may not have been right about the SNM desire to displace traditional elders, for government violence turned them into important conduits between the SNM and the common people. However, that the military strategy of the SNM helped sweep away any alternative to its own aggressive military approach and leadership cannot be refuted.

A second way in which the violence against civilians became part of the SNM political project was that the SNM (like the government, but on a much smaller scale) targeted for violence civilians whose clan backgrounds it associated with the Barre regime. Thus it committed clan-based violence against the diverse inhabitants of the refugee camps in the region (all reductively constructed as Ogaadeen and "from elsewhere"), as well as against numerous other Somalis who held low-level administrative positions in the towns of the Northwest.[3] These were now—selectively, on the basis of their clan—attacked, captured, and at times killed. The SNM did this, moreover, in spite of the fact that the government's bombardments of the towns had not spared these non-Isaaq civilians. The SNM leadership did not speak in one voice about the identity of those they considered the enemy. Its president at the time of the incursion, Axmed M. Maxamuud Silaanyo, who in 2010 became the head of the government of the self-proclaimed Somaliland Republic, in public emphatically identified the enemy as the government, not a clan enemy; others, however, had begun to emphasize the "Daarood nature" of the government, from hindsight clearly an ominous development.[4] For the secessionist project to succeed, the common people of the Northwest had to be forcibly unmixed; "punishing" civilians working for the government on the basis of their Daarood-ness was an important stage and a powerful political tool on the road toward bringing this about. Thus, although the clan-based violence the SNM committed against civilians must be understood against the background of the large-scale suffering of Isaaq civilians at the hands of the government, SNM policies and actions nevertheless represented political decisions and constituted a particular technology of power that part of the leadership and rank and file, like the Barre regime, adopted to forward its political goals.

Even outside the Northwest, the Barre regime continued its policy of using violence against civilians in the hope of terrorizing people into submission.[5] The execution in July 1989 of forty-seven middle-class men from Mogadishu—all Isaaq except for one man *assumed* to be Isaaq—who were abducted from their homes at night and executed close to the capital at Jasiira beach, is evidence of such a policy. Some believed that this was the regime's response to the rumored Isaaq role in the mosque demonstrations that had just taken place, while others saw it as an extension of its war against the SNM in the Northwest. Again others reported that the government's security branches were harassing, arresting, and executing suspected civilian supporters of all three active fronts, the SPM, SNM, and the USC,[6] and that the Jasiira massacre just happened to become public knowledge. However that may be, there is no doubt that Hawiye civilians in- and outside Mogadishu had come to be targets of government violence and that this targeting steadily increased in proportion to the USC political and military successes.

Whether, as Pacifico, Sica, and the Manifesto elders believed, there were indeed doves and hawks among Barre's top circle—those who were ready for meaningful political concession versus those who expected to beat down any opposition with military force—is again not fully clear. Was there ever any real chance that Barre would make meaningful concessions, let alone step down and leave the country before Mogadishu was swept up into war and chaos? From hindsight the answer appears to be negative. Had Barre stepped down, the political transition in Mogadishu might have been very different, as the campaign of clan cleansing might not have occurred in the absence of war, the breakdown of law and order, and the opportunity to loot and kill with impunity. Instead of leaving the capital city and protecting it from war, Barre's commanders instead intensified their clan-based violence against civilian supporters of the USC. As we saw in Chapter 2, the popular uprising that marked the beginning of the Battle for Mogadishu on December 30, 1990, was triggered by the government's brutal house-to-house searches for alleged USC supporters (read Hawiye civilians broadly construed), which involved plunder, rapes, other kinds of abuse, and perhaps executions, of the days before.[7]

The Battle for Mogadishu also marked the beginning of heavy government bombardments of residential neighborhoods, which by early January indeed harbored not only local USC fighters but also armed USC rebels from the countryside. The latter had captured heavy artillery on their way and used it to lay siege to central government strongholds such as Villa Somalia.[8] By then it must have been clear to regime commanders that their policy of targeting civilians had completely backfired and had, as had been the case in the Northwest, only deepened clan sentiment and radicalized USC supporters. These actions, which included attempts to mobilize support for the government through political appeals to *daaroodnimo* (the identity construct of Daarood-identity and solidarity), not only failed to save the regime but helped create the conditions that made the clan cleansing campaign that followed possible.

The Politics of Clan Cleansing During the USC Take-Over

The USC too used large-scale clan-based violence against civilians as an instrument for reaching its political goals. Analytically, however, as we saw before, this violence was different from what went before. The USC began to commit violence along a different axis than the one that had existed before and this violence was no longer delivered to its victims by way of state institutions but now involved civilians as victims *and* perpetrators. In other words, it was *communal* violence that the USC used as a political means toward its goals.[9] Given the sustained nature and geographical scope of the USC clan cleansing campaign, it exceeded in scale the violence inflicted on the Northwest by the Barre regime.

What did USC-Caydiid expect to achieve by adopting clan cleansing as its major political strategy? In the absence of direct testimonies by those who were close to Caydiid, one may deduct the following from USC actions. First of all, mobilizing rural fighters against "*the*" Daarood and promising them the wealth of Mogadishu because it was all "Daarood wealth" was a powerful motivating force and discursive strategy (to be further discussed below) and made the issue of compensating these *mujaahidiin* (as both the SNM and USC termed their fighters) moot. Second, by collapsing the terms of "Barre regime" and "*the*" Daarood into each other, the USC tried to make the participation of non-Daarood political clients and henchmen of the regime magically disappear from view. It made defection to the USC attractive for many members of the government and military, even high-ranking ones, as long as they belonged to the "right" clan. The third and for Caydiid himself probably the more important use of clan cleansing was that eliminating "*the*" Daarood would increase his chances of capturing the heights of the state for himself. The SNM, centered on the Northwest and with a strong secessionist faction, would not be a serious challenge to him in his ambition to take the power in Mogadishu. On the other hand, the top commanders of the SPM, who had defected from the government earlier or at roughly the same time Caydiid did, were serious potential rivals, in spite of the agreement of October 1990. As commanders of a front that was regarded as Daarood-based, they also objected to the USC clan cleansing campaign, which they perhaps did not see coming. Caydiid therefore tried to get rid of the SPM by unexpectedly attacking it from the back and trouncing it militarily only a few days after Mogadishu had been captured. Equally hard to avoid as a stakeholder in the post-Barre political order was the SSDF, which, though militarily severely reduced, could point at a much longer history of opposition to the regime than the USC. Moreover, the civilians making up its clan-base had been severely ill-treated by Barre at a time at which those associated with the USC had been allowed to prosper economically. A policy of clan cleansing against "*the*" Daarood was for men like Caydiid therefore, among other things, a strategy of making room at the top.[10]

However, Caydiid had other competitors as well, as became evident to the world when USC-Mogadishu proclaimed its own candidate for the position of transitional president only two days after Barre's expulsion from the city. In reality, as we saw above, part of the leadership of USC-Mogadishu had hoped to prevent full-scale war from reaching Mogadishu and had attempted to displace Barre politically through compromise. They did not think highly of Caydiid and considered him either insignificant or a threat to their organization. Moreover, it appears that they participated in, and condoned the clan cleansing campaign only when this hope of keeping the war outside the capital had been dashed[11] and when Barre's intransigence and the communal violence unleashed by callous warlords such as "Caato" (Cismaan Xassan Cali), "Qaybdiid" and "Shabeel" (of USC-Caydiid), and Galaal and "Nero" (of USC-Mogadishu) had destroyed any alternative to the option of full-scale war and clan cleansing. The more violence became the only game in the city and the country as a whole, the more indispensable Caydiid became to the USC, and the more real the gulf between "*the*" Hawiye and "*the*" Daarood in the experience of perpetrators and victims alike.

Michael Maren, then journalist for the *Village Voice* and someone who had spent many years as a foreign aid worker in Somalia, wrote about General Caydiid in November 1993, just as the general emerged victorious from the U.S./UN campaign to eliminate him. Maren noted both the centrality of Caydiid's political use of violence and the political quandary in which he found himself as a result of the large-scale violence over which he had presided. "Without violence or the threat of violence, Aidid becomes just one of the 15 faction leaders in Somalia, albeit the one who controls a large part of the capital," Maren wrote. On the one hand, he noted, "Aidid cannot compromise. He has power because he has delivered Mogadishu and its treasures to his people. If any sort of civil order is established in Somalia, his people are going to be asked to give back the loot, the cars, the houses, the farms they have seized. . . ." On the other hand, without compromise, Maren believed, Caydiid could never establish political prominence. For "a large majority of Somalis," Maren wrote, "Aidid is not an acceptable leader. Though he is a hero for ousting Siad Barre, *he will not be forgiven for the 30,000 or so deaths and wanton destruction of Mogadishu that he presided over at the end of 1991*" (Maren 1993: 22; my emphasis). In the context of this study, it is ironic that Maren referred only to the casualties of the war that broke out between Caydiid and Cali Mahdi in November of 1991; in "Darod-rein" Mogadishu, to use poet Togane's sarcastic expression, there may not have been enough people left to tell the story of the clan cleansing campaign over which Caydiid presided in 1991 (Togane 2006).

In her book *New and Old Wars*, especially the chapter called "The Politics of the New Wars," Mary Kaldor develops an argument that is relevant to the Somali civil war. Once one does not base one's political project on an idea or a cause that other people can be persuaded to join but on an identity that excludes others, she writes, then the only way of dealing with such others is to eliminate and expel them (2007: 104). This appears relevant to how Caydiid articulated the USC cause of overthrowing the dictatorship—in theory a cause all Somalis could join—as based in a particular oppositional identity (that of Hawiye-ness), which was moreover structured around active hatred of another particular identity (that of Daarood-ness). Since it was in most cases difficult to hold on to occupied areas inhabited by clan "others," a political project based on an identity rather than a cause made clan cleansing a more probable scenario.

New in the context of the USC's campaign of clan cleansing was the large-scale rape and sexual assault of women.[12] In the cases of former Yugoslavia (especially Bosnia) and Rwanda, where an estimated number of respectively 20,000 and 250,000 women and girls were raped, rape warfare has received considerable scholarly and legal attention (Alison 2007: 85, 87). International law has also defined it with increasing precision. Thus, the Rome Statute of the International Criminal Court, which came into force in 2002, considers it "a war crime and a crime against humanity." In the context of former Yugoslavia, the ICTY has recognized rape as "a distinct war crime," that is to say, a human rights violation committed in the context of war, while in the context of Rwanda, the ICTR has recognized rape as "potentially an act of genocide" (Alison 2007: 82–83). Such definitions are also relevant to the large-scale rape that was part of the clan cleansing in Somalia in 1991, which, although it preceded both Bosnia and Rwanda in time, has remained largely unexamined.[13]

In an article entitled "Rape and Rape Avoidance in Ethno-National Conflicts: Sexual Violence in Liminalized States," Hayden argues that sexual violence committed during war tends to occur when the state is liminal (hardly or nonexistent) and those who incite to or commit the rapes intend to communicate "that life together is finished" (Hayden 2000: 32). Both these conditions existed in 1991 in Somalia. As we saw in Chapter 3, there is evidence that leaders and commanders encouraged and condoned their fighters to rape. Making the latter complicit tied them more irreversibly to these leaders and their political agendas. However, one must still ask, as Benard does in the context of war rape in Bosnia, what caused "the willingness of very large numbers of presumably non-pathological men to use sex as an instrument of terror" (1994: 41). Alison relates large-scale rape during conflict to how national, ethnic, or clan conflicts bring about "drastic changes in the socially acceptable ways of being a man" (2007: 80). She speaks of an "ethnicised wartime construction of masculinity," by which she means that through rape the rapist asserts his dominance both as a man over a woman and as a man of a particular group over the enemy group (80). Thus, in Somalia, by violating women, the rapists destroyed the moral/ideal womanhood of their female victims, humiliated and demoralized the men who were unable to protect them, and asserted the dominance of their clan group over those of their victims.[14] By radically subverting the "cultural scripts" of both Somali custom[15] and Somali nationalism, according to which Somali men were to respect and protect Somali women and girls, the message that "life together is over" was powerfully communicated: "with women's bodies the vehicle of communication, the site of the battle and the conquered territory," as Alison puts it, rape became a powerful tool of creating and making absolute the clan constructs the architects of the clan cleansing intended to produce (81).

The War of the Militias and the Targeting of Civilians (1991-1992)

Maren's reference to the war between USC-Caydiid and USC-Cali Mahdi brings us to the third use of large-scale clan-based violence against civilians analyzed in this study, that inflicted by the factional militias that mushroomed in the immediate wake of the collapse of the state and the USC clan cleansing campaign. On both sides of the new political divide—now lining up "perpetrator clans" against "victim clans" irrespective of the actual acts and experiences of the individuals categorized this way—commanders mobilized clan-based militias against each other. As described in Chapter 3, most of these militias committed violence against civilians as a matter of habit; they had opportunity-with-impunity, were rarely paid or disciplined, and made robbing and otherwise violating civilians their way of life. However, violence against civilians often also had further political and strategic goals and functions, for example, when militias wanted to command the labor, farms, houses, and villages of "others" (as in inter-riverine areas) or eliminate civilian alternatives to warlord domination, as in Kismaayo in December 1992.

Some of this militia warfare represented the extension and continuation of the USC's clan cleansing campaign against Daarood individuals. However, in this stage of the civil war, the clan-based violence inflicted on civilians was part of a chain reaction that had been set into motion at the moment of the key shift. It set into motion a War of the Militias that can be said to continue until today.

That the violent acts visited upon civilians by the militias of all sides constitute war crimes and gross violations of human rights is irrefutable; its perpetrators are therefore no less condemnable and its victims no less deserving of public acknowledgement and social repair and reconstruction than those of the earlier episodes of violence discussed in this book. However, analytically, the violence of this seemingly unending militia warfare (that occurred both across the divide that opened up in 1991 and within each of the opposing groups) represented a tit-for-tat, a reciprocal brutalization of civilians perceived as part of the clan-bases of competing politico-military alliances in the wake of the key shift of 1991.[16] That the civilians of particular communities of victims initially sided with the USC or even participated in the clan cleansing campaign is an aspect that is often concealed by authors advocating for these groups (such as Mukhtar 1992 and Mukhtar and Kusow 1994). Pointing out that this was so does not excuse the injustice that was done to these communities but is a crucial analytical clarification of the different stages and contexts of Somali civil war violence.

Primes, Triggers, and Mythical Hate-Narratives

The Primes for Clan Cleansing

In his discussion of what kinds of circumstances have historically contributed to priming particular situations for genocide, that is to say, preparing the ground for it or intensifying the political volatility that enabled it, Alexander Hinton mentions "socio-economic upheaval, polarized social divisions, structural change, and effective ideological manipulation" (2002: 28). While these primes are relevant to Somalia in 1991, the conditions there were so grim that they overflow Hinton's categories and cannot be contained in them. Although the material conditions were laid out in Chapter 2, they deserve to be briefly summarized before we turn to the discursive priming for the clan cleansing campaign. In Somalia, economic collapse and the disintegration of state institutions went hand in hand. The role played in this by the regime's top administrative and military echelons, and increasingly, Barre's closest family, was blatantly illegal, immoral, and expressive of enormous contempt for the common people. The latter, meanwhile, grew more and more impoverished, whether they were residents of the ever-growing urban shanty-towns; middle-class professionals whose salaries could not even cover the gas for their cars, or farmers displaced by huge development projects that provided kickbacks to the top state elite and intensified competition for resources among nomads. All these conditions were exacerbated by the political injustice, corruption, and violent greed of the regime.

The outbreak of a full-blown war between the government and its people came on top of all this.[17] As law and order broke down in large parts of the country, the government retained and used its capacity to inflict political violence of unprecedented magnitude. Aiming to secure its absolute monopoly on power and suppress any opposition, it targeted people differentially on the basis of clan. This kind of political violence, which wrought enormous suffering and destruction, hardened clan identities and aggravated clan sentiments. Meanwhile, in the absence of freedom of the press, speech, assembly, and so forth, and with many of the educated driven into exile and educational institutions atrophying, any public civilian engagement of these looming problems inside the country was impossible.

The war in the Northwest had destroyed a whole region of the country, where in the aftermath any political and economic activities ceased except for the movements of the SNM fighters besieging the government troops in the towns and the latter's attempts at retaliation. From 1989 onward, there were armed rebellions and government counterattacks in central and south-central Somalia as well, with two armed fronts marching on the capital. By this time all armed fronts were clan-based, that is to say, recruited their fighters and commanders from a particular clan. And in at least two of the three fronts, the political "philosophy" used to fire up and motivate the fighters took the form of clan hate-narratives (to be discussed below). For ordinary Somalis, war and the threat of war constituted an important dimension of the situation. Moreover, as the fall of the regime began to loom, political and military competition and confusion escalated.

The situation in Somalia was clearly primed for further violence and was especially volatile in Mogadishu. There the primes for clan cleansing included a context of full-scale urban warfare and the omnipresence of different armed groups who were fighting on different sides of the conflict. The government's violent suppression of the opposition and the increasingly bold acts of disruption and destruction by the USC put an end to any semblance of law and order and simultaneously terrified and emboldened the opposition. Not only was there a very high level of violence, but also, at least until Barre had been expelled, great confusion, which in itself increased lawlessness. As the new axis of conflict—now articulated in terms of opposing clans, not of government and opposition—slid into place, different groups of people became aware of this (and began to act upon this awareness) at different times.

Some government soldiers were still fighting for the government. Others, however, made use of the opportunity to become USC *mujaahidiin*. While some government soldiers sold their uniforms and tried to blend in with the crowd, USC fighters at times donned Red Beret government uniforms and set out to attack government buildings in captured army jeeps. Other gangs, meanwhile, were operating purely for their own benefit. It was not always clear who was fighting whom and what the meaning and objectives of the violence that was being committed were at any point in time. In this murky situation, it has been said, influential individuals on different sides of the conflict purposefully fanned clan sentiments by sending out hit squads that misled their surviving victims about the clan background of the perpetrators.[18] Similarly, acts of violence by one side were sometimes publicized via *radio trottoir* as perpetrated by the other. In his memoirs, Italian diplomat Pacifico gave an example, blaming USC-Caydiid.[19]

> Thanks to a typical action of disinformation the Somali way, promoted probably by the guerrillas of Aidid, many were convinced that the authors of these kinds of violence were the Red Berets and other government soldiers who were trying to supplement their salaries with this uncommon kind of "second job." But the truth was different. Although the Red Berets were extremely capable of going out to plunder, kill and rape (and perhaps in a number of cases actually did so), the ones truly responsible for the climate of terror into which Mogadishu had been plunged were the bands of bandits recruited by Aidid who had infiltrated the capital and fought their war of liberation against the "bloody dictator," while plundering and killing the poor. (1996: 360–61)

Similar accusations have been levied against the Barre regime (Interviews 2 and 9). One survivor, a Manifesto elder, initially did not believe the news about anti-Daarood violence, as he was convinced this was another desperate strategy by the Barre regime to bring political opponents of Daarood clan backgrounds to its side (Interview 9).

Such actions and rumors of such actions helped prime the city for the communal violence that ensued and may even have served as triggers that propelled individuals into violence. Though they cannot be easily verified, their existence points to a complex web of meaning—a discourse or set of discourses—that constituted a crucial dimension of the priming for clan cleansing in Somalia in 1991. Analyzing the clan discourse that mediated the participation of fighters and civilians in this violence is the charge of what follows.

Mythical Group Hate-Narratives and Ethnic Cleansing

The concept of mythical group hate-narrative, developed by Ben Lieberman in his work on the nationalities (or ethnic groups) of former Yugoslavia, points at the transformation of existing stories about groups into rationales and justifications of group violence. Lieberman is interested in the role "national hate narratives" played in turning ordinary neighbors and friends into killers. Such narratives or discourses provide what he calls "cognitive frames," "a mental structure which situates and connects events, people and groups into meaningful narrative."[20] He identifies three characteristics of such mythical group hate-narratives. First, this group hate-narrative is a story in which the group is represented as *the* relevant unit of analysis, as having a discrete, "containerized" identity, which is characterized by its having been uniquely victimized by other, similar groups, which are therefore enemy groups. In the following quote, I have replaced Lieberman's references to "nationalism" with "*clannism*" and his mentions of "nation" and "national" with "*clan*":

> As an ideology of ethnic cleansing, *clannism* is more a story than simply a form of identity. Within *clan* narratives, the *clan* as an entity is viewed as the real protagonist. *Clan* narratives tend to be similar in their structures, in that they are compartmentalized; they present their hero, the *clan*, as unique in suffering; and they depict the *clan* narratives of rival *clans* as illegitimate. (2006: 299–300)

In his "Towards a Vocabulary of Massacre and Genocide," Semelin too comments on the relationship between such narrative production or story-telling and the "identitarian process" that is inherent in it. The story constitutes a way of constructing the in-group in terms of a moral sameness, while the out-group is depicted as an equally monolithic but evil threat (2003: 197). Semelin argues that

> The discourse of the other to be destroyed feeds upon a rhetoric of the threat that he represents. . . . Such a process is above all imaginary: "as they want to kill us, we must kill them first, as quickly as possible." . . . In sum, it is in the name of a vision of a collective self to be constructed and defended that massacre is perpetrated, on the basis of resentment, fear or revenge.

A second characteristic of such mythical hate-narratives, Lieberman argues, is their relationship to time, as they use the mythical long-term history of the group, a history that is constructed as at the core of this group's identity, to overwhelm that other time, that of everyday life, which neighbors, friends, classmates, colleagues at work, and so forth, had more or less peacefully shared irrespective of their group identities. Thus he writes:

> The stories of personal connections stress activities of the *quotidien*, of everyday life—eating, dating, playing sports, attending school— that take place in a chronology that can be described as every day time. Stories of ethnic hatred, in contrast, rely on a sense of the *longue durée*, though this may be very much imagined. (2006: 300)

It is by collapsing into each other the time of the mythical past of the group's unique, formative, and long-term grievances and the time of the everyday, that is to say, by collapsing "[h]istorical time and every day time, or past and present," Lieberman argues, that "the individual neighbour, classmate, teammate or acquaintance, becomes a member of an inherently evil group that deserves destruction. . . . With the fusion of historical and every day time, stealing, arson, and murder—all crimes in everyday life—can now be seen as righteous combat against an enemy nation" (300).

The third characteristic of such mythical hate-narratives, Lieberman points out, is that they tend to have two central themes: "themes of betrayal and victimization," and "economic and political resentments" (300). In the context of the hate-narrative, such grievances, which are presented as at the deepest and most sacred core of the group's history, can be resolved and compensated for in only one way: by attacking and exterminating the group enemy from its midst. Mythical hate-narratives claim that a group's deepest essence lies in grievances of the past; that this past has a mythical meaning and is, therefore, more significant than group members' everyday relationships in the present, and, finally, that other groups, defined in relationship to these grievances of the in-group, must be eliminated for those grievances to be redressed and for the in-group to obtain its rightful place.

The history or histories on which such hate-narratives draw are—and perhaps must be for them to do their work of generating hatred—a very complex phenomenon whose precise contexts and authorship remain obscure. A residue from older discourses and political "spin," drawing on fact and fiction to mediate historical experience, they are not only the political hate propaganda of the moment but also, as Lieberman (2006: 301) puts it, "stories told and retold within communities" and, in the words of Semelin (2003: 196), the "tales, rumours and memories of a culture." This is part of the mythical character and gives them their power. Mythical group hate-narratives do something unique with such "tales, rumours, and memories," for, as Hinton puts, it, they dress such "pre-existing cultural knowledge" up "in new ideological guises that maintain familiar and compelling resonances while legitimating new structures of domination and violence against victim groups" (2004: 11). It is usually impossible to attribute such older stories that "lie around" in a society and to which such mythical group hate-narratives give new meaning and urgency to particular authors. However, the responsibility for activating and transforming them at the moment communal violence breaks out lies with specific actors. Genocide scholars have noted a connection between the activation of group hate-narratives in situations primed for violence and the role of propaganda and the rhetoric of violence in the public sphere.[21]

In former Yugoslavia, a "rhetoric of exclusion" or "othering" became especially powerful when authority figures began to use it in the public sphere and combined it with the mongering of fear: "you will be duped if you do not act now" (Semelin 2003: 195–96; also Hinton 2002: 22). Directing violent comments against a publicly identified enemy can be a powerful prime for violence. It can serve, in the words of Semelin, as "a way of legitimating in advance the unleashing of an increasingly radical physical violence against this 'enemy.' . . . It creates de facto a climate of impunity and, as a consequence, an incitement to murder" (2003: 199). When journalists, scholars, artists, and religious leaders contribute to the normalization of such violent references to the "enemy," Semelin argues, this kind of "public declarations provide those who shall be involved in the massacres, in advance, with frameworks of interpretation and legitimization of their actions." All this is relevant to the Somali case.

In themselves, such public references to hate-narratives, which are often couched in euphemistic terms or thinly veiled code words for the "enemy," may not *cause* violence but they contribute, as Semelin puts it, to "the creation of a sort of semantic matrix that gives meaning to the increased force of a dynamic of violence that then works as a 'launching pad' for massacre."[22] In other words, they become part of what either primes a situation for violence against a particular out-group or, when the prime is already hot, may trigger such violence.

Clan Hate-Narratives and Clan Cleansing in Somalia

The concept of mythical hate-narrative is also a useful tool in analyzing and contextualizing the clan cleansing that occurred in Somalia. The embrace of clan as the relevant unit of analysis, of particular sets of grievances as at the heart of clan identity and the future well-being of the group, and the resulting urgent need to treat the friends, neighbors, and (nonpatrilineal) relatives of everyday life as the clan enemy that must be eliminated also marked the cognitive frame of clan cleansers in Somalia. However, this narrative did not consist of one monolithic story; it represented an absolute and monolithic conclusion drawn at this particular juncture of history from a multitude of clan stories and hate-narratives that were already available. Into these narratives were now rolled a vast array of grievances that were interpreted in terms of clan and seen as caused by factors to which clan was fundamental. The mythical hate-narrative became the master file into which were now uploaded grievances that were real and imagined, past and present, collective and individual, local/regional and national, as well as socioeconomic, ecological, and political. The cognitive frame—the dominant discourse—that ordered and provided a unified meaning to all these tensions, conflicts, grievances, and ambitions became that of the clan logic. It provided the blueprint for how the essence of clan identity could be asserted—must be asserted at this ostensibly crucial point in history—through violence.

The clan logic gained its strength from the intersection of three historical and contemporary realities. First, it fed on the political power of earlier interpretations of clan-based grievances and grudges of the past; in other words, it absorbed and gave new direction to the outcomes of earlier uses of clan and clan-based violence as a political instrument. Second, this discourse was now hitched to the political projects of political and military leaders who believed that clan cleansing could help them achieve their goals or was even indispensable to such an outcome. And third, the clan hate-narratives became a frame within which people of all kinds could fit their anger and pain about their political and socioeconomic plights. Grievances that derived from private and public, personal and professional, socioeconomic and political, and local and regional conflicts and inequalities now came to be interpreted in terms of mythical clan hate-narratives. Seen as expressions of the timeless essence of the identity and predicament of the group and rolled into a clan logic that saw the elimination of the clan enemy as the only assured remedy for such grievances, this clan discourse became a trigger for clan cleansing.

At the time of the clan cleansing campaign, such clan hate-narratives, much like the *guubaabo qabiil* discussed in the first chapter, circulated freely in private or semipublic spaces among people who shared the identities they reinforced and transformed. However, they also directly or indirectly entered the public sphere in Somalia in public speeches by politico-military leaders, in publicly performed or broadcast songs, and otherwise. They had three recurring themes. First, they equated those targeted for clan cleansing with the Barre regime irrespective of actual individual or group involvement with the political crimes of the regime. Second, they presented those targeted as allochthonous, that is to say as outsiders with no rights to reside any longer in the capital or other regions of central and south Somalia that were not regarded as the "original" homelands of their ancestors. Third, they were associated with the concept of "one hundred years of Daarood domination," which allegedly extended from the late precolonial period all the way to the end of the Barre regime. In the context of late 1990 and early 1991, these narratives came to constitute the clan logic and formed the rationales and triggers for clan cleansing.

The equation of the enemy to be cleansed with the Barre regime took a number of forms and included the use of code words to refer to that enemy. USC leaders and spokesmen tried to conceal the clan cleansing, as we saw above, even as it was unfolding around them. Thus, in their broadcasts on Radio Mogadishu, spokesmen for Cali Mahdi categorically denied the reports of Daarood being massacred in Mogadishu and elsewhere that began to reach BBC London in February and March 1991. However, they also purposefully used phrases that, while avoiding clan names to refer to the enemy, nevertheless, as code words, communicated and disseminated specific clan meanings into the public sphere.

Two code words infused with violent meaning figured prominently in the public political commentary of this time-period, namely those of "Faqash" and *haraadiga*. "Faqash," as we saw above, is an onomatopoeia describing the sound of someone running away as fast as s/he can. It appears to have originated with the SNM to counter the name-calling by the government, which referred to the armed opposition movements that broadcast through Radio Kulmis (Meeting Point) as Qurmis (Something Rotten). The pejorative name "Faqash" appears to have initially referred to exponents and backers of the government. However, the word "Faqash" was pregnant with the discourse that had developed when the SNM had responded to clan-based manipulation and scapegoating by the Barre regime with a clan-based hate-narrative of its own, namely that of MOD.

The political construct of MOD (Mareexaan, Ogaadeen, Dhulbahante) to refer to the Barre government emerged as follows.[23] Three political maneuvers helped shape this construct in the face of divisive and often devastating government clan manipulation. First, by articulating the concept of MOD domination, those who promoted this concept Misrepresented the fact that no clans were truly represented in the government and that Barre thus actively manipulated *perceptions* of such representation, for example, by attaching real rewards and punishment to his policy of clan division. Second, by Orchestrating the political campaign to make the MOD term stick, they turned the blame for the crimes and failures of the regime to clan "others" constructed in terms of "containerized," easy-to-hate clan identities. In doing so, they Denied and thus sidestepped any responsibility for the power they themselves—literally the very men who would ascend over time to the heights of SNM leadership—had exercised in the Barre regime as well as the civilian administrations before it.[24] Although the state under Barre must bear primary responsibility for continuing to turn political conflict into clan conflict, the SNM's embrace of a clan construct (MOD) to refer to the military government meant adopting this same framework. It went on to reduce Barre's complex, ever-changing, clan-manipulated network of political clients to the simplistic clan-based adjective of Daarood. It was by portraying the Barre dictatorship as a Daarood dictatorship that in 1990–1991 the word "Faqash" could become a code word for "the Daarood-enemy-to-be-exterminated-and-expelled." Behind this seemingly nonclan-specific term of "Faqash," clan cleansing could be concealed in wide-open public view.

The story of the term "Faqash" shows how the phrase gained its political power from its ability to help an opposition front rally popular support against an oppressive regime. In the context of a state that committed violence against subjects differentially on the basis of clan and an opposition front that included advocates of secession on the basis of clan, the conflict between the Barre regime and the SNM took on, that is to say, came to be experienced and articulated in clan terms. This contradictory mixture of lived experience and analytical and political misrepresentation and indoctrination boosted the term "Faqash" with a clan-specific meaning (i.e., the constructs of MOD and Daarood domination). This is how, in the particular circumstances of 1990–1991, it could and did become a prime and a launching pad for the clan cleansing of Daarood.

Canadian-Somali poet Mohamud Siyad Togane, quoted previously, is a merciless diagnostician of the virulent presence of clan hate-narratives in the

Somali body politic. One way of interpreting Togane's poetry is that the cure it proposes is to give Somalis "more of the same" in such undiluted doses that it will either cure or kill the patient. If one adopts the language of the clan hate-narratives, Togane suggests, then one must accept that the military dictatorship was indeed, as he puts it, a "Darod dictatorship" and a "Darod MOD tyranny & terror," and that, therefore, the "Hutu Hawiye holocaust" that followed was a (clan-)logical outcome and fully deserved (Togane 2003a). In other words, if one allows clan hate-narratives to stand in for analysis; if one accepts them emotionally or intellectually, one must admit that one embraces and justifies the destructive logic of clan cleansing. Refusing to take the former (namely, the regime's Daarood-ness) for granted, as this study does, does not in any way exculpate the Barre regime or underestimate its role in producing the other (namely, clan cleansing in the name of Hawiye-ness). However, this analysis insists that the opposition to Barre failed to oppose the categories of identity the regime, to protect its hold on power, violently reinforced. Instead, to assure their own hold on power, opposition leaders (especially those of the SNM and USC) embraced those categories and took clan-based violence, through the key shift, to the level of unmediated communal violence perpetrated by civilians against civilians.

Like "Faqash," *haraadiga* or *haraadiga Siyaad*, meaning "the remnants" or "the remnants of Siyaad's regime" also became a code word for those who were to be clan cleansed, especially used by the USC leadership. As we saw above, there were indeed remnants of the regime among those indicated by this name, including, up to May 1992, to mention the obvious, Barre himself. However, as a code word for *"the"* Daarood enemy this term concealed the evident fact that those who leveraged it politically had themselves been part of Barre's regime either until very recently or even up to the very moment of Barre's expulsion.[25] Using this term, leaders such as Cali Mahdi on Radio Mogadishu, Caydiid in public speeches, or SNM radio spokesman Yuusuf Sheekh Cali Madar,[26] could address the need to defeat and kill the enemy without attracting any opprobrium. Author Daahir Cali Cumar, who experienced the clan cleansing campaign in Kismaayo, reported on how it dawned on him only gradually that the phrase *haraadiga* did not just refer to what remained of the regime around the person of Barre, residing in the Gedo region. He writes, "The Daarood gave me a different explanation, namely that the USC, SNM, and their non-Daarood associates used that word to refer to people of Daarood descent" (1997: 206–7). Those targeted for clan cleansing as "remnants" or "remnants of Siyaad" understood the repeated public USC and SNM protestations that they would exterminate the remnants of the government that had been overthrown as public declarations that those among them who had survived the initial massacres in Mogadishu were fair game.

A second powerful theme of the clan hate-narratives of this period consisted of assertions by those who claimed to be native (autochthonous) to Mogadishu and its environs that *"the"* Daarood were allochthonous, foreign, from elsewhere, and thus an illegitimate presence on "their" land. Some of the people (especially Abgaal Hawiye) who had lived in and near Mogadishu before it became the capital of first Italian Somaliland and then the independent Republic of Somalia resented the presence of other Somalis who had migrated to the city in this period and some of whom, it is widely reported, often either took the local people who provisioned the city completely for granted or showed them disrespect. Even though these newcomers hailed from many different regions and clan backgrounds, at least some local eyes saw them as Daarood. The context of this migration of Somalis from the rural areas and the attitudes of those migrants who became commercially or politically successful deserves further study. The resentment may well have been based, at least in part, on fact. However, irrespective of fact or fiction, it is an example of a cultural narrative, a political commentary, and interpretation dating from an earlier era, that was available for absorption and transformation into something of a very different order, namely a mythical clan hate-narrative that made clan cleansing into a sacred group duty. As scholars such as Ceuppens and Geschiere have pointed out, accusations of allochthony to delegitimize particular groups or individuals—a common phenomenon in African politics in the last decades—often have less to do with the past than with making claims on the present (Ceuppens and Geschiere 2005). In the Somalia of 1990–1991, past and present were connected in such a way that past grievances became an imperative for the clan cleansing killing of tens of thousands of people in the present.

In 1990–1991, the old idea that *"the"* Daarood were outsiders and not fellow-Somalis residing in their country's capital and regional towns was combined with a more militant notion that was popularized in the public sphere by the famous Somali female singer of the nationalist era, Xaliima Khaliif "Magool." Putting her talent and popularity in the service of General Caydiid and the USC, "Magool" sang a war song that had once helped raise nationalist sentiment against Ethiopia in the 1977–1978 war, but now came to serve as an incitement to violence against the allochthonous insider, *"the"* Daarood. Its refrain said, as we saw in Chapter 1: "Death will befall him who has moved here from elsewhere . . . Does the land not belong to me? Chase them out, chase them out! God is Great!"[27] In the mindset promoted by propaganda such as this song, "*the*" Daarood were no longer fellow Somalis living and working within their country's national territory, but, like the Ethiopians in 1978, foreign occupiers whose defeat and removal was a moral and patriotic duty. What could illustrate the discursive shift from nationalist discourse to clan logic more powerfully than this casting of fellow Somali nationals as foreign occupiers? [28] At the hour of clan cleansing, clan hate-narratives became crystallized into this kind of public speech that directed popular feeling toward a particular goal: "We will drive them to the barbed wire (of the international boundary)"—*siliggaan geynaynaa*—as another song line put it.

In a poem that deals with the events of 1991 cited in Chapter 1, Mohamud Togane illustrates the viciousness and power of a clan hate-narrative that combines the ideas of "Daarood dictatorship" and allochthony, the concept of being non-native, not belonging. The Daarood were told to "move away from my country," he writes, and he goes on to describe in some detail how they left when they were expelled in 1991. The masses who fled on foot or somehow managed to find (and afford) transport by truck, car, or small boat hardly figure in Togane's description. Instead he invokes only the most hated henchmen and powerbrokers of the fallen Barre regime's top echelons: "Some fled by tanks! Some fled by Russian Migs! . . . Some fled by land cruisers." "On the beaches of Mombasa," the poet adds—implying and driving home the point that those fleeing were all beneficiaries of the regime—"their Darod dead bodies washed laden with American dollars!" (Togane 2003a). Once the USC clan hate-narratives had constructed all individuals who fitted into the genealogical construct of "*the*" Daarood as one monolithic group, namely as top perpetrators and beneficiaries of the Barre regime who, as foreigners, had no right to live and work where they did (or perhaps even to be alive), the rationale and justification for the acts that drove them to their deaths was in place. Why should USC supporters not gloat about the fates of their victims?[29]

A third influential strand of the clan hate-narratives that helped prime for clan cleansing consisted of the theme of "one hundred years of Daarood domination." This concept refers implicitly and explicitly to a historical narrative that includes (1) the establishment in the early 1980s of the fledgeling Majeerteen sultanate of Hoobyo, and thus the establishment of a small new ruling elite in what was at least in part considered Hawiye territory;[30] (2) the establishment in the southern coastal city of Kismaayo at about that time of what would become a Harti middle class of traders from the Northeast, which led to competition over resources and access to the sea between them and certain groups of nomadic livestock herders;[31] (3) the anticolonial jihad of Sayyid Maxamed Cabdille Xassan (1899–1921), which became further politicized after the fact because it became so central to the Barre regime's self-promoting nationalist interpretations of the past;[32] (4) the evolution of the Somali Youth League (SYL), the political party that played a dominant role in the movement for (and transition to) political independence; (5) the fact that the SYL, in spite of its opposition to Italy and because of its overwhelming popularity among Somalis, eventually won the political support of the departing Italian Trusteeship authorities at the expense of those who had been pro-Italian before (Mukhtar 1989: 80–81); (6) the constitution of the top leadership of the first independent Somali administrations of the civilian era (1960–1969), as well as the Barre regime,[33] and so forth.

In his book *Qaran dumay*, Daahir Cali Cumar comments on how "one hundred years of Daarood domination" became a powerful tool to spur USC fighters on to clan cleansing. These fighters, he writes, who were often either young men from the countryside (both farmers and herders) or unemployed urban youth (*dibjir*), all born since independence, were made to believe:

> that M.S. Barre and the Daarood people from whom he was born had oppressed their grandfathers, their fathers and them for at least 100 years; that they needed to take revenge in a self-sacrificing, courageous and dedicated way (mintidnimo) and to take back the wealth they had robbed from us and that is on display in the towns. They believed this, for I heard from very many Hawiye men: "The Daarood oppressed us for 100 years, so they should put up with what has happened to them." (1997: 131)

Historical grievances such as these are not devoid of significance and they deserve further study. Some studies—such as Hussein Bulhan's *Politics of Cain: One Hundred Years of Crises in Somali Politics and Society* (2008)—note the reference to "one hundred years"—dedicate themselves to explaining and justifying the political secession of the self-proclaimed Republic of Somaliland in the Northwest as well as the clan cleansing of 1991 by documenting "Daarood political dominance." They do this by counting top political positions in the various Somali administrations between 1955 and 1991 and proving that "*the*" Daarood were strongly overrepresented.[34] Such data are potentially very meaningful. However, unless accompanied by an analysis of important contextual factors, they are also simply political propaganda. For example, in the absence of any analysis of the actual significance and precise meaning of the clan background of political officials, such numerical data remain mute. To establish (rather than insinuate) the meaning of such data, a number of questions would need to be answered.[35]

First, one must empirically establish what kinds of tangible political or other benefits the holding of a political position bestowed upon the civilians of the groups that shared a clan background with such high officials. Such benefits undoubtedly existed, but most assuredly did not reach such groups as a whole. Second, one must establish to what extent the clan categories in whose name Barre, the SNM, the USC, and other clan-based militias from 1978 onward perpetrated large-scale violence had the same meaning in the period preceding such violence.[36] Third, was it *clans* that were represented in Barre's military and violently oppressive regime rather than *political clients* whose clan backgrounds the Barre regime manipulated? Were these political clients not temporary recipients of Barre's unpredictable political and economic patronage, the fruits of which they shared with a few other clients from their own clans as well as other groups? Did Barre not play a complex and eventually deadly game that involved (even if in unequal proportions) individuals of practically all clan backgrounds? If this included, especially in the mid- and later 1980s an active political manipulation of Daarood identity with real political consequences (which it did), how about the similarly manipulative favoring of Hawiye identity, with similarly real, especially economic benefits? And is it not equally imperative to study the involvement in this clan-manipulated system of political patronage of those very individuals who after 1991 came to hold the top positions of the self-proclaimed Republic of Somaliland without ever coming clean about their roles (and benefits) as Barre clients or ever questioning the clan hate-narratives they used to justify political secession?

The disentanglement of the fact and fiction on which mythical clan hate-narratives draw is, where a source base of written and oral documentation can be accessed or gathered in a systematic, scholarly way, a significant historical project. Trying to get to the bottom of what kind of political resource, strategy, and power Daarood identity represented under the Barre regime should be part of such a challenging historical project. However, basing one's proof for "one hundred years of Daarood domination" on a count of the clan backgrounds of top officials without pursuing these contexts, as Bulhan does, means using the same cognitive lens and adopting the same discourse that produced clan cleansing. This represents either faulty scholarly analysis or dishonest political entrepreneurship masquerading as scholarship.

The challenge of analyzing such historical phenomena and the clan narratives that draw on them is that one must, on the one hand, take them seriously (for they were and are a real political force) and on the other hand, reject them and refuse to take for granted the categories of group identity and the discourses that underlie and shape them. If one sidesteps such analysis and simply adopts the clan logic, as Bulhan does, then there is no need for empirical studies of the clan-manipulative divide-and-rule policies of the Barre regime or the agency and responsibility of the architects of the clan cleansing of 1991. Without such an analysis, moreover, the clan cleansing campaign and its relationship to the political project of the secession of the Northwest can both simply masquerade as the natural, inevitable, even legitimate results of "one hundred years of Daarood domination." We will come back to the mythical clan hate-narratives as obstacles to peace and postconflict reconstruction below.

In January 1991, these stories about real and imaginary grievances were spun into a mythical narrative that claimed to express a timeless truth about "*the*" Hawiye's deepest essence, namely that "we" have always been dominated by "them" and that the time to remedy this is to get rid of "them" now. It is in the context of this clan hate-narrative of "Daarood dominance" that the rare televised moment at which General Caydiid of the USC dropped his façade of being a nationalist statesman and let down his guard is so significant.[37] When he, publicly and on camera, snapped to the journalists who walked alongside of him in Afgooye in February 1991 that "the Daarood have become arrogant; they must be whipped," his remark reverberated with that notion of "Daarood domination."[38] Of course, hate-narratives do not have to be consistent or logical to be powerful. This is evident from another of Caydiid's stock-in-trade remarks of this period: that the Daarood were just 5 or 7 percent of the Somali population, that is to say, a minority that could be easily removed (Interviews 2, 3, and 4).

Two small anecdotes provide a glimpse of how the hate-narrative of "Daarood domination" was politically deployed. The first example of the political use of this particular thematic (that of "Daarood domination') comes from the Somali diaspora in the period 1989–1990. It illustrates a particular political strategy pursued at this time by the SNM, which, after the initial military defeat of 1988, was doing everything it could to extend the war against the regime to the rest of the country. At this moment there were many people who still hoped to protect Mogadishu from the fate that had befallen Hargeisa, which had been purposefully and totally destroyed by Barre's military. Overcoming this reluctance to take the war into Mogadishu thus became a political goal of the SNM. SNM speeches to Somalis residing in the Washington, D.C., area in this period were highly inflammatory. Playing on the notion of "Daarood dominance" and naming its flip-side, "Hawiye passive submission" to such domination, they compared those who opposed the wisdom of mounting an armed challenge to the dictator inside the capital with "animals that needed to be spurred to action"; those who were not armed at the hour of regime collapse, they warned, would not share in the new political arrangements.[39]

A second anecdote of a real-life incident, part of a wider genre of bitter, sarcastic stories told by survivors, is an eyewitness account that comments on the unexpected consequences of the hate-narrative about Daarood domination. It shows how effectively some USC's rural fighters had been indoctrinated with the idea that the Daarood had dominated the state and that all wealth was therefore "Daarood wealth." A particular Manifesto elder had managed to stay on in Mogadishu until after the clan cleansing had spent its greatest force. He related the following ironic incident. He and some acquaintances were sitting outside, in the shade of a building, when they saw a heavyset man coming in their direction. He was on foot and was huffing and puffing in the heat. They knew him and, when he came closer, asked him, "Why don't you use one of our cars?" referring to the property taken from them during the clan cleansing. The man complained about the unavailability of good-quality petrol and went on to give details about his destination. He was going to oversee the repair work on a building he owned, he explained. As he had been inspecting this building earlier, a USC gunman had come to threaten him. When he explained who he was—of the same clan as the gunman—the latter was stunned. He had been convinced that all nice buildings of the city were Daarood-owned and expressed regret about having participated in damaging the building now being repaired (Interview 4). Stories in this genre of tragicomedy abound.

Multiple Motives and Meanings

The complex intertwinement of grievous experience and the different layers of political interpretation and manipulation of such experience that underlie the historical development of clan hate-narratives are very difficult to disentangle. However, recent anthropological scholarship on Somalia offers insight into some of the material contexts that clan hate-narratives did not explicitly engage but that nevertheless shaped the specific forms clan-based violence took.

Among the reasons why clan hate-narratives could become so virulent, it was suggested above, was that they, like blood-sucking ticks, fed on the discontent and suffering produced by a range of contemporary conflicts, competition, and inequalities. The strong sentiments to which such discontent gave rise attached themselves to, and suffused the various meanings that clan took on at the moment of the clan cleansing campaign. Chapter 2 provided an analysis of such a material (economic) context at the level of the state. However, it is important to realize that different contexts gave rise to different primes for clan cleansing and produced different meanings and motives for the many small and large acts and episodes of violence that cumulatively produced it.[40] This study cannot provide a comprehensive reconstruction of such different contexts. Instead it will illustrate this point with four brief examples in which socioeconomic exclusion and decline or complex and multifaceted conflict over socioeconomic resources provided fertile ground for clan-based violence and the clan hate-narratives mediating it. These examples refer, on the one hand, to Somalia's urban and rural underclass, as well as its urban middle class of low-ranking government officials and professionals; and, on the other hand, to a particular regional context, that of Kismaayo.

Especially vulnerable to clan hate-narratives was Mogadishu's large urban underclass, especially its youth, whose conditions form an important dimension of the context that made violence possible, as is evident from their prominence among the perpetrators. Without access to proper schooling or work; often not part of stable families, as fathers might be migrant workers abroad with marriages breaking down as a result; often, moreover, forcibly recruited into the national army and without the resources to buy themselves out like richer youth; living in the poorest shanty-towns of the city but aware of the riches of other, luckier inhabitants; deprived of the economic capacity to get married, and without a cause in which to believe, members of this poor urban youth physically committed much of the violence and provided (and still provide) a bottomless source of gunmen and fighters (Mohamed-Abdi 2001; Marchal 1993; Bridges 2000: 183). The urban class divide was, therefore, an important dimension of the context for the violence of 1991 and after.

The same was true for many rural youth, who had been rallied to the cause in part with promises of access to the luxuries and fleshpots of the city. Together with their urban counterparts, these young men became the notorious

Mooryaan and Jirris of the civil war, easily attracted to violent political causes but not so easily disciplined. The fury of some of the rural gunmen when they first descended upon Mogadishu is very present in the memory of those who experienced it. One such person noted that the first wave of rural gunmen who attacked the houses of her neighborhood did not loot appliances or window frames in order to sell them—as was soon to become the norm—but just smashed everything. Rural anger at the ever-widening and increasingly visible urban-rural divide appears to have been a factor in shaping the dynamics of violence.[41]

Frustration also marked the lives, especially in the second half of the 1980s, of those middle-class families that were dependent on government salaries (as civil servants, teachers, or technocrats) but were not part of the Barre kleptocracy. These individuals also had a lowered resistance against political hate-narratives. In dire straits, with "salaries" that did not even cover their daily cup of tea and made a joke of their professional competence and aspirations, they were also barred from initiating any political, economic, or social change. Members of this socioeconomic group are consistently mentioned as those in charge of the practical organization of the clan cleansing campaign against their "enemy" peers, even systematically (by name) hunting the latter down in their homes or other places they frequented. However, middle-class men and women featured equally prominently as rescuers of neighbors, friends, and other individuals they knew personally.

The case of Kismaayo is a specific example of how socioeconomic competition and clan-based violence came to constitute each other.[42] The two factors provided "the axes of discontent," as Little puts it in his excellent study on the livestock economy of the Lower Jubba, that warlords could exploit and to which clan hate-narratives could be hitched (1996: 26). The economic picture Little presents about this rich agricultural area is one of increased economic competition between different groups, heightened in the 1980s by international development projects such as the Trans Juba Livestock Project.[43] The politicization and polarization of clan identities increased throughout the Barre era but especially in 1989–1990, when the Ogaadeen-based SPM took a large part of the area out of the control of the government. It became intertwined with the resource competition between the expanding urban middle class of traders (associated with a Harti and, to a lesser extent, Mareexaan clan identity construct), and different groups of Ogaadeen and Mareexaan herders, some of whom, moreover, also coveted Kismaayo as their natural outlet to the sea. No wonder that, in Kismaayo, the genealogical construct of Daarood-ness proved just as unstable a political template as Hawiye-ness in Mogadishu. It was moreover in the hinterland of Kismaayo, as Besteman, Declich, and Menkhaus have described with such passion, that the farming people we now call Somali Bantu suffered abuse and were squeezed off their land in local acts of clan cleansing targeted especially at them.[44]

The specific case of Kismaayo indicates how crucial local and regional contexts are to an understanding of the causes of the violence of state collapse as well as the forms it took. In general, such contexts have either remained largely unstudied and undocumented or have been presented in such incomplete and politically biased ways that they are not as informative as they could be.[45] Further research may throw more light on the different regional contexts of, and primes for clan-based violence.

The Triggers for Clan Cleansing

Apart from the concept of genocidal priming, Hinton also proposes that of genocidal activation as a heuristic tool. The pattern he discerns in comparative studies of genocide is that, even when a situation is "primed" for genocide, the latter does not begin until there is something that activates, sparks, or triggers it (2002: 30). In the Somali case, a detailed analysis of what kinds of factors triggered participation in clan cleansing will have to await comprehensive research into the oral accounts of how different participants in the clan cleansing—its architects, organizers, propagandists, perpetrators, bystanders, and rescuers—became involved in it. However, several triggers stand out and will be discussed in what follows: (1) the imminent fall of the Barre regime, and the perpetrators' sense of "now or never"; (2) the leadership provided by those who took charge of the practical organization of clan cleansing; (3) "horizontal" pressure by peers and the normalizing effect of committing violence in groups, and (4) opportunity-with-impunity, which also encompassed what has been referred to as the "business" dimension of ethnic or clan cleansing.

There is no doubt that at first the imminent fall of the Barre regime and then its actual collapse served as the major trigger for the clan cleansing and other clan-based violence in Mogadishu and its hinterland. It was the expectation of impending regime change that intensified the competition among those who hoped to control post-Barre Somalia, even as the regime hunkered down for its last violent hurrah. The SNM, USC, and SPM had expressed their intention to take over the government before Barre's expulsion. However, immediately after it, USC-Mogadishu claimed the presidency, USC-Caydiid heavily defeated SPM-Jees in a surprise attack, while in the SNM, those who had hoped to run the national government in partnership with the USC (such as Axmed M. Silaanyo)[46] lost out to those who were set on splitting the country and claiming all state power in part of it. Both USC and SNM scenarios were premised on seeing not just the Barre regime but also potential post-Barre competitors in clan terms (as Daarood) and, as a result, on seizing the moment and resorting to clan cleansing to preclude even the possibility of having to share power with other armed fronts or political factions in a unified state. The sense that rooting out "one hundred years of Daarood domination" was a matter of "now or never" appears to have served as an important trigger for the campaign of clan cleansing.

For many participants in the clan cleansing campaign it was its practical organization that triggered their actions, that is to say the directions and orders that emanated from the architects of the clan cleansing campaign as well as its midlevel leaders and organizers. The perpetrators of this campaign were of different kinds and consisted minimally of four groups: (1) the battle-hardened and militarily trained combatants who had either defected to the USC from the Somali National Army or had been recruited from the countryside by USC commanders; (2) the more hastily armed and militarily largely untrained urban and rural men, especially youth; (3) organized or semi-organized gangs of looters who worked for their own account, as described by Marchal (1993), and (4) armed and unarmed neighbors and acquaintances of those targeted. The first two categories of perpetrators appear to have been assisted by junior operators, who either themselves tracked down (or directed other gunmen toward) networks of their own (now "enemy") acquaintances: colleagues from work, neighbors, individuals with whom they had played soccer and attended school or whom they knew because they hailed from the same rural home town or region. The vignettes presented in Chapter 3 contain clear evidence of the organized nature of the clan cleansing: how gunmen were sent out to houses where Daarood families or individuals were known or reported to live, sometimes looking for their victims by name; that some houses were marked with the "D" of Daarood, thus publicly declaring them fair game; that many civilians (men and women) were collected from their houses and brought to USC commanders for further directions as to what needed to be done with them; how those who survived such abductions were keenly aware that they owed their survival to accident and to the perpetrators' desire to maintain deniability; how victims were rounded up in large numbers in the compounds of certain hotels or at traffic circles or checkpoints before they were killed. All these cases point at the organized nature of the violence and the direct or indirect impact of orders issued by men in charge.

There was another activator or trigger at work in Mogadishu that appears to have reinforced the orders and direction that the individuals who physically committed the acts of violence received. This was group pressure, as well as the normalizing impact of the behavior of other members of a group, at the very moment of violent action. Semelin refers to the phenomenon that perpetrators often "in fact cede to group pressure at the very moment of action" as "the horizontal functioning" of perpetrators (2003: 203). In Mogadishu, acts of looting and harming people were indeed often carried out by *groups* of men, especially younger men, and the concept and phenomenon of Mooryaan always refers to the plural, the group. Ceding to group pressure is what propelled Ali, the protagonist of the fictional *In the Name of the Fathers*, to join the fighting. In this story, which the author based on the experiences of his cousin, Ali is just a high-school student without any interest in politics or knowledge of clan constructs. He *becomes* a perpetrator when he joins the crew of a "technical," and the trigger for that decision occurs when he, surrounded by other related men in the family garage in which "technicals" are being outfitted, hears of the deaths "in battle" of his uncles. Even then, Ali is aware that one of his uncles refuses to join and resists the group pressure to which he himself gives in. As both Semelin (2003) and Fletcher, in his article "Becoming Interahamwe" (2007), suggest, many of the common people who participated in the acts making up genocide (or clan cleansing) were not by nature evil perpetrators who now found the opportunity to express their real essence but *became* perpetrators of evil acts when they, in colloquial parlance, got carried away in the context of a group. In other words, the group mediated both the first taking of a life and the habitual killing that followed.[47]

Finally, another trigger that appears to have propelled USC leaders and foot soldiers alike is one that can be termed "opportunity-with-impunity." If, for the leadership, opportunity meant the political opportunity to take control of the government or an area's resources, for common men and women it meant the opportunity to obtain direct material benefit of a smaller order, whether in the form of houses, farms, and cars, or such a simple household item as a *tawa* on which to bake the unleavened flat bread called *canjeelo* or *laxoox*. In the Rwandan context, the economic incentives that sometimes motivated perpetrators are referred to as "genocide business."[48] Clan cleansing too had its "business" dimension and opportunity-with-impunity meant that the perpetrators could expect to benefit from the violence and get away with it. Elders, intellectuals, women—as a category none were innocent. This is how Finnegan, writing for the *New Yorker*, represented the views of informants looking back on the violence of the civil war from the vantage point of 1995:

> The image of wise, community-minded, uncorrupted elders is seductive but ill-founded. Some well-informed (but discreet) observers, including Anogeel, even lay a large portion of the blame for the civil war at the feet of the elders, some of whom have been all too willing to help fill the armed ranks of the warlords with illiterate youths from their rural domains. . . . Like the elders, some intellectuals worked with the warlords . . ., advising them on matters like foreign funding. Not even women had been blameless: They sell their jewelry to buy arms, encourage their defeated fighters by singing, and perform victory screams [ululations] when there is a victory for their tribe. (Finnegan 1995: 69–70, 76)

Under the cover of war; in the shadow of the brutal regime of a Barre who, moreover, turned out not to be quite defeated; with spokesmen and advocates spinning clan hate-narratives on the one hand and preserving deniability on the other, and with waves of new violence rippling back and forth over large parts of the country, the instigators and leaders of the clan cleansing campaign appear to have felt assured of their impunity. They have so far been proven right. For the common male and female perpetrators of clan cleansing it was mostly the enormity of violent events in which they participated that provided impunity. With the victims successfully "cleansed" out of Mogadishu and large parts of south-central Somalia, with fellow perpetrators complicit and equally implicated, and with the attention of the world focused on the latest violence in Somalia and on not the "old news" of yesterday or last month, common participants—fighters and civilians alike—have not only enjoyed impunity but until today proudly honor as heroes those who orchestrated the violence.

Clan Cleansing and the Issue of Intent

What does all this imply for the intentionality of the process that led to clan cleansing and, more precisely, the intention of part of the USC leadership in initiating and overseeing that process? In its definition of genocide, article 2 of the UN Convention on the Prevention and the Repression of the Crime of Genocide, "intent to destroy" the targeted group is a crucial dimension of the violence to be so defined. If proving intent is equally significant to defining violence as ethnic or clan cleansing, then how would one go about establishing such intent and what would be considered sufficient evidence?[49] Scholars of genocide have struggled with this question. On the one hand, as Jacques Semelin argues, the legal focus on an individual's intent that is typical of a criminal court is not suitable (and would be simplistic) for scholarly analyses of the complex political processes that culminate in large-scale massacres (2003: 198). Those processes are more multifaceted and involve much more than individual acts and intentions. Even when individual organizers and perpetrators express their intentions explicitly (which is rare, as those responsible go to great lengths to cover their tracks), such expressions of intent are of limited relevance, Semelin argues, in comparison to the historical and contemporary contexts that make large-scale communal violence possible. Where does this leave scholars of genocide or ethnic and clan cleansing? When authority figures in Somalia made public reference to the mythical clan hate-narratives or used code words to express violent intent toward the targeted groups, is this not relevant to establishing their intent? Basing himself on the wider scholarship about genocide, Semelin discusses the potential value and inherent shortcoming of several approaches that are also relevant to the Somali case (199–200).

The public discourse of hatred by political leaders and other persons with authority is indeed significant, Semelin argues, for it provides the perpetrators with a "semantic matrix" that gives them direction and provides meaning and legitimacy to their actions. However, hate-speech is also just talk and becomes evidence of intent only when it can be connected to other evidence. For example, it can "attest . . . to the will of those who decide to massacre," Semelin argues, when it can be connected to either processes of decision-making (which are, however, often kept secret and thus difficult to discern) or the practical organization of the violence (which, once a general plan has been laid out, is often improvised).[50] This is relevant to the case of Somalia. There the relevance of the government's (or Barre's personal) decision-making processes is not in question for the periods 1978–1979 and 1988–1989, while, in the context of the USC clan cleansing campaign of 1991–1992, survivors' testimonies give ample evidence of its practical organization.

Nevertheless, the legal establishment of intent would require a legally oriented process and the extensive and systematic collection and examination of eyewitness accounts from all sides and different stages of the conflict that lies far beyond the scope and ambition of the analysis presented here. As a work of historical analysis and interpretation, this study offers the following conclusion. First, given the policies and acts of the Barre regime, there is no doubt that it purposefully (through decisions made at the top) set Somalis up against each other and that it used large-scale violence against the civilians of particular clan backgrounds at the same time that it raised to power and wealth individuals of other (or even the same) clan backgrounds. In the years following 1978, it purposefully committed large-scale violence against political opposition fronts and the civilians it associated with them (first, the SSDF, then the SNM, then the fronts that combined to form the SPM and, eventually, the USC). After 1982, in its attempt to hang on to its dictatorial power, it moreover actively promoted the political project and popular conception of Daarood identity and solidarity.[51]

As for the instigators and leaders of the clan cleansing campaign of 1990–1991, given the public statements made during this campaign; aspects of the practical organization of the violence and the acts that constituted it; the chronological order of atrocities committed; the denials and concealment of the clan cleansing campaign afterward; and, finally, its outcome (Mogadishu and large parts of south-central Somalia largely emptied of its Daarood residents), the intent of the leaders and ordinary participants in the clan cleansing of Daarood, however multifaceted and complex, is evident.

Conclusion

This study's heuristic use of recent genocide studies has brought out many analytical similarities between the Somali case and other episodes of large-scale violence against civilians. These include similarities in the wider causal contexts, the immediate triggers for the violence, the ways in which the violence developed and was carried out, and the roles in it of politico-military leaders and common civilians. This summary cannot do justice to the insights developed in the course of the narrative of this book but will list some of them by way of conclusion.

A comparison between the clan cleansing in the Somali case, the ethnic cleansing in former Yugoslavia (1991–1995), and the Rwandan Genocide (1994) shows the relevance of the following background factors. A first commonality is aspects of a colonial legacy that in Somalia did not so much elevate one group over another (as in Rwanda) but, in ways including collective "punishment," turned clan into the only tool of gaining access to the state and of competing with others for that access.[52] A second commonality is an economic context of precipitous decline in which the government played a blatantly unethical role. In Rwanda this decline included the steep decline of coffee prices, the disastrous consequences of the IMF and World Bank Structural Adjustment Plan of 1990, the threat posed by returning refugees to already increasingly scarce land and, to use Newbury's words, "a social polarization between rich and poor, and a strong awareness of increasing marginalization among urban poor and the majority of rural dwellers" (Newbury 1995: 15). Much of this and more (such as regional competition over resources and staggering corruption of the government) was also true for Somalia in 1991.

A third commonality is a context of political instability and the imminence of political transition. The details of this phenomenon differ between Rwanda, where the Habyarimana government was under acute international pressure to share power with the Rwandan Patriotic Front (invading from Uganda) and to hold multiparty elections; Yugoslavia, where the death of a long-term strongman triggered a struggle over the state; and Somalia, where the Barre regime was at its most brutal at the moment it was, in most other ways, at its weakest. In all cases politico-military entrepreneurs planned to use violence to monopolize power for themselves. A fourth commonality is an unresolved history of earlier large-scale violence against civilians on the basis of their group identity. In Burundi and Rwanda (between 1959 and 1991) and Somalia (from 1978 onward), such violence directly involved the state itself as perpetrator. A fifth commonality consists of the political propaganda and group victimization narratives that, once the primes for violence were hot, helped determine the form violence took and channeled economic and political grievances and resentments into perceptions of ethnicity (Rwanda), nationality and religion (former Yugoslavia), and clan (Somalia). These perceptions developed into the full-blown group hate-narratives that provided the rationale for the violence and accelerated its speed and intensity.

In terms of immediate triggers of the episodes of violence, the collapse of the regime and the outbreak of war were crucial to all three contexts compared here (Rwanda, former Yugoslavia, and Somalia). Armed violence and the breakdown of law and order swept away many people's adherence to normative ethical behaviors and cultural scripts. It lowered thresholds for violence for individuals and increased expectations of impunity. In all three cases, the orchestrators of the violence against civilians used it as a conscious political instrument. In the absence of another public agenda than their own group's political dominance, they could envision no role for members defined as "other"; simple logic then demanded their removal. As for the reasons that propelled ordinary civilians to participate in the violence, the Somali case has several factors in common with the other two areas: the adoption of hate-narratives that included the construction of the targeted groups as "foreign" and "from elsewhere"; political uncertainty and the fear that the in-group could obtain its rightful political position only by killing and expelling all individuals making up the out-group; obedience to the authority of clan bosses; peer pressure and pressure to conform and prove oneself to the in-group; being swept up in the moment—becoming clan cleansers not by long-term plan or premeditation but in the process of joining in with others, as Fletcher argues for Rwanda (2007); and opportunity-with-impunity or what Semelin has called, in the context of the Holocaust, "genocide business."[53]

The three areas also show similarities in the ways in which the violence was carried out. First, in all three cases, there is abundant evidence of how the campaigns of violence were actively organized and coordinated; this constitutes a strong indication of the perpetrators' intent. Second, in Somalia, as in former Yugoslavia, the clan/ethnic cleansing was at its most intense in the urban areas, which were the most cosmopolitan and where ethnic/clan backgrounds were not the dominant factor in defining the identities of many ordinary civilians. This was as true for Sarajevo as it was for Mogadishu. Third, in all three cases, the violence was communal, that is to say that ordinary civilians—mobilized, motivated, and organized by politico-military leaders—participated in the work of terrorizing and eliminating other ordinary civilians, often by joining informal or formal militias.

The fourth common factor, which is an aspect of the communal nature of the violence, is that the militarization of masculinity in the context of violent ethnic/clan conflict led to war rape on a large-scale. Part of the mobilization of men for violent ethnic/clan conflict was the transformation of the norms and expectations of moral masculinity (what it takes to be "real men" in a particular context). Men were implicitly invited and explicitly mobilized to commit large-scale war rape and many proved capable and willing to do so. This became a major instrument in the war. It contributed to the physical and psychological destruction of "enemy" women and the humiliation, defeat, and establishment of ethnic/clan domination over "enemy" men. In all cases, the orchestrators and perpetrators of such rapes appear to have communicated the lack of any expectation of future coexistence.

Fifth and finally, in Somalia and Rwanda the victory of "mythical time" over "the time of everyday life" (as explained above) was both powerful and incomplete. The latter meant that those who survived the violence often did so because individuals at that moment categorized as "other group" or perpetrators saved them, sometimes at great risk to themselves. Even so, those who rescued individuals they had personally known often participated simultaneously in genocide or cleansing of "other group" members not personally known to them (Hintjens 2009: 85).

Of course there are also many aspects of the Somali case that are unique. Of these the most striking is the enduring public silence and denial surrounding the clan cleansing of 1991–1992 and the complete impunity of all participants, whether organizers or lower-level executors of the violence. (The same can of course be said about the perpetrators of war crimes and gross human rights violations during the Barre regime, some of whom are the very same individuals.) The lack of meaningful public acknowledgement or any form of restorative justice for what happened in 1991–1992 is part of an undigested past that weighs heavily on the present.

The key shift of 1991, this study has argued, represented the abrupt reversal of the axis along which political violence had taken place before 1991 and the transformation of this violence from an armed struggle between a brutal military government and its armed opposition into an orchestrated campaign of communal violence, in which ordinary civilians turned against unsuspecting other civilians outside the institutions of the state. When I argue that it has continued to be a negative weight on the processes of reconstruction and reconciliation in Somalia, I am not simply saying that the "conflict identities" that shaped and were shaped by the clan cleansing campaign (those of Hawiye/Isaaq versus Daarood) are *at all times the only or most relevant* ones. Clan, in interplay with the appeals to nation and increasingly Islam, has continued to be a political instrument used by political and military entrepreneurs of all kinds and stripes in ways and at levels that continually change. However, the key shift of 1991 has transformed both the nature of the political competition in which clan remains a major instrument and the popular mindsets in Somalia. I will elaborate on this in what follows.

With regard to the changes in the central political objectives for which political entrepreneurs vie and have vied, there are many competing trends, two of which are most relevant here. One consists of political initiatives to reconstitute a federal or a strongly decentralized but unitary state—a trend first initiated during the Djibouti meetings of June–July 1991. One major break-line has underlain and still underlies the struggle for control over the central/federal state. This is the existence of the "conflict identities" that the key shift of 1991 hardened and transformed.[54] These have expressed themselves in the continued political mobilization of, on the one hand, Hawiye- and Irir-ness and, on the other hand, Daarood-ness. The reigniting of civil war violence in May 2006, when Cabdullaahi Yuusuf had become president of the Transitional Federal Government (2004–2008), was a result of the chasm that had opened up in 1991 and not only the Ethiopian military intervention the former SSDF strongman facilitated in December 2006. When, in the midst of resentment and panic expressed at the rise to power of a "Daarood president," politicians and intellectuals claiming to speak for Mogadishu successfully called for war (jihad) against the "foreign oppressors," the clan cleansing of 1991 resonated most powerfully (Kapteijns 2010a: 54–57).

A second political trend in what central political objectives politicians, using clan, vie for represents a radical departure from that prevailing in 1991. In 1991 the principal focus of political ambitions was the state, the central government, the position Barre had occupied until then. While this trend, as I just outlined, still exists, the key shift of 1991 enabled a radically different kind of political objective. This is the trend that aspires to the attainment of sovereignty, that is to say the power of state, over a part of the former Republic of Somalia, namely over a territory claimed in the name of clan as clan homeland. In regard to this trend, the clan cleansing of 1991–1992 has transformed the political terrain on both sides of the divide. For those targeted by the clan cleansing campaign, the unexpected betrayal, the intentional elimination and brutalization, the hate-narratives that constructed them as foreigners occupying other people's land, and their survival against many odds has given their "conflict identity," their "Daarood-ness" new significance; it has found expression in new territorial polities based on this identity such as Puntland. For many of those associated with perpetrating the clan cleansing, the enormity of what was attempted—to try to wipe out and expel "*the*" Daarood and subject survivors to USC-SNM government rule—makes political coexistence an unpalatable and perilous future to consider. The second political trend, enabled by 1991, has therefore been one toward a loose federation of territorially bounded clan-based states.

The first group to establish a territorially bounded clan-based state, until now not internationally recognized, was the Isaaq-based SNM in May 1991. At the level of popular sentiment this secession would have been impossible without the large-scale human rights violations the military Barre regime committed against enemies constructed as Isaaq. However, the political project of secession was not feasible (or even thinkable) until the key shift of 1991. The Northwest could secede only after violent chaos in the rest of Somalia had given it the political space to do so and after the clan cleansing campaign had set other Somalis at each other's throats. For the self-proclaimed Somaliland Republic, therefore, 1991 and not only 1988 represents the turning point.

There are currently other political trends in Somalia that are not direct results and expressions of the clan cleansing of 1991. For example, there are calls for creating a federal state based on regional and not clan representation, strong movements that aspire to establish an Islamic state of some kind, and warlords who control sets of resources that might revert to the control of the state whose reestablishment they therefore try to prevent. Only the future can tell which trend will prevail and whether politicians will be able to contain the destructive power of the legacy of the key shift.

On the level of popular mindsets also the divide that opened up as a result of the clan cleansing of 1991–1992, in combination with the lack of meaningful public acknowledgement, the ongoing denials of the nature of this violence, and the absolute impunity of those who orchestrated it and carried it out, has had a lasting and transformative impact. In the absence of systematic and reliable opinion polls, this is hard to substantiate. However, I propose that it expresses itself, for example, in the enduring power of the mythical clan hate-narratives; a blindness to anyone's past suffering or wrongdoing except that endured by the in-group, and an apprehensive ambiguity about the "conflict identities" among Somali youth of the "post-generation."[55] At the community level there are myriad initiatives to overcome the "conflict identities" reinforced and transformed by the clan cleansing of 1991–1992, with small victories offset by serious setbacks. So far, however, public calls for "mutual forgiveness," for "forgetting about the past" and "moving on" appear to lack a commitment to thinking through what a more comprehensive coming to terms with this past would mean and what mechanisms might be needed to support those working for peace and reconciliation. How to deal with the past and how "truth" may play a role in social repair and reconciliation is the burden of what follows.

Violence as a Subject: The Critical Issue of Representational and Analytical Strategies

In his "Staring at Suffering: Violence as a Subject," Donald Donham, as we saw in the introduction to Chapter 2, argues that violence is an especially challenging subject-matter to study. In part this is so, he proposes, because of the emotions attached to it both for those who experienced violence and those who study or write about it. This is all the more so when, as in the case of Somalia, the violence in question was a form of communal violence in which common people targeted other common people on the basis of a particular construction of the group identities of both. Moreover, twenty years after the collapse of the state and the political key shift of 1991, the Somali civil war is still ongoing in large parts of the former Republic of Somalia, now with Islamist agendas struggling for dominance with the discourses of clan and nation. This means, among many other things, that many former perpetrators have themselves become victims of civil war violence, while victims have at times become, or sided with perpetrators.

The subject-matter of the clan cleansing of 1991–1992 represents the kind of fraught discursive space to which Donham's essay refers and many scholarly analyses of this violence have, to use Donham's term, "joined the conflict" (2006: 29). What kinds of representational and analytical strategies the study of such a contested subject-matter might require is a topic to which Donham and scholars of genocide and large-scale communal violence such as Bowen (2002), Bringa (2002), Clark and Kaufman (2009), Eltringham (2004, 2006, 2009, 2011), Hinton (2002), Semelin (2003), Shaw (2007), and Strauss (2006) have given much thought. They conclude that three analytical steps are imperative. First, one must reject (that is to say, refuse to take for granted) the group categories in whose name violence was committed and ask how the violence and the construction of such group identities have shaped each other. If one accepts the identity constructs those who masterminded and directed the violence intended to impose (and, through violence, largely succeeded in imposing), then one adopts the discourse of the killers and cedes victory to them even in the aftermath. Second, one must contextualize as fully as possible how these categories of group identity became—could become—so lethal. In the case of Somalia, the failure to do so produces serious analytical pitfalls. If one ignores how the meanings and functions of clan as a construct of group identity and the large-scale violence perpetrated in its name shaped and transformed each other, then one distorts or overlooks the very processes by which clan became such a violent and near-genocidal force. Third, if one attributes single agency to clans and accepts the simple notion that whole clans oppressed or killed, then how does one account for those individuals who resisted the group hate-narratives and saved targeted victims when others killed? Has such a simplistic analytical view of agency not become a further obstacle to peace and social repair?

The failure, on the one hand, to reject the category of clan and, on the other, to take seriously and study its genesis and ongoing history as a political instrument and technology of power is precisely the analytical flaw that cripples evaluations of the clan hate-narratives on a scale of true and false. Clan hate-narratives do not describe transparent, self-evident realities, for they are premised on group categories that are designed to produce and justify violence between the groups they construct as meaningful. Accepting these categories as analytically sound means *buying into* the clan logic rather than trying to understand its genesis. The Barre regime was not ruled by and for clans; it ruled by purposefully using and manipulating clan as a political instrument and in this way treating individuals and groups differentially at different times. The patronage it bestowed upon its political clients and withheld from its political scapegoats had real and at times overwhelming consequences for individuals and groups and deserves further study. However, if one ignores that it was purposefully intended to create and intensify clan competition and hatred, then one just gives that manipulation and the clan sentiment it produced a further lease on life. Similarly, it was not whole clans that conducted the clan cleansing of 1990-1991 or other episodes of large-scale violence in Somalia, but individuals and groups acting on a particular construction of clan identities.

Competing Histories, Authoritative Truth, and the Prospects for Social Repair

The most discouraging discovery I made during the research for this book was how divergent and even diametrically opposed the memories and interpretations of what happened in 1991 are among what were then (and in some ways still are) the different Somali parties to the conflict. In other words, the mythical clan hate-narratives are alive and well and continue to underlie and shape Somali political and social realities. The demonization of the late president Maxamed Siyaad Barre is in some circles so complete that those who once played important roles in his regime but are not of Daarood background can indulge in it without anyone calling them out on their own involvement. In other circles the situation is reversed, with even those directly victimized by Barre—if of Daarood background—unwilling to criticize him or his surviving sons and other henchmen even for irrefutably established human rights violations and war crimes. The same is true for the late General Maxamed Faarax Caydiid, seen as guilty of crimes against humanity by survivors of the clan cleansing of 1991 but celebrated as a hero by others.[56]

Given that such divergent "truths," held with such passion, permeate the attitudes of many Somalis toward the past, each other, and the ongoing civil war, what would in such a context constitute meaningful truth and how might it relate to this study? This question of truth has received considerable attention in the scholarship about large-scale communal violence and other kinds of gross human rights violations in Latin America, Yugoslavia, Rwanda, and South Africa.[57] Many of the debates about such violent pasts have accepted as their premise that the truth must be brought out and made known. The reasons given for this are a combination of closely intertwined legal and moral arguments pertaining to perpetrators and victims, as well as the communities in which these two categories of stakeholders will have to coexist. Thus, it is argued, the truth must be brought into the light in order to hold the perpetrators accountable, to counter impunity and uphold or restore the rule of law, as well as to deter a repetition of the horrors of the past. The truth is also indispensable, it is said, out of respect for the victims and in order to do them justice, to help them "heal," come to terms with what happened to them, and regain trust in a shared moral and legal order. Not acknowledging their undeserved suffering is in the eyes of many analysts and scholars a new violation of their human rights. As for the communal and societal level, here the expectation is that authoritative truth can contribute to unifying a divided historical memory, to provide healing and reconciliation between perpetrators, passive bystanders, and victims, or, more modestly, to help people coexist in peace. In the absence of the public acknowledgment of the truth, it is said, perpetrators may be so emboldened and victims so resentful that both may be vulnerable to political entrepreneurs hoping to benefit from reigniting communal violence.

This is an unreasonably heavy workload to assign to "the truth." What kind of truth, brought out by whom, in what kinds of space and contexts could make a contribution to such a vast array of noble and necessary goals? Studies dealing with this question have, from a variety of disciplinary lenses, proposed ways to promote what is variously referred to as peace and reconciliation; truth and reconciliation; conflict analysis, management and transformation; social repair and reconstruction; moral repair, reclamation, and reparation; postconflict reconstruction; and so forth. Of particular relevance to this question of truth is Fletcher and Weinstein's (2002) "Violence and Social Repair: Rethinking the Contribution of Justice to Reconciliation," which focuses on the aftermath of communal violence such as the clan cleansing that is the subject of this book.

The first important argument these authors make is that efforts to bring about truth and justice give too much emphasis to legal approaches, which almost always focus on the individual. An example of such an approach is the International Criminal Court, established in 1998,[58] about which former U.S. Secretary of State Madeleine Albright so famously said: "Truth is the cornerstone of the rule of law, and it will point toward individuals, not people, as perpetrators of war crimes. And it is only the truth that can cleanse the ethnic and religious hatreds and begin the healing process" (Stover and Weinstein 2004: 1). Fletcher and Weinstein do not question that, in legal contexts, individuals should be found guilty of what they personally did, but they contend that a focus on the individual alone is not sufficient when it comes to dealing with the aftereffects of communal violence. This is so, they argue, because the latter constitutes violence that is "designed not only to kill but to terrorize and destroy the basis of community life" and involves large numbers of ordinary members of a community as perpetrators against other such community members (2002: 576). The authors fear that, if only specific individuals are considered guilty, "individuals and groups are offered the opportunity to rationalize or deny their own responsibility for crimes committed in their name" (601). In such a case, "individualized guilt may contribute to a myth of collective innocence" (580).

The authors do not, of course, advocate for collective punishment of the groups in whose name violence was perpetrated. Rather, they criticize the assumption of collective innocence implied in the individual focus adopted by judicial inquiries and major prosecutions. Such legal approaches, they argue, leave out of consideration many ordinary perpetrators who were not ringleaders but participated in the many small and large violent acts that make up episodes of communal violence or were passive bystanders who did nothing to stop or prevent them. They add, "The proposition that if everyone is guilty then no one is guilty ignores the possibility that holding everyone responsible for past atrocities may force a nation to come to terms with its past as well as to lay the groundwork for reconciliation" (601).

A second issue Fletcher and Weinstein raise with regard to truth, justice, and social repair is the question of what may constitute "the most authoritative rendering of the truth" for members of a community that has gone through communal violence. Many human rights specialists believe (or believed) that the most authoritative truth could be delivered by the judicial system as exemplified by the International Criminal Court (ICC) in The Hague. Fletcher and Weinstein contest this, however significant the ICC contribution to establishing a dependable historical record. In this context, they refer to a study of how individuals associated with legal institutions in former Yugoslavia felt about the truths that were being revealed by the International Criminal Tribunal for the former Yugoslavia (ICTY). The results of this study showed that, with the exception of Bosniaks (Bosnian Muslims), none of those studied, even though their professional identities were tied to the law, saw the findings of the ICTY as relevant or authoritative. All rejected the authority of "any aspect of the judicial 'record' that did not conform to their perspective on the 'truth' of what happened during the war" and emphasized the victimization of their own national group as the most relevant truth in need of public acknowledgment (600). One may say that they were trapped in what Yerkes calls "conflict identities" (2004: 933) and Hoffman "victimological memory" (2003: 295). This appears to hold true for the Somali case as well, with many people rehearsing the grievances about what they suffered at the hands of others and only few individuals willing to publicly reflect on, let alone take responsibility for, the violence committed in their name.

There are many Somalis who want to move on and look toward the future rather than the past. They emphasize the need to build strong and impartial government institutions and the (re-)establishment of social and economic relationships across the divides of the past. Fletcher and Weinstein partly agree with this, for in their "ecological" (that is to say, comprehensive) model for social reconstruction, "reconciliation" is only one of four broad processes that must be pursued simultaneously. The others are the establishment of justice (and thus safety), democracy, and economic prosperity and transformation (623–24). This is a tall order in any context and thus certainly also in that of Somalia. However, the Fletcher-Weinstein model is a sobering and necessary reminder that there are no shortcuts to social reconstruction in the wake of large-scale violence and that the pursuit of truths authoritative to all can only succeed in tandem with other efforts to build a strong economy and stable, robust, and impartial institutions.

Most relevant to the subject and scope of this study is the discursive dimension of efforts at social reconstruction and moral repair. Specifically, how might one engage and interrupt the clan hate-narratives that played such an important role in the violence of 1991–1992 and work toward shared authoritative truths about this divisive past. Here again comparative insights from the scholarship about genocide and other episodes of large-scale violence prove relevant. Thus students of Rwanda have reflected extensively on how memory, history, truth, and social reconstruction might relate to each other.

In recent years this superb historiography has undergone quite a shift. Initially, that is to say, relatively soon after the genocide, many authors emphasized the analytical imperative of rejecting the group hate-narratives and the rigid and static constructions of groupness on which they are premised.[59] The shift in emphasis has come in the wake of the Rwandan government's imposition of an official genocide narrative that, on the one hand, has made any mention of Hutu- and Tutsi-ness punishable by law but, on the other hand, indirectly constructs "*the*" Tutsis as righteous victims and "*the*" Hutu as unrighteous perpetrators. Now the scholarly call is to give "proper recognition to the plurality of perceptions of the past" (Lemarchand 2007: 28), to "elicit hidden transcripts (Eltringham 2009: 7), and to learn to "navigate different interpretations of the past" (Clark and Kaufman 2009: 8).

In proposing to bring out a plurality of interpretations of the past, these scholars do not assume that these interpretations are necessarily morally equivalent; rather they insist that these narratives are all in need of critical engagement. Cutting off the perpetrators' supply of "objective" oxygen" does not mean ignoring or suppressing the hate-narratives that mediated the violence (Eltringham 2006: 33). Lemarchand conceptualizes such a critical engagement of interpretations of the past as what Paul Ricoeur calls "le travail de mémoire" (critical memory work) and Sigmund Freud *durcharbeiten*, a "working though" and "coming to terms" with memory (2007: 29). Yerkes, writing about Serbian youth, uses another concept for similar processes and speaks of "facing processes" and the psychological challenges these bring along. She writes: "Initiatives that are based on rationality and that present 'facts' with the expectation that the receiver must believe them are unlikely to be effective. This is not simply a question of 'getting the facts straight'" (2004: 935). Hoffman, finally, speaks about the significance of "remembering rigorously" and impresses this duty of remembering anew on what she calls "the post-generation," the generation that follows that of the victims and perpetrators themselves, including the latter's children (25). She warns against "the temptation for the inheritors of the victims to derive a kind of referred rightness—which can so easily change to righteousness—from putatively belonging to the right side of history. There is no more reason for this than for collectively blaming the children of the aggressors for the sins of their parents" (296). Hoffman therefore asks the post-generation "to look beyond the fixed moment of trauma" and consider broader and longer-term historical processes. "I am not advocating a dispassionate forgiveness of past wrongs," she writes, but the kind of reflection that strives not to reproduce—by repetition or inversion—their legacy" (302). All these authors express their expectation or hope that critical memory work may produce shared authoritative truths about the past for a more peaceful future.

A number of scholars have used the discipline of ethnography to contribute to a critical working through of the phenomenon of "separate ethnic memory" that violence so often produces (Lemarchand 2007: 27). Eltringham (2011) and Hilker (2011) interviewed individual Rwandans about their views on Hutu- and Tutsi-ness in the light of the violence of the recent past. They made a twofold discovery. First they found that, on the one hand, the politicized constructs of group identity and the hate-narratives that had contributed to the genocide carried significant meaning for their respondents. They also learned that the latter's interpretations differed from person to person and were not homogeneous on either the Hutu or Tutsi side of the divide. Many people, especially youth, found these identity constructs deeply unsettling, as these identities, when they came to the fore, triggered mutual suspicion and prejudice among individuals of different backgrounds. This meant, the respondents explained, that they left ethnic identity as much unspoken as possible, even though it always underlay and structured their attitudes toward others. Their second ethnographic discovery was that, on the other hand, their respondents drew on their personal experiences during and in the aftermath of the genocide to develop views of Tutsi- and Hutu-ness that were much more nuanced and undermined the rigid and static group categories of recent political history and group hate-narratives. Such nuanced understandings of group identity were still "structured by ethnicity," Eltringham concluded, but not determined by it. Resituating and relativizing group identity in this way, he proposes, "disrupts ethnicity and in so doing disarms ethnicity of its deterministic binary qualities" (2011: 272). This opens the possibility for a creative reimagining of Hutu- and Tutsi-ness, he argues, and brings into play other factors that determine people's identity and social position in Rwanda. In other words, the truths of memories of personal experience undermine the authority and authoritativeness of the truths propagated by the group hate-narratives and genocide propaganda.

The propositions for social reconstruction and moral repair outlined above have a significant bearing on the case of Somalia. They put forward as a given that those who orchestrated and carried out war crimes and other crimes against humanity should be brought to justice. They propose moreover that other individuals and groups should refrain from indulging in the illusion of collective innocence and take some responsibility for the violence that was committed in their name, irrespective of the nature of their individual participation or lack of such. Such narratives and "facing processes" might disrupt the sterile recycling of group hate- and victimological narratives and show that the positions of perpetrator and victim have never been static and are occupied by different individuals and groups at different times. Paul Ricoeur put it as follows: "Past events cannot be erased: one cannot undo what has been done, nor prevent what happened. On the other hand, the meaning of what happened . . . is not fixed once and for all." What we can change about the past is therefore "its moral freight (*sa charge morale*), the weight of the debt it carries" (Paul Ricoeur cited in Lemarchand 2007: 29). Such critical memory work might draw on individual experiences of the meanings of clan constructs in people's personal lives and thus further relativize, resituate, and creatively reimagine those meanings.

In many Somali communities aspects of such critical memory work are pursued, in word and deed, and at the individual and small group levels, in private and public. With regard to Somali *public* engagement with the violence of the civil war, this has taken many forms, from poetry and fiction to academic and journalistic analysis and Web site commentaries. The poets with whose work this study opened contributed to such a public debate by insisting on clan as a tool of unscrupulous politicians and a diseased or insane popular mindset. The novels examined in the first chapter participated in the debate by showing their readers that the realities of individual lives could not be contained in the artificial and politicized constructs of clan and were harmed by them. Moreover, when poet Mohamud Togane calls for Somalis to join a "Clanaholics anonymous," his recipe for social reconstruction is not out of line with Fletcher and Weinberg's hope that "holding everyone responsible for past atrocities may force a nation to come to terms with its past as well as to lay the groundwork for reconciliation" (2003: 601).

All these renderings of civil war violence are mediations of this violence. That is to say that they represent and interpret aspects of this violence at the same time that they intervene in it by pursuing shared understandings and authoritative truths. The memories such mediations often make about the past shape their imagining of the future (Kapteijns 2010a). This book, which draws on these mediations, as well as many other Somali and non-Somali sources, also represents a particular mediation of this violence (that of 1991–1992), namely one using the conventions and interpretive tools of the academic field of history. It is not based on the premise that the truth about 1991 does not exist or cannot be recovered. In line with the scholarship about truth and postconflict reconstruction, it accepts, however, what Eltringham concludes in his study about Rwanda: "that the past is a contested place and that different interpretations of it should be explored (rather than dismissed) *because they reveal what actors hold to be current disparities*" (Eltringham 2004: 148, my emphasis). This is not an abdication of the responsibility of the historian. It is, rather, an acknowledgement that this historical analysis constitutes only one mediation of Somali civil war violence. The truths of the latter—the critical memory work that engages the moral freight in the present of what happened in the past—must and can in the long run only be pursued by Somalis who are willing to hold the truth dearer than anything else.

Time-Line of the Major Events Examined in This Book

1960: The British Somaliland Protectorate and Italian Somaliland achieved independence and united to form the Republic of Somalia.

1960–1969: The Era of the Civilian Administrations under Presidents Aadan Cabdulla Cismaan "Cadde" (1960–1967) and Cabdirashiid Cali Sharmaarke (1967–1969).

1969–1991: The Military Regime of Maxamed Siyaad Barre.

1979–1982: The Military Regime committed large-scale clan-based violence against civilians in Mudug.

1988–1989: The Military Regime committed large-scale clan-based violence against civilians in the Northwest.

1989–1990: The SNM committed clan-based violence against civilians (including refugees) in the Northwest.

1989–1991: The Military Regime further imploded into violence and retaliated against civilians for the successes of the armed opposition fronts active throughout Somalia to overthrow it.

July 1989: The Mosque massacre, followed by the Military Regime's mass execution of middle-class Isaaq civilians on the coast at Jasiira.

May 1990: The Manifesto Group submitted its Manifesto, a petition consisting of a list of concrete demands, to the Barre regime.

December 1990–January 26, 1991: The Battle for Mogadishu that ended with the expulsion of President M. S. Barre from Mogadishu and the collapse of the Military Regime.

January 1991: Unleashing of the USC's clan cleansing campaign in Mogadishu and central and south-central Somalia.

January 28, 1991: Cali Mahdi of USC-Mogadishu was hastily proclaimed president of a transitional administration. This was immediately contested by USC-Caydiid and the SNM.

February 6, 1991: Unexpected attack by USC-Caydiid on SPM-Jees in Afgooye. This attack represented a stage in the USC's clan cleansing campaign and marked the beginning of the War of the Militias.

February 26, 1991: An episode of clan cleansing by USC-Caydiid in Gaalkacyo.

March–May 1991: The SNF Alliance, formed in response to the USC's expulsion of Barre and the unleashing of its clan cleansing campaign, unsuccessfully tried to capture Mogadishu, committing violence against civilians on its way.

April 23, 1991: First USC capture of Kismaayo, a major stage in both the USC clan cleansing campaign and the War of the Militias.

April 1991: First outbreak of armed violence in Mogadishu between USC-Caydiid and USC Cali Mahdi. In November 1991, this turned into a full-scale war in which tens of thousands of civilians were killed. This armed conflict lasted beyond the U.S./UN intervention of December 1992.

May 18, 1991: The SNM formally seceded from the Republic of Somalia and proclaimed the independence of the Northwest as the Republic of Somaliland.

June–July 1991: Two national reconciliations meetings were held in Djibouti. They confirmed the presidency of Cali Mahdi.

January–May 1992: The SPM Alliance, including Barre, attempted to capture Mogadishu from the USC, committing large-scale clan-based violence against civilians on its way. Its defeat by USC-Caydiid spelled the end of Barre, who left the country definitively at the end of April 1992.

January–May 1992: Large-scale clan-based violence against the civilians of the interriver region by first the SPM Alliance and then the victorious SNA-Caydiid. In the Lower Jubba Valley, where the war also rolled back and forth, the Somali Bantu were targeted for clan-based violence by both sides. Famine resulted.

April 28–May 30, 1992: USC-Caydiid, driving the SPM-Alliance over the border, committed atrocities in Gedo.

May 14, 1992: Second USC capture of Kismaayo.

May 1992–May 1993: Large parts of Somalia fell prey to a devastating man-made famine that triggered the U.S./UN military humanitarian intervention of December 1992 (see Glossary under Operation Restore Hope and UNITAF).

August 1992: General Caydiid established SNA-Caydiid, an alliance of armed fronts based on a similar alliance established in February 1992.

October 1992: President Cali Mahdi established SNA-Cali Mahdi to counter SNA-Caydiid.

December 8–19, 1992: Last episode of clan cleansing examined in this book. Colonel "Jees," in alliance with General Caydiid, hunted down and massacred a large group of middle-class elders with clan backgrounds making up the Harti (a subcategory of Daarood) in Kismaayo.

Notes

Introduction

Epigraph: Breyten Breytenbach 1994: 163.

1. By "key shift" I refer both to a transformative political moment and, in a Foucauldian sense, to a momentous shift in the dominant public political discourse in Somalia. The key shift marked the slide into dominance of what I call the "clan logic," a discourse that not only identified its "other" as "other clan" but also articulated a rationale and agenda for clan cleansing (Kapteijns 2010a: 26–27; Mills 2009: 23; Foucault 1972: 175).

2. Clans refer to groups of people who trace descent from the presumed male ancestors of all Somalis through different nodes (intermediary forefathers) in that genealogical construct. Following Compagnon 1995 and as explained further below, this study deals with the political use and manipulation of this group identity. Lonsdale 1994 has attempted to distinguish between "moral ethnicity," constructive kinship-based social solidarity networks, and destructive "political tribalism." I focus on clan *as a political project* that uses specific constructions of cherished cultural commonalities and experiences to promote an agenda that, given the ways clan was hitched to state-formation in Somalia, has so far only been divisive. See also Kapteijns 2010b.

3. Group constructs like that of Daarood are conventionally referred to as clan families or clans. I avoid such terms as much as possible to resist the tendency to take such group constructs for granted, regard them as "natural," and assign simple agency to them.

4. This is used in Compagnon 1995. Lemarchand 1997 uses the term "ethnic entrepreneur."

5. The definition is too narrow because it excludes groups that are political (rather than national, ethnic, or religious) and too broad because any form of ethnically based communal violence can be made to fit. See Eltringham 2006: 67 n4 for three common criticisms of the definition by genocide scholars.

6. Hinton 2002: 6. The phrase "from the face of the earth" is not very clear. In the Somali case, one may say that perpetrators tried to annihilate victims from the face of the earth in Mogadishu and south and south-central Somalia but not in Nairobi or Washington.

7. Given that the violence at the center of this study was largely perpetrated by Somalis who, in all their diversity, constitute one national group, the term *ethnic* cleansing is not as appropriate as *clan* cleansing. Daahir Cali 1997 reports on terms the victims used in and after 1991: *xasuuq*, "genocide" (231), *ciribtir*, "extermination" (225), *gumaad*, "extermination" (220, 225), and *isir* or *qabiil safeyn*, "clan cleansing" (233).

8. The term is from Hayden 2002: 232; compare Bringa 2002: 205.

9. Lemarchand (1997: 185) too emphasizes the significance of triggers.

10. Cf. Mamdani 2002, who asks why and how so many individuals victimized as Hutu turned into killers.

11. This study addresses the international context of the events only in analyzing international support for Barre's military regime. Ethiopia's role in supporting and instigating the military incursions into Somalia by the armed opposition fronts that triggered large-scale violence and state collapse (SSDF in 1982, SNM in 1988, USC in 1990) remains understudied. For studies on the wider regional and international contexts of the events, see, for example, Doornbos 2006; Little 1996; Lyons and Samatar 1995; Markakis 1994; Rawson 1994.

12. This was true with regard to the SNM (associated with the Isaaq) and the emerging SDM (associated with the Raxanweyn), but not the SPM (associated with the Ogaadeen Daarood).

13. For example, Benaadiri groups such as the Reer Xamar and many of the Reer Brava (or Baraawe), the people of the city of Brava, have been constructed as outside the genealogical construct of Somaliness. This in spite of centuries of intense social interaction (including intermarriage) and cultural, religious, economic, and political contributions to (and sacrifices for) Somali state and society.

14. For this reason, some readers might insist on more detail than presented here. I indeed hope that such research will be forthcoming.

15. For a definition and history of Islamism, see Menkhaus 2004; Kapteijns 2010a: 54–55 ff. First manifesting itself in the mid-1970s as a movement for deepened personal religiosity in opposition to Barre's oppressive regime, it became an increasingly politicized and violent movement and discourse during the civil war. The al-Shabaab militias that dominate large areas of famine-stricken south and south-central Somalia in early 2012 exemplify this trend.

16. Although the Somali civil war has undergone many transformations since 1991, the deep divide that resulted from the clan cleansing campaign of 1991–1992 continues to underlie Somali political and social realities. It is also enshrined in the clan quota system adopted for the federal transitional governments in Somalia since 2000. Moreover, apart from the green zone protected by AMISOM (African Union Mission in Somalia) troops, Mogadishu and a good part of its hinterland remains clan-cleansed. I will return to the enduring legacy of the clan cleansing campaign in the conclusion.

17. See Kapteijns 2010b for an elaboration of this.

18. Compagnon 1995. For the concept of political entrepreneur, see 77–169 (Chapter 1); for his analysis of clan, see 453–86. Elsewhere (1998: 83), Compagnon conceptualizes

clanship (genealogical constructs of lineage segments, subclans, clans, and clan families) as a "ready-made ideology" that allows political entrepreneurs to pursue and mask personal political and economic goals.

19. It does, of course, question their premises and the categories of analysis implied in them.

20. He was proclaimed president of the transitional government by USC-Mogadishu January 28, 1991, two days after Barre's expulsion.

21. Accessed through Wellesley College Library Web site: http://0-infoweb.newsbank.com.luna.wellesley.edu.

22. A short account by a Somali journalist that stands out in this context is Afrah 1992. The author was long-term editor of the only English-language publication by the Ministry of Education and based his account partly on notes taken during the Battle for Mogadishu that began on December 30, 1990, which he witnessed firsthand. He completed the manuscript for the book in July 1991.

23. I interviewed eyewitnesses and survivors and their relatives especially with regard to the episodes of violence in Brava, Gaalkacyo, Kismaayo, Afgooye, and Gedo.

Chapter 1. Speaking the Unspeakable: Somali Poets and Novelists on Civil War Violence

Epigraphs: Michaels 1997: 161; Mills 1997: 17.

1. For the definition of popular culture in this context, see Kapteijns 2010a: 28.

2. For a more elaborate analysis of Somali poetry as "prestigious" (and gendered) speech intended to shape the political subjectivities of its audience, see Kapteijns 2010a.

3. The most relevant Web sites and poetry collections feature in the notes to the specific texts.

4. On November 26, 2011, Naaji's "Lament for Mogadishu," whose refrain any Somali over thirty can sing, had had 112,097 views. On that same date, Cabdi Muxumed Amiin's "To the Leaders of the USC," which had been uploaded to www.youtube.com as recently as February 6, 2010, had had 6,716 views.

5. For the Somali text of Masiibo, see Mohammed Sh. Hassan 1998: 98–102. No date is given.

6. The text is from an audiocassette of a live performance in Geneva, July 12, 1992. It is also known as "Baroordiiqda Xamar" ("Lament for Mogadishu"). My analysis of this poem overlaps with that in Kapteijns 2010a: 50–52, which also gives the Somali text as transcribed from that live performance. On November 26, 2011, the music video of this song on www.youtube.com had been viewed 112,097 times. On January 2, 2012, the only video that came up on www.youtube.com was "Axmed Naaji Sacad—Xamar yaa ku xaal marin doonaa," viewed 12,916 times in the three years since it had been uploaded.

7. This term is inspired by Fortier 1999: 43, who, in her attempt to "de-naturalize ethnicity," cites Paul Gilroy's concept of "ethnic absolutism." See also Wyschogrod 2005: 207.

8. For the Somali text, see Cabdi Muxumed Amiin 2006: 157–59.

9. For the Somali text of "Ragga USCyow" or "Ragga USC Daadahshow," 1991, see Cabdi Muxumed Amiin 2006: 150–56; also www.youtube.com, accessed November 26, 2010.

10. The text reads: "It is not that one is especially blessed or cursed or that it is just God's will. It is effort through which people outdo each other and what determines one's position here and in the hereafter."

11. "Afweyne" or "Big-Mouth" was Barre's nickname.

12. The reference to the proverb "the fire lit by a hypocrite will burn the believer," evokes unexpected consequences.

13. Transcribed from an audiotape obtained from RTD, Djibouti with the assistance of M. F. Afdub. The recording was made in Djibouti on January 18, 1999, and published (with minor differences) in Cabdulkadir Cabdi Shube 2007: 5–16.

14. The poet says, "How we were deceived by names and how did political fronts tear us apart like wild animals." Although all opposition fronts had the word "Somali" in their names, they did not, the poet appears to suggest, act in accordance with the values associated with "Somali-ness" and instead attacked and destroyed the common people.

15. The term is Hinton's (2002: 14).

16. In 1993, the poet performed this poem in front of USC leader Cismaan Xassan Cali "Caato," shortly after the USC attacks on Beledweyne. Given that Caato was deeply involved in the events described in the poem, this must be seen as a courageous act (Professor Abdiweli Ali, telephone conversation, February 15, 2010).

17. For example, Gassem (1994: 74) makes the same claim but as part of an account that tries to explain the clan cleansing away.

18. The SSDF spokesman in Nairobi grew into full awareness of the clan cleansing campaign only gradually. See Hasan Ali Mireh, "SSDF Leader Comments," BBC World Service in English, December 26, 1990 (FBIS 90-249, December 27, 1990); and "SSDF Rebel Leader on Collaboration with USC," BBC World Service in English, January 9, 1991 (FBIS, AFR 91 007, January 10, 1991); Interviews 3 and 9; telephone conversation with Hussein Yusuf, May 11, 2010.

19. I translate "dudid" as senseless fighting. The dictionary (Yaasiin C. Keenadiid 1976) gives "anger, without reason or understanding, of women and children."

20. These are the famous lines of Cabdillaahi Suldaan Maxamed "Timacadde"'s poem from the 1960s. See Boobe Yuusuf Ducaale 2006: 202–5; www.aftahan.com, accessed July 30, 2008.

21. For the rise of Islamism in Somalia, see Menkhaus 2004; International Crisis Group 2005; Kapteijns 2010a: 54–56.

22. The pioneer in studying Somali cyberspace is Issa-Salwe 2005.

23. For the Somali text, see www.golkhatumo.com, accessed March 11, 2008.

24. The poet appears to be using *umma* to indicate the community of Somali Muslims and *qaran* to indicate the community of ethnic Somalis as unified in a nation-state.

25. Abu Qaasim, tenth-century author of the law treatise called *al-Mukhtasar*. He belonged to the Hanbali *madhhab* or legal school.

26. For the Somali text, see www.somalitalk.com, accessed March 7, 2008.

27. There are many poems that illustrate this increased emphasis on Islam. See for example, Hibo Nuura's 1996 song entitled "Nation and Clan" (Qaran iyo Qabiil), authored in 1996, by the singer's father. A large part of this song is actually a prayer to God, www.somalilyrics.net, accessed March 26, 2008.

28. The emphatic use of the term *umma*, community of Muslims, in this case, Somali Muslims, is one indication of the importance the poet gives to an Islamic solution.

29. *Waali*, guardian, ruler; compare Arabic *wāli*.

30. *Weli* is a saintly person; compare the Arabic *wali Allah*, a "friend" of God.

31. *Fitna* (Arabic): discord, dissension, civil strife; also enticement, temptation.

32. This is also true for Cabdulqaadir Shube's "Sound, Drum of Wisdom," presented above.

33. This is a play on the phrase by the feminist poet Audre Lorde (1984) that "the master's tools will never dismantle the master's house."

34. See also Kapteijns 2010a: 66–67. In the nationalist era, popular songs did not mention clan. However, in men's poetry such as that constituting the poetry cycle of Hurgumo (c. 1978), poets spurred each other on to greater efforts in their opposition against Barre in explicit terms of clan and clan insults (Samatar 1988/1989). It is worth noting that the poetic discourse here is completely out of step with the actual public sphere of government in Somalia where, ever since the National Reconciliation Meeting in Djibouti in 2000, functions in the transitional administrations have been governed by clan quota in the form of the notorious 4.5 formula.

35. For this incident, see also Kapteijns 2010a: 25–26.

36. Ibid., 32–33, 68–69. The power of the conventions of prestigious speech has proven to be so strong that it appears to govern even the small body of women's poetry about civil war violence. This poetry is characterized by the triad of discursive strands examined above and observes the same constraints and silences (69).

37. See also Issa-Salwe 2005: 153–54.

38. For categorization of young men's orature as nonprestigious, see Axmed Cali Abokor 1993; Kapteijns 1999: 72–73.

39. Irir, the genealogical construct politically activated in 1991, encompasses (among others) the Hawiye and Isaaq, the clan bases associated with the USC and SNM.

40. Mohamed-Abdi 1994: 17–18, gives the French text of this short poem by Geelle Ismaaciil Macallin 1992. Aideed is the name of General Maxamed Faarax Caydiid of the USC, discussed further below. This is my translation from French. Morin 1997: 8 also gives this text.

41. Siyaad refers to Maxamed Siyaad Barre, the expelled president. The groups targeted for clan cleansing were constructed as all having collectively been allies and beneficiaries of his regime.

42. Osman 1996; Faysal Axmed Xasan 2000. An English translation of the latter is

forthcoming. The novels of the most famous Somali novelist, Nuruddin Farah, who has written two trilogies about the Somali civil war (*Blood in the Sun* and *Past Imperfect*) are in a class of their own and not considered here. The same is true for the recent novel *Madre Piccola* (translated as Little Mother) by Somali Italian novelist Cristina Ali Farah (Farah 2007, 2011). The latter deals primarily with Somali diaspora life in Europe and North America, but is also a very sensitive reflection about the clan cleansing of 1991 that drove the four main protagonists and narrators of the novel out of Mogadishu. For a review, see Kapteijns, *Canadian Journal of African Studies* 46, 1 (2012): 94–96.

43. The United Somali Congress (USC), led by Maxamed Faarax Caydiid, will be discussed extensively in Chapters 2–4.

44. The events surrounding the Manifesto Group that sent Barre an ultimatum in May 1990 will be discussed below.

45. Faisal Xasan Axmed 2000: 81–82, 84. See also Osman 1996: 102.

46. Faisal Xasan Axmed 2000: 80–81. The use of this song as an incitement to violence was confirmed to me by victims of the clan cleansing. It will be further analyzed in Chapter 4.

47. Not analyzed here are the novel's other themes, such as those related to the fates of the female characters.

48. I write "his," because Togane appears to address his accusations at men.

49. Because of considerations of space, in the citations below the line-breaks of the original poems are not always observed.

50. Togane 2006. "Darod-rein" and "Darod-frei" evoke Nazi terminology: "cleansed from," "free of Daarood."

51. Ibid. The concept of *nin belaayo ah* refers to a man who has the strength to force others to respect him and his personal space. Togane creates ambiguity about this term's positive connotation by translating it literally as "man of disaster."

52. In yet another twist, however, Togane concludes the poem with a final sneer, a reference to the words of statesman and political strategist Faarax Gololey, who prayed, "May the Daarood never eat dung, for, if they do, we all will."

53. The reference here is to the Isaaq of northwest Somalia.

54. MOD refers to the acronym introduced by the armed resistance front SNM to characterize the military regime in terms of the particular clan alliance on which it allegedly leaned (Mareexaan, Ogaadeen, and Dhulbahante Daarood). The term was part of a political strategy by which both regime and opposition came to collectively blame and punish whole clan groups for political acts and affiliations of individuals. This is further analyzed in Chapter 4.

55. During the Barre regime, Somalis had to address each other as "jaalle" or "comrade." Jaalle Siyaad or Comrade Siyaad refers to president Maxamed Siyaad Barre.

56. Il-jeex and Jaaji are slang references to particular clan groups. The former refers to a particular way of looking, namely looking around inquisitively for something to grab or interfere with, and was used to refer to the Habr Gidir Hawiye. Jaaji means "inferior, of low quality," and was used to refer to the so-called despised minorities.

57. *Bashbash* and *barwaaqo* are both words referring to prosperity and plenty.
58. Baydhaba or Baidoa, a town in south-central Somalia.
59. "Putridness and Clan."
60. Italian is widely spoken by Togane's generation of Somalis, as Italy's cultural influence and educational involvement in Somalia continued after Somalia achieved political independence.

Chapter 2. Historical Background to the Violence of State Collapse

1. For a fuller analysis, see Kapteijns 2010b. The most outstanding exception is Compagnon 1995, who both conceptualized clanship in a compelling way and traced its history as an instrument of patronage of the political elite from 1969 to 1991. The refusal to accept clan as a "natural" category does not imply denial of the social and emotional value of the shared experiences, common memories, and acts of mutual support and solidarity that characterize kinship relations in Somalia. Such refusal emphasizes how clan as a political project of political entrepreneurs struggling over the state exploits those cherished commonalities.

2. The concept and content of clan hate-narratives is further developed in Chapters 3 and 4.

3. In early August 2009, the UN invited generals Maxamed Cali Samantar, Maxamed Nuur Galaal, and others to Washington for a discussion about securing the Somali coastline. General Galaal, whose role in the clan cleansing of 1991 will be discussed in Chapter 2, objected to the participation of generals such as General Samantar who, he claimed, had been guilty of genocide in Hargeisa in 1988. On the one hand, this is the proverbial pot calling the kettle black; on the other hand, it is astounding that the UN would invite individuals involved in war crimes and worse to such a meeting. http://www.bbc.co.uk/somali/news/story/2009/08/090811_galaal.shtml, accessed January 18, 2010.

4. See Chapter 3. Issa-Salwe 1996 and Samatar 1991 form notable exceptions.

5. See, for example, Kusow 1994, Ahmed 1995, and Chapter 3.

6. See Lewis 2008: 74 for such a thoughtless use of the category of "*the*" Dhulbahante. See Kapteijns 2010b for further analysis.

7. Compagnon 1995 and Laitin and Samatar 1987 are exceptions.

8. This and the following sections draw on Kapteijns 2010b.

9. More detail is provided below. For a blistering and irrefutable critique of the nefarious role of food and other international aid played in keeping the dictator in power and in undermining state and economy, see Maren 1997.

10. Compagnon 1995: 843–54, App. 3. Compagnon shows that even the army and NSS, where the notion of MOD dominance carried *some* meaning, had high-ranking officers who did not belong to the so-called MOD clans (1995: 464 ff.). Compare Laitin and Samatar 1987: 156.

11. Especially between 1989 and Barre's expulsion on January 26, 1991, other collective clan-based punishments of civilians took place in the country that have not been

properly documented and therefore do not get the attention here that they deserve. Some occurrences will nevertheless be mentioned below.

12. Compagnon explains this in two ways. First, he sees it as evidence of Barre's own clannist mindset and paranoia, as he saw himself as having taken over the state from "*the*" Majeerteen, because the assassinated president of the last civilian administration had been of that clan background. Second, he sees it as a political strategy to turn popular sentiment against Majeerteen political clout. The regime's political propaganda and "spin" used something that may well have been true for some individuals to depict (and then treat) a whole group as guilty of "tribalism" and "arrogance."

13. See Samatar 1991; Jama Mohamed Ghalib 1995: 128; Issa-Salwe 1996: 94–97. Of course, Barre neither targeted only Majeerteen nor targeted Majeerteen as Majeerteen only. Individuals who in this period refused to toe the line or expressed ideas of their own (including intellectuals and writers such as Nuruddin Farah, Maxamed Daahir Afrax, Maxamed I. W. Hadraawi, and many others) were driven into exile or harassed and imprisoned.

14. Issa-Salwe (1996: 93–94) also mentions the execution of six high-ranking officers in Hargeisa for alleged disobedience.

15. To be precise, sixteen of the executed were Majeerteen by clan background; the seventeenth was a nephew of the leader of the coup, colonel Maxamed Sheekh Cismaan "Cirro." See Issa-Salwe 1996: 94.

16. Compagnon (1995: 433) notes that there were several officers who were Hawiye and Isaaq by clan background among those sentenced to prison-terms.

17. Issa-Salwe 1996: 95–96. A number of young women had been put onto trucks and driven to the local military camp to be raped. One girl had been able to save herself by jumping from the moving truck and was, as a result, still disabled (Personal information, London, summer 1991).

18. Jama Mohamed Ghalib 1995: 128 (quote), 84, 179.

19. Kusow (1994: 31) constitutes evidence of such scapegoating: "Similarly, clanism in Somalia is a system of stratification whereby the members of the clan in power assume the role of the bourgeois class and thus avail themselves of a greater share of the resources. . . . For example, between 1960–1969, the Majerteen (Darood clan) dominated both the economic and the political scenes of the country." He attributes the notion that nationalism produced a pyramid with "*the*" Daarood on top to Hussein Adam's public lecture "Rethinking the Somali Political Experience," presented as a background paper at the Workshop on Political Reconciliation and Reconstruction in Somalia, U.S. Institute of Peace Public Friday, October 6, 1992, Washington, D.C. (32). In a later article (Mohamud and Kusow 2006: 19), Kusow presented a different interpretation of such clan-based accusations against "*the*" Majeerteen, without, however, formally retracting the earlier hate-narrative: "In attempts to consolidate power and marginalize less supportive individuals and clans, Siad Barre instituted a plan to eliminate supposedly 'treacherous and treasonous' individuals in the government and categorized some clans as natural enemies of the revolution."

20. In this context, Compagnon concludes somewhat cynically that the military regime's devious strategy of charging the Majeerteen with "tribalism" had more success than his references to Marx and Engels (1995: 463).

21. "Dhafoorqiiq" ("with steam coming from their ears"), that is, so emaciated that their temples stood out either from hunger or because of their extraordinary feats as warriors.

22. See Compagnon 1995: 532–52 for an analysis of this history.

23. Africa Watch 1990: 36–37, a memorandum sent to Barre by a group of twenty-one Isaaq elders March 30, 1982. Compagnon 1995: 529 ff.

24. Bridges (2000: 116) writes about population growth and erosion in Hargeisa. Between 1984 and 1986, he visited the unofficial Gannet camp on the edge of the city, which did not have toilets or clean water. For government recruitment of refugees, see Amnesty International (1988: 16), which reports that 7,000 may have been forcibly recruited into the army in August and September 1987 and several were detained when they tried to evade recruitment. See also Africa Watch 1990: 34. Gersony (1989: 62) may have underestimated the numbers, but he writes that "Before May 1988 several hundreds and perhaps more of the 100,000 refugees in northern Somalia were given guns by government and induced to become paramilitary groups on behalf of the government."

25. Compagnon (1995: 519 ff.) mentions the sudden abolition of the franca valuta system, the withholding of import-export licenses from merchants who specialized in this trade, and the prohibition of *qaat* growing and the destruction of *qaat* farms. In this same period, Saudi Arabia stopped all livestock imports from Somalia, allegedly because the animals were diseased.

26. According to Compagnon (1995: 544–48), Maxamed Xaashi "Gaani," related to Barre's second wife, had been in charge of the twenty-sixth military sector since 1980. His name is associated with the state of emergency of 1982–84 and the human rights violations committed against the Isaaq population in this period. In March 1986, he was replaced with General "Morgan," who, until December 1986, followed a more lenient policy of reconciliation. However, when the head of the NSS for the Northwest was assassinated by the SNM on December 19, 1986, the regime went back to all-out war on the SNM (1995: 668). The document in which "Morgan" proposed to Barre to make the area separating the government forces and the SNM uninhabitable by destroying water tanks and villages is very likely not authentic, although Compagnon (669) believes it is. Even so, as Amnesty International (1988: 38) concludes, "the measures advocated in it seem to be precisely the same as those carried out by the government's security forces along the frontier with Ethiopia in the northwest region."

27. Apart from the testimony gathered by Africa Watch 1990, Gersony reports many rapes even before May 1988 (1989: 31).

28. See Chapter 4 for further analysis.

29. According to Pacifico 1996: 228, General Aadan Cabdullaahi Nuur "Gabyow," his son-in-law Colonel Bashiir "Bililiqo," and Colonel Axmed Cumar "Jees" commanded some of the government forces sent to fight the SNM.

30. See Somaliland Research Society & SomalilandNet.com, Unpublished Sources; also the video by Ibraahim Ahmed, "Somaliland: Genocide, Holocaust, War Crimes, Faqash History," www.youtube.com, accessed December 23, 2011.

31. Issa-Salwe 1996: 107, 103 (poem).

32. This information is from the introduction to Dhoodaan's poem (see www.doollo.com, /mainpage/boggasuugaanta/dhoodaan/duraaqsi.htm, accessed August 28, 2010). I am grateful to Abdisalam Issa-Salwe for pointing this source out to me even beyond its mention in his book (1996: 103). Barre's effort to create political Daaroodism was also confirmed by Interview 2.

33. Gersony 1989: 45. On 46 he lists by name a number of UNHCR Refugee Camps in northern Somalia before 1988: Adiades, Agabar, Arapsio, Bixin, Biyoley, Dam, Darimaan, Dawaale, Las Dhure, Sabaad, and Tug Wajale. Of the 65 former inhabitants he interviewed, 74 percent identified as Ogaadeen, Oromo, and Gadabursi, 19 percent as Geri, Sheekhaal, and Hawiye.

34. The hostile reception of the refugees by part of the local population is generally not reported but enters into the emergence of this negative relationship.

35. Gersony (1989: 53–55) found that the government recruited many inhabitants of refugee camps into the army by force, especially in 1985–1986. As for the war of 1988, he found that former residents of the camps denied they or their co-residents had joined government forces in the war against the SNM, arguing that they could not have left their families alone in the face of SNM attacks on the camps. They claimed it was only after these SNM attacks that some received some arms from the government. Witnesses on the other side of the argument, however, insisted that camp inhabitants had received arms and were seen with government officials during this period.

36. Gersony interviewed former residents of eleven of the twelve camps, nine of which the SNM reportedly attacked (1989: 49–52).

37. Compagnon 1998: 78. Maren makes a reference to the camp at Beledweyne and recounts the expulsion, deportation, and execution of refugees residing in the camp of Jalalaqsi by Hawaadleh Hawiye-based USC militias during the period of a month in late 1990. His informant, who lost one daughter and all his possessions, estimates the number of camp residents who were executed and dumped into the Shabeelle River at 2000. He himself was saved by a Hawaadleh friend (1997: 99, 113–15).

38. Compagnon mentions that there were many men who were Raxanweyn and Hawiye by clan background in the rank-and-file (1995: 601) and mentions Hawiye officers deserting in the aftermath of the government's transition to full-scale war in the Northwest (1995: 603, 680).

39. See Compagnon 1995: 606–30 for an excellent summary; Rawson 1994; Pacifico 1996: 271.

40. Only the production of bananas for export was again on the increase (Samatar 1994).

41. Compagnon (1995: 501) mentions that $1.5 million was paid this way by a British firm to which the Somali government awarded the contract for the Jubba Sugar Factory.

42. For the enormous poaching scandal, see Compagnon 1995: 500, 621. For the Craxi scandal, see idem, 625. The Craxi scandal also involved the road built between Bosaaso, Garoowe, and Gaalkacyo, which, on the Somali side, was overseen by General Caydiid.

43. Compagnon 1995: 620. Nur Ali Qabobe, who worked at the Central Bank in the 1980s, gives a withering account of Fadumo Maxamed Siyaad Barre's role at the Central Bank (2002: 125–37). He also mentions the high position of Canab, the daughter married to General "Morgan," at the Foreign Exchange Department of the Ministry of Finance (134). Compare Afrah, who reports Fadumo as holding both positions (1992: 10–11).

44. Compagnon 1995: 627, referring to Jean-François Bayart, *L'État en Afrique: La politique du ventre* (2006).

45. Rawson 1994: 164–69. Compagnon reports average U.S. economic aid of about $40 million a year in 1982–1987, then a decline in the context of budget cuts in the United States. In 1988, he reports, this economic aid, which had amounted to $34.1 million in 1985, had been reduced to $6.5 million (1995: 644–45).

46. Bridges reports for 1984–1986 that "Our total aid to the country was running at around $120 million a year, the largest set of American aid programs in sub-Saharan Africa. About twenty-five million of this was military." The embassy staff in this period numbered 218 (with 179 family members), which Bridges found excessive (2000: 60, 80, 169–72). For the size of the USAID mission, also see Rawson 1994: 169.

47. Brons (2001: 187) also reports on the estimated numbers of refugees and states that $133 million was sent to Somalia through UNHCR, including $66 million for food. Maren recounts that neither the government nor the international aid organizations really wanted to have the refugees counted. Business as usual was profitable for both sides (1997: 125–30).

48. ION 367, January 28, 1989, "Somalia: Diplomatic Offenses Everywhere." Barre traveled to Egypt, Iraq, and Kuwait. Samantar traveled to Britain where he was told that the government would not restore British aid until the Somali government achieved reconciliation with the North. Xusseen Kulmiye Afrax traveled to Italy on behalf of the military regime and promised "a sound leadership and administration" in the North (ION 368, February 4, 1989: 7 "Somalia: Kulmieh Afrah Visits the EEC").

49. Cabdi Muxumed Amiin 2006: 129. For an early performance of the song by Saado Cali, see www.youtube.com "Saado Cali Land Cruiser (Hees)," accessed August 28, 2010.

50. This book largely consists of dates; references to it will therefore often just be to the date (and not the page number). In this case the date is the end of December 1989.

51. Compagnon 1995: 601, about the summer of 1989.

52. Krech 1989; Compagnon 1989: 76 (for "Jees").

53. Compagnon 1995: 590. "Gabyow" was demoted in February 1989 (*Africa Confidential*, 30, 4, February 17, 1989, "Somalia: Army Purge"). According to ION, he was arrested in July 1989 (ION 393, July 29, 1989: "Somalia: Two Ministers Arrested").

54. Amnesty International 1992: 4; Krech 1989: September 12, 1989.

55. ION 375, March 25, 1989: "Somalia: Dissident Army in the South."

56. ION 380, April 29, 1989. "Somalia: Unclear Situation in the South."

57. ION 394, August 26, 1989. "Somalia: A Fragmented Country." A similar accusation, that the government provoked a fight and then sided with one side, is made by General Caydiid in Ruhela 1994: 81.

58. Maren mentions the army's violence against Hawiye civilians in Beledweyne in early 1990: "In early 1990, several aid agencies withdrew foreign staff from Beledweyne after Hawiye soldiers in the town defected from the army, which then retaliated by attacking civilians. Soldiers rounded up local men, burned houses, killed villagers, and executed a number of refugees" (1997: 179). Compare Ruhela 1994: 160, which mentions one hundred (instead of two hundred) killed, and places what appears to be the same event in May 1990. Ruhela 1994 has parts written or dictated to Ruhela by Caydiid.

59. Typescript document, "Shir-waynihii Kowaad ee Badbaadinta Ummadda Soomaaliyeed lana qabtay 7 dii illaa 12 kii Jannaayo 1989, Hotel Helios, Roma, Italiya," in possession of the author.

60. Ruhela 1994: 168; Interview 2; Brons, citing Cumar Salaad Cilmi, refers to Dhumoodle (east of Garoowe and northwest of Eyl) and Hanan-Weylood as early USC military bases (2001: 207); Pacifico 1996: 270.

61. Daahir Cali Cumar refers to this agreement as the "saddex geesood" or "three-sided" agreement (1997: 180). See also Krech 1989, December 17–18, 1989.

62. Krech 1989, September 23 and October 1989, reports that the government, for example, retook Dhoobley and Afmadow.

63. Issa-Salwe mentions 200 Hawiye civilians killed in Dhuusamareeb (1996: 106–7).

64. The example of the Abris group in the area of Afmadow, mentioned above, is a case in point.

65. Issa-Salwe 1996: 106. Pacifico reports such conflicts for the central region of Somalia (Hiiraan and Middle Shabeelle), as well as the north-central and northeastern regions for June–July 1990. Upper and Lower Jubba had slipped out of government control already before then (1996: 337). Many of these conflicts did not follow the Daarood-Hawiye axis that became dominant in 1991–1992 (Little 1996).

66. According to Rawson (1994: 164), U.S. military aid since 1978 had "followed a formula of modest defensive materials and training." However, this formula nevertheless provided the Barre regime with $18.1 million for a M113 TOW missiles program, $11.6 million for M198 howitzers, and $2.7 million for a M47 tank rebuild program. Before 1978, the Soviet Union had provided even more weapons. Toward the end Libya and Saudi Arabia appear to have provided arms to the Barre regime.

67. The term is Compagnon's (1998: 83), who writes: "Kinship helps to form a political arena, but does not capture the essence of competition: the language of kinship, rather, provides a *ready-made ideology* through which combatants stigmatize the enemy (especially in oral poetry), ascribe unthinkable violence to the other side, and in turn justify their own atrocities, while claiming to uphold the social values of clan solidarity."

68. Axmed M. Silyano [sic] 1991 (Bibliography, Unpublished Sources).

69. Samantar's trusted position, apart from his competence and ruthlessness, also derived from the fact that he was from a so-called minority group, which made it less likely that he would develop a constituency independent from Barre.

70. U.S. Military n.d. (See Bibliography, Unpublished Sources). See also Pacifico 1996: 126.

71. See Compagnon (1995: 469) for biographical information.

72. Sica and Pacifico describe him using epithets such as incompetent, debauched, and dissolute (Sica 1994: 93; Pacifico 1996: 307, 309). See Compagnon 1995: 580 for some biographical information.

73. See also Faisal Xasan Axmed's novel *Maandeeq* (2000).

74. Pacifico 1996: 305. See also the interview Abdirahman Jama Du'ale (n.d.) conducted with Ibrahim Ali Barre "Canjeex": "Interviewed in Nairobi, Canjeex Denied the Allegations," www.angelfire.com/tn3/sdwo/news71.htm, accessed August 2, 2009.

75. Even this political resource of Barre's appears to have been disintegrating. Compagnon reports a delegation of Mareexaan top officials (including "Gaani," but excluding Maslax and Cabdiraxmaan Jaamac "Buluq Buluq") who presented Barre, first on May 26 and again in August 1989, with an ultimatum and demanded reforms such as a national unity government and free elections (1995: 596–97).

76. Pacifico describes him as unprincipled and basing his political positions on opportunism (1996: 98).

77. Yasmeen Maxamuud (2010) based her article on interviews with the survivors. See also Nur Ali Qabobe, who comments on other criminal acts by Maxamed Sheekh Cismaan's son and refers to the vast property in real estate of his wife (2002: 113). Maren visited and interviewed him in Mogadishu in late 1992 or 1993. Maren writes that Maxamed Sheekh had earned the Barre regime's support in part by testifying against so-called "traitors": "Ultimately it led Mohamed Sheikh to a real estate empire of more than 100 buildings in Mogadishu, and other holdings in Dubai. These buildings include numerous houses and offices rented by NGOs and the UN Operation in Somalia, from which the total rent is said to exceed $500,000 a month." As for the looting of humanitarian supplies in 1992–1993, Maxamed Sheekh was not impressed: "This looting today, a few lorries and the relief food, is nothing compared to what happened here before. This is not looting. I know about looting" (1997: 176).

78. Ambassador Bridges says about Caddow that "he bought a huge house for his daughter in Washington on Foxhall Road, the second-largest real estate deal in D.C., where he was Somali ambassador for ten years" (2000: 185). Bridges, who served as U.S. ambassador in Somalia from 1984–1986, recounts how, in Mogadishu, Caddow's wife Caasha tried to blackmail him into renting a villa from her for $6,000 a month, payable in dollars. When he refused, she threatened to rent it to the Libyans instead. Caasha succeeded in renting the villa to a CONOCO oilman who stayed on even after the U.S. embassy was evacuated in January 1991. The same villa became the residence of Ambassador Oakley during UNITAF. See also Ruhela 1994: 87.

79. On July 21, 1989, United Press International reported that the religious disturbances of the week before had led to over 300 killed, including 46 on Jasiira beach, and that 2,000 people had been arrested. Krech reported that the "army mounted house-to-house searches for two days...and seized hundreds of civilians" and 24 people had been killed, 60 wounded, and 2,000 arrested (Krech 1989, July 14–17, 1989). See also *Africa Confidential*, 30, 15 (July 28, 1989), "Death in Mogadishu." Pacifico (1996: 305) and Jama Mohamed Ghalib (2000: 206–7) believed that Isaaq organizers played an important role in the demonstration.

80. Pacifico 1996: 299, 305. Somaliland Research Society & SomalilandNet.com gives a list of fifty-five names (Bibliography: Unpublished Sources). The victims included one man who was of a different northern clan background but closely related to them. One man survived because he was concealed by another man's dead body. See also Africa Watch 1990, Appendix 2.

81. Barre's disingenuousness is obvious both in the case of the Cairo reconciliation meeting Italy and Egypt unsuccessfully tried to organize for November 1990 and in May that year, when he promised to submit the new constitution to a popular referendum. Both incidents are discussed below.

82. The Commission for the Reform of the Constitution consisted of Ismaaciil Jumcaale Cossobleh; Axmed Ashkir Bootaan, head of the political office of the party; Axmed Cali Salaax, juridical adviser for the presidency; Abud Musacad Abud, pro-rector of the National University of Somalia, and Maxamed Cali Tuuryare, head of the faculty of jurisprudence, who were known as moderate people with the most excellent professional qualities. Professor Antonio La Pergola, later president of the Constitutional Court in Italy, briefly came from Italy to assist (Pacifico 1996: 322–23). See also Sica 1994: 40.

83. Pacifico 1996: 361; Sica 1994: 46, 56–57. Sica's information about the casualties of the bloodbath of June 28, 1990, was that seventy people had been killed and ten times as many wounded.

84. Sica (1994: 57) notes that the regime claimed seven deaths and tens of wounded, but "that eye witnesses reporting to the embassy and the doctors in the hospitals said ten times as many." See also Krech 1989 and Pacifico 1996: 361.

85. Axmed Suleemaan "Dafle" replaced Barre as head of the party (Krech 1989, October 11). Maslax was replaced as minister of defense and head of the armed forces by "Morgan," and so forth (Krech 1989, November 15, 1990; Sica 1994: 93)

86. Cabdiraxmaan Jaamac Barre "Buluq-Buluq," Barre's cousin, became deputy prime minister and minister of finance (Pacifico 1996: 376). According to Sica (1994: 75), Madar's appointment was the result of "enormous pressure of Italy, western countries, IMF and World Bank."

87. Krech 1989, October 12, 1990, and October 23, 1990, reported three people dead and thirty-six wounded.

88. This is the so-called Galgalo incident. See *Africa Confidential*, 32, 3 (8 February 1992), "Somalia: Where Do We Go from Here?" and Sica 1994: 94. Jaamac Cumar Ciisa (1995: 134) blames the USC. "Morgan" replaced Barre's son Maslax.

89. FBIS December 3, 1990, Radio Mogadishu, December 2, 1990, "Prime-Minister Announces Security Measures;" FBIS December 27, 1990, Radio Mogadishu, December 24, 1990, "Interior Minister Adds Details."

90. FBIS December 31, 1990, Radio Mogadishu, December 30, 1990, "Prime Minister Briefs Parliament on Security."

91. The following is based on the text of the Manifesto itself. See "Somali Manifesto" in Bibliography (Unpublished Sources). For a published copy of the original, see Bongartz 1991: Appendix 1.

92. In the sense of aspiring to be "modern." See Kapteijns 2009: 104, drawing on Donham 2002.

93. The SNM was not represented. According to Interview 3, there was only "one Isaaq" who signed the Manifesto but was explicitly "only representing himself."

94. No. 68 of Compagnon's list (1995: 858).

95. See Jama Mohamed Ghalib 1995: 209. They are respectively No. 10 and No. 20 on Compagnon's list (1995: 866, 856).

96. No. 74 on Compagnon's list (1995: 858).

97. Interview 4. The attack on Caydiid's house occurred on July 12, 1993.

98. Literally, "people barred from inheriting from each other." Information from Mursal Farah, Wellesley, July 17, 2010.

99. Interview 3. The respondent had himself been a signatory of the Manifesto.

100. Krech 1989 reports that it met with a number of constituencies in the city (intellectuals and businessmen) on September 4 and 10. On January 16, 1991, the seven members of the Reconciliation Committee included at least three prominent signatories of the Manifesto, Axmed Maxamed Darmaan, Xusseen Xaaji Maxamed Bood, and Cabdulcasiis Nuur Xirsi (FBIS January 17, 1990, Radio Mogadishu, January 16, 1991, "Reconciliation Committee, USC Rebels Meet").

101. There is some mention of Article 82 of the Constitution that might allow for Barre to step down with honor in the videotaped conversation of what appears to be a meeting of USC-Mogadishu and the government at the time Maxamed Hawaadleh was prime minister ("U.S.C. 1991, Shocking Video Part 1" (Unpublished Sources), http://www.youtube.com/watch?v=o1sqeMut24s, accessed August 28, 2010.

102. *Christian Science Monitor*, December 31, 1990, Mogadishu, Robert M. Press, "Somali Dissidents Detail Government Wrongdoings."

103. Cali Shiddo Cabdi, No. 7 on the list of Compagnon 1995: 855, who had been ambassador to France before the military takeover; Axmed Maxamed Darmaan, No. 44 (857), who had been ambassador to China in that same period; Jaamac Cali Jaamac, No. 104 (858).

104. Though initially against the secession of the northwest, Cigaal later accepted the presidency of the Republic of Somaliland (1993–2002).

105. Compagnon 1998: 81. Sica 1994: 60. The former died in February and the latter in July 1990.

106. His name is 2nd/4th on the original list of signatories, that is to say, the number

by his name is 2, but numbers 1a and 1b were added by hand after the list was typed. See Sica 1994: 42.

107. On January 17, 1991, BBC World summary presented Axmed Maxamed Darmaan as a USC member.

108. Sica 1994: 69. Pacifico mentions Axmed "Shuqul," [Ismaaciil] Jumcaale Cossoble, lawyer Benvenuto, Cismaan Rooble, and Maxamed Yuusuf Aadan "Muuro" as his friends (1996: 335–36).

109. Sica 1994: 69. Interview 4 confirmed this.

110. The literal meaning is "native colonial soldier," a concept Pacifico held very high.

111. Pacifico 1996: 360–61 (for the murder of Bishop Colombo on July 9, 1989, idem, 295–86). See also Jama Mohamed Ghalib 1995: 204–5. Pacifico criticized the USC for its disinformation campaign that blamed all violence on the Red Berets instead of its own fighters (1996: 360).

112. *Economist*, September 29, 1990.

113. Pacifico describes Mogadishu in February–March 1990 as "a city where both by day but especially at night armed bands made the rounds undisturbed committing with relative ease aggressions and lootings" (1996: 334; see also 375).

114. *Economist*, September 29, 1990.

115. Also the building of the representative of the European Community.

116. According to Interview 4, Xusseen Bood never was a Member of Parliament.

117. *Africa Confidential*, 32, 3 (February 8, 1992), "Somalia: Where Do We Go from Here?" See also Daahir Cali Cumar 1997: 131, who writes that this militia was trained in Aadan Yabaal and Cadaale (Middle Shabeelle).

118. For SNM support for Caydiid, see Interview 4. See Daahir Cali Cumar 1997: 161 for SPM military activities in Bay and Bakool.

119. According to Pacifico (1996: 383), who was close to USC-Mogadishu: "The decision, therefore, to avoid a head-on collision in the capital seemed shared by all the most moderate and reasonable political personalities of the USC and, as far as can be known, by men such as General Nur Galal and the mythical Colonel Shebel who later found themselves, almost against their will, in the position to lead the guerrillas in the Battle for Mogadishu. And of course the major objections against unleashing an open confrontation in the city came from the Abgaal, who lived in the city. Aidid, with his Habr Gidr militias, wanted instead to launch the final attack against the heart of the regime in Mogadishu, but had until then not succeeded in making his point of view prevail." Pacifico's reflections on the initial intentions of General Galaal and Colonel "Shabeel" may be correct but cannot be verified. Both indeed played crucial roles in the clan cleansing of 1991–1992 (Chapter 3).

120. FBIS December 13, 1990, Radio SNM, December 11, 1990, "USC Chairman's Statement on Cairo Meeting." The videotape recorded in Mogadishu on or about January 9, 1991, shows that he sticks to this point during a meeting between a delegation including Xusseen Xaaji Maxamed Bood (and thus either of representatives

of USC-Mogadishu or the Reconciliation Committee). See Bibliography, Unpublished Sources, Disc 3.

121. For example, according to Krech 1989, the USC conquered Jowhar three times in the period September–November 1990.

122. FBIS, January 21, 1991, Radio SNM, "USC Rebels Report on Situation, Position." It is probable that the USC claimed this victory on behalf of its ally, the SPM led by Colonel "Jees."

123. FBIS February 1, 1991, Paris AFP in English, January 31, 1991, "Official Says 600 Refugees Killed in Somalia": "Six hundred were shot dead while many others panicked and jumped into Wabi Shabeele River where they perished in the floods, Mr. Mersa [a Ethiopian government spokesman] said adding that 20,000 others had managed to cross into Ethiopia." Compagnon (1998: 78) writes: "The USC had massacred Daarood/Ogadeen refugees in November 1990, when they took control of the region between Belet Ouen and Jowhare along the Shebelle River." This policy is reminiscent of the attacks on the refugee camps in the northwest by the SNM, closely allied with Caydiid, which was discussed above. See Maren 1997: 113–14 for the events at the refugee camp at Jalalaqsi.

124. *Guardian*, January 23, 1991, Nairobi, Peter Biles, "Hunger and War Drive Refugees to Somali Border" (includes interview with Dr. Murray Watson).

125. Agence France Presse, December 2, 1990.

126. *Christian Science Monitor*, December 24, 1990, Mogadishu, Robert Press, "Rebels Close in on Somalia Capital."

127. *New York Times*, December 12, 1990 (Dateline Nairobi, December 11), Jane Perlez, "Unrest Fills Somalia's Capital as Rebel Groups Press Drive to City."

128. BBC Summary of World Broadcasts, December 24, 1990 (Dateline Nairobi, December 21): AFP in English, "Horn of Africa in Brief: Somalia Foreign Diplomats Speak of 'Total Anarchy' in Mogadishu." There are several reports of soldiers firing into crowds, once in an open market and once at the airport when a crowd surged forward to meet a plane.

129. *New York Times*, January 4, 1991, Nairobi, Jane Perlez, "Effort to Evacuate Foreigners from Somalia Stalls." FBIS December 31, 1990, Radio Mogadishu, "Prime Minister Briefs." Mohamed Jama Ghalib 1995: 210 about the incident that sparked the popular uprising.

130. FBIS January 2, 1991, Radio Mogadishu, "Premier Says Mogadishu District Rid of Rebels."

131. *Washington Post*, January 1, 1991, Nairobi, December 31, 1990, Neil Henry, "Rebels Force Somali Leader Out of Capital." In the "U.S.C. 1991 Shocking Video Part 1," someone who appears to be a USC representative denounces the practice of hunting down people in their houses on the basis of their clan background with great urgency.

132. Sica 1994: 103. Interview 2.

133. Pacifico 1996: 383–84.

134. Pacifico 1996: 384. Interview 2.

135. *Africa Confidential*, 32, 3 (February 8, 1992), Somalia: "Where Do We Go from Here?" In 1992, Afrah wrote about this moment: "But the man who really directs the military operation in Mogadishu is veteran soldier/politician Brig. Osman Halleh whose command post is kept secret" (1992: 51). However, in 1994 he wrote: "The man who directs the guerilla operations against the government in the capital is the veteran military/politician, General Mohammed Noor Galaal" (1994: 40).

136. *Africa Confidential*, 32, 3 (February 8, 1992), Somalia: "Where Do We Go from Here?"

137. Mohammed Nur Galal 2005.

138. See Bibliography, Unpublished Sources, Disc 3.

139. FBIS, January 2, 1991, BBC World Service in English, December 31, 1990, Focus on Africa: Interview with Mohamed Robleh (Maxamed Roobleh), USC representative in London.

140. Ibid.

141. *Toronto Star*, January 3, 1991, Paul Watson, "Ex-Somali Leader's Son Prays for Justice." Watson reports on an interview with the son of the last civilian president Cabdirashiid Sharmarke. He was rejoicing that Barre's fall was near and organizing other Somalis to send aid to Mogadishu. Within two weeks, his relatives would be hunted down in the streets of Mogadishu by USC fighters. The person quoted here is the late brother of Cumar Cabdirashiid Sharmarke, who briefly served as prime minister of the TFG under president Sheikh Shariif Xassan in 2009–2010.

142. Pacifico (1996: 401) defines the term "Faqash" at this point in time as follows: "a nickname which most recently had been affixed to all government soldiers who committed indiscriminate acts of banditry and violence against the common people." I translate this pejorative term as "government scum" and analyze the clan hate-narrative of which it became a part in Chapter 4.

143. *Washington Post*, January 7, 1991 (Dateline Mombasa, January 6), Neil Henry, "Evacuees Tell of Somalia's Chaos, Carnage."

144. Pacifico reports remembering how, in January, when all was lost, General "Morgan" begged Barre to let himself be moved outside Mogadishu while there still was hope; how Barre growled, almost like a wounded lion, that he would die where he was. Pacifico does therefore not believe that Barre, when he left Mogadishu on January 26, 1991, did so voluntarily. He met Barre for the last time on January 4, 1991 (1996: 159).

145. In the *Guardian* of December 31, 1990, "Somali Rebels Fight in Streets of Capital: Tribal Insurgents Reject Dictator's Offer of Peace Talks," Rakiya Omaar wrote that both sides use rocket-propelled grenades. See also Afrah 1992.

146. Pacifico 1996: 378–80. The FBIS radio transcripts for this period also deal with this conference.

147. In this context, four Manifesto/USC-Mogadishu leaders were briefly arrested for "spying for a foreign embassy," including Xusseen Bood, the head of USC-Mogadishu, Axmed Maxamed Darmaan, who was to be a Manifesto delegate to the

Cairo conference, as well as Xaaji Cali Shiddo and Maxamed Cumar Jaamac "Dhigic-Dhigic" (Sica 1994: 95).

148. Sica 1994: 96–97; FBIS January 4, 1991, Radio Mogadishu. Speech by Barre announcing that the reconciliation meeting would be held in Mogadishu (instead of Cairo, as was being negotiated by Italy and Egypt), that he would adhere to any resulting resolution and would pay costs and guarantee security.

149. FBIS January 2, 1991: The elders mentioned were Cumar Xusseen Cabdi Qorey, Xaaji Axmed Xaaji Bageh, Cabdullaahi Gacal Sabriiye, and Xaaji Cumar Macallin.

150. FBIS January 8, 1991, AFP in English, David Chazan, "Flights Postponed." Chazan claims that they had been given radios by the police commander called Cabdiraxmaan; and that, when they used it, a rocket fired at the place of meeting killed the two elders, while two others were seriously wounded. Also Sica 1994: 118. Afrah reports: "Eyewitnesses said that the men, carrying white flags, passed peacefully into rebel-held territory and that the device went off as soon as they sat at the conference table. Other members of the group were seriously injured in the blast" (1992: 52). Xaaji Muuse Boqor's family believes that he was killed by the USC, as Barre was hoping to use the ceasefire negotiations to buy time and because the elders were meeting in a USC-held area of the city (Mohamed Kassim, January 17, 2010; also Interview 4).)

151. BBC Summary of World Broadcasts, January 12, 1991. According to this news report, the Ceasefire Committee consisted of three government representatives (the ministers of Finance, Interior, and Transport), and ten generals: Xusseen Xassan Cali, Axmed Maxamed Sheekh, Maxamed Xusseen Daa'uud, Cali Ismaaciil, Maxamed Aadan, Maxamed Jaamac Aabi (or Xarbi), Muusa Xassan Sheekh, Maxamed Saalax, Maxamed Jaamac Biixi, and General Cali Xaashi Cilmi Barre. See also FBIS January 11, 1991, Radio Mogadishu, January 10, "Information Minister Stresses Rapid Cease-Fire."

152. Sica 1994: 115. This is confirmed by BBC Summary of World Broadcasts, February 2, 1991, excerpt from Kenya Television Network.

153. Sica 1994: 116. For USC-Rome spokesman Cabdulqaadir Maxamed, see idem, 117. For USC-London spokesman Cumar Xassan, see BBC Summary of World Broadcasts, January 11, 1991, quoting an AFP dispatch from Nairobi of January 9. For SSDF spokesman Xassan Cali Mirreh, see FBIS January 10, 1991, London BBC World Service in English, January 9, 1991, Focus on Africa Program, and "SSDF Rebel Leader on Collaboration with USC."

154. FBIS January 17, 1991, Radio Mogadishu, January 16, "Reconciliation Committee, USC Rebels Meet: Cease-fire Resolution Adopted." The other members were Mawlid Macaani Maxmuud, Ibraahim Cabdalla Xassan "Eso," and Mahad Dirir Guuleed (spelling corrected).

155. BBC Summary of World Broadcasts, January 16, 1991, "Somali Rebel Radio Says Peace Effort Is Doomed as Fighting Intensifies." This had been reported on SNM Radio on January 14, 1991.

156. FBIS January 17, 1991, "Reconciliation Committee." Also BBC Summary of

World Broadcasts, January 18, 1991, Radio Mogadishu, January 17, 1991, "Somali Information Minister Announces Cease-Fire: Committee Named."

157. BBC Summary of World Broadcasts, January 22, 1991, Radio Mogadishu, January 17, 1991, "Somalia President Reportedly Ready to Accept Changes Proposed by Committee." The brigadier shared the clan background of those against whom the campaign of clan cleansing was getting underway (personal information from Professor Abdiweli Ali Gaas, by email, September 9, 2010).

158. Peter Biles, "Somali Rebels Reject Peace Plan," *Guardian*, January 22, 1991, Nairobi; "Reject Prime Minister Appointment," FBIS BBC World Service in English, January 21, 1991.

159. "Reject Prime Minister Appointment."

160. On January 9, 1991, Xusseen Bood had been part of a delegation meeting with General Caydiid in a northern neighborhood of Mogadishu, at which Caydiid had refused any accommodation with the government as long as Barre did not resign. See Disc 3.

Chapter 3. Clan Cleansing in Mogadishu and Beyond

1. "Somalia foreign diplomats speak of 'total anarchy' in Mogadishu," BBC Summary of World Broadcasts, December 24, 1990, Horn of Africa in Brief. See also Peter Biles, "Somalia rebel clans gathering for the kill: all foreigners reported evacuated from the city," *Observer*, January 14, 1991, Nairobi. He means foreigners from the West.

2. Sica 1994: 137; Pacifico 1996: 405; Bridges 2000: 204: U.S. ambassador Bishop had wanted to evacuate the local Somali embassy staff separately to a place outside the city. But this did not happen and several local staff members left behind in the embassy compound were killed.

3. Pacifico 1996: 416–18. See also Disc 1.

4. Reid G. Miller, AP, January 29, 1991, Mogadishu, January 28. Miller interviewed Wilhelm Huber and wrote, "Barre turned his hill-top villa into a fortress defended by his personal guards, the Red Berets. Armed with tanks, mortars and 105 mm cannons, they had a panoramic view of the city beneath them and used their vantage point to shell every quarter, Wilhelm and other witnesses said."

5. Ambassador Bishop had to negotiate with an armed (and probably drunk) army officer during the evacuation of the embassy (Bridges 2000; Bishop 1995).

6. A U.S. State Department official, noting that "superpower competition is a thing of the past," characterized the conflict as "a tribal affair without international implications." See Jane Perlez, "Fighting Subsides in Somalia's Capital," *New York Times*, January 1, 1991, Nairobi. A Western diplomat sounded the same theme: "A lot of people just can't wait to get back at the Marehan" (Neil Henry, "Both Sides Claim Control in Somalia; Some Experts Fear Period of Anarchy," *Washington Post*, January 3, 1991, Nairobi).

7. Sica, who continued to be blasted by the USC (and others) for having engaged Barre diplomatically until the very end, found this criticism particularly galling from those who actually had been key players in that regime only days or weeks before (1994: 137–38).

8. Sica 1994: 137–38. Astonished at the brazen opportunism of politicians who had served Barre just weeks before, Sica recounts how he met Cabdiqaasim in Djibouti in March 1991 and made reference to the latter's exile: "'What exile,' he responded, 'I am on an official mission for the government of Mogadishu'" (138).

9. The term is Pacifico's (1996: 446).

10. See Concerned Somalis, Bibliography, Unpublished Sources.

11. Ibid. The document gives Maxamed Xassan "Shabeel" instead of Maxamed Xaashi "Shabeel."

12. Some of those targeted by the USC had indeed worked with and for the regime. Apart from those who had been welcomed into the USC, the most prominent Barre supporters had either escaped earlier, left with Barre, or made their way out separately by car or plane.

13. Paul Watson, "Ex-Somali Leader's Son Prays for Justice," *Toronto Star*, January 3, 1991.

14. Less eloquent but equally revealing are the words of a woman interviewed by Cindy Horst about how she first experienced the war. Ayaan said: "When the war in Somalia started, it began as a political issue against the government. But when it reached Mogadishu, it changed the focus on clan issues" (Horst 2006: 56).

15. In Dadaab refugee camp in Kenya, Horst (2006: 60) interviewed Ubax Cabdi, who was twelve when the war started. She saw USC fighters rape and seriously injure a woman who was their neighbor and worked as a policewoman. They did so in front of both the neighbors and her husband, also a policeman.

16. Interview 5. Siciid Cismaan Keenadiid (2013: 15–16) witnessed a neighborhood "court" punishing the crime of being Daarood with death.

17. Interviews 2 and 5; see also Compagnon 1998. Mohamed Jama Ghalib dilutes the question of accountability by writing about Dr. Abyan that he was "murdered by mindless clan militia drunk on Darood-Hawiye animosity" (1995: 221).

18. Compagnon also writes that "a video showing the arrest and execution by USC guerillas of a Daarood man in civilian attire was welcomed with laughter by the [Hawiye] Abgaal people with whom I watched it" (1998: 78 n. 8).

19. According to "Interclan Fighting, Chaos Reported in Mogadishu," FBIS January 2, 1991, Nairobi, KTN Television in English, Barre's wife Khadiija had arrived in Geneva. Jane Perlez reported that a military plane had landed in Kenya without permission presumably carrying members of the Somali government and their families ("Somalia, Abandoned to Its Own Civil War with Others' Weapons," *New York Times*, January 6, 1991). According to Inter-Press Service, March 18, 1991, Mombasa: "some wealthy refugees [were] living it up in beach hotels" as well as in Nairobi. Peterson (2000: 41) reported about Barre that, after he fled to Kenya in April 1992, "he and 20 aides took temporary asylum in Nairobi's luxurious Safari Park Hotel."

20. Some *laheystayaal* were captives held by their captors to labor for them or provide sex. Of the latter, some ended up as wives of their captors.

21. Personal information from MA, a close friend of this individual's son, Boston, March 7, 2009.

22. Xassan Dimbil is No. 26 on the list in the Appendix of Compagnon 1995: 855-60. The abducted men were Cabdullaahi Hoolif, Cabdixamiid Islaan Faarax, and Cabdullaahi Matukade, respectively Nos. 68, 88, 98. The narrator, Cabdiasiis Nuur Xirsi (Interview 4) is No. 27.

23. Information from BI, the girl's brother, Wellesley, August 12, 2010. The girl, now married with children, lives in Minnesota.

24. See Chapter 4 for further analysis of rape warfare.

25. Information from MY, her brother, Wellesley, September 28, 2010.

26. Information from AD, her son, Wellesley, July 10, 2010.

27. Interview 7. The Sheikh Sufi family was attacked in May 1991.

28. Todd Shields, "The African land the world forgot sinks into anarchy; Somalia's collapse reflects a continent's decline," *Independent*, January 20, 1991. Shields noted that the fighting and chaos that erupted on December 30 had continued but that after January 12 no foreigners were present to comment on it. As we will see below, the BBC briefly reported on Somali allegations that the USC was engaging in clan cleansing on February 7 and March 5, 1991.

29. Shields refers to the journalists' "rebel guides" (Todd Shields, "In Somalia Only the Children Can Be Trusted," *Independent*, February 3, 1991), while Henry had a USC representative called Abdul Osman, a thirty-three-year-old economist, as his guide (Neil Henry, "War Guts Capital of Somalia; Looting, Stench of Death Pervade Mogadishu After Fall of Ruler," *Washington Post*, January 30, 1991, Mogadishu, January 29, 1991). Shields reported on January 20 ("The African Land") that "even a few weeks before [the war engulfed the capital], visitors could join guerrillas for a tour of 'liberated Somalia' that wound from city centre through road blocks, to rebel-controlled countryside, and back to the nominally government-controlled capital."

30. Henry, "War Guts Capital"; Reid G. Miller, AP, January 30, 1991; Aidan Hartley, "New Leader Offers Olive Branch amid Carnage and Looting of Wrecked City," *Guardian*, January 30, 1991, Mogadishu, January 29.

31. Henry, "War Guts Capital."

32. Hartley, "New Leader Offers."

33. Reid G. Miller, AP, January 29, 1991, Mogadishu, January 28.

34. Robert M. Press, "Somalia's Leaders Look for Ways to Keep Peace," *Christian Science Monitor*, February 5, 1991, Mogadishu.

35. Henry, "War Guts Capital."

36. Shields, "In Somalia Only the Children."

37. Hartley, "New Leader Offers."

38. Michel Sailhan, "More on Conference," FBIS February 4, 1991, Paris AFP in English, February 2, 1991.

39. Ibid.

40. Amnesty International 1992; "Somali Tells of Month-Long Massacre,"

Independent (London), August 5, 1992, Interview 9 (on Northwest); Professor Abdiweli Ali Gaas, phone conversation, July 15, 2009 (on Gedo). Professor Mohamed Kassim, Interview 7 (on Brava). For Brava and Gedo, also see below.

41. Chris McGreal, "The Lost Continent: A Nation Waits for Famine and Revenge," *Independent*, April 7, 1991.

42. "Interim President Speaks at Inauguration," FBIS January 30, 1991, Radio Mogadishu, January 29.

43. "Ali Mahdi Meets with Reconciliation Committee," FBIS January 31, 1991, Radio Mogadishu.

44. "Addresses Reconciliation Committee," FBIS January 30, 1991, Radio Mogadishu, January 29, 1991.

45. "Interim Prime Minister Addresses Committee," FBIS January 30, 1991, Radio Mogadishu January 29, my emphasis.

46. "Somalia Former President Appeals for End to Killings," February 14, 1991, BBC Summary of Broadcasts.

47. "Interim Prime Minister Addresses Committee," FBIS January 30, 1991. See also Nur Ali Qabobe 2002: 101; Ismail Ali Ismail 2010: 290. Cumar Carta may have seen this as a step toward a power-sharing arrangement between SNM, SPM, and USC-Caydiid, agreed on in October 1990. However, Cali Mahdi's decision *not* to try to preserve the national army was seen by many as an endorsement of the clan cleansing campaign.

48. "Spokesmen Rejects Allegation," FBIS February 11, 1991, Radio Mogadishu, February 7, 1991. Reference is to Africa and the Week, BBC World Service in English, February 6, 1991.

49. BBC World Service in English, Focus on Africa, March 5, 1991. Only a summary is available of this program.

50. "Official Dismisses Reports on Ethnic Massacres," FBIS March 14, 1991, Radio Mogadishu, March 11, 1991.

51. "Somali News Agency Denies Claims of Opposition to USC made in BBC Interview," BBC Summary of World Broadcasts, March 18, 1991, Radio Mogadishu, March 15, 1991.

52. There was no formal response from Mogadishu to the public accusations of genocidal violence in Somalia by groups in Washington and Toronto discussed below.

53. Personal information from Alifaisal Dirir Farah, who attended this meeting in Mogadishu (Wellesley, July 10, 2010).

54. This split turned violent in April 1991 and then, more lethally, in November. Examples would include Daniel Compagnon, Abdisalam Issa-Salwe, Kenneth Menkhaus, and Said S. Samatar.

55. A noncomprehensive list includes Africa Watch and Physicians for Human Rights 1992: 4; Bradbury 1994: 14–15; Bridges 2000: 204; Greenfield 1991; Human Rights Watch June 1993: 4 and 1995: 2, 14; Markakis 1994; Mohamed Diriye Abdullahi 2001: 39; Mukhtar 2003: 151–52 ("Mogadishu"); Prendergast 1994b; Samatar 2001: 18.

56. For example, Lyons and Samatar 1995: 21; Adam 2008: 92. Ismail Ali Ismail assigns no explicit agency (2010: 292), but on the other hand suggests that a form of ethnic cleansing took place: "Ethnic alliances for political gain in peacetime are palatable. But when violence becomes politics by other means, such alliances can only lead to ethnic cleansing" (290).

57. For a denial of intent, see also Brons 2001: 223.

58. Hussein Ali Dualeh served as ambassador of the Barre regime in Uganda and Kenya and then became a wealthy businessman in Mogadishu. In 2010 he was minister of finance of the self-proclaimed Republic of Somaliland.

59. Hussein Ali Dualeh 1994: 125–26 (my emphasis). He also writes that "the Hawiye . . . chased them [the Daarood] out of Mogadishu and forced them to leave all their properties behind" (126).

60. Omaar 1992: 232; see also Africa Watch 1992: 3. For other half-truths and falsehoods, see Gassem 1994: 74; Ghalib 1995: 211.

61. Amnesty reported: "In the first three months after Siad Barre's overthrow, hundreds of Darod clan members were killed and Darod women raped in Mogadishu and their property looted, mainly by troops loyal to General Aideed" (1992: 4).

62. FBIS February 6, 1991, SNM Radio of February 3, 1991; February 1, 1991, BBC Summary of World Broadcasts, SNM Radio of January 30. The latter reported that 600 soldiers surrendered in Berbera and Cadaadley and that in Burco the remaining Barre soldiers were wiped out.

63. Khaled Haidar, FBIS February 25, Paris AFP in English; "SNM Fighters Destroy 'Enemy' Force in Borama," FBIS February 6, 1991, Radio SNM of February 5, 1991; idem, "SNM Conducts 'Mopping Up' Operations in Awdal."

64. See (1) Immigration and Refugee Board of Canada, Somalia: Information on the Current Situation of the Gadabursi in Somalia and in Somaliland, September 1, 1992, SOM11602, http://www.unhcr.org/refworld/docid/3ae6ad8e24.html, accessed August 5, 2010; (2) Mohsin Mahad, "SNM as Seen from the Other Side," and "Speaking as a Faqash," April 22, May 13, 2005, http://www.wardheernews.com, accessed January 13, 2009; (3) Cabdale [sic] Faarah Sigad, "My Memory of February 4 in 1991 and Borama's Genocide," http://harowo.com/2007/01/16, accessed August 5, 2010.

65. Saturdays Only, BBC World Service in English, FBIS February 9, 1991.

66. The fighting reportedly occurred on February 7, 1991, and the SDM was explicitly mentioned as allied with the USC ("Somalia: Siyad Loyalists Involves in Clashes in South," BBC Summary of World Broadcasts, February 11, 1991, Radio Mogadishu of February 8, 1991). See also two other news reports: "Somalia: Fighting Reported Between USC and SPM Forces; Jibuti Appeals for Aid," BBC Summary of World Broadcasts, February 12, 1991"; and Robert M. Press, "Somalia Tries to Pick Up the Postwar Pieces," *Christian Science Monitor*, February 19, 1991.

67. Two young men who fled Mogadishu at this time and passed through (and, in one case, spoke with) the SPM militias believed that the latter were caught unaware by the clan cleansing of Daarood. Personal information from Hussein Yusuf (by telephone

from Columbus, Ohio, January 17, 2010), and Abdikarim Hassan (San Diego, January 8, 2010). The SPM was considered Ogaadeen-based but, at this moment, appears to have had fighters of many clan backgrounds in its ranks.

68. David Chazan, "SSDF Chief Says We Can Take Mogadishu," FBIS March 27, 1991, Paris AFP in English, my emphasis.

69. Bakr Ogle, "Renewed Fighting Ensues Between USC, SPM, 210 Dead," FBIS February 11, 1991, *Nairobi Standard of Sunday*, February 10.

70. Michel Sailhan, Mogadishu, "USC Troops Capture City," FBIS February 11, 1991, Paris AFP in English, February 10, 1991.

71. Ibid.

72. "USC's Aidid Not to Recognize Interim Government," FBIS March 5, 1991, London BBC World Service in English, Focus on Africa, February 28, 1991.

73. Michel Sailhan: "USC Mounts 'Wide-Scale' Operation to South," FBIS February 11, 1991, Paris AFP in English, my emphasis.

74. Ibid.

75. See Military Communiqué, Unpublished Sources.

76. "SDF to Attend Conference," FBIS February 23, 1991, Radio Mogadishu: "The SSDF, with ninety-seven representatives from Benaadir, Galguduud, Mudug, Nugaal and Bari regions, met with Maxamed Abshir Muusa, Cali Mahdi's Minister of Planning, in Gaalkacyo between 14 and 19 February, 1991. Here the SSDF announced it would attend the February 28 conference in Mogadishu. The SNM refused to attend." See also "Ministry Reports Fighting in Gaalkacyo District," FBIS February 28, 1991, Radio Mogadishu. According to the BBC Summary of World Broadcasts, March 2, 1991, "Radio Mogadishu reported on 28 February that the Somali Internal Affairs Ministry said that fighting had broken out among residents of Gaalkayco [sic] district in Mudug region, central Somalia." "The Ministry appealed for an end to the fighting, adding that the problem should be solved by peaceful means." In addition, "The USC Threatens Siad's 'loyalist troops,'" FBIS March 2, 1991, AFP, reported fighting between Hawiye and Majeerteen in Gaalkacyo.

77. See Concerned Somalis, Unpublished Sources. Caydiid's communiqué gives the total enemy losses as 550 killed, 320 wounded, and 200 captured. The press release must have quoted Caydiid's communique. According to Interview 4, the elders taken away and never heard of again were sixteen, including Maxamuud Xaaji Xassan.

78. Interview 4; personal information from Professor Abdiweli Ali Gaas, part of the Concerned Somalis at that time (February 14, 2010).

79. "USC's Aidid Not to Recognize Interim Government," FBIS March 5, 1991, London BBC World Service in English, Focus on Africa, February 28, 1991.

80. FBIS March 1, 1991, Radio Mogadishu of February 28, 1991, "SDM Chairman Comments."

81. Personal information from Professor Abdiweli Ali Gaas, who mentioned the murder in Baydhaba of local Majeerteen bank employees and a wealthy merchant called Warsame Doos. The latter, together with other men, was murdered close to the tomb of

Sheikh Uways (telephone conversation, February 14, 2010). Also Daahir Ali 1997: 190, 247–48, 262.

82. Information from Hussein Ali Yusuf, telephone conversations, January 16–17, 2010.

83. Information from Siyaad Sheikh Daahir, telephone conversation, February 10, 2010, and in Wellesley, Massachusetts, October 10, 2010. In 2007 Barbaar Amar was governor of Baydhaba.

84. Mukhtar and Kusow 1993: 8; Mukhtar 1992: 4. The authors go as far as to claim that the Dighil and Mirifle represent "at least two-thirds of the Republic's population." According to Horst (2006: 47), "The refugees in Dadaab mainly originated from the interriverine area between the Jubba and the Shabeelle," adding that 80 percent were Daarood.

85. Peter Biles, "Somalia's Leader Flees as Capital Falls to Rebels," *Guardian*, January 28, 1991, Mombasa.

86. Chazan, "SSDF Chief Says."

87. "Thousands of Somali Refugees Reportedly Arriving," February 21, 1991, UPI; FBIS March 28, 1991, Nairobi KTN Television in English of March 27, 1991.

88. Personal information from Abdikarim Hassan, San Diego, January 8, 2010. The story goes that his killers could not be sure what the author's clan background was, as his northern accent was not clan-specific. The killers reportedly said: "It is better that we mistakenly kill an Isaaq man than that we let a Daarood man go free." While this story may well be apocryphal, it powerfully evokes the realities of the time period.

89. "More Than 150 Killed When Boat Carrying Somalis Sank," March 4, 1991, AP, Nairobi (for quotations). See also UPI, March 2, 1991 (which reported 100 Somali refugees drowned); and "130 Somalis Said to Drown as Refugee Boat Founders," *Washington Post*, March 4, 1991.

90. MV stands for "Motor Vessel," a prefix commonly used in the Merchant Navy.

91. Chazan, "SSDF Chief Says."

92. Kismaayo's population had swollen to 400,000 or 500,000 people according to Didrikke Schanche, "Government Forces Seize Major Southern, Western Cities," AP, April 24, 1991.

93. Daahir Ali referring to February 1991 (1997: 248).

94. FBIS April 11, 1991, London BBC World Service in London, April 9, 1991, Focus on Africa. This alliance consisted of militias of the SPM, the SSDF, and what would later become the SNF (a Mareexaan-based front).

95. McGreal, "The Lost Continent."

96. "SSDF, SPM Forces Said Advancing to Mogadishu," FBIS March 25, 1991, Paris AFP in English, March 22, 1991, Nairobi.

97. "Demonstrations Reported in Mogadishu 21 March," FBIS March 25, 1991, Paris AFP in English, March 22, 1991.

98. Chazan, "SSDF Chief Says."

99. The same sentiment was expressed by SPM political spokesman Cumar Macallin.

The *Kenya Times* reported him as saying that Barre would not be allowed to take power again because of his "dictatorial orgy," adding that the SPM and SSDF "accused the present interim government in Somalia of deliberate killing of the members of the Darod clan; instigating terror on the populace; and recent massacre of 500 innocent women and children in Galcaio" ("Moallim denies that Kismaayo and Baidoa have fallen to the USC," *Nairobi Kenya Times*, April 26, 1991).

100. This is probably Cabdullaahi Maxamuud Axmed "Gardheere," commander of the group of hardened soldiers called "Dhafoorqiiq" (Professor Abdiweli Ali Gaas, telephone report from Garowe on inquiries held there, August 1, 2010). Daahir Cali (1997: 174–79), speaks about this campaign and Major-General Cabdullaahi "Gardheere" in detail.

101. Chazan, "SSDF Chief Says."

102. Ibid.

103. McGreal, "The Lost Continent."

104. FBIS April 10, Paris AFP in English, April 8.

105. Daahir Ali (1997: 169–79) gives a detailed description of the SNF-Alliance to take back Mogadishu, though he does not use this name for the combined front. For his views of the internal betrayal, see 178.

106. By April 13, 1991, they had been driven back beyond Brava (120 miles southwest of Mogadishu) after fierce fighting on April 10–11. Another group of fighters had been driven back to west of Baydhaba (110 miles northwest of Mogadishu). See also Michel Sailhan, "Loyalist Forces Repulse Attacks near Mogadishu," FBIS April 15, 1991, Paris AFP in English, April 13, 1991.

107. Daahir Cali (1997: 179) comments on the fate of those who tried to make their way back to Kismaayo.

108. According to Bradbury (1994: 54), "The front between the USC and the SPM/SNF passed through the Juba valley three times between February and April 1991." Local residents may not always have had the choice to remain neutral or may have been perceived as siding with the other side even when they did not. Daahir Cali asserts the leaders of the communities of Lower Jubba sided against the people of Kismaayo (1997: 188), as did Professor Cali Fiqi, telephone conversation, November 26, 2010.

109. "SDM Chairman Comments," FBIS March 1, 1991, Radio Mogadishu of February 28, 1991.

110. Personal information from Professor Ali Fiqi, telephone conversation, November 26, 2010.

111. The song is called "Lament for Brava." Issa-Salwe quotes two lines of the song (1996: 120). It was also played during the Bravanese-Somali community gathering I attended with members of the Sheikh bin Sheikh family in Toronto on October 14, 2011.

112. Professor Mohamed Kassim (Interview 7), speaking on the authority of his father-in-law, then mayor of Brava. The date of this is uncertain. See also Daahir Cali 1997: 169.

113. Information from Professor Mohamed Kassim (Interview 7) who heard this from the wife herself.

114. Ibid.

115. Alessandra Vianello, reporting on inquiries among members of the Bravanese diaspora, by telephone from London, January 23, 2010. See also Daahir Cali 1997: 199.

116. Ibid. In April–May 1992, during what may be called Barre's last hurrah, Brava changed hands between the warring parties twice (Daahir Cali 1997: 205, 227–28).

117. The former prime minister of the penultimate civilian administration, who had been living and working in the United States, spells his name Abdirazak Haji Hussen.

118. McGreal, "The Lost Continent."

119. "Deputy-Prime-Minister Leaves for Kismaayo," FBIS March 29, 1991, Radio Mogadishu of March 28; "Warring Parties Agree on Cease-Fire," FBIS April 8, 1991, Paris AFP in English, April 6, 1991; "Fighting Reported Between Rival Factions," FBIS April 10, 1991, Paris AFP in English, April 8, 1991.

120. Daahir Cali notes that cars with megaphones telling people to leave as they would all be killed also traversed the city. He points out that Kismaayo was politically not united and the Islamist Ittixaad organization, in charge of the port, petrol, and food, may have encouraged such disunity to gain power for itself (1997: 187).

121. Ibid. Xiirey Qaasim is No.75 on the list of Manifesto signatories by Compagnon (1995: 858).

122. The following relies in good part on Daahir Cali, who describes the capture of Kismaayo in detail (1997: 185–94).

123. The Saleebaan are a subgroup of the Habr Gidir Hawiye and thus perhaps had the power to offer those who were being pursued asylum.

124. FBIS April 30, 1991, *Nairobi Sunday Times* in English, April 28. See also Daahir Cali 1997: 190.

125. Sica 1994: 148–51. Somali accounts emphasize that Maxamed Abshir had a half-brother who was Hawiye, but such a kinship relation did not always offer protection. It is more likely that his political usefulness to the USC had not run out. Former Prime Minister Cabdirasaaq was reportedly among those who fled Kismaayo by the "Habaar waalid" road.

126. "Kismaayo, Baydhaba Taken from Siad Barre's Troops," FBIS April 24, 1991, Radio Mogadishu of April 23, 1991 (my emphasis). Didrikke Schanche, "Government Forces Seize Major Southern, Western Cities" (April 24, 1991, AP), quotes the Cali Mahdi administration as (falsely) stating: "The interim government reports it took Kismaayo and Baidoa *with little fighting and no harm to civilians*" (my emphasis). This misinformation also reached Amnesty International 1992, which reported: "In contrast [to Mogadishu], when they [the USC] captured Kismayu in May 1992 and on other occasions, those commanding Aideed's forces are said to have prevented them from committing abuses."

127. Interview 1. Maxamed Sheekh Faruur had been wounded in the incident that killed two other Manifesto members on January 8, 1991, and had fled separately from his wife by boat.

128. The same happened after the flight and expulsion of the people of the Northwest.

129. Horst writes that 400,000 Somalis arrived in what became the three refugee camps in Dadaab in 1991–1992 (2006: 19). Hussein Ali Dualeh's claim that all were Daarood is undoubtedly an exaggeration (1994: 126). See also the moving photographs with texts by Sheikh 2001.

130. Bradbury and Davies 1991: 2, 22, 6 (for quote). In Gardo, Bradbury and Davies found 26.6 percent of children between one and five years old significantly malnourished (1991: 36). According to African Rights 1993, Ethiopia put fewer obstacles in the way of the refugees than Kenya, though it initially provided few services.

131. By July 1992, Rogge estimated the number of those internally displaced as a result of "ethnic cleansing" at 280,000, mostly urban Somalis, containing "a large proportion of Somalia's remaining merchant, administrative, and professional classes" (1992: 37).

132. Africa Watch and Physicians for Human Rights 1992.

133. Personal information from Hussein Ali Yusuf, who lived in Gedo in this period.

134. Ibid., 15. The authors do not give a date. It is therefore not clear whether this violence occurred in spring 1991 or after "Jees" returned to Caydiid's camp some time before August 1991.

135. Africa Watch and Physicians for Human Rights 1992: 19; Menkhaus 1991; Prendergast 1994a.

136. Besteman 2009. Prendergast, who visited the Lower Jubba area in the summer of 1993, reported that many Bantu Somalis had been displaced and that UNITAF should beware of trying to organize local district councils in the absence of the former Bantu Somali residents (1994a: 7). In this context this study would characterize the violence Besteman calls genocide as episodes of ethnic or clan cleansing. Bantu Somalis trace descent to East African peoples speaking Bantu languages. Socially discriminated, they nevertheless enjoyed considerable political and economic opportunity in post-independence Somalia.

137. Amnesty International August 1992: 1. See also "Somali Tells of Month-Long Massacre," *Independent*, August 5, 1992.

138. Compare Daahir Cali (1997: 228) on what happened when the USC reached Maandheera. According to unconfirmed Somali oral reports, Lieutenant-Colonel "Shabeel" was responsible for killing General Mohamed Jama Bihi (Maxamed Jaamac Biixi), whose body was reportedly tied to a car, dragged through the town, and left unburied.

139. Amnesty International August 1992. One victim mentioned by name was a schoolteacher from Mogadishu, Cabdullaahi Aabi Faarax.

140. Personal information from the person who survived this ordeal.

141. Daahir Cali 1997: 228. This author also reports on atrocities committed outside of Kismaayo just before the city was captured in March 1992. He regarded these incidents as part of terror warfare that aimed at causing panic among the survivors, driving them out, and replacing them with other inhabitants (1997: 226). He does not specify whether the targets of this terror warfare were Wagosha (now Bantu Somali), although the latter certainly formed a significant part of the population of this area (see Menkhaus 1991; Prendergast 1994a).

142. For the underlying causes of conflict in Kismaayo, see Chapter 4.

143. Jane Perlez, "Somali Clans Planning Last Grab for Advantage," *New York Times*, December 9, 1992. See also *Africa Watch* 1993: 5.

144. The four are the Deshiishle, Dhulbahante, Majeerteen, and Warsangeli.

145. Africa Watch (1993: 7) received a list of 126 names killed by fighters of "Jees" and reported that refugees in Kenya claimed that as many as 600 had been killed.

146. Jane Perlez, "Witnesses Report a Somali Massacre before U.S. Arrival," *New York Times*, December 29, 1992. Of the individuals whose bodies were found in Gobweyn the following were mentioned by name: Mohamed Abdi Hersi, Gura Hadj (Gurey Yuusuf Xaaji), and Ali Warabe. Dr. Mohamed Muse Sugulle, one of Kismaayo hospital's five doctors, was shot in front of his family. One person was said to have lost seventeen family members (Perlez, "Witnesses Report").

147. Keith B. Richburg, "Somalis' Battle for Kismaayo Is Biggest Threat to a Fragile Peace," *Washington Post*, April 12, 1993.

148. Perlez, "Witnesses Report" quotes "the Harti" as saying that "they have deep roots here and . . . that they regard other clans as occupiers." Richburg, "Somalis' Battle for Kismaayo," quotes the Ogaadeen elders removed from Kismaayo to protect them from "Morgan" as claiming "they are the true indigenous inhabitants of Kismaayo." The recurring use of autochthony/allochthony arguments as rationales for political and economic rights is further analyzed in Chapter 4.

149. That this fear was not unfounded is suggested by the murder on January 2, 1993, of the head of the UNICEF office in Kismaayo, twenty-eight-year-old Sean Devereaux, whose testimony about the massacre had been widely quoted in the international press (Alison Mitchell, "U.S. Army Investigating Killings in a Somali Port," *New York Times*, January 5, 1993).

150. Perlez, "Witnesses Report."

151. There are many precedents in the Somali civil war. One example is the Barre regime's brutal repression of "the Hargeisa Group," a group of professional middle-class men who established a self-help project to improve public facilities and social services for the residents in Hargeisa in late 1981 and early 1982 (Africa Watch 1990: 37–40). Another is the massacring of the peace party in Gaalkacyo at the end of February 1991. At the time of writing, this policy of targeting educated middle-class men and women as potential peacemakers is still pursued by the Islamist al-Shabaab militias dominating part of south and central Somalia.

152. The expression "genocide by force of habit," used in the context of Darfur, is Alex De Waal's (2004: 724).

Chapter 4. The Why and How of Clan Cleansing: Political Objectives and Discursive Means

Epigraph: Michaels 1997: 166.

1. The term "moral irrepair" is inspired by the title of Walker 2006.

2. Indirectly, however, the indifference or even gloating (*schadefreude*) that had characterized the attitudes of many Somalis at the time of the attacks on Majeerteen civilians of Mudug may have emboldened Barre's clan-based collective "punishment." See Chapter 2, "The State's Clan-Based Violence Against Civilians in the Northeast (1979–1982)."

3. The government was still a major employer at this time; teachers, journalists, clerks, and other low-level administrators of all kinds were government employees transferred by their ministries to different parts of the country, including the Northwest.

4. That the terms "Faqash" and "Daarood" to describe the SNM enemy were merging is clear from speech reported in the March 4, 1989, issue of *Indian Ocean Newsletter*, that the leaders of the SNM "refuse to contemplate any talks with the present regime, who they consider only represent Darod Somalis." "Somalia: Issaq Administration in the North," ION 372, March 4, 1989.

5. Whether the orders and decisions always originated with Barre himself rather than with his closest associates in the last years of his regime (especially after his car accident of 1986), is not fully clear.

6. Pacifico 1996: 299, 305; Interview 2.

7. Pacifico 1996: 384. "USC 1991 Shocking Video," Unpublished Sources.

8. Afrah 1992 lists the equipment the guerrilla forces captured when Barre was expelled: "over 45 million Dollar in U.S. supplied military hardware including 25,000 M16 rifles, 15,000 AK47, thousands of hand grenades and landmines, 20 Soviet made T55 tanks, 35 artillery pieces, 36 rocket launchers, 40 armoured personnel carriers, 6 Chinese-made Migs, 5 hawk hunt[ers] (damaged)."

9. The communal nature of the clan cleansing campaign remained particularly pronounced until May 1991, the aftermath of the first USC capture of Kismaayo.

10. Whether Caydiid himself saw clan cleansing as mostly a political instrument or personally believed the clan hate-narratives that were marshaled in its service is a subject of debate. Without the clan cleansing campaign, the USC would most likely have gained control of the presidency in any case. However, in the absence of further warfare, Caydiid himself might have had less power than he actually obtained because of his talent for military strategy and his willingness to use violence. It is likely that Caydiid saw the main rivals of his career (including Barre and other professional military men and military coup makers such as Cabdullaahi Yusuf of the SSDF) as Daarood rivals. A psychological portrait of this central character is beyond the scope of this study; it would potentially add significantly to our insights into this stage of the civil war.

11. As mentioned above, Barre's intransigence also played a role in dashing their hopes.

12. Rape had been part of the military government's clan-based violence against civilians in Mudug (1978–1979) and the Northwest (1987–1988), as attested to by oral accounts and Africa Watch 1990. The scale and context of USC rape warfare, however, constituted a new departure.

13. Exceptions are Yasmeen Maxamuud 2006 and Gardner and El Bushra 2004, which deals with rape by government forces and officials in the Northwest.

14. As Alison puts it, "Groups are often targeted for destruction or domination through their women, because of women's roles as biological reproducers of the collectivity, transmitters of its culture, and signifiers of ethno-national difference" (2007: 80).

15. See, for example, Kapteijns 2010a: 51.

16. Ahmed has spoken of "the mimetic quality of violence," which might also be relevant in this context (2004: 216).

17. This draws on the title of Africa Watch 1990, *Somalia: A Government at War with Its Own People*.

18. Relevant incidents make up part of the narrative of Chapters 2 and 3. See "Somalia: A Fragmented Country," ION August 26, 1989; Ruhela, 1994: 81; Nur Ali Qabobe 2002: 44.

19. Pacifico wrote this in summer 1989.

20. Lieberman 2006: 299. Lemarchand uses the concept of "mythico-histories," which he defines as "a mixture of fact and fiction designed to offer each community retrospective validation of its own interpretation of the genesis of ethnic conflict" (1994: 19). His book on Burundi deals explicitly with how "political discourse as a system of possible definition of ethnic selves" can be transformed and then be "mobilized, and ultimately incorporated into the horrors and irrationality of genocidal violence" (xxvi).

21. Lemarchand notes in this context that "evolving perceptions of 'otherness'—*l'imagination constituante*, to borrow Paul Veyne's phrasing—are a constitutive element of ethnic strife" (1996: xxix), which ethnic entrepreneurs manipulate to their political advantage (176).

22. Semelin 2003: 199. Lieberman similarly argues that the activation of such hate-narratives does not only provide the motives or rationales for ethnic cleansing but also accelerates transitions to violence (2006: 300).

23. See the discussion of MOD in Chapter 2.

24. The initial letters of these three political maneuvers (**M**isrepresentation, **O**rchestration, and **D**enial) also form the acronym of MOD. Making an argument easier to summarize is a technique on which political campaigns of information and misinformation thrive.

25. See Chapter 3 for further analysis.

26. This is implied in Daahir Cali Cumar's report on the BBC Radio commentary of Yuusuf Sheekh Cali Madar, August 28, 1991 (1997: 253). For Caydiid's use of the term *haraadiga*, see 135.

27. See Chapter 1 for discussion of Faisal Axmed Xasan's novel *Maandeeq*.

28. Ironically, but with tragic consequences, several hate-narratives would blow

up in the face of USC-Caydiid itself. For example, USC-Cali Mahdi later constructed Caydiid's own Habr Gidir clan base, in its turn, as not native to Mogadishu and "from elsewhere."

29. See the poetic taunt from 1992 by Geelle Ismaaciil Macallin that was cited in Chapter 1 and whose French text is given in Mohamed-Abdi 1994: 17–18.

30. Battera (2004: 91–141) shows and explicitly argues (111) that relations between the different groups were much more complex than later hate-narratives have claimed and cannot be reduced to a Daarood-Hawiye binary or to military force at the exclusion of collaboration and cooptation. This does not mean the historical grievances expressed by those incorporated into this emerging mini-state have no validity. However, it underlines that such grievances helped the transformation of incomplete and imprecise interpretations of the past into a program for immediate violent action.

31. See the discussion of Kismaayo above. Here the break-lines came to be articulated in terms of subdivisions of the genealogical construct of Daarood.

32. The term "dervishization" draws on the name of Sayyid Maxamed's armed followers, the Daraawiish or Dervishes. Ahmed 1995 blames the Barre regime for "dervishization" of Somali history and society as a whole and produces a thinly concealed anti-Daarood clan hate-narrative.

33. Bulhan 2008; for a critique of this aspect of the hate-narrative, see below.

34. Compagnon 1995 (Appendix) uses the same method of counting top members of the regime but argues that there was no such MOD or Daarood dominance under Barre, although he appears to make an exception for the army and other security forces. More importantly, Compagnon refuses to take the categories for granted.

35. In the following, I especially focus on the Barre regime (1969–1991). In Mukhtar 1989 and 2003, referencing a count of clan backgrounds of leading politicians takes the place of an analysis of the latter's actual politics and policies (including their use of clan as a political instrument and the political patronage they may have bestowed). Such counts, which are moreover largely unspecified, lead Mukhtar to claim first (1989: 95) that the majority of the founding members of the Somali Youth League (SYL) in 1947 were from the inter-river region and non-Daarood, and then (2003: 24) that it was "a Daarood party" from 1947 to 1953, "a Hawiye party" from 1953 to 1960, a broad-based party from 1960–1963, and a party that was "exclusively Daarood" from 1963 to 1969. See also my critique of Bulhan 2008 below.

36. In this context it is significant that Bulhan 2008 distinguishes between "clan" and "Klan," with the latter referring to those who made dishonest and divisive use of clan solidarities and sentiments. He does not, however, apply or maintain this distinction in a consistent way, so that for this author all individuals with Daarood clan backgrounds become "Klan" members.

37. In Ruhela (1994: 42 ff.), Caydiid consistently presents his vision as a comprehensive and democratic restoration of state and society. The term "Daarood" barely figures. However, it is striking that he regularly uses the term "Irir," a then less commonly used genealogical construct within which the lower-level constructs of Isaaq and Hawiye

(and, in this context, therefore the SNM and USC) are unified. For example, Caydiid refers to the "Hawiye Irir Tribe" and the "Isaq Irir Tribe" (48).

38. Information from Abdirahman Nur (Boston) and Mursal Farah (Wellesley), who saw this video independently from each other in early 1991.

39. This was a common SNM theme, which was sounded, for example, during the speech of an SNM spokesman held on July 1, 1989, in the Washington, D.C., area.

40. The oft-repeated insight that a civil war is never just one war, but many wars and that (in Rwanda) each person has a unique "genocide story" is also relevant to the Somali case (Eltringham 2009: 5).

41. Alessandra Vianello, personal information. Nuruddin Farah has also made this argument (2007 and in various oral presentations).

42. For Kismaayo, see also Chapter 3, "Kismaayo Again."

43. Little 1996: 45. See also Menkhaus and Craven 1996.

44. See Besteman 2009; Besteman and Cassanelli 1996; Declich 2001; Menkhaus 1989, 1991; Menkhaus and Craven 1996.

45. Other relevant contexts include tensions due to resource conflicts and differential state patronage between local inhabitants and the vast numbers of refugees settled in their midst after the drought of 1974 and the 1977–1978 war, as discussed in Africa Watch 1990 and Maren 1997, and conflict over land, as discussed in Besteman and Cassanelli 1996.

46. See Axmed M. Silyano [sic], Unpublished Sources.

47. Compare Strauss 2006 and Waldorf 2007 for similarities with Rwanda.

48. The term "genocide business" is from Semelin (2003: 204).

49. In the ethnic cleansing campaign against Bosnian Muslims in former Yugoslavia, the question of the intent of the Serbian government turned out hard to prove legally, though Alison 2007, Allen 1996, Benard 1994, and Bringa 2002 report many specific aspects of the violence that suggest that government and army authorities not only turned a blind eye but instructed Serb militias to kill, rape, and expel.

50. Semelin (2003: 200). Practical organization, he writes, "attests best to the will of those who decide to massacre."

51. It did so even as it purposely manipulated individuals and subgroups on all sides against each other as well.

52. The exception here is perhaps the British administration of the Northwest (the Somaliland Protectorate) that consistently favored what it considered its "friendlies," that is to say "*the*" Isaaq, whose political agency was nevertheless of course never static or single.

53. Semelin 2003. See also Strauss 2006 and Waldorf 2007. Apart from the fictional character of Ahmed in Faisal Hasan's novel *Maandeeq*, there is so far no evidence of perpetrators being coerced into participation in the violence by armed force, though such evidence may still emerge.

54. The term is Yerkes's (2004: 933).

55. The term is Hoffman's (2003: 295).

56. Www.youtube.com carried a music video presented by Xogta Media and entitled "Caydiid Hees." The song praises General Caydiid: "We miss you, Caydiid. If you had been here today, al-Shabaab would not have existed," accessed December 9, 2010.

57. Among the many studies I have found useful are Boraine, Levy, and Scheffer, 1994; Cohen 1995; Eltringham 2011; Fletcher and Weinstein 2002; Gibson 2004; Johnstone 2003; Ross 2003; Walker 2006.

58. The date of the "Rome Conference." The "Rome Statute" came into force July 1, 2002.

59. Examples are Newbury 1995, 1998; Eltringham 2006.

Glossary

Faqash: Pejorative term initially used by the SNM to refer to exponents and backers of the government ("government scum"). However, it became a code word in the campaign of clan cleansing and then indicated those to be clan-cleansed, namely all individuals of all clan backgrounds making up the genealogical construct of Daarood.

Gabay: Name of one of the most prestigious Somali poetic genres. (See also Orwin and Riiraash 1997; Samatar 1982.)

Guubaabo qabiil: literally "cheering on, or inciting, one's clan," a kind of poetry whose raison d'être is to take sides and support or vilify specific clans or subclans. The Somali poetic canon does not regard this kind of poetry as prestigious.

ICC (International Criminal Court): An independent international organization that is not part of the United Nations system and is governed by the Rome Statute. The latter was adopted in 1998 and entered into force on July 1, 2002, after it had been ratified by sixty states. (See http://www.icc-cpi.int/Menus/ICC/About+the+Court.)

ICTR (International Criminal Tribunal for Rwanda): Court of law established by the UN Security Council in 1994 to deal with the genocide and other serious violations of international law committed in Rwanda in 1994. (See http://www.unictr.org.)

ICTY (International Criminal Tribunal for Former Yugoslavia): Court of law established by the UN Security Council in 1993 to deal the war crimes committed in former Yugoslavia in the first half of the 1990s. (See http://www.icty.org.)

Laheystayaal: "Hostages," "people in the power and protection of others." This was the term used for those individuals who during the clan cleansing campaign were either hidden and protected or kept and exploited by those who at that moment had the power to do so.

MOD: Acronym introduced by one of the armed resistance fronts (the SNM) to characterize the military regime in terms of the particular clan alliance on which it allegedly leaned (the Mareexaan, Ogaadeen, Dhulbahante Daarood). The term was part of a nefarious political strategy by which both the regime and the opposition came to collectively blame and punish whole clan groups for the political acts and affiliations of individual political or military leaders.

Mooryaan: This term's original meaning is "poor, destitute." The name was applied to the young men who physically committed much of the violence in Mogadishu in the period under study. (See also Marchal 1993; Mohamed-Abdi 2001.)

Mujaahidiin: "Fighters" or "fighters of jihad" (Arabic). Both the SNM and USC used this term to refer to their fighters.

Operation Restore Hope (also called UNITAF): UN-sanctioned military humanitarian intervention in Somalia that was multi-national but in which the U.S. was the dominant force. This study often refers to it as the U.S./UN international intervention. It was officially called UNITAF from December 3, 1992, to May 4, 1993. At that date it became UNOSOM II, which lasted until March 1995, although the United States pulled out most of its troops in March 1994.

***Qaat*, *qat* or *khat*:** Leafy plant (*catha edulis*), whose leaves or twigs are chewed as a stimulant. It prevents chewers from getting sleepy or feeling tired but can also make them reckless and impulsive.

SDM (Somali Democratic Movement): Armed front based in the inter-river region that sided with USC Caydiid in January 1991 but soon divided into pro- and anti-Caydiid factions.

SNA-Caydiid (Somali National Alliance led by General M. F. Caydiid): Alliance of armed fronts founded in August 1992 but based on a similar alliance established in February 1992.

SNA-Cali Mahdi (Somali National Alliance led by Cali Mahdi): Alliance of armed fronts established by Cali Mahdi in October 1992 to counter SNA-Caydiid.

SNF (Somali National Front): Armed front founded in March 1991 in opposition to the USC and especially active in the Southwest. Between March 1991 and the USC capture of Kismaayo at the end of April 1991, the name SNF or SNF Alliance was also used for the broader Daarood-based Alliance that tried to capture Mogadishu in this period (See "SNF or SNF Alliance").

SNF or SNF Alliance (Somali National Front or Somali National Front Alliance): Daarood-based alliance that formed in response to the USC clan cleansing campaign in March 1991 and was defeated by USC-Caydiid and the SDM at the end of April 1991.

SNM (Somali National Movement): Armed front founded in 1982 in opposition to the military regime of Maxamed Siyaad Barre and especially active in the Northwest.

Somali Bantu: Somalis who trace descent from Bantu-speaking peoples. It came into use after the collapse of the Somali state. Before this date, the term used in scholarship about Somalia was Wagosha (people of the forested river banks).

SPM (Somali Patriotic Movement): Armed front founded in 1989 in opposition to the military regime of Maxamed Siyaad Barre and especially active in the Southwest. The name was used by rival warlords mobilizing different clan bases (e.g., SPM-Jees or SPM-Morgan).

SPM-Alliance: The broad Daarood-based alliance that made a last attempt to capture Mogadishu in spring 1992. At its defeat Barre was definitively driven out of the country.

SSDF (Somali Salvation Democratic Front): First opposition front that took up arms against the Barre regime and based itself on the Ethiopian side of the Somali-Ethiopian border. It increasingly drew its support from north-central and northeast Somalia.

SSF (Somali Salvation Front): Armed front founded in Nairobi in 1978 in opposition to the military regime of Maxamed Siyaad Barre. It was absorbed into the SSDF (see above).

UNITAF (United Task Force): See Operation Restore Hope.

USC (United Somali Congress): Armed front founded in 1989 in opposition to the military regime of M. S. Barre and especially active in south-central and southern Somalia. The division between USC-Caydiid and USC-Cali Mahdi led to full-scale war in November 1991.

Bibliography

See the Introduction for a discussion of the source base of this study (including the fieldwork that helped generate it) and areas of scholarship on which this book draws. Detailed references are given in the notes. The following collections of unpublished materials deserve separate mention:

Unpublished Sources

ORAL INTERVIEWS

The following are interviews the author conducted with eyewitnesses and survivors of clan cleansing in Mogadishu, Baydhaba, Kismaayo, and Gedo.

Interview 1: Geello Xirsi, Frankfurt, July 2004.

Interview 2: Maxamed Aadan Yuusuf, Wellesley, Massachusetts, January 23, 2009.

Interview 3: AH, former Manifesto elder who spoke to me by phone on the condition that I would not use his name. April 8, 2009.

Interview 4: Cabdulcasiis Nuur Xirsi, signatory of the Manifesto Group, Boston, May 3, 2009.

Interview 5: Eng. Maxamuud Cali "Cadami" and Saciid M. Shire "Suugaan," Columbus, Ohio, June 15, 2009.

Interview 6: Abshir Maxamed Cali, by phone from Virginia, August 29, 2009; about USC capture of Kismaayo in April 1991.

Interview 7: Mohamed Kassim, by telephone from Sharja, August 23, 2009, and January 17, 2010; about the different episodes of violence experienced by the Benadiri people, especially the residents of Brava.

Interview 8: Siyaad Sheekh Cumar Sheekh Daahir, by phone from Boston, mid-February 2010.

Interview 9: Cabdulcasiis Nuur Xirsi, signatory of the Manifesto Group, Wellesley, November 17, 2010.

AUDIO-VISUAL PRIMARY SOURCES

The following are audio-visual primary sources not available on the Internet and in possession of the author. They consist of informally videotaped recordings of events in

Somalia in 1991–1992 by USC journalists, copies of which were provided to me by Eng. Maxamuud Cali "Cadami" and Fadumo Dheel. Relevant to this study are three discs:

Disc 1 contains footage of a USC film crew driving through the Huriwaa neighborhood of Mogadishu before Barre's expulsion on January 26, filming what they see and occasionally interviewing groups of people and commanders about what is happening and how they see the situation. They also interview some Italian families who are evacuated by helicopter on tape. This tape also contains a brief Italian TV program shot in Mogadishu on February 2, 1991, and footage of the demonstration by Somalis in Toronto, probably in March 1991, including speeches about the massacres in Mogadishu and the plight of the expelled.

Disc 2 overlaps with, but has some footage other than Disc 1.

Disc 3 contains a set of interviews the film crew held with USC commanders, female nurses, and wounded men at General Caydiid's temporary headquarters. Having interviewed these individuals in the field, the film crew followed Caydiid's car and entourage via Jowhar to Mogadishu, where on January 9–10, 1991, Caydiid held a series of meetings with leading politicians of USC-Mogadishu and the Reconciliation Committee (Cumar Carta Ghaalib, Xusseen Xaaji Maxamed Bood, and Cali Mahdi) and top USC military men, of whom generals Nuur Caddow, "Nero," Galaal, Axmed Sahal "Ciriiri," and Cabdullaahi Warsame are identified by name. Then the crew filmed Caydiid as he left for "the central regions," including Beledweyne. On YouTube, Keymedia gives January 24 for this event (Gen. Aidid with Sulux and Manifesto Readers).

OTHER UNPUBLISHED SOURCES

Silyano [sic], Axmed M. 1991. "A Proposal to the Somali National Movement on a Framework for a Transitional Government in Somalia." London, March. Typescript in possession of the author.

Canadian Network on Human Rights in Somalia. 1991. Press Release, Toronto, March 9. www.somaliawatch.org, accessed May 19, 2009

Concerned Somalis. 1991a. "Genocide in Mogadishu: Mogadishu after the ouster of Barre's dictatorship," with Victim List. March 11. www.somaliawatch.org, accessed March 21, 2009.

———. 1991b. "Genocide in Galkayo (USC assault in the Mudug region)." March 19, including USC Military Communiqué "Galkio Falls into the U.S.C. Hands." March 3. www.somaliawatch.org, accessed March 21, 2009.

"Mogadishu Massacre." 1991. Document forwarded to me privately by email March 29, 2009: list of 229 names of victims of "clan cleansing" (mostly men but some women) probably put together in Nairobi c. March 1991.

"Kismaayo Massacre." 1992. Document forwarded privately by email March 29, 2009: list of 77 male and female victims (6 to 82 years), killed in Kismaayo, December 1992.

Military Communiqué. 1991. Ref. No.USC/DD/3/3/91, March 3: Galkio [Gaalkacyo] falls into the U.S.C hands. From Genocide File, www.somaliawatch.org, accessed March 21, 2009.

Mukhtar, Mohamed Haji. 1992. "Ergada Mission to the Horn of Africa (The Inter-River Regions of Somalia). August 18–September 14."
Mukhtar, Mohamed Haji and Abdi Mohamed Kusow. 1993. "The Bottom-Up Approach in Reconciliation in the Inter-River Regions of Somalia: A Visiting Mission Report of August 18 to September 23."
Somali Manifesto I. 1990. To: General Mohamed Siad Barre, President of the Somali Democratic Republic, *Mogadishu*; Subject: Recommendation Aimed at Bringing About National Reconciliation and Salvation." For a published copy of the original, see Bongartz 1991, Appendix 1. For a list that gives the clan backgrounds of the signatories, see Compagnon 1995: 858 ff.
Somaliland Research Society & SomalilandNet.com and Mohamed-Aar Abdillahi Mohamed. 2001. "War Crimes Committed Against the People of Somaliland," presentation of Somaliland Research Society & SomalilandNet.com at Somaliland International Meeting, London, and "Unique Question to Abdiqaasim Salaad Hassan." Original date of posting given as Tuesday, January, 23, 2001; posted on Somalia Watch under rubric "The Genocide File-Forgive But Not Forget," May 19, 2007, accessed March 21, 2009.
"U.S.C. 1991 Shocking Video Part 1." 1991. Videotaped conversation among what appear to be members of the Reconciliation Committee and USC-Mogadishu, among them Xusseen Bood, accessed August 21, 2010. There is no Part 2.
U.S. Military. n.d. "Somalia: Operations Other Than War," Special Edition 93-1. http://www.globalsecurity.org/military/library/report/call/call_93-1_appxa.htm, accessed August 28, 2009.
Somali Community in the Americas. 1991. "Genocide in Mogadiscio." March 18. www.somaliawatch.org, accessed March 21, 2009.

Secondary Sources

Adam, Hussein. 2008. *From Tyranny to Anarchy: The Somali Experience*. Trenton, N.J.: Red Sea Press.
Afrah, Mohamoud Mohamed. 1992. *Target Villa Somalia*. Karachi: [n.p.].
———. 1994. *The Somali Tragedy*. Mombasa: Mohamed Printers.
Africa Watch. 1990. *Somalia: A Government at War with Its Own People: Testimonies About the Killings and the Conflict in the North*. New York: Africa Watch Committee.
———. 1992. *Somalia: A Fight to the Death? Leaving Civilians at the Mercy of Terror and Starvation*. Washington, D.C.: Africa Watch, February 13.
———. 1993. *Somalia: Beyond the Warlords: The Need for a Verdict on Human Rights Abuses*. Washington, D.C.: Africa Watch, March 7.
Africa Watch and Physicians for Human Rights. 1992. *No Mercy in Mogadishu: The Human Cost of the Conflict and the Struggle for Relief*, written by Alex de Waal and Jennifer Leaning. Boston: Physicians for Human Rights, July.
African Rights. 1993. *The Nightmare Continues . . . Abuses Against Somali Refugees in Kenya*. London: African Rights, September.

Ahmed, Akbar S. 2004. "'Ethnic Cleansing': A Metaphor for Our Time." In *Genocide: An Anthropological Reader*, ed. Alexander Laban Hinton, 211–30. Malden, Mass.: Blackwell.

Ahmed, Ali Jimale. 1995. "'Daybreak Is Near, Won't You Become Sour?': Going Beyond the Current Rhetoric in Somali Studies." In *The Invention of Somalia*, ed. Ali Jimale Ahmed, 135–16. Lawrenceville, N.J.: Red Sea Press.

Ali, Ayaan Hirsi. 2007. *Infidel*. New York: Free Press.

Alison, Miranda. 2007. "Wartime Sexual Violence: Women's Human Rights and Questions of Masculinity." *Review of International Studies* 33: 75–90.

Allen, Beverly. 1996. *Rape Warfare: The Hidden Genocide in Bosnia-Herzegovina and Croatia*. Minneapolis: University of Minnesota Press.

Amnesty International. 1988. *Somalia: A Long-Term Human Rights Crisis*. New York: Amnesty International, September.

———. 1990. *Somalia: Report on an Amnesty International Visit and Current Human Rights Concerns*. London: Amnesty International, January 25.

———. 1992. *Somalia: A Human Rights Disaster*. London: Amnesty International.

Axmed Cali Abokor. 1993. *Somali Pastoral Work Songs: The Poetic Voice of the Politically Powerless*. Uppsala: Department of Social and Economic Geography, Uppsala University.

Battera, Federico 2004. *Dalla Tribù allo Stato nella Somalia nord-orientale: Il Caso dei Sultanati di Hobiyo e Majeerteen, 1889–1930*. Trieste: Edizioni Università di Trieste.

Benard, Cheryl. 1994. "Rape as Terror: The Case of Bosnia." *Terrorism and Political Violence* 6, 1: 29–43.

Berman, Bruce J. 1998. "Ethnicity, Patronage and the African State: The Politics of Uncivil Nationalism." *African Affairs* 97, 388: 305–41.

Berman, Bruce J. and John Lonsdale. 1992. *Unhappy Valley: Conflict in Kenya and Africa*. Book 2, *Violence and Ethnicity*. London: James Currey.

Besteman, Catherine. 2009. "Genocide in Somalia's Jubba Valley and Somali Bantu Refugees in the U.S." http://hornofafrica.ssrc.org/Besteman.

Besteman, Catherine and Lee V. Cassanelli, eds. 1996. *The Struggle for Land in Southern Somalia: The War Behind the War*. Boulder, Colo.: Westview Press.

Bishop, James K. 1995. "Escape from Mogadishu in 1991." In *Embassies Under Siege*, ed. Joseph G. Sullivan, 149–66. Washington, D.C.: Brassey's.

Bongartz, Maria. 1991. *Somalia im Bürgerkrieg: Ursachen und Perspektives des innenpolitischen Konflikts*. Hamburg: Institut für Afrika-Kunde.

Boobe Yuusuf Ducaale. 2006. *Diiwaanka Maansada Cabdillahi Suldaan Maxamed (Timacadde)*. 2nd ed. Addis Ababa: Flamingo Press. (1st ed., Mogadishu, 1983).

Boraine, Alex, Janet Levy, and Ronel Scheffer, eds. 1994. *Dealing with the Past: Truth and Reconciliation in South Africa*. Cape Town: Institute for Democracy in South Africa.

Bowen, John R. 2002. "Culture, Genocide, and a Public Anthropology." In *Annihilating Difference: The Anthropology of Genocide*, ed. Alexander Laban Hinton, 382–95. Berkeley: University of California Press.

Bradbury, Mark. 1994. *The Somali Conflict: Prospects for Peace*. Working Paper. Oxford: Oxfam.

Bradbury, Mark and Rick Davies. 1991. *A Report by the Assessment Mission to Bare, Nugaal and Mudug Regions of Somalia from September 17th to September 30th to the Inter-NGO Committee for Somalia (UK)*. October.

Breytenbach, Breyten 1994. "Afterword." In *Dealing with the Past: Truth and Reconciliation in South Africa*, ed. Alex Boraine, Janet Levy, and Ronel Scheffer, 160–65. Cape Town: Institute for Democracy in South Africa (IDASA).

Bridges, Peter. 2000. *Safirka: An American Envoy*. Kent, Ohio: Kent State University Press.

Bringa, Tone. 2002. "Averted Gaze: Genocide in Bosnia-Herzegovina, 1992–1995." In *Annihilating Difference: The Anthropology of Genocide*, ed. Alexander Laban Hinton, 194–225. Berkeley: University of California Press.

Brons, Maria H. 2001. *Society, Security, Sovereignty and the State. Somalia: From Statelessness to Statelessness?* Utrecht: International Books.

Bryden, Matt and Martina I. Steiner. 1998. *Somalia Between Peace and War: Somali Women on the Eve of the 21st Century*. Nairobi: UNIFEM.

Buckley-Zistel, Susanne. 2006. "Remembering to Forget: Chosen Amnesia as a Strategy for Local Coexistence in Post-Genocide Rwanda." *Africa* 76, 2: 131–50.

Bulhan, Hussein A. 2008. *Politics of Cain: One Hundred Years of Crises in Somali Politics and Society*. Bethesda, Md.: Tayosan International.

Cabdi Muxumed Amiin. 2006. *Diiwaanka Hilin Hayaan: Suugaanta Abwaan Cabdi Muxumed Amiin*, ed. Yuusuf X. Cabdullaahi (Sheekhulcasri). Spanga (Sweden): Omhassan.

Cabdulkadir Cabdi Shube. 2007. *Durbaan Garasho: Gabayadii iyo Maansooyinkii Abwaan Cabdulkadir Cabdi Shube*. Stockholm: Scansom.

Ceuppens, Bambi and Peter Geschiere. 2005. "Autochthony: Local or Global? New Modes in the Struggle over Citizenship and Belonging in Africa and Europe." *Annual Review of Anthropology* 34: 385–407.

Clark, Phil and Zachary D. Kaufman, eds. 2009. *After Genocide: Transitional Justice, Post-Conflict Reconstruction and Reconciliation in Rwanda and Beyond*. New York: Columbia University Press.

Cohen, Stanley 1995. "State Crimes of Previous Regimes: Knowledge, Accountability, and the Policing of the Past," *Law & Social Inquiry*, 20, 1: 7–50.

———. 2001. *States of Denial: Knowing About Atrocities and Suffering*, Cambridge: Polity Press.

Compagnon, Daniel. 1992. "Dynamiques de mobilisation, dissidence armée et rébellion populaire: Le cas du Mouvement National Somali (1981–1990)." *Africa* 47, 4: 502–30.

———. 1995. "Ressources politiques, régulation autoritaire et domination personnelle en Somalie: Le régime de Siyaad Barre (1969–1991)." Ph.D. dissertation, Political Science, Université de Pau et des Pays de l'Adour.

———. 1998. "Somali Armed Movements: The Interplay of Political Entrepreneurship and Clan-Based Factions." In *African Guerrillas*, ed. Christopher Clapham, 73–89. Oxford: James Currey.

Cooper, Frederick. 2006. "The Politics of Citizenship in Colonial and Postcolonial Africa." *Studia Africana* (16 Octubre):14–23.

———. 2008. "Possibility and Constraint: African Independence in Historical Perspective." *Journal of African History* 49: 67–196.

Daahir Cali Cumar (Deyr). 1997. *Qaran Dumay iyo Qoon Taalo-Waayey* [sic]. Nairobi: Mam & Bros.

De Waal, Alex. 2004. "Counter-Insurgency on the Cheap." *Review of African Political Economy* 31, 102: 716–25.

Declich, Francesca. 2001. "When Silence Makes History: Gender and Memories of War Violence from Somalia." In *Anthropology of Violence and Conflict*, ed. Bettina E. Schmidt and Ingo W. Schröder, 161–75. London: Routledge.

Dolby, Nadine. 2006. "Popular Culture and Public Space in Africa: The Possibilities of Cultural Citizenship." *African Studies Review* 49, 3: 31–47.

Donham. Donald L. 2002. "On Being Modern in a Capitalist World: Some Conceptual Issues." In *Critically Modern: Alternatives, Alterities, Anthropologies*, ed. Bruce M. Knauft, 241–57. Bloomington: Indiana University Press.

———. 2006. "Staring at Suffering: Violence as a Subject." In *States of Violence: Politics, Youth, and Memory in Contemporary Africa*, ed. Edna G. Bay and Donald L. Donham, 16–33. Charlottesville: University of Virginia Press.

Doornbos, Martin. 2006. *Global Forces and State Restructuring: Dynamics of State Formation and Collapse*. New York: Palgrave Macmillan.

Eltringham, Nigel. 2004. *Accounting for Horror: Post-Genocide Debates in Rwanda*. London: Pluto Press.

———. 2006. "Debating the Rwandan Genocide." In *Violence, Political Culture & Development in Africa*, ed. Preben Kaarsholm, 66–91. Oxford: James Currey.

———. 2009. "Introduction." *Journal of Genocide Research* 11, 1: 5–10.

———. 2011. "The Past Is Elsewhere: The Paradoxes of Proscribing Ethnicity in Post-Genocide Rwanda." In *Remaking Rwanda: State Building and Human Rights after Mass Violence*, ed. Scott Strauss and Lars Waldorf, 269–82. Madison: University of Wisconsin Press.

Fadumo Ahmed Alim. See Xaawa Jibriil.

Faisal Axmed Xasan. 2000. *Maandeeq*. Scarborough, Ont.: Markham Litho., 2000.

Farah, Cristina Ali. 2007. *Madre piccola*. Rome: H. Frassinelli.

———. 2008. *Barni en Domenica*. Trans. from Italian to Dutch Carolien Steenbergen. Amsterdam: Sirene.

———. 2011. *Little Mother: A Novel*. Trans. from Italian Giovanna Bellesia-Contuzzi and Victoria Offredi Poletto, Intro. Alessandra di Maio. Bloomington: Indiana University Press.

Farah, Nuruddin. 2000. *Yesterday, Tomorrow: Voices from the Somali Diaspora*. New York: Cassell.

———. 2007. "Of Tamarind and Cosmopolitanism." *Halabuur: Journal of Somali Literature and Culture* 2, 1–2: 34–37.
Fearon, James D. and David D. Laitin. 2000. "Violence and the Social Construction of Ethnic Identity." *International Organization* 54, 4: 845–77.
Feldman, Allen. 1995. "Ethnographic States of Emergency." In *Fieldwork Under Fire: Contemporary Studies of Violence and Survival*, ed. Carolyn Nordstrom and Antonius C. G. M. Robben, 224–52. Berkeley: University of California Press.
Finnegan, William. 1995. "Letter from Mogadishu: A World of Dust." *New Yorker* 20: 64–77.
Fletcher, Laurel E. and Harvey M. Weinstein. 2002. "Violence and Social Repair: Rethinking the Contribution of Justice to Reconciliation." *Human Rights Quarterly* 24, 3: 573–639.
Fletcher, Luke. 2007. "Turning Interahamwe: Individual and Community Choices in the Rwandan Genocide." *Journal of Genocide Research* 9, 1: 25–48.
Fortier, Anne-Marie.1999. "Re-membering Places and the Performance of Belonging(s)." *Theory, Culture, Society* 16, 2: 41–64.
Foucault, Michel. 1972. *The Archaeology of Knowledge and the Discourse of Language.* New York: Pantheon.
Freedman, Sarah Warshauer, Harvey M. Weinstein, K. L. Murphy, and Timothy Longman. 2011. "Teaching History in Post-Genocide Rwanda." In *Remaking Rwanda: State Building and Human Rights After Mass Violence*, ed. Scott Strauss and Lars Waldorf, 297–315. Madison: University of Wisconsin Press.
Gardner, Judith and Judy El Bushra, eds. 2004. *Somalia—The Untold Story: The War Through the Eyes of Somali Women.* London: Pluto Press.
Gassem, Mariam Arif 1994. *Hostages: The People Who Kidnapped Themselves.* Nairobi: Central Graphics.
Gersony, Robert. 1989. *Why Somalis Flee: Synthesis of Accounts of Conflict Experience in Northern Somalia by Somali Refugees, Displaced Persons and Others.* Washington, D.C.: Bureau for Refugee Programs, Department of State, August.
Ghalib, Jama Mohamed. 1995. *The Cost of Dictatorship: The Somali Experience.* New York: Lilian Barber Press.
Gibson, James L. 2004. *Overcoming Apartheid: Can Truth Reconcile a Divided Nation?* New York: Russell Sage.
Greenfield, Richard. 1991. "Somalia's Sad Legacy." *Africa Report* 36, 2: 13–18.
Hartley, Aidan 2003. *The Zanzibar Chest: A Story of Life, Love, and Death in Foreign Lands.* New York: Atlantic Monthly Press.
Hayden, Robert M. 2000. "Rape and Rape Avoidance in Ethno-National Conflicts: Sexual Violence in Liminalized States." *American Anthropologist* 102, 1: 27–41.
———. 2002. "Imagined Communities and Real Victims: Self-Determination and Ethnic Cleansing in Yugoslavia." In *Annihilating Difference: The Anthropology of Genocide*, ed. Alexander Laban Hinton, 231–53. Berkeley: University of California Press.
Hilker, Lindsay McLean. 2011. "Young Rwandans' Narratives of the Past (and Present)."

In *Remaking Rwanda: State Building and Human Rights After Mass Violence*, ed. Scott Strauss and Lars Waldorf, 316–25. Madison: University of Wisconsin Press.

Hintjens, Helen. 2009. "Reconstructing Political Identities in Rwanda." In *After Genocide: Transitional Justice, Post-Conflict Reconstruction and Reconciliation in Rwanda and Beyond*, ed. Phil Clark and Zachary D. Kaufman, 77–99. New York: Columbia University Press.

Hinton, Alexander Laban. 2002. "The Dark Side of Modernity: Toward an Anthropology of Genocide." In *Annihilating Difference: The Anthropology of Genocide*, ed. Alexander Laban Hinton, 1–40. Berkeley: University of California Press.

———, ed. 2004. *Genocide: An Anthropological Reader*. Malden, Mass.: Blackwell.

Hoffman, Eva. 2003. "The Balm of Recognition: Rectifying Wrongs through the Generations." In *Human Rights, Human Wrongs: The Oxford Amnesty Lectures 2001*, 278–303. Oxford: Oxford University Press.

Horst, Cindy. 2006. *Transnational Nomads: How Somalis Cope with Refugee Life in the Dadaab Camps in Kenya*. New York: Berghahn.

Human Rights Watch. 1993. "Somalia." In *The Lost Agenda: Human Rights and UN Field Operations*, 107–32. New York: Human Rights Watch.

———. 1995. *Somalia Faces the Future: Human Rights in a Fragmented Society*. 1, 2. April.

Hussein Ali Dualeh.1994. *From Barre to Aideed: Somalia, Agony of a Nation*. Nairobi: Stellagraphics.

International Crisis Group. 2005. "Somalia's Islamists." *Africa Report* 100, 12.

Ismail, Ali Ismail. 2010. *Governance: The Scourge and Hope of Somalia*. Victoria, B.C.: Trafford.

Issa-Salwe, Abdisalam M. 1996. *The Collapse of the Somali State: The Impact of the Colonial Legacy*. London: Haan.

———. 2005. "Electronic Communication and an Oral Culture: The Political Dynamics of Somali Websites and Mailing Lists." Ph.D. dissertation, Thames Valley University.

Jaamac Cumar Ciisa (Aw). 1995. *Qaranjabkii Soomaaliya*. Mombasa: n.p.

Johnson, John J. 1974. *Heellooy, Heelleellooy: The Development of the Genre Heello in Modern Somali Poetry*. Bloomington: Indiana University Press.

Johnstone, Gerry A., ed. 2003. *Restorative Justice Reader: Texts, Sources, Contexts*. Cullompton, Devon: Willan Publishing.

Kaldor, Mary. 2007. *New and Old Wars*. 2nd ed. Stanford, Calif.: Stanford University Press.

Kapteijns, Lidwien. 1994. "Women and the Crisis of Communal Identity." In *The Somali Challenge: From Catastrophe to Renewal?*, ed. Ahmed I. Samatar, 211–32. Boulder, Colo.: Lynne Rienner.

———. 2001. "The Disintegration of Somalia: A Historiographical Essay." *Bildhaan: International Journal of Somali Studies* 1: 11–52.

———. 2009. "Discourse on Moral Womanhood in Somali Popular Songs, 1960–1990." *Journal of African History* 50, 1: 101–22.

———. 2010a. "Making Memories of Mogadishu in Somali Poetry about the Civil War."

In *Mediations of Violence in Africa: Fashioning New Futures from Contested Pasts*, ed. Lidwien Kapteijns and Annemiek Richters, 25–74. Leiden: Brill.
———. 2010b. "I. M. Lewis and Somali Clanship: A Critique." *Northeast African Studies* n.s. 1, 1: 1–25.
———. 2013. "Black Hawk Down: Recasting U.S. Military History at Somali Expense." In *Framing Africa: Portrayals of a Continent in Contemporary Mainstream Cinema*, ed. Nigel Eltringham, 39–71. New York: Berghahn.
Kapteijns, Lidwien, with Maryan Omar Ali. 1999. *Women's Voices in a Man's World: Women and the Pastoral Tradition in Northern Somali Orature, c. 1899–1980*. Portsmouth, N.H.: Heinemann.
Kapteijns, Lidwien and Annemiek Richters. 2010. "Introduction." In *Mediations of Violence in Africa: Fashioning New Futures from Contested Pasts*, ed. Lidwien Kapteijns and Annemiek Richters, 1–23. Leiden: Brill.
Krech, Hans. 1989. *Der Burgerkrieg in Somalia (1988–1996): Ein Handbuch*. Berlin: Dr. Koster.
Kusow, Abdi M. 1994. "Peace and Stability in Somalia: Problems and Prospects. *Ufahamu* 22 1/2: 25–40.
Laitin, David D. and Said S. Samatar. 1987. *Somalia: Nation in Search of a State*. Boulder, Colo.: Westview.
Lemarchand, René. 1972. "Political Clientelism and Ethnicity in Tropical Africa: Competing Solidarities in Nation-Building." *American Political Science Review* 66, 1: 68–90.
———. 1994. *Burundi: Ethnocide as Discourse and Practice*. Washington, D.C.: Woodrow Wilson Press.
———. 1996. *Burundi: Ethnic Conflict and Genocide*. Washington, D.C.: Woodrow Wilson Center Press.
———. 1997. "Patterns of State Collapse and Reconstruction in Central Africa: Reflections on the Crisis in the Great Lake Region." *Africa Spectrum* 32, 2: 173–93.
———. 2007. "Genocide, Memory and Ethnic Reconciliation in Rwanda." In *Collection l'Afrique des grands lacs*, ed. S. Marysse, F. Reyntjens, and S. Vandeginste, 21–30. Paris: l'Harmattan.
———. 2009. *The Dynamics of Violence in Central Africa*. Philadelphia: University of Pennsylvania Press.
Lewis, Ioan M. 2008. *Understanding Somalia and Somaliland: Culture, History, Society*. New York: Columbia University Press.
Lieberman, Ben. 2006. "Nationalist Narratives, Violence Between Neighbours and Ethnic Cleansing in Bosnia-Herçegovina: A Case of Cognitive Dissonance." *Journal of Genocide Research* 8, 3: 295–309.
Little, Peter D. 1996. "Conflictive Trade, Contested Identity: The Effects of Export Markets on Pastoralists of Southern Somalia." *African Studies Review* 39, 1: 25–53.
Lonsdale, John. 1994. "Moral Ethnicity and Political Tribalism." In *Inventions and Boundaries: Historical and Anthropological Approaches to the Study of Ethnicity and*

Nationalism, ed. Prebend Kaarsholm and Jan Hultin, 131–50. Roskilde, Denmark: Roskilde University.

Lorde, Audre. 1984. *Sister Outsider: Essays and Speeches*. Trumansburg, N.Y.: Crossing Press.

Lubkemann, Stephen C. 2008. *Culture in Chaos: An Anthropology of the Social Condition in War*. Chicago: University of Chicago Press.

Lyons, Terrence and Ahmed I. Samatar. 1995. *Somalia: State Collapse, Multilateral Intervention, and Strategies for Political Reconstruction*. Washington, D.C.: Brookings Institution.

Mamdani, Mahmood. 1996. *Citizen and Subject: Contemporary Africa and the Legacy of Late Colonialism*. Princeton, N. J.: Princeton University Press.

———. 2002. *When Victims Become Killers: Colonialism, Nativism, and the Genocide in Rwanda*. Princeton, NJ: Princeton University Press.

———. 2009. *Saviors and Survivors: Darfur, Politics and the War on Terror*. New York: Pantheon.

Marchal, Roland. 1993. "Les 'Mooryaan' de Mogadiscio: Formes de violence dans un espace urbain en guerre." *Cahiers d'Études Africaines* 33, 130: 295–320.

Maren, Michael. 1993. "Aidid's Endgame." *Village Voice*, November 30, 22.

———. 1997. *The Road to Hell: The Ravaging Effects of Foreign Aid and International Charity*. New York: Free Press.

Markakis, John. 1994. "Ethnic Conflict and the State in the Horn of Africa." In *Ethnicity and Conflict in the Horn of Africa*, ed. Katsuyoshi Fukui and John Markakis, 217–37. Athens: Ohio University Press.

Maxamed Sheekh Xassan, ed. 2007. *Murti Dumar: Kaalinta Suugaanta Haweenka Soomaaliyeed (Women's Wisdom: Somali Women's Literary Role)*. Stockholm: Scansom.

Meintjes, Sheila, Aku Pillay, and Meredith Turshen. 2001. "There Is No Aftermath for Women." In *The Aftermath: Women in Post-Conflict Transformation*, ed. Sheila Meintjes, Aku Pillay, and Meredith Turshen, 3–19. London: Zed Books.

Menkhaus, Kenneth. 1989. "Rural Transformation and the Roots of Underdevelopment in Somalia's Lower Jubba Valley." Ph.D. dissertation, Political Science, University of South Carolina.

———. 1991. *Report on an Emergency Needs Assessment of the Lower Jubba Region (Kismaayo, Jamaame, and Jilib Districts) Somalia*. Nairobi: World Concern.

———. 2004. *Somalia: State Collapse and the Threat of Terrorism*. Oxford: Oxford University Press.

Menkhaus, Kenneth and Kathryn Craven. 1996. "Land Alienation and the Imposition of State Farms in the Lower Jubba Valley." In *The Struggle for Land in Southern Somalia: the War Behind the War*, ed. Catherine Besteman and Lee Cassanelli, 155–78. Boulder, Colo.: Westview.

Michaels, Anne. 1997. *Fugitive Pieces*. New York: Knopf.

Michnik, Adam. 1994. "Why Deal with the Past?" In *Dealing with the Past: Truth and*

Reconciliation in South Africa, ed. Alex Boraine, Janet Levy, and Ronel Scheffer, 15–18. Cape Town: Institute for Democracy in South Africa.
Mills, Sara. 1997. *Discourse*. London: Routledge.
Mohamed-Abdi, Mohamed. 1994. *Apocalypse: Poèmes somalis*. Trans. Mohamed Mohamed-Abdi. Montelimar: Voix d'Encre.
———. 2001. "De Gaashaanqaad à Mooryaan: Quelle place pour les jeunes en Somalie?" *Autrepart* 18: 69–84.
Mohamed Diriye Abdullahi. 2001. *Culture and Customs of Somalia*. Westport, CT: Greenwood.
Mohammed Nur Galal. 2005. "Interview with Mohammed Nur Galal." *Journal of Middle Eastern Geopolitics* (Rome) 1, 2: 135–42.
Mohammed Sh. Hassan, ed. 1998. *Gurmad: Diiwaanka Gabayada Soomaaliyeed*, vol. 2 Stockholm: Scansom. See also Maxamed Sheekh Xassan.
Mohamud, Abdinur S. and Abdi M. Kusow. 2006. "Why Somalia Continues to Remain a Failed State." *African Renaissance* 3, 5: 13–23.
Morin, Didier. 1997. "Littérature et politique en Somalie." *Centre d'Etude d'Afrique Noire, Travaux et Documents* 56: 1–32.
Mubarak, Jamil Abdalla. 1996. *From Bad Policy to Chaos in Somalia: How an Economy Fell Apart*. Westport, Conn.: Praeger.
Mukhtar, Mohamed Haji. 1989. "The Emergence and Role of Political Parties in the Inter-River Region of Somalia from 1947 to 1960 (Independence)." *Ufahamu: Journal of the African Activist Association* 17, 2: 75–95.
———. 2003. *Historical Dictionary of Somalia*. New ed. Lanham, Md.: Scarecrow Press.
Neier, Aryeh. 1994. "Why Deal with the Past?" In *Dealing with the Past: Truth and Reconciliation in South Africa*, ed. Alex Boraine, Janet Levy, and Ronel Scheffer, 1–8. Cape Town: Institute for Democracy in South Africa.
Newbury, Catharine. 1995. "Background to Genocide: Rwanda." *Issue: A Journal of Opinion* 23, 2: 12–17.
———. 1998. "Ethnicity and the Politics of History in Rwanda." *Africa Today* 45, 1: 7–24.
Nordstrom, Carolyn and Antonius C. G. M. Robben, eds. 1995. *Fieldwork Under Fire: Contemporary Studies of Violence and Survival*. Berkeley: University of California Press.
Nur Ali Qabobe. 2002. *Somalia: From Nation-State to Tribal Mutiny*. New Delhi: Pharos Media.
Omaar, Rakiya. 1992. "Somalia at War with Itself." *Current History* 91, 565: 230–34.
Orwin, Martin and Maxamed Cabdillahi Riiraash. 1997. "An Approach to Relationships Between Somali Meter Types." *Journal of African Cultural Studies* 10, 1: 83–100.
Osman, Abdirazak Y. 1996. *In the Name of the Fathers: A Somali Novel*. London: Haan.
Pacifico, Claudio. 1996. *Somalia: Ricordi d'un mal d'Africa italiano*. Citta di Castello: Edimont SRL.
Perouse de Montclos, Marc-Antoine. 2000. *Villes en guerre en Somalie: Mogadiscio et Hargeisa*. Paris: CEPED 59.

Peterson, Scott. 2000. *Me Against My Brother: At War in Somalia, Sudan, and Rwanda.* New York: Routledge.
Prendergast, John. 1994a. *The Bones of Our Children Are Not Yet Buried: The Looming Spectre of Famine and Massive Human Rights Abuse in Somalia.* Washington, D.C.: Center of Concern, January.
———. 1994b. *"The Gun Talks Louder Than the Voice": Somalia's Continuing Cycles of Violence.* Washington, D.C.: Center of Concern, July.
Rawson, David. 1994. "Dealing with Disintegration: U.S. Assistance and the Somali State." In *The Somali Challenge: From Catastrophe to Renewal?* ed. Ahmed I. Samatar, 147–87. Boulder, Colo.: Lynne Rienner.
Robben, Antonius C. G. M. and Carolyn Nordstrom. 1995. "The Anthropology and Ethnography of Violence and Sociopolitical Conflict." In *Fieldwork Under Fire: Contemporary Studies of Violence and Survival,* ed. Carolyn Nordstrom and Antonius C. G. M. Robben, 1–25. Berkeley: University of California Press.
Rogge, John. 1992. "The Displaced Population in South and Central Somalia and Preliminary Proposals for their Reintegration and Rehabilitation." Report to UN Development Programme. Winnipeg: University of Manitoba Disaster Research Unit, September 4.
Ross, Fiona C. 2003. *Bearing Witness: Women and the Truth and Reconciliation Commission in South Africa.* London: Pluto Press.
Ruhela, Satya Pal, ed. 1994. *Mohammed Farah Aidid and his Vision of Somalia.* New Delhi: Vikas.
Samatar, Ahmed I. 1994. "Empty Bowl: Political Economy in Transition and the Crises of Accumulation." In *The Somali Challenge: From Catastrophe to Renewal?* ed. Ahmed I. Samatar, 65–92. Boulder, Colo.: Lynne Rienner.
———. 2001. "Introduction: Somali Catastrophe: Explanations and Implications." In *Variations on the Theme of Somaliness,* ed. Muddle Suzanne Lilius, 7–30. Turku, Finland: Åbo Akademi University.
———. 1988. *Socialist Somalia: Rhetoric and Reality.* London: Zed Press.
Samatar, Said S. 1982. *Oral Poetry and Somali Nationalism: The Case of Sayyid Mahammad 'Abdille Hasan.* Cambridge: Cambridge University Press.
———. 1988/1989. "Oral Poetry and Political Dissent in Somali Society: The Hurgumo Series." *Ufahamu: Journal of the African Activist Association* 17, 2: 31–52.
———. 1991. *Somalia: A Nation in Turmoil.* Minority Rights Group Report. London: Minority Rights Group, August.
Schlee, Günther. 2003. *Identities on the Move: Clanship and Pastoralism in Northern Kenya.* New York: Manchester University Press.
Semelin, Jacques. 2003. "Toward a Vocabulary of Massacre and Genocide." *Journal of Genocide Research* 5, 2: 193–10.
Shaw, Martin. 2007. "The General Hybridity of War and Genocide." *Journal of Genocide Research* 9, 3: 461–73.
Sheikh, Fazal. 2001. *A Camel for the Son.* By the artist.

Sica, Mario. 1994. *Operazione Somalia: La dittatura, l'oppozitione, la guerra civile nella testimonianza dell'ultimo ambasciatore d'Italia a Mogadiscio.* Venezia: Marsilio.

Siciid Cismaan Keenadiid. 2013. *Xusuuqor: Dagaallada Sokeeye (Dis. 30/1990–Juun 1994.* Ed. Yuusuf Nuur Cismaan. [London:] EAIRC.

Stover, Eric and Harvey M. Weinstein, eds. 2004. *My Neighbor, My Enemy: Justice and Community in the Aftermath of Mass Atrocity.* New York: Cambridge University Press.

Strauss, Scott. 2006. *The Order of Genocide: Race, Power, and War in Rwanda.* Berkeley: University of California Press.

Togane, Mohamud. 2003a. "The Phenomenon Called Al-Hajji Mudane Musse Soodi Yellahow." http://www.somaliawatch.com, posted in 2003, accessed February 14, 2008.

———. 2003b. "The Darod Fire Back." http://www.somaliawatch.com, posted January 11, 2003, accessed February 14, 2008.

———. 2003c. "Afweyne's Swansong." http://www.mudulood.com, posted February 26, 2003, accessed February 14, 2008.

Togane, Mohamud. 2006. "Why the Darod Will Never Return to Mogadishu: A Candid Tête-à-Tête with Mohamed Dhere." http://www.mudulood.com, posted January 12, 2006, accessed February 14, 2008.

Umm Kulthum: A Voice like Egypt (1996). Produced, written and directed by Michal Goldman. Arab Film Distribution. Waltham, Mass.: Filmmakers Collaborative.

Waldorf, Lars. 2007. "Ordinariness and Orders: Explaining Popular Participation in the Rwandan Genocide." *Genocide Studies and Prevention* 2, 3: 267–70.

Walker, Margaret Urban. 2006. *Moral Repair: Reconstructing Moral Relations After Wrongdoing.* New York: Cambridge University Press.

Walsh, Langton Prendergast. n.d. *Under the Flag and Somali Coast Stories.* London: Andrew Melrose.

Willemse, Karin. 2005. "Darfur in War: The Politicization of Ethnic Identities?" *ISIM Review* 15 (Spring): 14–15.

———. 2007. *One Foot in Heaven: Narratives on Gender and Islam in Darfur, West-Sudan.* Leiden: Brill.

———. 2009. "The Darfur War, Masculinity and the Construction of a Sudanese National Identity." In *Darfur and the Crisis of Governance in Sudan: A Critical Reader,* ed. Salah Hassan and Carina Ray, 213–32. Trenton, N.J.: Africa World Press.

Wyschogrod, Edith. 2005. "The Warring Logics of Genocide." In *Genocide and Human Rights: A Philosophical Guide,* ed. Joseph K. Roth, 207–19. New York: Palgrave Macmillan.

Wolf, Eric.1982. *Europe and the People Without History.* Berkeley: University of California Press.

Xaawa Jibriil. 2008. *Saa Waxay Tiri: Maansadii iyo Waayihii Xaawa Jibriil (And Then She Said: The Poetry and Times of Hawa Jibril).* Trans. and Intro. Faduma Ahmed Alim. Toronto: Jumblies Press.

Yaasiin C. Keenadiid. 1976. *Qaamuuska Af Soomaaliga*. Mogadishu: Wasaaradda Hiddaha iyo Tacliinta Sare.

Yasmeen Maxamuud. 2006. "Rape: A Conspiracy of Silence." January 23. http://www.wardheernews.com.

Yerkes, Maryanne. 2004. "Facing the Violent Past: Discussions with Serbia's Youth." *Nationalities Papers* 32, 4: 921–37.

Zur, Judith N. 1998. *Violent Memories: Mayan War Widows in Guatemala*. Boulder, Colo.: Westview Press.

Name Index

Aadan Cabdulle Cismaan "Cadde," 150
Abdirazak Haji Hussen (Cabdirasaaq Xaaji Xusseen), 173, 270nn117, 125
Abgaal, 61, 63–66, 118–19, 155, 213, 258n119, 263n18
Abshir Kaahiye Faarax, 112, 115
Abyan, Ibrahim, 139–41, 263n17
Adam, Hussein, 154, 250n19
Addis Ababa, 16, 22, 187
Afgooye, 124, 140, 157, 159–60, 163–65, 169–70, 185, 217, 245n23, 265n47
Afrah, Mohamoud Mohamed, 137–38, 245n22, 253n43, 260n135, 261n150, 273n8
Africa Watch, 18, 84–85, 87, 89, 91, 155, 179, 251n23, 256n80, 265n55, 272nn145, 151, 274n12, 276n45
African Rights, 18, 166–67, 177, 71n130
Ahmed, Ali Jimale, 275n32
Ali, Ayaan Hirsi, 178
Alison, Miranda, 201–2, 274n14, 276n49
Amnesty International, 18, 102, 109, 146, 184–85, 251nn24, 26, 266n61, 270n126, 271n139
Axmed Jilacow Caddow, 104, 133–34
Axmed Maxamed Darmaan, 114–15, 118, 127, 129, 257nn100, 103, 258n107, 260n147

Baardheere, 182, 186–87
Bakool, 99, 118–20, 160–61, 163, 182, 258n118
Bantu Somalis (Somali Bantu), 158, 164, 170, 184, 221, 271nn136, 141
Barbaar Amar, 164, 268n83
Bari, 80, 176, 179, 267n76
"Bari Bari," Maxamed Yuusuf Ismaaciil, 152
Barre, Maxamed Siyaad, 1–3, 5–7, 9, 12,
17–18, 23, 25, 29–30, 33, 40, 55–56, 61–64, 66–68, 75, 77–86, 88–89, 93, 95–97, 99–109, 112–30, 132–37, 141, 143–44, 146–47, 151–52, 154–56, 158–59, 162, 165, 168–71, 176–77, 181–86, 192–200, 203, 210–12, 214–18, 220–22, 224–27, 229–30, 233, 250nn12, 19, 253nn43, 48, 255n75, 256n85, 260n144, 262nn160, 4, 7, 263n19, 272n151, 273nn2, 5, 10, 275n35
Bay, 119–20, 160–61, 163–64, 176, 182, 258n118
BBC (British Broadcasting Corporation), 123, 151–52, 210, 264n28, 267n76
Benard, Cheryl, 23, 201, 276n49
Bood, Xusseen Xaaji Maxamed, 115, 118–20, 127, 129, 132, 139, 150, 153, 257n100, 258–59n120, 260–61n147, 262n160
Brava, 16–17, 149, 158–59, 161, 163–65, 168, 170–72, 176, 182–84, 187, 244n13, 245n23, 265n40, 269nn108, 111, n112, 270n115
Baydhaba, 66, 97, 120, 128, 159, 163–65, 170, 176, 182–86, 249n58, 267n81, 268n83, 269nn99, 106, 270n126
Beledweyne, 91, 99, 119–20, 246n16, 252n37, 254n58
Besteman, Catherine, 136, 141, 221, 271n136, 276n45
Biles, Peter, 18, 151, 166, 262n1
"Bililiqo," Bashiir, 96, 172, 251n29
Bosnia, 5–6, 190, 201, 236, 276n49
Bridges, Peter, 94, 104, 251n24, 253n46, 255n78, 262n5
Bringa, Tone, 13, 56, 232, 276n49
Bulhan, Hussein A., 215, 275n36
"Buluq-Buluq," Cabdiraxmaan Jaamac, 104, 151, 255n75, 256n86

Burco, 86–87, 158, 266n62
Buulo Xaawo, 184–85, 187

"Caato," Cismaan Xassan Cali, 145, 200, 246n16
Cabdi Muxumed Amiin, 16, 29–30, 34, 40–42, 44, 50–51, 69, 95, 109, 245n4, 246n16
Cabdiqaasim Salaad Xassan, 105, 108, 112, 133, 263n8
Cabdirasaaq "Jurile," 141, 176
Cabdulcasiis Nuur Xirsi, 127, 257n100, 264n22
Cabdullaahi Axmed Caddow, 105, 133–34, 255n78
Cabdullaahi Axmed "Cirro," 129, 152
Cabdullaahi Hoolif, 112, 264n22
Cabdullaahi Yuusuf Axmed, 83, 153, 230, 273n10
Cabdulqaadir Aadan Cismaan, 173
Cali Mahdi, 18, 112, 115–16, 118, 133–34, 139, 141, 149–52, 158, 160–63, 171, 173, 177, 180–81, 186–87, 200, 210, 212, 267n76, 270n126
Canab Maxamed Siyaad (Barre), 110, 253n43
"Canjeex," Cabdullaahi Jaamac Warsame, 104, 106
Caydiid (Aideed), Maxamed Faarax, 54, 98, 100, 113, 115–17, 119–21, 123, 134, 143, 148–49, 153, 157–58, 160–63, 167, 170–71, 173–75, 177, 180–90, 199–200, 205, 212–13, 217, 233, 247n40, 253n42, 254nn57, 58, 258n118, 259n123, 262n160, 266n61, 267n77, 270n126, 271n134, 273n10, 274n26, 275nn28, 37, 277n56
Cibaar, Maxamed Cali, 44, 45, 48, 50
Cigaal, Maxamed Ibraahim, 114, 257n104
Chazan, David, 18, 159, 167, 169, 261n150
Cohen, Stanley, 154, 156, 277n57
Colombo, Salvatore, 106, 117
Compagnon, Daniel, 2, 9, 90, 93, 97, 140, 194, 244n18, 249nn18, 110, 250n12, 251nn20, 26, 254n67, 255n75, 263n18, 275n34
Cumar Carta Ghaalib (Qaalib), 119, 121, 127, 129, 150, 151, 265n47
Cumar Macallin, 173, 261n149, 268n99

Daahir Cali Cumar "Deyr," 17, 159, 161–64, 168, 174, 176–77, 182, 187, 212, 215, 244n7, 254n61, 258n117, 269nn100, 105, 107, 108, 270nn116, 120, 122, 271nn138, 141, 274n26
Daarood, 2, 4, 10–11, 54–56, 58–59, 61–67, 78, 88–89, 98, 100, 119, 134, 140–45, 149, 151–57, 159, 161–65, 167–71, 173–74, 176, 179–82, 184–85, 187–88, 191, 197–202, 205, 210–18, 221–22, 226, 229–30, 233, 243n3, 10, 248n54, 250n19, 252n32, 259n123, 263nn17, 18, 266nn59, 61, 67, 268n84, 269n99, 273nn4, 10, 275nn30–37
"Dafle," Axmed Suleemaan, 89, 103, 155, 256n85
"Dhigic-Dhigic, Maxamed Cumar Jaamac, 141, 151, 176, 261n147
Dhoobley, 96, 175–76, 178, 254n62
Dhoodaan, Cadullaahi Macallin, 89
Dhulbahante, 78, 89, 170, 172, 211, 249n6, 272n144,
Dhuusamareeb, 99, 120, 254n63
Donham, Donald, 14–15, 71–72, 74, 83, 92, 153, 231–32, 257n92

Egypt, 126–27, 152, 253n48, 256n81, 261n148
Eltringham, Nigel, 7–8, 14–15, 72, 232, 237–38, 240, 243n5, 276n40, 277nn57, 59
Ethiopia, 5, 11, 16, 23, 78, 81, 83–87, 89–91, 96, 98, 100, 109, 120, 157, 162, 166–67, 179, 194, 213–14, 230, 244n11, 252n26, 259n123, 271n130

Faarax M. J. Cawl, 160
Fadumo Maxamed Siyaad (Barre), 93, 110, 263n43
Faisal Axmed Xasan, 55, 58–60, 69, 276n53
Farah, Cristina Ali, 178, 248n42
Farah, Nuruddin, 136, 248n42, 250n13, 276n41
Fletcher, Laurel, 15, 234–36, 239, 277n57
Fletcher, Luke, 223, 228

Gaalkacyo, 5, 82, 99, 151, 157, 160–63, 173, 245n23, 253n42, 267n76, 269n99, 272n151
"Gaani," Maxamed Xaashi, 84, 103, 152, 157, 168, 172, 251n26
"Gabyow," Aadan Cabdullaahi Nuur, 96, 159–60, 169, 176, 251n29, 253n53
Gadabursi, 89, 262n33, 266n64
Galaal, Maxamed Nuur, 81, 118, 121, 123, 140, 168, 200, 249n3, 258n119, 260n135

Name Index 299

"Gardheere," Maxamed Maxamuud Axmed, 169, 269n100
Garoowe, 82, 162, 253n42, 254n60, 269n100
Gersony, Robert, 86–87, 89, 251nn24, 27, 252nn33, 35, 36
Gedo, 5, 54, 149, 157–58, 160–61, 168, 170, 176–77, 181–84, 186–87, 191, 212, 245n23, 265n40, 271n133
Ghalib, Jama Mohamed, 82, 155, 263n17
Gobweyn, 189, 272n146

Habr Gidir, 62, 119, 155, 248n56, 258n119, 270n123, 275n28
Hargeisa, 85–87, 96, 101, 117, 152, 158, 218, 249n3, 250n14, 251n24, 272n151
Harti, 188–89, 214, 220, 272n148
Hartley, Aidan, 18, 147–49, 265n41
Hawiye, 4, 11, 54, 56, 61–66, 96–100, 116, 118, 121, 123, 125, 132, 134, 141–42, 145, 149, 152–56, 161, 169–71, 180, 185, 191, 197–98, 200–201, 221, 214, 216–18, 221, 229–30, 247n39, 250n16, 252nn38, 58, 254n63, 263n17, 266n59, 267n76, 270n125, 275nn30, 35, 275–76n37
Hayden, Robert, 6, 201.
Henry, Neil, 18, 124–26, 147, 262b6, 264n29
Hiiraan, 99, 161, 254n65, 258n117
Hinton, A. L., 5, 7, 14, 203, 208, 221, 232, 243n6, 246n15
Hoffman, Eve, 236–37, 276n55
Huber, Wilhelm, 131, 160, 262n4
Hussein Ali Dualeh, 16, 155, 266nn58, 59, 271n129

Ibraahim Meygaag Samatar, 115
ICRC (International Committee of the Red Cross), 167, 186–87, 189
ICTY (International Criminal Tribunal for Former Yugoslavia), 201, 216, 236
IMF (International Monetary Fund), 94–95, 102, 104, 227, 256n86
In the Name of the Fathers (novel), 55, 223
Irir, 39, 54, 180, 247n39, 275–276n37
Isaaq, 4, 54, 65, 83–90, 92, 105, 121, 140, 161, 195–97, 229–31, 244n12, 247n39, 248n53, 250n16, 251nn23, 26, 256nn79, 93, 268n88, 273n4, 276n37, 52
Islamic Courts movement, 9
Ismaaciil Jumcaale Cossobleh, 115, 256n82, 258n108

Issa-Salwe, Abdisalam, 14, 74, 81–82, 99, 171, 246n22
Italy, 17, 93, 97, 106, 115–16, 125–27, 215, 249n60, 253n48, 256nn81, 82, 256n86, 261n148

Jannaale, 131, 163–64
"Jees," Axmed Cumar, 96, 98, 119, 123, 159–60, 172, 181, 183, 188–91, 251n29, 271n134
Jilib, 161, 165, 173
Jowhar, 120, 163–64, 259nn121, 123
Jubba, 93, 99, 120, 131, 158, 170, 176, 182–84, 220, 254n65, 268n84, 269n108, 271n136

Kenya, 5, 11, 93, 96, 109, 136, 155, 157, 162, 166–67, 175, 177–79, 182, 184, 186–87, 262n15, 263n19, 270n130, 272n146
Kismaayo, 5, 17, 96, 132, 141, 152, 157–62, 164, 168, 170, 173–77, 180–84, 186–91, 202, 212, 214, 219–21, 243n9, 245n23, 268n92, 269nn99, 107, 108, 270nn119, 120, 122, 125, 126, 271n141, 272nn146, 147, 149

Laitin, David D., 77, 79, 80, 88, 194, 249nn4, 7, 10
Lemarchand, René, 14, 19, 237–39, 243n4, 244n9, 274nn20, 21
Lewis, I. M., 155, 249n6
Lieberman, Ben, 14, 206–8, 274n22
Little, Peter, 220, 254n65

Maandeeq (novel), 55, 58–60, 255n73, 274n27, 276n53
Majeerteen, 81, 83, 89, 185, 195, 214, 250nn12, 13, 5, 19, 20, 267nn76, 81, 272n144, 273n2
"Mama" Khadiija (Macallin), 93, 104, 263n19
Mareexaan (Marehan), 65, 78, 96, 122, 125, 138, 147, 172, 183, 185, 187, 211, 220, 248n54, 255n75, 262n6, 268n94
Maren, Michael, 90, 94, 99, 200, 249n9, 252n37, 253n47, 254n58, 255n77, 259n123, 276n45
Maslax Maxamed Siyaad (Barre), 93, 97, 104, 157, 255nn72, 75, 256nn85, 88
Maxamed Abshir Muuse, 114, 126, 160, 173, 176, 267n76, 270n125
Maxamed Abshir Walde, 162

300 Name Index

Maxamed Hawaadleh Madar, 107, 121, 127, 129, 150, 256n86, 257n101
Maxamed Saciid "Gentleman," 126, 261n150
Maxamed Sheekh Cismaan, 104, 133, 255n77
McGreal, Chris, 149, 168–69, 173
Menkhaus, Ken, 99, 221, 265n54
Merca, 101, 163–65
Michaels, Anne, 21, 192
Miller, Reid, 18, 147, 262n44
Mogadishu, 9, 10, 17–18, 23, 25, 28–33, 39–40, 42, 44, 50, 54–56, 58–62, 68–69, 75, 77, 84–85, 95, 98–99, 101–2, 104–8, 114–32, 135–37, 140, 142–43, 145–46, 149–50, 152–62, 164, 167–70, 173–74, 176–79, 181–82, 184–85, 187–89, 191–93, 197–200, 204–5, 210, 213, 218, 220–21, 223–24, 226, 228, 230, 243n6, 244n16, 255n77, 258nn113, 119, 260n144, 262n160, 275n28
Mohamed-Abdi, Mohamed, 16, 53, 276nn48, 50
Mombasa, 124, 166, 175, 178, 214, 263n19
"Morgan," Maxamed Saciid Xirsi, 83–84, 97, 99, 103, 108, 118, 120, 127, 144, 152, 157, 168, 172, 176, 187–91, 251n26, 253n43, 256nn85, 88, 260n144, 272n148
Mudug, 11, 80, 82, 86–87, 99, 160, 162–63, 176, 179, 195, 251, 267n76, 273n21, 274n12
Mukhtar, Mohamed Haji, 182–83, 185, 203, 215, 265n55, 268n84, 275n35
Mustafa Sheekh Cilmi, 23, 38, 40, 43, 165
Muusa Boqor, 126, 261n150
Muuse Islaan, 162

Naaji, Axmed Sacad, 23, 28, 39, 42–43, 50, 245n4
"Nabaddoon," Cumar Cabdinuur Nuux, 44, 47, 50
Nairobi, 16, 18, 23, 56, 115, 127, 141
"Nero," 157, 200
Newbury, Catherine, 14, 15, 227
Northwest, 3, 9, 11, 80, 84–89, 92–96, 101, 103, 105–6, 109, 149, 152, 159, 165, 195–99, 204, 215, 217, 231, 251n26, 252n38, 265n40, 270n128, 273n3, 274nn12, 13, 276n52
Nugaal, 80, 82, 162, 176, 179, 267n76
Nur Ali Qabobe, 151, 253n43, 255n77, 265n47, 274n18
Nuurto Xaaji Xassan, 17, 116, 152

Oakley, Robert, 190
Ogaadeen, 78, 89, 91–92, 96–97, 121, 139, 172, 185, 196, 211, 220, 252n33, 259n123, 267n67, 272n148
Oromo, 97, 252n33
Osman, Abdirazak Y., 55–56, 60, 69

Pacifico, Claudio, 17, 95, 98, 104–6, 116–18, 120, 122, 124, 126, 133–34, 139, 196–97, 205, 254n65, 255nn72, 76, 256nn79, 82, 258nn108, 110, 111, 113, 119, 260nn142, 144
Perlez, Jane, 18, 166, 188, 190, 262n6, 263n19, 272nn146, 148
Press, Robert, 18, 114–15, 147
Peterson, Scott, 186, 263n19
Puntland, 176, 230

"Qaybdiid," Abdi Hasan Awale (Cabdi Xassan Awaale), 98, 157, 200

Radio Mogadishu, 17, 59, 108, 118, 126, 128–29, 150–51, 162, 164, 170, 176, 210, 212, 261nn148, 154, 262n157, 267n76
Raxanweyn, 160–61, 164–65, 182–83, 185, 252n38
Reer Xamar, 145, 158, 171, 244n13
Richburg, Keith, 189, 272n148
Rwanda, 7, 16, 63, 72, 201, 226–29, 234, 236, 238, 240, 276n40

Sailhan, Michel, 120, 148–49, 160–61, 171
Samantar, Maxamed Ali, 81–82, 103, 106–7, 134, 249n3, 253n48, 255n69
Samatar, Said S., 77, 79–80, 82, 88, 194, 247n34, 249nn4, 7, 10, 265n54
SDM (Somali Democratic Movement), 156, 160, 164, 170, 176, 182–84, 187, 244n12, 266n66
Semelin, Jacques, 206, 208, 223, 225, 228, 276nn48, 50
Al-Shabaab, 172 244n15, 272n151, 277n56
"Shabeel," Maxamed Xaashi, 123, 134, 148–49, 157, 171, 187, 200, 258n119, 271n138
Shabeelle, 120, 161, 163, 182, 254n65, 259n123, 268n84
Shaw, Martin, 6, 14, 232
"Shiddo," Xaaji Cali, 114, 126, 257n103, 260–61n147
Shields, Todd, 18, 147, 264nn28, 29

Shube, Cabdulqaadir Cabdi, 16, 23, 35, 42–43, 50
Sica, Mario, 17, 106–7, 116, 119–20, 122, 126–27, 133, 141–42, 175–76, 197, 255n72, 256nn83, 84, 86, 258n106, 262n7, 263n8
Silaanyo, Axmed Maxamuud, 197, 222
Siyaad Sheekh Daahir, 164–65
Somali Armed Forces. *See* Somali National Army
SNA (Somali National Alliance)-Cali Mahdi, 187, 189–90
SNA- Caydiid, 183, 187–89
SNA Somali National Army, 86, 88, 90, 92, 98, 109–11, 129, 151–52, 222
SNF (Somali National Front), 182, 184–87, 268n94
SNF Alliance, 118, 169–72, 182–83, 269nn105, 108
SNM (Somali National Movement), 2, 31, 54, 79, 84–92, 96, 98–99, 101, 103, 113–15, 117, 119, 120, 123, 126–29, 133, 151, 158, 176, 186, 195–97, 199, 204, 210–13, 216–17, 221–22, 226, 230, 244nn11, 12, 247n39, 251nn26, 27, 252n35, 267n76, 273n4 276nn27, 39
Somaliland, 155, 252n30, 266n64; British, 276n52; Italian, 75, 213, 251; Republic of, 176, 197, 215–16, 231, 257n104, 266n58
SPM (Somali Patriotic Movement), 2, 4, 96–99, 101, 119–20, 123, 129, 133, 151, 157, 159–61, 168–69, 173, 186–89, 197, 199, 220–21, 226, 258n118, 266n67, 268n94, 269nn99, 108
SPM Alliance, 176–77, 179–85
SPM-Jees, 182, 187, 188, 222
SPM-Morgan, 187
SSDF (Somali Salvation Democratic Front), 81–85, 87, 89, 127, 151–52, 157, 162–63, 168–69, 173, 176, 179, 194–95, 199, 226, 230, 244n11, 246n18, 267n76, 268n94, 269n99, 273n10
SYL (Somali Youth League), 109, 112, 275n35

Togane, Mohamud Siad, 60–66, 68–70, 79, 145, 200, 211–12, 214, 239, 248n51, 248n52

Transitional National Government, 45
Transitional Federal Government, 43, 153, 230

UN (United Nations), 4, 74, 224, 249n3
UNITAF, 179–80, 187, 189, 242
UNHCR, 78, 90, 94, 252n33, 253n47
U.S. State Department, 86, 94, 262n6
USAID, 94–95, 102, 110, 253n46
USC (United Somali Congress), 2, 4, 10, 17, 25, 29, 30–31, 33–34, 40–41, 43–44, 53, 55–56, 58–60, 91, 96–98, 100–102, 106–8, 115–22, 124–29, 132–33, 135, 137, 139–49, 151–87, 197–204, 210, 212–17, 221–26, 230, 244n11, 252n37, 258n119, 259nn123, 131, 262n7, 263n18, 266n66, 273n10, 276n37
USC-Cali Mahdi, 18, 154, 157, 163, 179, 181, 187, 191, 202, 275n28
USC-Caydiid, 18, 99, 101, 115, 119, 126, 133, 154, 157, 163, 170, 179–81, 191, 196, 198, 200, 202, 205, 221, 274n28
USC-Mogadishu, 115–16, 119, 121, 123, 125–28, 130, 132, 135, 138, 140, 153, 158, 199–200, 221, 245n20, 258n119, 258–59n120

Wardhiigley, 108, 121–22, 125, 146
"Wardhiigley," Cali Maxamed Cossobleh, 97, 115
Weinstein, Harvey M., 15, 234–36, 239, 277n57
World Bank, 227, 256n86

Xaashi Weheliye Macallin, 126, 261n150
Xassan Cali Mirreh, 162, 246n18, 261n117
Xassan Dimbil, 143, 264n22
Xiirey Qaasim Weheliye, 174
Xuddur, 120, 163, 182
Xusseen Kulmiye Afrax, 103, 108, 133–34, 253n48

Yasmeen Maxamuud, 255n77, 274n13
Yemen, 28, 166, 179
Yerkes, Maryanne, 236–37, 276n54
Yugoslavia (Former), 5–6, 201, 206, 208, 226–28, 234, 236, 276n49
Yuusuf Sheekh Cali Madar, 212

Subject Index

aid, 78, 83–84, 93–95, 102, 106, 110, 131, 136, 200; food, 78, 90, 94–95, 141, 166, 181, 186, 188, 249n9, 253n47, 255n7; military, 94–95, 106, 254n66, 273n8
armed fronts, 2, 10 12, 22, 25, 38, 40, 89, 96–100, 129, 133, 157, 159, 161, 169–70, 180, 187, 191, 193, 244n11, 246n14
arms, 45, 85, 89, 99–100, 121–23, 125, 161, 181, 224, 252n35, 254n66. *See also* weapons

Battle for Mogadishu, 102, 114, 117–18, 120–21, 124, 137, 198, 245n22, 258n119

children, 38, 45, 73, 79, 124–25, 128, 134, 137–38, 147, 160, 163, 166–69, 171, 174–75, 178–79, 237, 264n29, 269n99, 271n130
clan hate narratives, 8, 12–13, 53–54, 59, 61, 63, 66, 69, 74, 79, 144, 164, 193, 203–4, 209–14, 216–20, 224–25, 227–28, 230–33, 236, 273n10, 274n28, 275n30
clan logic, 13, 29, 51, 60, 69, 79, 90, 92, 209–10, 212, 214, 217, 233, 243n1
clan-based militias, 10–11, 89–90, 156–57, 160, 164, 202, 216
collapse: of armed forces, 121, of banks, 110; of economy, 47, 203; of regime, 7, 10, 17, 18, 132, 134, 154, 156, 192, 195, 218, 221, 227, 241; of state, 1, 3, 9, 12, 15, 21–23, 35, 38–40, 42–44, 50, 69, 71, 73–75, 79–80, 92–93, 156, 194, 202, 221, 232, 244n11
collective "punishment," 2, 9, 80–81, 86–87, 90, 184, 191, 194, 227, 235, 273n29
colonial, 2–3, 15, 75–77, 80, 109, 136, 194, 226, 258n110
communal violence, 3, 5, 7–8, 10, 12–13, 15, 18, 51, 60, 72, 92, 130, 192–93, 198, 228–29, 232, 234–35, 273n9

conflict identities, 229–31, 236
corruption, 57, 78, 93, 104, 110–11, 203, 227, 253n42
cosmopolitan, 6, 58, 228

denial, 15, 149, 153–56, 226, 229, 231, 249n1, 266n57, 274n24; blatant, 154; interpretive, 155–56
discourse, 1–2, 4, 8–9, 12–13, 21, 29, 39, 50–51, 60–61, 69, 74, 77, 91, 136, 191, 193, 205–6, 209–10, 214, 216, 225, 232, 243n1, 244n15, 247n34, 274n20
discursive, 8–9, 12–13, 44, 52, 89, 101, 192–93, 199, 203, 214, 232, 236, 247n26

elders, 29, 56, 82, 89, 107, 109–10, 112–15, 117, 126–27, 133, 135, 139–41, 143, 162–63, 183, 189–90, 195–97, 224, 242, 251n23, 261nn149, 150, 267n77, 272n148
ethnic cleansing, 5–6, 154, 156, 206, 226, 228, 244n7, 266n56, 271n131, 274n22, 276n49

famine, 11, 18, 179, 184, 186–87, 242, 244n15, 265n41
faqash, 124, 162, 210–12, 252n30, 260n142, 266n64, 273n4

genocide, 4–7, 18, 72, 87, 92, 134, 154, 156, 162, 165, 184, 201, 203, 206, 208, 221, 223–26, 228–29, 232, 236–38, 243n3, 244n7, 249n3, 252n30, 266n64, 271n136, 272n152, 276nn40, 48
genocide business, 223, 228, 267n48
guubaabo qabiil, 53, 210

Habaar Waalid road, 175, 177, 270n125
haraadiga Siyaad, 128, 133–34, 150, 160–61,

Subect Index   303

168, 176, 212–13. *See also* remnants of Barre
human rights, 110, 115, 134, 154, 179, 184, 190, 245; organizations, 18, 80, 83, 110, 155–56, 181; violations, 12, 74, 82, 87–88, 94, 100, 102–3, 109–10, 161, 185, 190, 201–2, 229–30, 233–34

impunity, 52, 104, 145, 171–72, 198, 202, 208, 221, 223–24, 227–29, 231, 234
intellectuals, 82–83, 85, 98, 109, 140, 150, 224, 230, 250n13, 257n100, 263n16
intent, 4, 5, 59, 63, 91, 117, 154, 156, 196, 221, 224–26, 228, 230, 258n119, 266n57, 276n49
internet, 23–24, 45, 48
Islam, 9, 13, 22, 42–45, 48, 50, 111, 128, 150, 172, 175, 229, 231, 247nn27, 28
Islamism, 13, 44, 172, 175, 232, 244n15, 246n21, 270n120, 272n151

Jasiira massacre, 104–6, 197, 256n79
journalists, 10, 18, 120, 137–38, 146–48, 153, 160–61, 163, 166, 168–69, 171, 186, 200, 208, 217, 264n29, 273n3
justice, 11, 15, 24, 26, 32, 37, 42, 135, 149, 226, 229, 234–36, 238, 260, 263n13; restorative, 15, 229

key shift, 1–5, 12, 30, 56, 60, 133, 149, 192, 202–3, 212, 22932, 243n1

laheystayaal, 143, 153, 263n20
large-scale violence against civilians, 3, 11, 15, 18, 73, 130, 192, 194–95, 198, 202, 226–27

Manifesto, 107, 109–12, 114–18, 140–41, 153, 197, 205, 218; Manifesto group/elders, 56, 102, 107–9, 111–15, 119, 125–26, 135, 139, 143, 151, 173–74, 177
masculinity, 60, 201, 228
memoirs, 16–17, 98, 124, 126, 137, 153–55, 186, 196, 205
memory, 15, 19, 26–27, 73, 172, 220, 234, 236–40; critical, 237–40
middle class, 6, 105, 113, 140, 174, 181, 188–91, 197, 203, 214, 219–20, 272n151
minorities, 10, 138, 145, 157, 172, 217, 248n56, 255n69

MOD, 64–66, 78–79, 211–12, 248n54, 249n10, 274n24, 275n34
moral (ir)repair, 1, 12, 15, 193, 234, 236, 238, 273n1. *See also* social repair; social reconstruction
Mooryaan, 25, 27, 38, 54, 59, 220, 223
Mosque massacre, 102, 105–6
mujaahidiin, 98, 163, 199, 204

nation, 9, 13, 17, 27, 29, 31, 34–36, 39, 41–50, 68–69, 89, 128, 150, 206, 229, 232, 235, 239, 246n24, 247n27
national reconciliation meetings, 25, 35, 42, 45, 109, 112–13, 126–27, 153, 160, 162, 169, 177, 181, 247n34, 256n81, 261n81
niman magacleh, 140, 188
novel, 55–56, 58–60, 166, 178, 239, 248nn42, 47, 255n73, 274n27, 277n53

"one hundred years of Daarood domination," 210, 214–17, 222
opportunity-with-impunity, 145, 202, 221, 223, 228

patrimonial, 2, 77–79, 84
poetry, 8–9, 16, 18, 21–23, 30, 40–45, 51–53, 60–63, 69–70, 88, 212, 239, 245nn2, 3, 247nn34, 36, 254n67
political entrepreneurs, 3, 6, 13–14, 38, 42, 76–77, 92, 165, 192–93, 227, 229, 234, 249n1
postconflict reconstruction, 15, 180, 217, 240. *See also* moral repair
post-generation, 231, 237
prose fiction, 4, 8, 16, 22, 53, 55

qaat (khat), 25, 57,159, 183,251n25

rape, 3, 5, 12, 24–25, 38–39, 58–59, 82–83, 85, 104–5, 122, 141, 143–45, 169, 171, 174–75, 177, 183, 185, 198, 201–2, 205, 228, 250n17, 263n15, 273nn12, 13, 276n49
reconciliation, 15, 48, 63, 106–9, 119, 127, 129, 162–63, 229, 231, 234–36, 239, 250n19, 251n26, 253n48
Reconciliation Committee, 107–8, 111, 114–15, 118–20, 127–29, 141, 150, 257n100, 259n120, 261n154, 265n43, 265n44
Red Berets, 78, 104–5, 107, 111, 121–24, 127, 135, 138, 146, 205, 258n111, 262n4

refugees, 84–86, 90–92, 94, 119–20, 136, 161, 165–67, 175, 177–79, 196, 251n24, 252nn33, 35, 253n47, 259n124, 263nn15, 19, 268nn84, 89, 271nn129, 130, 276n45
religion, 24, 26–27, 29, 37, 39, 42–43, 69, 112, 128, 149, 227
religious leaders, 16, 29, 42, 49, 82, 105, 109, 112, 150, 183, 188, 205
"remnants of Barre," 128, 133–34, 150, 160–61, 168, 176, 212–13. See also *haraadiga Siyaad*
restorative justice, 15, 229

social reconstruction, 1, 12–13, 236, 238–39. See also moral repair
social repair, 15, 202, 231–32, 234–35. See also moral repair
Somali cyberspace, 16, 22, 166, 246n22. See also internet; Web sites
song, 16, 18, 21–23, 28–30, 33–34, 51–52, 59, 66, 95, 109, 171, 210, 213–14, 245n6, 247nn27, 34, 248n46, 253n49, 269n111, 277n56

technology of power, 1, 9, 14, 75–76, 83, 88, 91, 197, 233

traders, 109, 110, 214, 220
truth, 8, 15–16, 36, 46, 60–61, 124, 132, 155, 159, 187, 192, 205, 217, 231, 233–36, 238–40, 266n60

War of the Militias, 10–11, 157–59, 167, 170, 179–80, 184–85, 191, 202
war crimes, 74, 87, 92, 94, 100, 149, 190, 202, 229, 233, 235, 238, 129n3, 252n30
weapons, 58, 100, 120–21, 125, 139, 148, 154, 254n66, 263n19. See also arms
Web sites, 23, 44, 239. See also internet; Somali cyberspace
women, 13, 22, 24–26, 28, 33–34, 38, 40, 57–59, 78, 82–85, 122, 124–25, 128, 137–38, 141, 144–48, 163, 166–67, 174, 178, 183, 185–86, 201–2, 220, 222–24, 228, 246n19, 247n36, 250nn10, n17, 263nn15, 16, 266n61, 269n99, 272n151, 274n14

youth, 25, 47, 78, 109–10, 112, 137, 172, 186, 215, 219, 222, 224, 231, 237, 238

Acknowledgments

A multiyear project like this accumulates many debts of gratitude. In Addis Ababa, I would like to express my heartfelt gratitude to Wafa Neguede (with Mounay and Ato Sbhat) not only for opening her home to me but also for her friendship, wisdom, inspiration, and encouragement. Thank you Amira and Akram for your friendship, hospitality, and encouragement. At UNESCO Addis Ababa, I owe a debt of gratitude to Nureldin Satti, Wafa Neguede, and Tseday Bemenet. My association with you in an intellectual environment otherwise not optimal for the study of Somali history anchored my research in Ethiopia in more than one way. My warmest thanks also to Xusseen Cabdulqaadir Qaasim (Hussein Kasim), Mukhtaar Sheekh Cumar Aadan, and Ayaan Cabdalla Xaashi, without whose help I could not have visited Jigjiga; I am still awaiting your counter visits! I thank Member of Parliament Korfa Garane for his help and hospitality, and for smoothing the paths of bureaucracy for me. I thank the Institute of Ethiopian Studies at the University of Addis Ababa for granting me an affiliation for the duration of my stay in Ethiopia.

In Djibouti, my thanks go, first and foremost, to my close friend and colleague of twenty years, Maxamed Daahir Afrax, director of the Halabuur Centre for Culture and Communication in the Horn of Africa. At the Centre and among "Bahda Halabuur," that is to say, those associated with literary creativity as represented by the Halabuur Journal, Radio-Television-Djibouti, SomaliPEN, and the University of Djibouti, I found a home away from home and a social and intellectual context that was conducive to my research. In this context, my gratitude goes out to Maxamed Cabdillaahi Riraash, also a cherished and long-standing friend and colleague, Xaashi Cabdillaahi Orrax, Cabdalla Xaaji, and Burhaan Daahir, Aadan Xasan Aadan "Belelo," Khadar Cali Diraneh, Nimcaan Cabdillaahi, Hibaaq Cismaan, Fadumo Maxamuud, and others. I cannot thank enough Zahra Cabdi, who opened her apartment in uptown Djibouti to me and inspired me with her low-key and principled kindness toward the people surrounding her. I also thank the women of Group Sitti, Mustafa Yare and the other artists of Deegaan, singer and performer Cabdinuur Allaale, and the late Cumar Macallin for their kindness and hospitality. At Zahra's house, Xaliima's open-hearted kindness was a source of joy for me, as was, at Afrax's quarters, that of Ifraax.

In Yemen, I thank Alessandra Vianello and her now late husband, Dr. Abud Musa`ad Abud (who passed away in London in 2009), as well as their extended family residing in al-Mukalla. My immersion in the lives of a Bravanese family in exile allowed me to witness what family and Qaadiri devotion means to them. I also have fond memories of our morning outings to the sea and the delights of traditional Bravanese cuisine.

In the Netherlands, I spent four months at the Netherlands Institute for Advanced Study in the Humanities and Social Sciences (NIAS) as a member of the theme-group Mediations of Violence in Africa. I thank the NIAS staff as well as the theme-group members and other colleagues in the Netherlands, especially Paul Doornbos, Anke van der Kwaak, Annemiek Richters, and Karin Willemse, from whose knowledge, wisdom, genuine interest in the work of others, and generosity of spirit I have learned and benefited.

I thank Wellesley College, especially Provost Andrew Shennan, for making such a productive sabbatical possible. I also express my gratitude to my colleagues in the History Department (especially Alejandra Osorio and Quinn Slobodian), and the staff of the Library (especially Susan Goodman, Karen Jensen, Dale Katzif, Ravi Ravishankar, Laura Reiner, and Susan Richman), Copy Center (especially Vicky Mutascio), and the Controller's Office. Sarah Zaidi (Class of 2011) kindly read the manuscript. Anne Wasserman helped prepare the final manuscript.

I thank Maxamed Aadan Yuusuf (Boston), Maxamuud Cali "Cadami" (Columbus) and Cabdulcasiis Nuur Xirsi (Boston), who kindly read a draft of the manuscript. I am grateful to colleagues and friends in the United States and Canada who have answered questions, helped out with translations, and dug up information. Professor Cabdiweli Maxamed Cali-Gaas (Abdiweli Ali or Abdiweli Ali Gaas) of Niagara University and, at the time of writing, Prime Minister of Somalia's Transitional Federal Government, has answered my questions and connected me to knowledgeable individuals for over three years. I also thank my friends and colleagues Abdisalam Isse-Salwe (Medina), Abdourahman Waberi (Claremont and Paris), Anwar Diriye (Minneapolis), Abdikarim Hasan (San Diego), Abdirahman Nur (Boston), Burhan Ismail Yusuf (Boston and Minneapolis), Faisal Axmed Xasan (Toronto), Faisal Abdi

Roble (Los Angeles), Fowsia Abdulkadir (Ottawa), Maxamed Sheekh Xasan (of Scansom, Toronto), Abdullahi and Leila Kassim (Kitchener), Mohamed Kassim (Toronto and al-Sharja), Mohamud Togane (Montreal), Said M. Shire "Suugaan" (Columbus and Toronto), Siyaad Sheikh Daahir (Boston), Alessandra Vianello (London and al-Mukalla), Huseen Ali Yusuf (Washington, D.C.), and Yasmeen Maxamuud (San Diego). Nuruddin Farah, the accomplished novelist, dramatist, and essayist, has influenced and inspired me through his persistent rejection of clan as a valid category of analysis and refusal to reduce individuals to the clans that claim them.

I have experienced writing about violence as a lonelier undertaking than my earlier projects and it is in this context that I am especially grateful to Bert B. Lockwood, Jr. (Professor and Director, Urban Morgan Institute for Human Rights, University of Cincinnati College of Law), Series Editor of the Pennsylvania Studies in Human Rights, and Peter Agree, University of Pennsylvania Press Editor-in-Chief, for their approachability and intellectual encouragement. I also gratefully acknowledge the anonymous reader's comments on the manuscript elicited by the Press. Of course, I alone am responsible for the contents of this book.

I gratefully acknowledge the Fulbright-Hays Faculty Research Abroad Program, the National Endowment for the Humanities, the Netherlands Institute for Advanced Study in the Humanities and Social Sciences, the Halabuur Centre for Culture and Communication in the Horn of Africa, and Wellesley College for supporting my sabbatical research in 2007–2008.

I formally thank the following individuals and institutions for allowing me to cite copyrighted materials: Nuruddin Farah, excerpt from *Yesterday, Tomorrow: Voices from the Somali Diaspora* (New York: Cassell, 2000); Abdirazak Y. Osman, excerpts from *In the Name of the Fathers: A Somali Novel* (London: Haan, 1996); Mohamud Togane, excerpts from four poems: "The Phenomenon Called Al-Hajji Mudane Musse Soodi Yellahow," "The Darod Fire Back," "Afweyne's Swansong," and "Why the Darod Will Never Return to Mogadishu: A Candid Tête-à-Tête with Mohamed Dhere"; The Rector and Visitors of the University of Virginia for excerpts from Donald L. Donham, "Staring at Suffering: Violence as a Subject," in *States of Violence: Politics, Youth, and Memory in Contemporary Africa*, ed. Edna G. Bay and Donald L. Donham (Charlottesville: University of Virginia Press, 2006: 16–33); and Koninklijke Brill NV (Brill Publishers) for an excerpt from Lidwien Kapteijns, "Making Memories of Mogadishu in Somali Poetry About the Civil War," in *Mediations of Violence in Africa: Fashioning New Futures from Contested*

Pasts, ed. Lidwien Kapteijns and Annemiek Richters (Leiden: Brill, 2010: 25–74) and the United Nations for the map of Somalia (No. 3690, Rev.10).

Finally, I thank my six siblings and their families in the Netherlands, always a source of strength and inspiration, and Mursal Farah for his consistently critical engagement and unfailing support.

www.ingramcontent.com/pod-product-compliance
Lightning Source LLC
Chambersburg PA
CBHW030523230426
43665CB00010B/742